VIRTUAL MODERNISM

Virtual Modernism

* * * *

Writing and Technology
in the Progressive Era

Katherine Biers

University of Minnesota Press
Minneapolis
London

The University of Minnesota Press gratefully acknowledges financial assistance provided for the publication of this book from the Department of English and Comparative Literature at Columbia University.

An earlier version of chapter 3 was previously published as Katherine Biers, "Syncope Fever: James Weldon Johnson and the Black Phonographic Voice," *Representations* 96 (Fall 2006): 99–125; reprinted with permission of the University of California Press.Portions of chapter 4 were previously published as "Djuna Barnes Makes a Specialty of Crime: Violence and the Visual in Her Early Journalism," in *Women's Experience of Modernity, 1875–1945*, ed. Ann L. Ardis and Leslie W. Lewis (Baltimore: The Johns Hopkins University Press, 2002); copyright 2002 The Johns Hopkins University Press.

Copyright 2013 by the Regents of the University of Minnesota

Published by the University of Minnesota Press
111 Third Avenue South, Suite 290
Minneapolis, MN 55401-2520
http://www.upress.umn.edu

Library of Congress Cataloging-in-Publication Data
Biers, Katherine.
Virtual modernism : writing and technology in the Progressive Era / Katherine Biers.
Includes bibliographical references and index.
ISBN 978-0-8166-6754-3 (hc) — ISBN 978-0-8166-6755-0 (pb)
1. American literature--20th century—History and criticism. 2. Modernism (Literature)—United States. 3. Literature and technology—United States—History—20th century. 4. Popular culture—United States—History—20th century. I. Title.
PS228.M63B54 2013
810.9'112—dc23
2013018885

Printed in the United States of America on acid-free paper

The University of Minnesota is an equal-opportunity educator and employer.

20 19 18 17 16 15 14 13   10 9 8 7 6 5 4 3 2 1

Contents

Introduction: The Promise of the Virtual   1

1. Stephen Crane's Abilities   35

2. Realizing *Trilby*: Henry James, George du Maurier, and the Intermedial Scene   71

3. Syncope Fever: James Weldon Johnson and the Black Phonographic Voice   109

4. Wonder and Decay: Djuna Barnes's New York   139

5. Gertrude Stein Talking   173

Acknowledgments   199

Notes   201

Index   257

The Promise of the Virtual

To be potential means: to be one's own lack, to be in relation to one's own incapacity.

—Giorgio Agamben

HENRY JAMES'S 1898 NOVELLA "In the Cage" follows the travails of an impoverished young female telegraph operator working at a busy post office in a fashionable district of London. She gets through her day by indulging alternately in romantic fantasies and world-weary cynicism about two well-heeled customers who are using her as a go-between to conduct an adulterous affair. But working at top speed to code their handwritten messages and those of the larger "herd" gives her little time to think. So sometimes she slows down her work in order to read and interpret what she is only supposed to write and send. As she takes her time with one particular missive, given her by the dazzlingly handsome male half of the couple in question, "the sense of every syllable he paid for was fiercely distinct; she indeed felt her progressive pencil, dabbing as if with a quick caress the marks of his own, put life into every stroke."[1] Writing *and* reading the message allows the telegraph girl to imagine herself as the male sender and her attractive customer as the receiver, engaged together in an act of erotic, rather than merely communicative, exchange. Slowing down her "progressive pencil," she gains a fleeting sense of the potential to become someone other than who she is, or could possibly ever be. The telegraph girl thereby discovers a new kind of experience that is the subject of this book.

Virtual Modernism: Writing and Technology in the Progressive Era argues that American writers developed a poetics of the virtual in response to the rise of mass culture and mass communications technologies before World War I. The writers I discuss turn to ideas of the virtual and virtuality because they are competing with immersive multimedia experiences and spectacular amusements on offer within the burgeoning culture industry.

They recreate such experiences for readers by evoking them in language, through shifts in grammatical tense, modality, subjunctive mood, disjunctive juxtapositions of genre, compositional principles of assemblage, and elliptical and indirect forms of audience and reader address. The writers in this study are therefore modernists, emphasizing the formal properties of language in reaction to modernity and its new technologies. But they also retain a faith in the correspondence of language and reality more characteristic of realism and naturalism. For they do not dispense with reference itself, but slow it down, virtualizing the objects to which they refer. Like the telegraph girl's progressive pencil, a virtual poetics seeks to unleash a hidden capacity for objects in language to become other than what—or who—they are.

The virtual poetics of the writers in this study was part of a larger "virtual turn" in the United States in the pre–World War I period, when a fascination with the writings of Henri Bergson, William James, and vitalist philosophy swept the country. Vitalist ideas such as "creative evolution" or "pure experience," as I note later in this introduction, became a way for some intellectuals to sanctify industrialization, urbanization, cultural nationalism, and a host of new technologies, including media technologies. But I argue that what was in many ways a retrograde spiritualization of modernity in the wider culture became in the literary text a way of achieving an important critical purchase upon it. The aspiration to save the idea of progress through a recourse to the virtual in language, and particularly to a virtual experience *of* language, opens a window on the qualitative dimension of historical change. This window is particularly revealing for cultural critics immersed in the early twenty-first century's fascination with all things virtual.

In what follows, I use the terms *virtual, virtuality,* and, occasionally, *virtual reality* in an idiosyncratic way that needs to be distinguished from how such terms are more commonly used today. As Marie-Laure Ryan has noted, the term *virtual* tends to oscillate between two poles of meaning in contemporary parlance—the "fake" and the "potential."[2] Understood as the fake, the virtual is closely associated with the optical image, where it often—as in Plato's cave—carries connotations of the double, the illusion, and the simulacrum. By contrast, the virtual as *potential*—the meaning closer to my usage—originates with Aristotle and medieval scholastic philosophers and designates not the absence of existence, but the potential or force to come into existence. The acorn, to cite Aristotle's example, contains a virtual oak. As Ryan points out, the virtual-as-potential, in contrast to the virtual-as-fake, carries largely positive connotations of "productivity, openness, and diversity."[3] Most important, neither definition is equivalent to the digital.[4] The digital definition was initially only a technical term to describe the difference between a computer's internal operations and its user interface.[5] It has since grown to encompass anything computer related. As Katherine Hayles puts it, the virtual-as-digital is best understood simply as "the cultural perception that material objects are interpenetrated by information patterns."[6]

It has been largely forgotten, however, that long before digital technologies were developed, and in close dialogue with the well-established but radically changing field of experimental psychology, Henri Bergson and William James sought to rethink *experience* as virtual, in order to find an alternative to the battle between idealism and empiricism in the nineteenth century. Their use of the term, not included in the preceding taxonomy, is the one I draw on throughout this book. Virtual experience for Bergson and James is not a fake experience. Neither, however, is it identical with the virtual-as-potential of Aristotle and the scholastics, nor with the definition of *virtuality* found in Gilles Deleuze's philosophy (which is partly based on Bergson), nor with the informational definition of the virtual-as-digital. The difference lies in the emphasis placed on experience.[7] A virtual experience for both philosophers is one that both belongs to the self and extends beyond, occupying a liminal position at the fringes of self and world. It both exists and does not exist: the subject can grasp it, via introspection or intuition, but only fleetingly, just before it becomes assigned to the position of subject or object. Most important, it is an experience that cuts across spheres of experience defined separately from one another within modernity—religious, aesthetic, narrowly empirical—and that offers a route back to a shared life world.[8]

The authors in this study, however, turned to the virtual experience of *language* in order to carve out a value for the literary, both with and against the rise of mass entertainments and the new technologies that made them possible. William James, as I discuss following, placed special weight on the way language offered evidence for the reality of virtual experience. One hypothesis about James's preference for language and literature as examples in his essays and lectures, and about the philosophy of pragmatism James founded more generally, is that it was an attempt to both rethink and defend the traditional locations of cultural status and authority that had been upended by the rise of consumer society.[9] I suggest that new media technologies in particular were jeopardizing language's special status as the predominant means of structuring experience. I show that the authors in this study often claim, in implicit and explicit ways, that the experience of language's *potential* to refer offers the best way to find common ground in a world governed by media other than print. The virtual thus becomes, throughout *Virtual Modernism,* a redemption for literature with the advent of mass culture.

To make this argument, in the following pages I draw equally upon the fields of media studies and American literary studies. Media studies and media theory have offered literary critics valuable insight into the tremendous impact that the storage, transmission, and entertainment capabilities of new media technologies such as film had on literature beginning in the late nineteenth century.[10] Cultural studies of technology in particular during this period have argued that both mass culture and new media technologies were dispossessing forces for the self; technology uncovered the alterity, exteriority, and materiality that constituted subjectivity, dethroning the idea of the self as stable, self-present, and unchanging. American literary studies has shown, however, that many American writers already conceptualized *language* as the site of a radical self-dispossession, long before the rise of mass media technologies and industrial modernity, often by virtue of its connection to the divine.[11] I argue that mass culture and mass media were thus eerily familiar in their effects to many American writers, for they confirmed that experience itself was transitional, much as Ralph Waldo Emerson had argued—a matter of active processes and energies that dispossess the self. *Virtual Modernism* argues that it was a technologically inspired *re*engagement with experience, rather than the invention of new technologies or the extension of old ideas about experience, that was formative for American modernism.

Of necessity, then, my analysis also speaks to a body of criticism that for several decades has been interested in trying to understand the relationship between modernist writers and the forms of mass and popular culture they so often claimed to reject. The cultural phenomena in question include "media" conventionally defined, such as newspapers, magazines, film, and photography, as well as more "popular" forms of entertainment, such as burlesque shows, circuses, panoramas, spectacular theatrical events, and public re-creations of battle scenes and disasters. The modernists' oppositional stance was first explored as a problematic nexus by Andreas Huyssen, who saw in it an ambivalent rejection by elite male writers of a threatening and contaminating feminized other.[12] It was subsequently rethought by a variety of critics as a pervasive and strategic set of convergences or borrowings between "high" literary and "low" popular and mass cultural modes.[13] Recent accounts, which have been formative for my concerns in these pages, have understood this relationship instead to consist of a conflicted, critical encounter over the location of the public sphere. Contra Habermas, the argument goes, the late nineteenth century did not experience the decline and fall of a rational public sphere with the rise of a sensation-seeking mass culture, but instead came to have a proliferation of competing publics with competing participants, all clamoring to be heard in venues other than literature and print.[14] Nancy Bentley has provided the most extensive account of this encounter in the American context, charting a series of clashes at the turn of the century between literary elites, who embraced a restricted definition of public culture as both literary and national, and competing, extraliterary (and sometimes transnational) sites of "low" or popular public discussion and debate.[15] Most important, she shows that an active contestation among publics—rather than either an invasion of elite culture by mass culture or an erosion of the different sites of cultural production—shaped the concerns of literary authors in late nineteenth-century America.[16]

In what follows, I build on this recent work by reframing the competition and contestation between a mass public and a literary public in the United States as a rivalry over experience.[17] I argue that Americans took early mass culture seriously as an intellectual problem not just because of the growth of new civic institutions (as Bentley argues) but because the rise of mass culture did not violate a clear boundary between public reason and private sensory experience to begin with, as Habermas tends to imply. That boundary had long been conceptualized instead, in the American context, as a conversion or turning from one realm to another. Emerson notably distinguished the work of the "American scholar," in distinction from the European, as "a strange process . . . by which experience is converted into thought, as a mulberry-leaf is converted into satin."[18] Writers and intellectuals like William Dean Howells and W. E. B. Du Bois thus were led to acknowledge the alarming possibility that—for example—a spectacular, jingoistic re-creation of a Spanish-American War battle, or a bowdlerized recording of the black spirituals, might "convert" experience into thought in just the same way as a realist short story or a classical concert.

As these methodological stakes suggest, I approach what I am calling the late nineteenth-century "virtual turn" and its significance for literature in a highly synoptic way, drawing on literary criticism, philosophy, media studies, and cultural history. While this significantly limits the specificity of my historical claims, by bringing together such broad areas of inquiry I am able to illuminate the ways that the writers in my study were themselves making use of ideas that spanned many different disciplines. In fact, one way to understand the concept of virtual experience is to see it as an attempt on the part of James, Bergson, and others to hold together different areas of inquiry that the emergence of disciplinarity was rendering irreducible, even sometimes hostile, to one another, such as behaviorist psychology, psychoanalysis, philosophical phenomenology, political theory, and communications research. To grasp the way these different realms interpenetrated requires, at the end of the day, something of a synchronic historical approach—even though, as I discuss at the end of this introduction, such an approach is in fact inimical to the fundamental presuppositions of both a philosophy and a poetics of the virtual.

This book stems from a set of frankly presentist concerns. First, the virtual is ubiquitous today as a term designating primarily digital technologies and the forms of culture they enable. My hope is that attention to the late nineteenth- and early twentieth-century virtual will put the pervasive equation between the virtual and the digital to rest. This prior turn anticipates our present moment in interesting ways, although, for reasons to be elaborated at the end of this introduction, I try to resist making claims about similarities and differences between then and now. Moreover, although James and especially Bergson are routinely invoked in discussions of the ontology of the digital, neither media studies nor American literary studies has acknowledged how widely an interest in vitalist philosophy once held sway in response to a similarly fluid and transitional period in media history.[19] Finally, as Martin Jay has recently pointed out, it is often forgotten how important the philosophical search for virtual experience, which he calls "experience without a subject," undertaken particularly by pragmatism, would be to twentieth-century thinkers central to critical theory and poststructuralist theory.[20] The chapters that follow explore an early incarnation of the quest to define experiences without subjects, showing both that it was closely connected to historical and technological changes at the turn of the century, and that it was inseparable from literary modernism.

A variety of authors and texts might have been chosen for this study. Willa Cather and Wallace Stevens were captivated in different ways by Bergson's arrival in America; Henry Adams's autobiography offers an eloquent and sardonic testimony to the virtualization of experience; Kate Chopin's *The Awakening*, with its close attention to the limits of conscious experience, the pleasure economy of the late nineteenth century, and the flowing aesthetics characteristic of Wagner, Schopenhauer, and Nietzsche, also belongs within the conversation I am establishing here.[21] Yet in comparison, the writers I have chosen turned to a poetics of the virtual out of a more direct engagement and participation in early mass culture, thus illustrating the links between the two. Stephen Crane and Djuna Barnes earned their livings writing for newspapers and magazines from a young age; James Weldon Johnson wrote for one of the most successful black songwriting teams of the 'teens; Gertrude Stein embraced celebrity in the 1930s and wrote essays for newspapers and magazines throughout her American tour; and Henry James—although perhaps the most skeptical of all of these writers about mass culture—found in the sudden mass frenzy over the work of a close friend, I argue, a significant inspiration for the formal innovations he undertook in his later years. From the point of view of hindsight, each writer thus becomes a historically illuminating holdover. In each, a "modernist" formal experimentation, inspired by the deforming and subject-defying energies of mass culture, is still tied to realist and naturalist convictions about the representational power of language, the importance of progress, the viability of the public sphere, and the reality of common experience.

The rest of this introduction elaborates some of the ways in which the idea of the virtual became important in turn-of-the-century America as a means to address the claims of the literary, both in the sense of the claims of literary reference per se and literature's claims to rival other media. At the center of this story of an earlier "virtual turn" is the notion of experience elaborated by James and Bergson and taken up by intellectuals and social reformers in America in the years before World War I. As I show in the first section, James, Bergson, and others embraced the idea of virtual experience—an experience without a subject—as a way to contest the impoverishment of human agency and moral responsibility inherent in grand nineteenth-century systems of historical and evolutionary progress. The significance of this development for American literature then makes up the subject of the second section by way of a further reading of Henry James's "In the Cage." James's story is an exploration of the philosophical idea of virtual experience, I show, as much as an exposé of the changes the telegraph wreaked on late nineteenth-century life. I close, in the third section, by developing further some of the methodological implications of my reading of "In the Cage," and specifically of this book's larger quest to bring together the fields of American literary studies and media studies through the idea of the virtual, in its late nineteenth-century rather than its contemporary sense.

To Be and Not to Be: Virtual Experience

The closing decades of the nineteenth century were a time of significant intellectual ferment among philosophers and political and social theorists in the United States and Europe. Discontent had long been growing with the grand nineteenth-century systems of positivist science, which were dedicated to explaining all phenomena with reference to the inevitable and deterministic "progress" of Darwinian evolution. Equally untenable, however, were explanations of the world offered by religious thought, which saw phenomena only in the light of an ideal realm accessible through spiritual revelation. Figures as different in outlook as William James and John Dewey in the United States; Friedrich Nietzsche and Wilhelm Dilthey in Germany; Alfred Fouillée and Henri Bergson in France; and Thomas Hill Green and Henry Sidgwick in England sought instead to call a truce to the irreconcilable conflict between empiricism and idealism.[22] The aim of intellectuals became to discover a workable philosophy appropriate to everyday experiences of choice and free will, especially those of an emerging professional class navigating the problems of urban and industrial societies at the turn of the century. An average member of that class, as William James noted, "wants facts; he wants science; but he also wants a religion . . . . Now what kinds of philosophy do you find actually offered to meet your need? You find an empirical philosophy that is not religious enough, and a religious philosophy that is not empirical enough for your purpose."[23]

Whether they sought to mediate between religion and science; socialism and laissez-faire economics; ethical intuitionism and utilitarianism;

or idealist and empiricist epistemology, the diverse solutions found by late nineteenth-century intellectuals to the problem posed by James had something significant in common. All were determined in some way to revitalize and rethink the category of experience itself. A philosophy based not on grand systems but instead on experience seemed the only way to end the nineteenth century's interminable philosophical battles.[24] For each side of the various schisms noted earlier had relied on narrow and specialized notions of experience, from the stimulus reported by the experimental subject in the laboratory, to the sensory confusion synthesized in the act of aesthetic or moral judgment, to the pious awe of a religious vision. This specialization of experience itself could be chalked up to the advent of modernity, which had carved up a shared life world into different disciplines and areas of expertise. As the essays of Montaigne demonstrated, by contrast, an examination of experience as such could be a warrant to range freely over natural science, philosophy, religion, and art. The attempt to restore a lost totality of experience was marked by technocratic optimism as much as antimodern polemic and could rest on appeals to the ordinary Jamesean "amateur" or the extraordinary Nietzschean superman.

But in order to rethink experience, late nineteenth-century philosophers and social theorists also had to confront a profoundly altered conception of subjectivity, which was the legacy of nineteenth-century empirical psychology. Previous philosophical investigations of experience, in the specialized sense noted earlier, tended to be premised on a notion of stable subjectivity. As Martin Jay puts it, experience, historically, "was always that of and for a subject, whether that subject was characterized as transcendental or immanent, universal or particular, collective or singular, punctual or temporally extended."[25] Late nineteenth-century discoveries in psychology about the processual nature of perception and identity made such assumptions problematic. As German psychologists and philosophers such as Franz Brentano and Ernst Mach argued in the 1870s and 1880s, and James himself pointed out in *Principles of Psychology* in 1890, we do not "see" the world as it really is. Instead, we create the objects of our perception by integrating partial and distorted sensory input to construct a whole picture. As with the object, so, too, then, with the subject. Psychologists argued that the sense of a stable and coherent self that is continuous over time does not precede perception but is dependent upon integrative habits of perception, such as attentiveness.[26] Consciousness becomes a construct of the body's life processes and its vital and unbroken transactions with the environment—less a sovereign ego than a rider, in Nietzsche's phrase, "hanging in dreams on the back of a tiger."[27]

The new psychology, as Judith Ryan has pointed out, created something of a crisis. It entailed a disturbing subjectivism, for if the self was no more than a bundle of sensations, then an "object . . . did not exist except with referent to the act of seeing" and "perception itself could not exist absolutely, but only with reference to an object."[28] It also made vision—the sense constitutive of the sovereign ego—into "only one layer of a body that could be captured, shaped, or controlled by a range of external techniques," such as those deployed in large-scale industrial production, social control, and new technologies of spectacle and recording.[29] Finally, as the German media theorist Friedrich Kittler has shown, empirical psychology at the turn of the century was busy clearing a path for a systems-based understanding of language, particularly in Germany. In a disturbing development for philosophy itself, just as subject and object were becoming matters of function, so too were sender and receiver, writer and reader.[30]

An answer to the dilemma of systems without subjects, however, was to embrace *experiences* without subjects.[31] By suggesting that thoughts and things occupy the same ontological order, the new psychology seemed to offer a solution to the quest for a more unified form of experience adequate to modernity. For the irreducibly interactive relationship between the perceiving subject and the object of perception could be accounted for with reference neither to idealism nor to empiricism. A conception of psychological experience beyond the duality of subject and object—experience as a fluid zone of indetermination between subject and world—emerged to become the lynchpin of the thought of James and the American pragmatists in particular, as well of that of Bergson, Dilthey, Nietzsche, and the transatlantic philosophical, cultural, and literary movement loosely termed "vitalism."[32] This notion of experience could accommodate ideas of individual agency and rational choice, while still allowing for the reality of empirical physical processes that exercised a determining force on mind and subjectivity—provided, that is, that it was possible to accept a measure of uncertainty and doubt about what could be known in any absolute sense.

The philosophical implications that the new devotees of experience extracted from psychology had profound consequences for art and literature.[33] To grasp the notion of an experience without a subject, it was necessary not only to redefine experience as a term, but to formulate methods of inquiry distinct from the narrow empiricism and specialization of function characteristic of psychology itself. As a result, aspects of experience that had been narrowly defined as outside the purview of reason—including introspection, emotion, dreams, and other suspensions of conscious perception—became reimagined much more expansively in the late nineteenth century as a way to restore a lost totality of experience. It is thus not surprising to find that, as numerous studies have shown, the ideas of empirical (pre-Freudian) psychology inspired new techniques, structures, and approaches to depicting subjectivity in literature, art, drama, dance, film, and photography at the turn of the century, helping to birth the transatlantic movement we have come to call modernism.[34] In the United States, a long-standing rhetoric of experience as definitional for American identity gave a distinctive flavor to the American literary response to vitalism, as well as to the way American writers and cultural critics interrogated and integrated vitalist claims with reference to modernity. Among the vitalists, it was Bergson and James who, in my estimation, had the greatest influence in America, both on the broader culture of progressivism during the pre–World War I period, and on the writers I discuss in this book.

Both philosophers arrived at their revitalized notions of experience out of markedly different contexts, but also in communication with each other.[35] Despite significant differences, both can be described as attempting to produce a form of what James called "radical empiricism."[36] Radical empiricism is distinguished from ordinary empiricism by its attempts to recognize the relations between sense data, without subsuming them under an abstract principle or concept.[37] James's name for those relations was "pure experience." Pure experience is an "instant field of the present . . . as yet undifferentiated into thing and thought."[38] It is also a "flux . . . of things conjunct and separated," continually in movement (49). While such terms suggest otherwise, James denied that pure experience should be understood as a primal or ultimate reality and was willing to accept uncertainty about what that reality consisted of. What was perhaps most important, given the importance of psychological evidence to James, is that pure experience be understood as in some way prior to consciousness and constitutive of it. In pure experience:

> There is no self-splitting of it into consciousness and what the consciousness is "of." Its subjectivity and objectivity are functional

attributes solely, realized only when the experience is "taken," *i.e.* talked-of, twice, considered along with its two different contexts respectively, by a new retrospective experience, of which that whole past complication now forms the fresh content. (12)

Here subjectivity and objectivity are properties *of* experience rather than the other way around. In a conceptual and stylistic reversal of expectations for philosophical discourse, experience now occupies the subject position in James's sentences. Through this grammatical shift, James not only describes but demonstrates his belief that, in Jonathan Levin's words, "an underlying continuity structures the perception of every particular discontinuity."[39] Every discrete experience is "fringed" with "a *more* that continuously develops," undermining even the discontinuity foundational to philosophy itself—that of knower and known (37).

Bergson, in a more extensively developed philosophical system, described his conception of the conjunctive relations within experience as a part of his larger elaboration of a metaphysics of time. Time, he argued, should be rethought as *durée*, or duration, in order to grasp its essence, which consists not only of changes in degree—quantitative, measurable differences that are familiar from the divisions on a clock or calendar— but also changes in kind, qualitative differences like those in the color spectrum, which are continuous and interpenetrating. Past, present, and future are thus distinct *and* continuous elements of experience, for Bergson. The intellect always spatializes and homogenizes time, cutting up its undifferentiated flow into a series of stills, like a film camera, and then reassembling them to make a whole.[40] It was thus the task of philosophy to consider time in terms of its long-neglected qualitative and variable aspect. Time, he famously declared, is a life force, or "élan vital," entailing unpredictable creative divergence and the emergence of the new.[41]

Despite the significant differences between duration and pure experience, James and Bergson use the same term to describe the challenge each concept poses to the atomism of ordinary empiricism—the *virtual*.[42] In *Matter and Memory*, a study of the relations of body and mind, Bergson describes the mental image as virtual, because it is a subtraction from the *durée*, not a product of discrete sensory impressions. Memory and intellect screen out the continuous changes of time-as-duration, Bergson argues, in order to produce mental representations that are tailored to the adaptive and evolutionary needs of the organism. As a result, "representation is there, but always virtual," always ready for a "conversion from the virtual to the actual" performed by the body (36).[43] Given that external stimuli mix together with memory and bodily capacity to condition what the organism perceives, Bergson concludes that the body is a creative "center of indetermination" whose ability to delay the relation between a stimulus and its response corresponds to the organism's place on the evolutionary ladder.[44]

In *Creative Evolution*, Bergson expands his discussion of duration beyond questions of mind, which had been the subject of his first two books, *Matter and Memory* and *Time and Free Will*. Offering a sustained philosophical challenge to the determinism and mechanism of Social Darwinism, *Creative Evolution* argues that evolution itself comprises the movement of duration. Evolution should not be understood as a change in degree, he argues, in which what already exists has more existence added to it. The present is not a kind of phantom latent in the past, fully formed and lacking only in existence; instead, the present and future emerge via creative innovation or change.[45] As Gilles Deleuze has argued, at the heart of Bergson's reworking of Darwin (and challenge to many of Darwin's followers) is a distinction between the possible and the virtual. To describe a change as "possible" is to assume that the change to come is already fully formed, waiting in the wings to be realized on the stage of existence. To describe a change as "virtual," by contrast, is to abandon the fiction that the new is ever fully constituted in advance. Evolution is not a process whereby the possible becomes real by addition, but one in which the virtual becomes actual by creative elaboration.[46]

James follows Bergson in *Matter and Memory* to describe the mental image as virtual. Echoing Bergson, he claims that what we see is a reflection of the potential but also very real actions we *might* take in response to our surroundings, as creatively elaborated or invented by our bodies. James's examples of such actions, however, are less adaptive and evolutionary than ordinary and everyday—like taking a walk or having a conversation. For instance, he illustrates his notion of the virtual mental image via an example drawn from his presumed readers' everyday experience on the Harvard campus. How do we know that we all have the same image in mind, he asks, when we use the words "Memorial Hall"? Even in regard to this unmistakable building, James notes, we cannot be sure that we are discussing the same thing. However, once we travel to the building, we discover "the knowing really was there, as the result now shows.

We were *virtual* knowers of the Hall long before we were certified to have been its actual knowers, by the percept's retroactive validating power" (36).[47] In other words, there is no absolute correspondence between the name "Memorial Hall" and the thing, or the thinker and the object of his thought, but just an "instant field"—full of the potential for reference. Therefore, the arrival at the hall *makes* the meaning, splitting that field retroactively into "two parts, a 'consciousness' and its 'content,' and the content corrected or confirmed" (39). "Memorial Hall" is a virtual mental image that reflects the capacity to walk to the building, no more, no less; the words stand in for the action, offering a substitution that is more practical and efficient. Nevertheless, James argued, the potential action for which the words substitute is somehow also real.[48]

James often seemed to place the greatest weight on the evidence of virtual experience that could be provided by language. He argued, for instance, that the word *feeling* makes clear that transitions between subject and object are real, for we use *feeling* to designate either something experienced from within *or* measured from without (74). Aesthetic appreciation also provides such evidence. When describing loveliness and ugliness, James noted, adjectives tend to "wander," "as if uncertain" whether to "fix" themselves to the subject or the object. "Shall we speak of seductive visions or of visions of seductive things?" he asked (18).[49] One is tempted to conclude that language *is* pure experience for James. For only language is able to offer both direct experience *of* the virtual—in the faculty or capacity for reference emphasized by wandering adjectives, or shifts of grammatical subject—and knowledge *about* it, such as the very knowledge James himself is providing us.

Virtual or potential experience, for this very reason, poses a significant problem for *philosophical* discourse. Because to speak of a faculty or a capacity is to speak of something that is both present and absent at the same time, it is also to speak of something that necessarily evades the presuppositional structure of linguistic predication.[50] Grammatical predication itself thematizes and substantializes, elevating the virtual into the ideal, despite both philosophers' stated opposition to idealism.[51] Moreover, by inviting comparison, the use of metaphors and examples—as in Bergson's description of consciousness as cinematic or James's illustrative personal stories—engages the reader in precisely the conceptual and spatializing work of the intellect both are keen to downplay. Evidence of the problem can be seen especially in the way both Bergson and James find intentionality and freedom in experiences that are supposedly irreducible to the subjective or personal. What often seems to be at stake in both philosophers' discussion of the virtual mental image, for instance, is a particular *subject's* freedom to choose. The subtraction of the mental image from the *durée*, Bergson argues, "signifies choice, and consciousness mainly consists in this practical discernment."[52] The multiplicity of stimuli impinging on the organism from without, "make an appeal to my will and put, so to speak, an elementary question to my motor activity."[53] James famously, and notoriously, described belief itself as a matter of "will." It remains unclear in what sense "will" and "motor activity" can be defined as choices, if there is no subject doing the choosing.

A philosophy of the unsayable will perhaps inevitably fail by converting the unsayable into what is said. Perhaps this is why there often seems to be a melancholy quality to James's attempts to develop a metaphysics based on experience, as, too, in Emerson's meditations on the concept.[54] This melancholy can be detected in some of James's metaphors, which serve to illustrate his points when more straightforward language fails. For instance, James's Christian colleague C. S. Peirce's solution to the idealist/ empiricist schism was the logical argument that belief should be defined as simply that on which we are prepared to act.[55] This idea is inherent in James's account of the virtual mental image of Memorial Hall, but he establishes the ungrounded nature of belief in that discussion not through logic, but through the image of a solitary ship, far from home:

> As each experience runs by cognitive transition into the next one, and we nowhere feel a collision with what we elsewhere count as truth or fact, we commit ourselves to the current as if the port were sure. We live, as it were, upon the front edge of an advancing wavecrest, and our sense of a determinate direction in falling forward is all we cover of the future of our path. . . . Our experience, *inter alia*, is of variations of rate and of direction, and lives in these transitions more than in the journey's end. (36)

The functional nature of consciousness makes belief perpetually provisional, an ongoing journey with no certain destination. Although there is no absolute certainty to ground our beliefs, James suggests that we can take solace in the fluidity of subjectivity itself, for we can have "experiences of tendency" that link our mental images with the external world that our bodies unconsciously navigate. As the poignant uncertainty of this lonely, and lovely, image conveys, however, it remains to be seen how a "sense of a determinate direction in falling forward" can be experienced *by* a subject, much less understood as an example of "will," because it is the very action that, for James, brings the subject itself into being.[56]

The tendency to reduce virtual experience to qualities possessed by a subject or subjects was also characteristic of many writers and critics during the career of philosophical vitalism in America, when the ideas of James, Bergson, and Nietzsche enjoyed a broad vogue beginning roughly around 1911, with the translation of Bergson's *Creative Evolution*.[57] For theologian and social reformer Lyman Abbott, Bergson's philosophy was "a philosophy of progress," indebted to neither "the fatalistic scientist nor the fatalistic theologian" and confirming that "God is a living god; and is creating living men and women."[58] For the publicist Gerald Stanley Lee, a Bergson-esque concept of creative evolution offered a way to celebrate the prosthetic effects of technology: "We are not only inventing new machines," Lee wrote to an eager new audience drawn from the nascent disciplines of advertising and public relations, "but our new machines have turned upon us and are creating new men. The telephone changes the structure of the brain. Men live in wider distances, and think in larger figures, and become eligible to nobler and wider motives."[59] Philosophical vitalism in the United States during the prewar period quickly became a way to covertly salvage a faith in progress itself, or to champion an emerging consumer economy, or to retrofit manifest destiny. The effect was to reinstall the subject at the center of a supposedly subjectless experience, as the idea of virtual experience became a way to reimport spirituality into notions of progress that had long chafed within a mechanistic or finalistic cast.[60]

Among those who made the most sophisticated and creative use of vitalist ideas were two public intellectuals who studied with James and with John Dewey: Randolph Bourne and Walter Lippmann.[61] Both turned to virtual experience to inject a tolerance of uncertainty, an embrace of pluralism, and a spirit of open-ended experiment into debates about culture and politics in the wake of industrial modernity. Randolph Bourne, as I discuss in chapter 3, reworked William James's notion of the real as a "flux . . . of things conjunct and separated," into a theory of American culture and identity as "transnational," made up of immigrants who retain their cultural identity while joining together into a larger national democratic community.[62] Walter Lippmann, in his first book, *A Preface to Politics*, used both Bergson and Nietzsche to forward an anti-foundational theory of democratic politics. Whatever "credit or reverence" we give to government, Lippmann argued, should be based on its ability to enable will and freedom—defined in the radically empiricist sense. Rather than being based on moral law, governmental authority should spring from its "utility in ministering to those concrete experiences which are as obvious and as undefinable as color or sound."[63] As I discuss in chapter 5, these are very different terms than Lippmann would come to adopt after World War I. In his much more influential book *Public Opinion* (1922), he would launch a devastating and influential critique of the possibility of an informed public from an idealist standpoint, prefaced with a lengthy quotation from Plato's Allegory of the Cave.

This early twentieth-century American "virtual turn," and the problem of potentiality and progress that lies buried within in it, had a significant influence on each of the five writers in my study. It is possible to *demonstrate* the reality of virtual experience—as William James implied, and as these writers show—through the greater flexibility of literary language, which can evade or undercut the substantializing and thematizing effects of predication. What Crane, Henry James, Johnson, Barnes, and Stein have in mind when they make use of this flexibility, however, is not a demonstration (or a celebration). Rather than translating vitalist philosophy into literature and thereby illustrating its tenets, these writers turn to the virtualizing powers of language in response to the troubling problems posed by a decentered subjectivity in the context of mass culture and new media technologies—problems that remain largely unaddressed in vitalism itself. These writers, too, can therefore be understood as attempting to preserve an outdated ideal of progress, by means of the virtual poetics found in their fiction, essays, and reportage. But I argue that what is in many ways a failing for philosophy, strictly speaking, especially when disseminated throughout American culture, becomes instead, in the literary text, profoundly revealing historically.

In examining the way that the literary treatment of virtuality or potentiality can enable a critical stance toward modernity, I follow the lead of Walter Benjamin, who criticized the ideas of the European vitalists as they appeared in the philosophical works of the time, but who found in the literature influenced by them something of significant value. In a 1940 essay on Baudelaire, Benjamin describes the vitalist attempts "to grasp 'true' experience" since the late nineteenth century as a "strange situation" for philosophy.[64] Any search for a "purer" or more holistic notion of experience is always at least implicitly opposed, for Benjamin, to the kind of experience that "manifests itself in the standardized, denatured life of the civilized masses" (314). Such attempts run the risk of sliding into fascism, for "their point of departure, understandably enough, has not been the individual's life in society" (ibid.). However:

> Towering above this literature is Bergson's early monumental work, *Matière et mémoire*. . . . Of course, the historical determination of memory is not at all Bergson's intention. On the contrary, he rejects any historical determination of memory. He thus manages to stay clear of that experience from which his own philosophy evolved, or, rather, in reaction to which it arose. It was the alienating, blinding experience of the age of large-scale industrialism. In shutting out this experience, the eye perceives a complementary experience—in the form of its spontaneous afterimage, as it were. Bergson's philosophy represents an attempt to specify this afterimage and fix it as a permanent record. His philosophy thus indirectly furnishes a clue to the experience which presented itself undistorted to Baudelaire's eyes, in the figure of his reader. (ibid.)

Benjamin's recourse to the metaphor of the afterimage suggests, on the one hand, that Bergson represses "the individual's life in society." Just as an eye reflexively shuts out a damaging stimulus that threatens to disable or blind it, so too do the philosophers of "life" shun the technological and mediated environments—the rhythms of factory work, the anonymity of the crowd, the ubiquity of the photograph and film—that were shaping life as they knew it. Those conditions then return in the reified concepts of philosophical inquiry, much as the relations of production are reified in the mirror-like form of the commodity. But, on the other hand, by adopting a metaphor for the act of reification drawn from Bergson himself—the cinematic consciousness of *Creative Evolution*—Benjamin suggests that Bergson's revolutionary philosophy of time in fact does offer important insights into *modernity* for the historical materialist critic.

Benjamin's acknowledgment of Bergson's "indirect" value was closely related to the fact that in the final years of his life he was seeking to effect his own vitalist synthesis—in his case, of materialism and theology.

In his late writings, Benjamin's quest for this synthesis led him to formulate an account of *history* that resembled Bergson's account of the *durée*. Running through "On the Concept of History," the series of theses in which he famously links civilization to barbarism, is a conception of history as duration, and of historians—history's victors, for Benjamin—as the Bergsonian intellect, dividing up the spoils of the continuous past and categorizing it according to their present needs. Benjamin suggests in this elliptical and provocative work that the past, like Bergson's *durée*, has a qualitative dimension that connects it, unbeknownst to history's victors, to the present. The past as such thus never passes away, for "nothing that has ever happened should be regarded as lost to history."[65] It therefore has a political relevance, as a force that, when unleashed, can bring about a future that is qualitatively different than the present.[66] Quite unlike Bergson, however, Benjamin describes the force of the past as a "secret index" or a "secret heliotropism," suggesting that the vital force of becoming always latent in the past is inseparable from the moments in which the past becomes an object that can be cited, translated, or reproduced—troped—in language (390). "Only for a redeemed mankind has its past become *citable* in all its moments," he notes (ibid.) (emphasis mine). Benjamin thereby suggests that language, by potentializing the objects to which it refers, can unleash their capacity to become other than themselves, or to differ from themselves.[67] Benjamin finds this redemptive power of language both politically valuable for the historical materialist critic, and when encountered in the literary or dramatic text, historically revelatory.

Put more simply, it is history rather than experience that needs to be rethought, for Benjamin, as creative emergence as well as repetition, as potentiality as well as possibility, and as indivisible continuity as well as something to be measured or counted. In turn, it is history, rather than "pure experience," that becomes available, for Benjamin, in dreams, in altered mental states, and in works of art and literature. Benjamin sees the potentializing language of Baudelaire, Proust, Karl Kraus, and the authors of seventeenth-century German baroque theater, among others, as striving to make European history citable. In what follows, I see the potentializing language of turn-of-the-century American writers as striving to make American history citable. The writers in this study thus did more than reflect the vogue for the virtual in their historical moment. They also sought to atone for the technological alienation that underlay it. By way of introduction, in the following section I turn to a further discussion of Henry

James's short story "In the Cage." James's story, like Baudelaire's poems, according to Benjamin, offers us an "undistorted" view of the "experience" from which vitalist philosophy "evolved."[68] As such, it furnishes us with a means by which to think about both the continuities and the changes that link the late nineteenth-century experience of the virtual to that of today.

Before the Frame and the Wire: "In the Cage"

"In the Cage," first published in 1898, strikingly anticipates our contemporary moment. It portrays an information worker trapped in something resembling a cubicle, whose job is to send out messages via a binary communications technology—the "sounding" telegraph—hooked into a larger network. Much as James's own recently hired typist processed his dictated words into typescript, the nameless telegraph girl *encodes* her customers' handwritten messages, transforming them into discrete bits of information that she—or anyone else who knows the code—can manipulate at will. Sender, receiver, and medium are virtual in the informational sense of the word; they become defined as functions within a larger system. The real scandal of this telegraph office—which is also a post office—seems to be that anyone, even a working girl, *might* occupy the place of the aristocratic lovers' exclusive "address."[69]

The character's very thoughts throughout the story can also be described as virtual in another contemporary sense of the term. They are simulacra, illusory visions given form by the apparatus itself. As several recent critics have pointed out, the protagonist's position in the cage, which she describes in the first line of the story as a "framed and wired confinement," seems to exercise a determining force on the way she interprets events (174).[70] She continually alternates between romantic fantasies of subjective merger with her customers—the "wire"—and a more disillusioned, objective, and even mercenary view of their affair—the "frame." The character herself would seem thus on some level to be inseparable from the machine she operates. Thoughts and feelings come not from within in this story, as in the romance novels the protagonist herself reads, but from without.

Other readings of "In the Cage" less attentive to the medium of the telegraph have focused on the telegraph girl's close association to writers and artists portrayed in James's other short works in the late 1890s, who also find themselves in states of ecstatic or eroticized exclusion from a dazzling social scene. Like them, she is a writer, of sorts. And like them, she cannily mitigates her isolation and penury by her masterful skill at imagining—even willfully fabricating—stories from the merest glimpses into her customers' lives. In this she is much like James himself, who all but makes explicit his identification with her in his preface to the New York edition. One reason may be that he too was suffering rejection from the world of fashionable London around this time, due to the failure of his ambitions to write for the theater. Just as the telegraph girl has to consciously try to make the best of her exclusion from the social scene by enjoying and cultivating her creative insight into it to the fullest extent, so does he.[71]

In what follows I bring together this critical focus on the medium's determining force and on the telegraph girl's aesthetically productive social isolation to read her predicament instead as a fictional refashioning of the idealist/empiricist schism, and her aesthetic solution to her own isolation as a version of the turn to "virtual experience" undertaken by Bergson, William James, and other late nineteenth-century vitalists. "In the Cage" thus discloses, as Benjamin notes in regard to Baudelaire and Proust, the "experience" of modernity—here specifically the experience of modern communications media—from which vitalist philosophy "evolved." Given the parallels between James himself and the telegraph girl, we can also understand the story as reflecting James's own emerging interest in the vitalist notion of virtual experience. As I suggest in more detail in chapter 2, however, for James, the virtual is not a way to transcend a technologized modernity, but instead a way to potentialize it from within, unleashing its hidden capacity to become other than it is.

The telegraph girl's alternation between a "wired" and a "framed" understanding of her customers' affair is inseparable from a larger alternation in the story between an idealist and a narrowly empirical point of view on the events in the shop more generally.[72] When she becomes aware of the affair between Captain Everard and Lady Bradeen, for example, she imagines the two of them in perfect rapport not only with her, but with one another. They stand "shoulder to shoulder in their high encounter with life," their talk is "that of the very happiest of people," and their telegrams give "a wondrous image" of their relationship (183). In turn, when she surmises that their affair is growing more dangerous, she sees Captain Everard as caught up "in the grip of a splendid dizzy fate; the wild wind of his life blew him straight before it," while Lady Bradeen becomes a stylized tableau of feminine distress borrowed from a romance novel: "The white begemmed hand bared to write rose in sudden nervousness to the side of the wonderful face" (208, 212). Her aristocratic customers, in other words, are walking ideals—fittingly enough for aristocrats, they are paragons of a timeless beauty, driven by an unknown destiny, whose moral character and beauty she aspires to love and to judge disinterestedly.

This rather exalted mood, however, stands in stark contrast to another, darker turn of mind, which gives the telegraph girl a wholly different take on what she calls the "animals" who frequent her shop. Her proximity to so much intrigue often leads her to formulate a more general theory of her customers' behavior that is based not on the winds of fate but a desire for mates. Like a positivist sociologist or an evolutionary naturalist, "her eye for types amounted . . . to genius" (187), and, storing her observations in her "small retentive brain," she "arrives at a philosophy of her own" (189). "It was literally visible," she reports, "that the general attitude of the one sex was that of the object pursued and defensive, apologetic and attenuating, while the light of her own nature helped her more or less to conclude as to the attitude of the other" (189). The telegraph girl does not spare herself from this altogether more base, but no less abstract, account of her customers' motives as driven by the laws of sexual selection—comically reversed as they are from Darwin's schema of active males and passive females.[73] She even describes her work in the cage as akin to "the life of a guinea-pig or a magpie" and goes on to liken the cage to a "fence" between herself and those she observes. The fence, it turns out, is necessary, for as she artfully supplies Lady Bradeen with a missing piece of her special lovers' code, thereby opening up the possibility of blackmail, the guinea pig in her becomes a tiger: "It was as if she had bodily leaped—cleared the top of the cage and alighted on her interlocutress. . . . Yes, she had made Juno blush" (213).

The telegraph girl's radically opposed interpretations are reinforced by her highly symbolic positioning within the story, both in the immediate scene of the shop itself and in the story's larger narrative arc. In the shop, she sits "sandwiched" in between the telegraphic apparatus of the "sounder," on the one hand, whose metaphorics of wordless, ideal communication pervade the text, and the counter clerk, on the other, who is "reduced to idiocy by the effect of his passion for her" and who gazes at the female customers with "a mere male glance," his "intention unmistakably low"

(209, 180, 195). Heightening the sense that James is providing us with a portrait of different interpretive positions, which the telegraph girl takes up at different times, she, the counter clerk, and the sounder itself have something of the quality of an audience at the theater. They all face the space of the shop across a permeable boundary, like an audience gazing over the footlights.

This hallmark of James's later style—the use of the dramatic "situation"— also places the telegraph girl in between different symbolic *denouements* to her story. The story's dramatic tension, conventionally enough, derives from her choice between two different possible suitors or lovers, yet the latter also figure the two warring positions within the central philosophical debate of James's time. The telegraphist only encounters Captain Everard after her fiancé, the grocer Mudge, who works with her, has been promoted to a better position, but in a more downscale telegraph shop. Mudge views the world entirely in terms of a materialistic calculus, seeing even his own fiancée's flirtation with the aristocracy in terms of its possible exchange value—"The more flirtations, as he might roughly express it, the more cheese and pickles" (203). The telegraph girl, as a result, faces either a marriage with the materialistic Mudge or an ecstatic communion with Everard beyond material want. Even the different locations associated with these prospective mates have empirical and ideal connotations. "Chalk Farm" is the mundane, working-class neighborhood where Mudge has relocated, while "Park Chambers" is the upscale Mayfair home of Everard, which the telegraph girl aptly describes as "the ideal setting for the ideal speech" (209).

The scenic construction, and the alternating worldviews, allow James to portray the telegraph girl therefore as confronting a very similar problem to that of the philosophers and social theorists discussed earlier. She continually shuttles back and forth between opposing explanations for a reality that is in fact riven by a fundamental and ineradicable uncertainty. That uncertainty, and the shifting and irreconcilable systems of thought to which she is drawn in order to explain it, have much to do with the fact that she is a messenger, or go-between, for two lovers, and that she works at a telegraph shop where messages are sent out but not received.[74] However, neither her uncertainty nor her shifting interpretations are reducible to the material facts of telegraphy, nor even to the "cage" itself, not least because such a reduction would in turn be a version of the narrow empiricism to which she herself occasionally subscribes. James instead invites us to follow the telegraph girl's experience of interpretation—what he calls her "'subjective' adventure"—as she moves from one point of view to another.[75] That experience might be aptly described as one of "variations of rate and of direction," as William James puts it. By virtue of her work in the cage, she is a virtual knower, "living in [the] transitions more than in the journey's end" (36).

The telegraph girl also finds confirmation of, as well as compensation for, the virtual nature of her knowledge through intuition and introspection, just like Bergson and William James. The delay necessary for both is an important means of making her "caged and wired confinement" bearable.[76] Bergson likens the mind to a telephonic exchange for its ability—in more evolutionarily developed organisms—to productively and creatively slow down the response to a stimulus. The telegraph girl sees her own capacity for delay in similar terms. A "literal prolongation" of the action of sending and receiving messages, as Bergson puts it, allows the telegraph girl to feel superior to the other "animals" in the shop: "She was rigid in general on the article of making the public itself affix its stamps, and found a special enjoyment in dealing to that end with some of the ladies who were too grand to touch them. She had thus a play of refinement and subtlety greater, she flattered herself, than any of which she could be made the subject" (188). Delay also allows the telegraph girl to demonstrate her play of refinement and subtlety to Captain Everard over the matter—literally—of his handwriting; this demonstration too allows her to transcend the evolutionary fray. "By the blessing of heaven," she notes, "... he formed some of his letters with a queerness—!" (206). In order to live a little longer in this heaven and to "bring their heads together" over the "fence," she pretends not to be able to read some of his missives. The telegraph girl's love for Captain Everard, therefore, is inseparable from the exercise of her powers of creative invention. With him, "everything, so far as they chose to consider it so, might mean almost anything" (205).

It is not simply interpretive freedom that is at issue in the telegraph girl's delaying tactics, then, but the access that this freedom gives her to the potentiality of her own experience. The "progressive pencil" mentioned in my opening pages may serve as a case in point. The very first time the telegraph girl encodes a message for the dazzling captain, she finds herself devoid of the ability to think at all. Rushing to complete his telegrams, her feelings become dissociated from her thoughts, because the job demands that words be counted rather than read. "Her immediate vision of himself had the effect, while she counted his seventy words, of preventing intelligibility" (182). Yet, as always, the opposite conclusion is also possible, especially in retrospect: "she *had* taken him in; she knew everything: she had made up her mind" (183) (emphasis mine). Upon Everard's return the next day, she rebels against interpretation itself by allowing her pencil to travel more slowly across the page. As she "[feels] her progressive pencil, dabbing as if with a quick caress the marks of his own, put life into every stroke," the telegraph girl experiences the emergence of her thoughts themselves from an indeterminate—and erotic—zone of bodily sensation, movement, and feeling, and thus exercises what Bergson might call "choice" or "free will." The erotic potentiality encoded by this scene of encoding is therefore inseparable from the experience of shifting interpretive frames. It takes on a special significance in light of the story's engagement with philosophical themes because an erotic experience of thinking—especially, perhaps, if it involves an identification with the opposite sex—can be reduced neither to animalistic desire nor idealized love.

But James might just as easily be drawing on the ideas of his brother, William, as Bergson in the way he describes the rewards of the telegraph girl's delaying tactics. For what her slowness gives her when coupled with introspection is access to a form of "pure experience" in the transitions between the momentary "stops" of conceptual thought. During her first encounter with Lady Bradeen, "she found her curiosity going out with a rush, a mute effusion that floated back to her, like a returning tide, the living color and splendour of the beautiful head, the light of eyes that seemed to reflect such utterly other things than the mean things actually before them" (180). Lady Bradeen's eyes function as a kind of endless, mirroring *mise en abyme*, because the "mean things" that should appear there are, logically, both the telegraph girl and her circumstances. Presumably the "utterly other things" that *do* appear there are also reflections of the telegraph girl, but are idealized self-images that she unknowingly projects onto, or rather into, the reflective eyes. This scene might thus draw us into endless speculations about the nature of the identification and desire between both parties. In a significant echo of the traps James sets for his reader in "The Turn of the Screw," published the same year, we are positioned in between the main character's point of view and an omniscient point of view by the use of free indirect speech, making the former's real thoughts tantalizingly unknowable.

The tidal metaphor for "curiosity," however, suggests that there is something else to be found in this scene than an endless, mirroring regard from which there is no escape for character or reader. For one thing, the tide dissociates curiosity from the telegraph girl herself, who is its putative location, turning it into a strangely impersonal force that departs and returns without her control, in the form of a movement or transition that transcends them both. The effect is to make the character's mental images into *virtual* mental images; an intellect somehow flows *in between* the telegraph girl and Lady Bradeen, rather than originating in one mind or the other. Fluid syntax reinforces this impression, as the simultaneously transitive and intransitive verb "floated" merges the mental image of Lady Bradeen's "beautiful head" with the tide of curiosity in which it floats. Whereas William James's sense of an experience "fringed" with "more" redeemed an atomized experience for philosophy, here a telegraph girl's experience of her own curiosity about her customers redeems the Victorian post office.

The same watery, fluid reality laps at the edges of the telegraphist's thoughts when, while reading the telegrams, she takes up the position of the absent lover in the exchange. The imagery James uses suggests that the transition she continually undergoes from the positions of subject to object to medium of communication throughout the story, often noticed by critics, should be considered just as real as each of those three positions themselves: "Our young friend's perusal of her ladyship's telegraph was literally prolonged by a momentary daze: what swam between her and the words, making her see them as through rippled shallow sun-shot water, was the great, the perpetual flood of 'how much *I* know—how much *I* know!'" (212). It is impossible to decide whether the momentary daze signals the telegraphist's imagination of perfect communicative transparency with either of the two lovers or of her intention to blackmail them with evidence of their illicit affair. But by emphasizing that "how much *I* know—how much I know!" *swims* in between the telegraphist and the page, this passage implies that certainty in either case is a creative self-elaboration born out of a pure experience that links subject and world.[77] It is as if she can feel the constitution of her own subjectivity, as a watery, fluid, and immersive transition or movement from position to position.

These intuitions of a watery but real connection between observer and observed, born out of delay and introspection, are, finally, embraced by the telegraph girl in an attempt to get beyond a notion of *discrete* sense perceptions altogether: "She had surrendered herself . . . of late to a certain expansion of her consciousness; something that seemed perhaps vulgarly accounted for by the fact that, as the blast of the season roared louder and the waves of fashion tossed their spray further over the counter, there were more impressions to be gathered and really . . . more life to be led" (178). In acknowledging the vulgarity of accounting for an expansion of experience as a matter of accumulating impressions, the telegraph girl makes a move that resembles the radical empiricist critique of empiricism. The previous passage suggests that minds do not "gather" discrete impressions through the windows of the senses, like a watcher on the beach who feels the drops of the spray. Such a Lockean or associationist account of sense perception is literally vulgar because of its emphasis on the quantification and materialization of experience and on the idea that experiences can be confined within the self. The gathering of impressions, for instance, reflects the gathering of money that Mudge imagines will result from his fiancée's increasing closeness with Captain Everard. The idea of a watery transition or tide flowing between subject and object, as the origin of the discrete drops of spray, instead allows the telegraph girl to emphasize the reality of the tie she feels to her unknowing and unreachable customers.

It seems clear, therefore, that the telegraph girl is cannier than many critics have given her credit for. She is not blinded by her infatuations with her customers. "The flashes, the quick revivals" of her interest in them, she tells us at one point, are "absolute accidents all, and neither to be counted on nor to be resisted" (178). Instead, she takes such moments as the occasion for an introspective meditation on the processes of her own perception, much as vitalist philosophers suggest, and thereby discovers what she calls a "queer extension of her experience" that can serve as an alternative to toggling back and forth between empiricist and idealist worldviews. However, she does all this because she is a telegraph operator trapped in the Victorian post office, where she has only the materials available immediately to hand: slowing down her work of transcribing handwriting into the dots and dashes of binary code. The story thus emerges as less a reflection of vitalist ideas than a testing ground for their historical character. For the telegraph girl's self-experimentation and the knowledge that emerges are portrayed in this story as a necessary form of accommodation to the historical emergence of new media like the sounding telegraph, and more particularly to the experiences of intermedial exchange that they enabled.

We are justified, then, in reading the telegraph girl as a figure for her author, but not, as some critics have suggested, because her imagination allows her fully to transcend the materialities of her existence. Instead she reveals the ways in which James himself was beginning to turn to the idea of the virtual or the potential to achieve a form of redemption from within an otherwise imprisoning media-technological order. Around the time of writing "In the Cage," as I show in chapter 2, James was also becoming preoccupied with generating a sense of latency and delay, albeit at the level of the sentence, via grammar and syntax. While the opacity and digressiveness of late Jamesian style has been credited to a variety of factors, I argue that it is best understood historically as an appropriation of the media transpositions—from theater, to film, to drama, to photography, to novels—characteristic of a highly multimedia mass culture and mass public sphere at the turn of the century. While the new citability of media forms threatened the cultural authority of artists and writers, when appropriated by the language of the literary text, it offered a way to potentialize the emerging media-technological order from within. I suggest that, through style, James seeks to unleash what Benjamin called the "hidden index" in new mass-cultural forms, such as illustrated bestsellers or photography, and thereby to open up a different future than the ones such forms themselves contain, particularly as regards the artists and writers whose cultural authority they place on the line. Insofar as the telegraph girl's "progressive pencil" allows her to delay the arrival of a future in which words are only numbers, therefore, that pencil is very much James's as well.

Literature, Media, and the Afterlife of Writing

My reading of "In the Cage" significantly complicates two influential recent accounts of what happened to the category of experience in American literature beginning in the late nineteenth century. The first of these comes from the tradition of literary criticism inaugurated by Stanley Cavell and his revisionary reading of Emerson as a radical philosopher of experience.[78] For critics writing about American modernism in the wake of Cavell, nothing *did* happen to the category of experience in American literature.[79] Critics influenced by Cavell have argued that convictions about the transitory, dependent, and evanescent nature of the self and subjectivity—precisely what modernity itself is often understood to traumatically introduce into literary representation—were already at the heart of the American literary tradition. Authors writing in the Emersonian mode already understood selfhood and subjectivity to be receptive, passive, processual, and experimental—like the tide of curiosity on which Lady Bradeen's head floats—rather than fixed, immutable, stable, and constant. Such convictions have been traced not only to the works of Emerson, but also to those of Jonathan Edwards, Herman Melville, Henry David Thoreau, and others.[80] Keeping the American tradition of thinking through experience in mind leads to the conclusion that late nineteenth-century psychological discoveries discussed earlier did not undermine—they in fact confirmed—long-standing insights at the heart of the American literary tradition.

According to a second body of recent criticism, however, something very significant did in fact happen to the category of experience in the late nineteenth century. For critics influenced by the "media discourse analysis" of Friedrich Kittler, whom I mentioned earlier, new media technologies circa 1900 dethroned subjectivity and undermined long-cherished conceptions of language, literature, and the arts.[81] As literature was forced into competition with film, photography, and phonography, writing lost its special status as the receptacle of a mysterious prelinguistic truth, and hermeneutics itself lost its legitimacy. Literary modernism arose as a compensatory preoccupation with the purity, specificity, and technical capacities of the literary or artistic medium. While the materiality of mind and the fluidity of subjectivity are seen as intrinsic to much of American literature by Cavell and later critics writing in his wake, Kittler—who ignores pragmatism—credits such notions instead to the invention of late nineteenth-century media technologies. For Kittler, however, in the wake of media, experience vanished entirely. Subjectivity gave up the *Geist*.[82]

Neither of these explanations fully does justice to the telegraph girl's experience. The defiant slowness of her Jamesian pencil suggests that by 1900, literature was most certainly in competition with new media technologies; language could no longer be understood to possess what Richard Poirier memorably called, in regard to Emerson, the "aboriginal power of troping."[83] In addition to pen, paper, and voice, the self could find itself, and be founded in, what Emerson might have called the "low" and "common" materials newly to hand, including the typewriter, the news photograph, the silent film, and the phonograph. At the same time, the telegraph girl's canny making-do in her cage suggests that hermeneutics, of the radical kind practiced in the Emersonian tradition, was not entirely vanquished by media systems, either, as media studies especially in the Kittlerian vein might have it. Instead it had to be actively claimed as an alternative to what American literary elites, including Henry James, viewed as more impoverished forms of self-making and self-abandonment on offer in an emerging media-technological order. Devotees of experience as they already were, American writers understood mass culture and new media technologies as the occasion not for a debasing fall from the ideal into the real, but instead for the rise of a rival "thinking language."[84] The literary turn to potentiality figured in the "progressive pencil" thus emerges as a form of redemption for literature itself, and as a claim for the value of the transitional experience of selfhood found there, *against* the fluid, passive, processual, and experimental experiences of selfhood solicited by a technologized modernity.

The chapters that follow tell the story of these encounters and claims. Chapter 1, "Steven Crane's Abilities," further explores what I have set out as a conflict over experience by examining the metaphorics of writing and of color that run throughout Crane's work. Crane's violently disfigured faces, forms, and landscapes, I show, should be understood not as allegories of writing per se, but instead as allegories of socially informed realist writing at the dawn of mass culture. As Crane's texts show more vividly and starkly than most, the idea that the self is mediated by the materialities of language and media was not news to American writers. What was new was the uncanny—even horrifying—similarity between the experience of new spectacles, such as the immersive and entertaining news coverage of the Spanish–American War, and that of the "living" word or book of nature in the American Protestant tradition. Crane zeroed in on the ironies of this overlap in his fiction, but he was troubled by it as well. I argue that the textual representation of color allowed Crane to recreate the feeling of incipience characteristic of divine dispossession by the word and to restore to literary writing and the author some margin of their formerly sacred mission and abilities.

Chapter 2, "Realizing *Trilby*: Henry James, George du Maurier, and the Intermedial Scene," examines the emergence of Henry James's late style from an unusual perspective—his friendship with du Maurier, whose *Trilby* was one of the bestselling illustrated novels of the 1890s. Looking at James's late work through the lens of "Trilbymania" reveals the importance of what I call "mass pictorialism" to James—the citation or "realization" of a scene or situation across theater, film, photography, texts, and illustration—as he set about retooling his literary method in the wake of his failure as a dramatist. The distinctively intermedial quality of early mass culture inspired James's distinctive grammar of latency, as I argued earlier, but I also see the energies of intermedial transformation as lying at the root of his utopian social imaginary, in which sexual identity and selfhood are understood to be irreducible to psychology.

The intermedial in its utopian dimension is also important to James Weldon Johnson, the subject of chapter 3, in his quest to achieve cultural "uplift" for African Americans during the "nadir" of race relations in the 'teens. In "Syncope Fever: James Weldon Johnson and the Black Phonographic Voice" I argue that ragtime music—a much-adulterated and much-recorded mass cultural form—was at the center of Johnson's generically innovative 1912 novel, *The Autobiography of an Ex-Colored Man*, passages from which were reused in his later essays and prefaces about black contributions to the arts. In Johnson's work, ragtime bridges the gap between the *phone* and the graph, speech and writing. I argue that Johnson creates a virtual voice in his novel that mimics the "phonographic" logic of ragtime itself. This voice signifies the unspeakable legacies of slavery through its very inarticulacy, while at the same time acting as a crucible for interpretive possibility. Johnson thus uncovers what Benjamin called the "hidden index" in ragtime that ties this debased mass cultural form to an alternative future that has yet to arrive.

Chapters 4 and 5 take up two more conventionally "modernist" writers: Djuna Barnes and Gertrude Stein. I read them, however, less as avatars of the new than—like all of the authors in this study—historically illuminating throwbacks, or holdovers. In chapter 4, "Wonder and Decay: Djuna Barnes's New York," I argue that Barnes's much-noted baroque literary style can be traced not to the interwar movement of the neobaroque in Europe, but instead to some of her earliest written work in pre–World War I New York, as a reform-minded newspaper reporter covering cultural and social events. I show that Barnes's portraits of everyday life in Progressive Era New York make thorough use of her digressive ornamental style and her compositional principles of assemblage; as in her later work, she also depicts history itself as secondary and unreal, the product of a debasing fall into duality. I make the case that Barnes's style and her dualistic and vertically oriented cosmological vision emerged as a way of negotiating a broader cultural conflict she saw firsthand in her youth, between the "good works" enjoined on the public by reform journalism and the passivity simultaneously being solicited from them by the consolidation of film and an emerging media industry.

Chapter 5, "Gertrude Stein Talking," uses as its jumping-off point
Stein's 1934–35 lecture tour of the United States in which she talked about
the philosophy of her writing, its distinctively "American" quality, and a
variety of social issues of the day. By reading other works that are often
overlooked, I argue that Stein's lectures were not just a statement of what
she had always been doing in her writing. Instead, they offered a refinement and crystallization of her pragmatist and radically empiricist aesthetics—in the light of her experience of mass media–inflected celebrity.
Exploiting the paradox inherent in her own celebrity, in which she was
heralded simultaneously for the clarity and obscurity of her speech and
writing, Stein engages with contemporaneous debates about the function of communication in society. She offers an idiosyncratic model of
communication as vitality and force, engaging both emotion and reason.
Stein's writings of the 1930s thus provide perhaps the clearest example of
the ways in which the rise of mass culture and new media technologies
were second nature to American writers. Appropriating the power of the
celebrity image, Stein didn't just describe her distinct place in the pantheon of American writers but brought it into being.

A final set of caveats are in order. The analysis I offer of the late nineteenth-
century "virtual turn" raises a number of methodological problems and
questions having to do with the paradox of "historicizing"—that is, spatializing and quantifying—an idea usually used or invoked precisely to *oppose* cognitive acts of spatializing and quantifying. My concern for history
as qualitative transformation or becoming, a concern I claim is shared by
the authors in this book, is arguably undermined by a frequent tendency
to treat history itself as linear. Throughout, it might be charged that I effectively deflate the potentializing aspirations for the literary that I uncover in
each writer by tracing them to mass culture at a particular historical moment announced in the subtitle: the "Progressive Era."

As a way to compensate for these reductions inherent in the paradigm
of the "virtual turn," I resist making claims about continuity or change between the multimedia culture of pre–World War I America and the present
moment, tantalizing as those parallels are. Instead, my goal is to let literary
language do the work of unleashing the "hidden index" of the past, which I
hope will thereby connect itself "secretly," as Benjamin might put it, to a variety of contemporary concerns. At the same time, my discussion of mass
culture and technology in each of the following chapters seeks to avoid

promoting the common view of mass culture as a forward march of media with ever more sophisticated technical specifications or attributes. For this reason, I have not organized the chapters according to different media technologies but have focused instead on different authors and events. The discussion of technology that I do undertake focuses on qualitative transformations or tensions *between* media forms and between media and the arts—such as those found in the pictorialist films of "Trilbymania," for instance, or the theatrical re-creations of Spanish–American War photographs. These intermedial and multimedial aspects of pre–World War I culture have largely been neglected within media studies, in part because transformations between media are considered, paradoxically, to define the *digital* as a medium. Another motivation for focusing on authors and events rather than technologies comes from a desire to bring media studies and American literary studies into conversation. In so doing, I hope to infuse a sense of both change and continuity into our understanding of the relationship between the late nineteenth-century "virtual turn" and today.

To see how the virtualizing power of literary language is able to do this, let us return one last time to the telegraphist's progressive pencil. The autoerotic overtones James imparts to the act of "marking up" handwriting for telegraphic transmission makes the new ability to transmit messages instantaneously via the "sounding" telegraph and the consolidated Victorian postal system appear in both its qualitative and quantitative dimensions—as both the emergence of the new and a repetition of the same. The sounder and its system are new, James suggests, much as affective and erotic states are new; both technology and feeling "progress" or change from one state to the next without measurable stages in between. But the sounder and the system are also a repetition of the same much as the telegraphist is also a copyist—the mission of both the girl and her machine is to keep the message the same while increasing its speed. Telegraphy is thereby virtualized by the figure of the pencil that writes itself, in the sense that its emergence becomes irreducible to preexisting possibilities latent in handwriting and waiting to be made real. It is to a closer examination of this strange afterlife of writing, with its power to transform the possible into the potential, that I now turn.

CHAPTER 1

Stephen Crane's Abilities

I cannot help vanishing and disappearing and dissolving. It is my foremost trait.

—Stephen Crane, letter to Ripley Hitchcock, March 15, 1896

S TEPHEN CRANE has long been hard to place within a specific literary tradition or period. His commitment to portraying social types and typical events in his fiction, his interest in embodied cognition, his preoccupation with problems of faith and skepticism, and his drive to experience the "strenuous life" all place him firmly within the canon of the realists and naturalists. Yet his impressionistic style, so redolent of film and photography, along with his fascination with the mediated nature of perception and with the shocks administered by war, have made him, for many, a herald of the international modernist movement in literature and the arts that arose during and after World War I. One solution to this problem is to understand Crane as a radical empiricist and his fiction as an illustration of ideas that have much in common with those of C. S. Peirce and William James—a long-neglected parallel that I emphasize in the final section of this chapter. Ultimately, however, in the pages that follow, I show that Crane turns to a poetics of the virtual—and in particular to a poetics of color—to gain a critical purchase on forms of technological alienation that the philosophers of "virtual experience" remained unable to address.

One of the most commonly reported facts about Crane, whose signature subject was the experience of war, is that before writing his most acclaimed novel, *The Red Badge of Courage,* he had never seen a war. Contemporaneous reviewers nearly always commented on Crane's inexperience, either praising his amazing capacity for imagining how war feels or condemning him for being only a "theoretical soldier."[1] Crane's mentor, William Dean Howells, tended to take the latter view. Howells, the most influential critic of the day and a champion of the realist novel, was to note (after Crane's death) that in writing *Red Badge,* his protégé had "lost himself in a whirl of wild guesses at the fact from the ground of insufficient witness . . . though it was what the public counted a success."[2] Criticisms like these evidently had an effect on Crane, who only grudgingly produced further war stories on demand and avidly sought to become a war correspondent following *Red Badge*'s publication, first in the Greco–Turkish War of 1897, and then in the Spanish–American War. Yet even in the context of war reporting, Crane's lack of direct experience continued to be the most salient fact about him for others. His well-known ability to convincingly depict an experience of battle without having seen one led editors to market him as a striking witness to the "reality" of war. "That Was the ROMANCE: 'The Red Badge of Courage.' This is the REALITY: A Battle of To-Day in Greece. By STEPHEN CRANE," the *San Francisco Examiner* trumpeted in 1897.[3]

Crane's ability to depict war without having seen one has often been credited by contemporary critics to his facility at thematically and formally incorporating media images of war into his writing, particularly since the Spanish–American and Philippine conflicts were arguably the first "media wars" in American history. Bill Brown has documented Crane's many references to war imagery and has argued that Crane's texts show the ways in which, during wartime, the public sphere became less a site for the exercise of deliberative reason than for a "mass subject" to be "produced by, by bearing witness to, an image ubiquitously reproduced."[4] Amy Kaplan has argued that Crane deliberately presented war as a mediated spectacle or image to be consumed in *Red Badge* in order to challenge rampant discourses of U.S. imperialism in the 1890s.[5] In a highly influential reading, Michael Fried has argued that the metaphors of violent writing running throughout Crane's texts allegorize the material work of his own writing, and by extension that of the photographic treatment of reality to which both journalism and realist fiction aspire.[6] Such readers emphasize the ways in which technology and spectacle in Crane's work disclose the alterity of the self and its reliance on the materiality of writing and representation. They position Crane as moving away from realism and toward a new set of literary aspirations and abilities that might be more properly described as modernist or avant-garde.

Yet Crane's embrace of such aspirations and abilities was by no means uncomplicated, as suggested by his persistent compulsion to witness war in order to write about it, which likely killed him.[7] This chapter argues that

Crane's conflicts in regard to realism had to do with his awareness of an uncanny overlap between the emerging mass public sphere and a rather different set of principles still informing his own writing. As earlier studies have suggested, the depiction of identity in Crane's work—and even his own identity as a writer, as the epigraph to this chapter suggests—has much in common with the prophetic, intermediate, selfhood-in-process characteristic of the Puritan and Protestant traditions.[8] Crane was also aware, I contend, that a radical empiricism had often been central to the intermediate Puritan self, in both its spiritual and secular incarnations. Borrowing from John Locke's sensationalism, Jonathan Edwards had discovered the presence of the divine in the feeling of typological interpretation, as he searched the Old Testament for words to describe the unfamiliar natural forms he encountered in the New World.[9] Critics writing in the wake of Stanley Cavell, as I noted in the introduction, have established that, a good half-century before mass culture inaugurated a postliterary public sphere, Emerson, Melville, and Thoreau were exploring the ways that the continuities between thoughts and things could be experienced in the changing and turning of the literary trope.[10] Late nineteenth-century American intellectuals such as Crane's mentor, Howells, therefore, may have taken mass culture as seriously as they did because they already considered experience itself to be transitional and fluid, and thoughts and things to belong to the same ontological order. While many critics argue that it took the burgeoning mass cultural sphere to reveal the alterity of the self and its construction by writing and representation, I hold that these ideas were in fact already familiar in Crane's intellectual milieu.

The influence on Crane's work of this contestation over experience is my subject in this chapter. I begin, in the first section, by laying out in more detail the conflicting realist and prophetic tendencies in Crane before turning to the ways in which these conflicting tendencies played out on a larger historical canvas with which he was intimately familiar: the spectacular news coverage of the Spanish–American War. Media spectacles of war were particularly troubling for realism, as I suggest with reference to Howells's short story "Editha," because—as distinctively immersive, theatrical events—they confused distinctions between the virtual self of the American public sphere, in progress toward the fulfillment of a reasoned plan for social justice, and the virtual self solicited for commercial gain in the emerging mass public sphere, in thrall to spectacularized war. In the second section, I unpack the ways in which this confusion was also palpable in *The Red Badge of Courage* (which may be why Howells was dissatisfied with the book). The remainder of the chapter pursues a reading of the disfigured faces and forms in Crane's texts as allegories of Crane's own struggle over the question of his realist "abilities," with a focus on the immersive, yet unlocatable, *qualia* of color. My reading reveals that Crane's conflict with realism was not over "writing as such," but over the unstable boundary between writing, which had historically functioned to convert private experience into forms of public reason for the American man of letters, and new spectacular forms of mass culture, which increasingly performed a very similar kind of conversion for the purposes of commerce or social control.

Realism, Mass Culture, and the Spectacle of War

It was not, of course, as the newspapers and early critics of *Red Badge* would have it, that Crane had a miraculous ability to accurately intuit the truth of experiences he had never had. Writing for Crane was less a means of creating a fidelity or correspondence to experience, as it was for Howells, than a means of realizing or actualizing experience, like a baseball batter warming up for a swing. *Red Badge,* for instance, shaped what Crane was later to see as a war correspondent, supplying him with images and themes that he later recycled in his newspaper dispatches from the front and in his supposedly more informed later war fiction.[11] *Maggie: A Girl of the Streets,* a novel about a girl forced into prostitution by poverty, shaped Crane's actions in a more personal way. Crane moved to the Bowery in order to finish the novel, where several years later, scandalously, he became involved in a court case defending a prostitute.[12] He eventually fell in love with a madam, Cora Taylor, and lived with her until his death. Crane's practice of visualizing his own life events ahead of time through writing gave his fiction an uncannily prophetic air. For instance, long before he himself spent thirty hours at sea in a lifeboat off the coast of Florida on a failed expedition to Cuba, an ordeal that became the subject of his short story "The Open Boat," he had written a short story about four men stranded in a boat, trying to reach land after a shipwreck.[13] As Christopher Benfey notes, "If most writers tend to write about their experience, however disguised, Crane did the reverse: he tried to live what he'd already written."[14] It was as if Crane felt his identity to be forged anew in the act of writing, lending his texts a prophetic quality.

This tendency in Crane can be traced to two influences. After leaving Syracuse University, he worked as a reporter on the Jersey shore for his brother's newsgathering agency, and later for the New York newspapers. His journalism experience taught him, much as it had Howells, to see and to represent character and situation in terms of what is typical or representative. References to types, as a result, came to suffuse his fiction. Crane's descriptions abstract the general from the specific, and his characters have names that are characteristics, such as "The Swede" in "The Blue Hotel," or "the correspondent" in "The Open Boat." A fundamental assumption behind the new form of "realist" fiction that Crane practiced was that the synoptic view it provided had a social efficacy, and the analysis it offered of the social world was often shared with the journalistic exposé.[15] Yet while champions of social realism like Howells emphasized the necessity of direct experience for the disillusioning portrayal of typical events, a talent for seeing types in fact made such experience unnecessary. In writing *Red Badge*, for instance, Crane was able to effectively extrapolate from passing references by Civil War veterans, from memoirs by Union and Confederate officers, and from his experience at military school.[16] Having grasped the basic general pattern, he derives a particular experience from it, whether in fiction or in life. As Larzer Ziff puts it, "Events were a test of [Crane's] consciousness, not its instructor."[17]

But Crane's capacity to see the general in the particular, and especially his tendency to test out his writing in experience, can also be traced to the tradition of American Protestantism and specifically Puritanism that underlay it.[18] This tradition, as noted earlier, tended to see in the very ability to interpret the sensory experiences of biblical words, or in the perception of nature itself, evidence of the working out of America's divine or cosmic plan. Crane was intimately familiar with such ideas due to the influence of his father, the Reverend Jonathan Townley Crane, whose oft-noted criticism of fiction reading was based on a conviction about the divinely sanctioned social and self-transformations that could be effected by direct contact and shared experience across classes.[19] His writings and ministry were inseparable from the progressive challenge to the depredations of industrialism and financial speculation in the late nineteenth century. This was a cause that the younger Crane embraced, whatever he otherwise thought of his father's attitude toward fiction or his larger spiritual mission.[20]

Cosmic polarities and portentous symbolism drawn from this tradition suffuse Crane's fiction and nonfiction, as has often been noted. Such devices are often deployed ironically—as they are to a lesser extent in Howells's work—in the service of cultivating analytic and resolutely secular insights on typical characters and social situations. In contrast to the typical or representative pilgrim who can experience the divine in the act of biblical exegesis, the strictly social type in a realist or naturalist novel is blind to the way his judgments are shaped by his feelings and by the workings of the material environment upon him. Often, what makes the representative or the typical individual and social situation "real" in Crane is precisely this ironic disjunction between social and material typicality and a character's own personal prophetic typology.[21] Yet Crane also portrays his characters' discovery of their material circumstances as horrifying, suggesting he still found meaning in ideas of transcendent destiny.

Mass culture, specifically the nature of Crane's work as a war reporter, posed a threat to both his divine and his secular mission. The period just following *Red Badge*'s publication saw the advent of the Spanish–American War and the Philippine War, which were represented and discussed in the news and also in pageants, plays, spectacular re-creations, and early films. As many cultural historians have noted, the war spectacles presented an iconography of typical figures—the American soldier, the Cuban revolutionary, the Spanish general, and the war correspondent—in ways wholly detached from their context. War was becoming virtual, as Brown notes earlier, a matter of images circulating in a closed system of meanings. Importantly, however, war was also becoming a virtual *experience*. The theatrical aspect of the war coverage placed great weight on what it *felt like* to witness war. The emphasis on experience in mass entertainments circa 1900 threatened to deprive the Puritan transitional self of its home in language; meanwhile, realism's hope to cultivate an enlightened literary public came to seem unlikely. A glance at the newspaper coverage and many spectacular public events surrounding the Spanish–American War illustrates the nature of the problem that mass culture presented to the writer's mission, as Crane inherited it.

It is something of a myth that the U.S.–Cuban conflict was started by the newspapers. As the story goes, a circulation battle between William Randolph Hearst, the newspaper magnate and editor of the *New York Journal*, and Joseph Pulitzer, of the rival *New York World*, led both papers to whip up "war fever" or "hysteria" in the populace with their use of illustrations, huge "scare" headlines, and fake news stories. Thus they pushed a reluctant president William McKinley into war, feeding a resurgent nationalism, a nascent consumer society, and the beginning of American global hegemony.[22] This myth of the "newspapers' war" or the "correspondents' war" was likely born after World War I, a war that demonstrated the widespread effectiveness of centralized government propaganda although it in fact banished the war correspondent from the front lines.[23] The myth may well have been reinforced during and after World War II, with the massive vertical integration of the media empires of Hearst and Henry Booth Luce, as portrayed by Orson Welles in *Citizen Kane* (1941); the consolidation of what Adorno and Horkheimer called the "culture industry" more broadly in the interwar period; and finally the rise of realpolitik during the Cold War, which rejected the hold of emotion and moral compass alike as motivations for U.S. foreign intervention.[24]

In reality, the rallying cry of "Cuba Libre" was less an ideological master narrative through which a centralized media machine confused the populace and controlled the government than a loose script for the production of sensational effects in a wide variety of venues in media including print. A survey of the broader cultural landscape in the United States during the period, such as that found in Bonnie Miller's excellent history of the visual and popular culture of the war, reveals that "mass" media, including newspapers and the first newsreels, were often consumed in local and variable performance venues where news and a great variety of other amusements inextricably mingled. Hearst and Pulitzer loom larger in our imagination now because of the later, postwar context of *Citizen Kane* than they did in the late 1890s, when both reached only 3 percent of the population.[25] Miller shows that pageants, plays, spectacular re-creations of war scenes, vaudeville, panoramas, and minstrel shows worked in tandem with local newspapers and film to depict Cuban suffering, U.S. "heroism," the infamy of the Spanish colonialist government, and the details and strategies of various battles, as well as sometimes to undertake serious debate about the origins and aims of U.S. intervention. During the run-up to hostilities with Spain in 1898, for instance, theaters were important venues for distributing information procured by reporters, via either war plays based on very recent news stories or announcements to audiences. In turn, panoramas and battle reenactments often sought to convey detailed information from press reports and illustrations.

These productions mark a significant contrast in their variability and distinctly local appeal with the later control over distribution and consumption achieved by more integrated networks of cultural producers

after World War I via newspapers, newsreels, radio, and eventually television. For instance, although the war helped to birth the film industry
and to launch the newsreel, as many scholars have shown, the meaning
of those first films was also dependent on highly theatrical "attractions"
generated at the context of their reception.[26] Footage of the wreckage of
the *Maine* explosion was shown accompanied by emotive orchestral accompaniment. Newsreels of American troops rushing into battle, which
were often themselves clearly reenactments, were shown in auditoriums
filled with imitation gun smoke and the piped-in sounds of musketry
fire.[27] While it is common to claim that film, photography, and news reports in this period were exemplary of press propaganda, the theatrical
artifice of the news was in fact publicly affirmed and indulged as a result of
its close connection to these spectacular events and restagings. The media
coverage of the Spanish–American War, in other words, was a multimedia
performance, demonstrating the highly complex encounter between the
bourgeois public sphere and mass culture during this period.

Throughout its run, as Miller documents, the 1898 Omaha World's Fair
featured a scale model of the warship *Maine* exploding daily on the fair's
"lagoon." Spectators first watched a slideshow of the wreckage, the cleanup,
and funeral processions—gleaning information, newsreel style—before
then witnessing the ship destroyed in front of them.[28] The impulse to stage
such events was undoubtedly indebted to the highly profitable "thrill of
watching forms implode," as Nancy Bentley notes of 1890s spectacles more
generally.[29] However, such events were not quite entertainment, either,
for they aspired to convey news and information, particularly given their
synergy with newsreels and the close relationship between real events and
their re-creation in model form.[30] The unsettling nature of the spectacle
of the exploding *Maine* comes, in other words, not from the way it treats
war and disaster as entertainment, but instead from the way it collapses
distinctions between the consumption of the spectacle and the exercise of
deliberative reason constitutive of the public sphere.

The slippage between these two realms can be explained by the fact
that the simulation of war for pleasure, jingoism, commercial gain, and
news made little distinction between the truth value of the simulation
and the truth value of the *experience* of the simulation. Entrepreneurs
used newspaper articles to back up the facts they were presenting, but the
press, in reporting these shows, seemed mainly concerned with whether

they provoked an authentic emotional response in the spectator. The aptly named Henry J. Pain, a specialist in the art of pyrotechnics, constructed a popular battle re-creation of "The Battle of Manila" several weeks after the battle itself in 1898, featuring firing cannons, burning ships, "screeching shells," and reproductions of Philippine forts and of U.S. and Spanish battleships.[31] The point was to create a functionally equivalent experience of battle for those who watched. Such experiences, and not the facts themselves, were often verified by the reporters who had served as eyewitnesses to the event. Pain's touring conflagrations were so "realistic," according to one paper, that they kept spectators in "a frenzy of excitement and anticipation."[32] The *New York Journal* praised another re-creation of the Battle of Manila in Madison Square Garden in terms that suggested it had placed viewers in the position of its own reporters. The event was reproduced "with such historical accuracy that New Yorkers see the blockade and battles as effectively almost as though they had been on board a *Journal* dispatch boat."[33]

In order to bring home the Cuban conflict to audiences, as many scholars have documented, the unsettling thrills brought by film and other mass entertainments were harnessed to a very familiar story of American identity in progress toward a definite and well-justified end—that of empire. The visual conventions of melodrama, with its logic of the racial other threatening an imperiled white femininity, structured representations of the Spanish Empire as bloodthirsty and effete, the Cuban *reconcentrados* as helpless and feminine, and the American soldier as inviolable and manly. Such narratives of manifest destiny and American empire were ubiquitous, although more contested in public venues than we have tended to remember.[34] However, those in the anti-imperialist movement that formed with the annexation of the Philippines—and which included realist writers such as Crane's mentors William Dean Howells and Hamlin Garland— were also troubled by something rather different. The prophetic feeling that the war spectacles engendered had no intrinsic relationship to the mission of social justice the spectacles professed. Nor, for that matter did they really have a necessary link to justifications for American empire, or to anything at all.[35] The language of empire and manifest destiny could be disturbingly dissociated from feeling, as illustrated by the ease with which advertisers transferred feelings associated with the Cuban cause to a huge variety of commercial products that had little or nothing to do with it.[36]

To the distress of realist writers devoted to cultivating analytic insight into the social world, the thrill of mass witnessing could attach itself, and be attached to, almost anything.

Such is the accusation of an antiwar short story written by William Dean Howells in 1905. "Editha" suggests that the contamination of judgment by feeling defines the problem of mass-mediated war. The story then subtly offers its own analysis of the war news spectacles and their effects on the mind as a solution. "Editha" tells the story of a young engaged couple in which the eponymous bride-to-be urges her fiancé to join up for an unspecified foreign conflict that strongly resembles the Spanish–American War. Initially George, the fiancé, questions Editha's faith in what she calls the "order of Providence," and her conviction that he should take up arms in a "sacred" war.[37] Eventually, however, George becomes converted to the cause and departs for the front, where he is killed in the first skirmish. Far from a hero's death, George's demise is "telegraphed as a trifling loss on our side" (222). The story closes as Editha is confronted by George's mother, who fails to take solace from his heroic sacrifice. With bitter irony, she condemns Editha for sending off her son to war.

The story criticizes the spectacularization of war by borrowing a familiar tableau from the mass press—the melodramatic image of the soldier departing for the front and leaving behind his anxious bride-to-be—and making it serve a socially illustrative function. In an ironic reversal, it is the bride who has been whipped into a frenzy by the spectacle of war and her fiancé who is ambivalent about enlisting. Howells thereby indicates the degree to which the uneven intersection of mass culture and the public sphere confused social categories and identities. With the advent of war as popular and mass-mediated spectacle, it is the woman who becomes hungry for news and attuned to world events and the man who remains strangely languid and diffident, even in the face of what Editha calls a "crime and shame at our very gates," an often-repeated claim about the state of affairs in Cuba (216).[38]

Howells's main criticism of the war news spectacles concerns their dangerously ungrounded appeal to the material mind. Editha never persuades George of the rightness of the cause; instead, he enlists because he gets caught up in a kind of mass hysteria after attending a boisterous rally at the town hall that culminates in a raucous parade through the streets. While explaining his decision to Editha later that night, this formerly calm, skeptical, and ironic character is barely in control of himself; he "drank goblet after goblet of . . . ice-water without noticing who was giving it, and kept on talking, and laughing through his talk wildly"(219). Howells borrows a familiar argument among liberals at the time, such as his friend E. L. Godkin, that nervous exhaustion and "excitability" was the cause of the public's hunger for war.[39] The scene indicates the degree to which Howells took mass culture seriously as a source of insight into the embodied nature of cognition. Rather than identifying with the heroic image of himself as a representative type destined to fulfill the "order of Providence," George goes to war because he loses his cognitive capacity for judgment altogether. "Editha" charts perhaps the only recorded case of pretraumatic stress disorder.

George's night with the mob ultimately invites readers to draw a firm distinction between the virtual self of the American public sphere, prophetically remade in the service of a more just society, and the virtual self solicited by the war news spectacles, dangerously fascinated with the thrill of spectacularized war. What actually changes his mind about enlisting is learning about the exciting new technologies of warfare: "Why, I believe I was the first convert to the war in that crowd to-night!" George notes breathlessly. "I never thought I should like to kill a man; but now I shouldn't care; and the smokeless powder lets you see the man drop that you kill" (219). The reference to smokeless powder, or cordite, recalls the new smokeless guns that had just emerged prior to the Spanish–American War. As Cynthia Wachtell has pointed out, the elimination of the clouds of smoke from the battlefield had the effect of making the source of the enemy's fire invisible while making the carnage inflicted upon him—via ever deadlier rifles and improvements in the machine gun—highly visible.[40] By describing George as a "convert" to these technologies because of their ability to make violence into a spectacle, Howells invites readers not to reject the idea of conversion altogether, but to distinguish between true and false conversions—those beholden to reason, self-awareness, and the pursuit of justice, and those beholden, like George's, to nothing more than excitement. Editha's conversion to war has also clearly been of the latter variety. As George struggles initially to decide between loyalty to her idealism or to his own loathing of war and killing, the narrator tells us "It all interested her intensely; she was undergoing a tremendous experience, and she was being equal to it" (218). Editha's "experience" echoes the emphasis placed on participatory witnessing characteristic of the war news spectacles. The absence of an object—*What* does Editha experience?—is its most telling quality.

By situating George's conversion both to war and to spectacle within a mob scene, Howells also takes up the distinction between the emerging mass public sphere, devoted to detaching sensation from reason and from language, and the literary public sphere, in which short stories like "Editha" invite the public to see—and distinguish themselves from—"modern" figures like George and Editha. Too addled by the spectacle to distinguish between real war and mass-mediated war, George is typically unable to consider the rightness or wrongness of the cause. In a mind under sway of the mob, Howells suggests, the social and material constraints on the exercise of judgment are simply too great. Readers, however, might take a cue from Editha and school themselves differently to meet modern sociopolitical problems. At one point, the story suggests that the overwrought Editha does in fact possess an innate capacity for judgment, for she is aware of the ways in which her thoughts are being influenced. "She was conscious of parroting the current phrases of the newspapers," the narrator tells us, "but it was no time to pick and choose her words" (216). Editha has been reading the papers, not attending rallies and watching films; as a result, she knows her mind is not fully her own, but George doesn't. The implication is that had Editha cultivated her insight further—perhaps by reading realist fiction—she might not have sent the hapless George to war.

Howells's invitation to readers to draw these distinctions, however, finally trades on an underlying similarity between the literary public sphere safeguarded by analytic fiction and the mass public sphere. For both in "Editha" and in the war news spectacles, the self is understood as perpetually in process, and what becomes most decisive and meaningful for the outcome is not the ability to distinguish between real and representation, but an immersive experience of communal witnessing. George's nervousness makes him a representative American, albeit not of the kind for which Editha longs. His condition portends not a heroic death but a pathetic one. Mediated not by the feeling of prophetic symbolism but by the thrill of mob witnessing, he is en route not simply to his end within the story, as a "statistic" of war, but to the ending—and hence to the analytic insight—of the story itself, which Howells expertly forecasts from the first page onward. An illustrative instance for realist fiction, rather than for the coming American empire, George's death embodies an ironic reversal from spiritual to material prophecy that undercuts the hopes for civic cultivation to which the story is otherwise devoted. George's thoroughly virtual self not only invites us to understand the causes of war; in the same gesture it also announces the limitlessness of the spectacle's power over the embodied mind.

The Prophet of the Material World

Howells's comment in regard to *The Red Badge of Courage* that the inexperienced Crane had "lost himself in a whirl of wild guesses at the fact from the ground of insufficient witness" suggests that he saw his young disciple as a combination of George and Editha. Disoriented by his own sensory experience of mediated war, Crane has written a novel that fails to analyze the real and instead engages in a dangerous form of "divination."[41] Perhaps one reason why Howells might have seen Crane in these terms is that, by the time he penned these remarks in 1902, he would have known Crane as a war correspondent whose marketability traded on his experience neither of war, nor of reporting, but of writing *Red Badge* itself. Moreover, if Howells did feel that *Red Badge* presented war as a dangerously disorienting spectacle, other critics' comments would likely have only reinforced his opinion. Reviews of the novel frequently discussed parallels between Crane's style and photography, film, and the coloristic techniques of the Impressionist painters, understanding all of them as ways of creating immersive and therefore realistic effects. One critic noted that Crane's use of color aimed "to affect the mind through the eye"; another wrote that Crane "stages the drama of war . . . within the mind of one man, and then admits you as to a theater"; and still another described Crane as "a Muybridge" and *Red Badge* as a "photographic revelation."[42]

Far from celebrating sensory experience on its own, however, Crane, like Howells, repeatedly emphasizes in *Red Badge* that sense impressions can be dangerously separated from the exercise of judgment. Much as Howells did in "Editha," Crane presents the main character's decision to join up as the result of somatic excitement brought about both by media and by the mob. "The newspapers, the gossip of the village, his own picturings, had aroused him to an uncheckable degree," the narrator tells us of the private Henry Fleming. "They were in truth fighting finely down there."[43] Like Editha, Henry is half-aware of the effects of external impressions upon his thoughts; Crane's use of free indirect discourse suggests that he both knows and doesn't know that he is "parroting phrases from the newspapers." War is equally devastating and meaningless in *Red Badge* as it is in "Editha," precisely because the disorientation it produces in the embodied mind is ungraspable, making it inseparable from the experience of war as spectacle. Instead of heroic memories of Henry's exploits, "bits of color . . . had stamped themselves unawares upon his engaged senses" during the fight, leaving him with a purely material and mechanical experience that is drained of significance (94).[44] "His mind took a mechanical but firm impression," we are told at one point of his charge into battle, leaving him convinced later "of everything . . . save why he himself was there" (86).

Through ironic reversals very similar to those in "Editha," *Red Badge* again and again reduces the prophetic to the material. On several occasions, Crane leads us to see how Henry's feelings of immersive witnessing make him believe he is destined for heroism. Before he has seen battle, he longs to be one of the "chosen beings" as he gazes at more seasoned soldiers. Often, "swift pictures of himself, *apart, yet in himself,* came to him—a blue desperate figure leading lurid charges with one knee forward and a broken blade high" (emphasis mine, 51). The "swift" pictures, as many critics have noted, resemble those of a film.[45] But Crane is referencing film here specifically as an interactive and an immersive theatrical entertainment because he suggests that its images are illusory *realizations* produced by embodied observation. It is not the "swift pictures" themselves but Henry's feeling of interpreting them that makes him think he will become a hero. The fact that they emerge from the body lends them their spurious truth. They are *both* separate from Henry and yet generated from within him.

The passage also suggests that the prophetic feeling in question is the product of unconsciously gathered sense perceptions from Henry's immediate environment. As he imagines his future exploits, for instance, he is described as marching in a column of men, suggesting that the army, frequently described through the text as a giant body, is also *his* body. Sensory input from the soldiers close around him helps to shape his mental images: "In his ears, he heard the ring of victory. He knew the frenzy of a rapid successful charge. The music of the trampling feet, the sharp voices, the clanking arms of the column near him made him soar on the red wings of war" (51). The Army "corps" is a kind of theatrical surround whose stimuli accompany, enhance, and partially help to generate the images he sees. It is hard to understand why else Crane might have felt the need to emphasize "in his ears" or the fact that the sounds are proximate to Henry's position in space. The spatial orientation of the character suggests an environmental source for Henry's mental images of heroism. At the same time, Crane makes clear that Henry is equally reliant on his internal bodily environment. For the images he sees correspond directly to his body's pain and fatigue: "Various ailments had begun to cry out. In their presence, he could not persist in flying high with the red wings of war; they rendered it almost impossible for him to see himself in a heroic light" (51).

In contrast to Howells, however, for Crane there is often something profoundly uncanny, even horrifying, about the would-be hero's visions, which suggests that they *are* a form of prophecy. It is clear, on the one hand, that Henry's mental images proceed from his manifestly embodied mind, for he sees one kind of prophetic image while aroused and on the march and another kind when in a semi-conscious state. Waking from slumber and perceiving a "motionless mass of men" asleep around him, he momentarily understands himself to be "in the house of the dead" and cannot move "lest these corpses start up, squalling and squawking." "His disordered mind," the narrator specifies, "interpreted the hall of the forest as a charnel place. . . . In a second, however, he achieved his proper mind. He saw that this sombre picture was not a fact of the present, but a mere prophecy" (66). Henry sees the sleeping soldiers as animate corpses because he has himself just awoken, and he understands prophetic typology to be the product of a disordered mind—"mere" prophecy. Yet, on the other hand, the horror of this moment introduces a new note that suggests Henry's vision is prophetic, both within the text, and—strangely—outside of it as well. It is not lost on the reader that Henry himself may well end up the same way as the soldiers he initially thinks he sees. But the "motionless mass of men, thick spread on the ground, pallid and in strange postures" also looks forward to the photographs of the Civil War dead that would begin to circulate more widely to audiences in the late 1880s and that were likely one of Crane's inspirations for the novel.[46] Henry's disordered mind *is* prophetic, in a way the character could not know but 1890s readers can; it has become the source of a material, rather than a spiritual prophecy that extends outside the text to history itself. The reader is drawn into a mysterious temporal loop whereby a fictional character is able to unknowingly envision a real history that is already past by the time of the reading itself.

Henry's disordered mind is also uncannily prophetic in a passage near

the end of Crane's original manuscript where the character reflects backward on his experiences. "In spectator fashion" he examines his memories
as if he is watching a film or attending a parade; his "performances" march
before him as "gilded images of memory," their mechanical and material
nature once again belying the significance he accords them (106). Troubled,
however, by haunting memories of having acted with less than perfect
heroism, Henry consoles himself with a prophetic image drawn from the
Bible. "It had been necessary for him to swallow swords that he might
have a better throat for grapes. Fate had in truth, been kind to him; she
had stabbed him with benign purpose and diligently cudgeled him for his
own sake" (ibid.). Here Henry makes a rather muddled reference to the
New Testament Book of Revelation, where the Word of God, depicted as a
rider on a white horse, issues from his mouth "a sharp sword with which to
smite the nations."[47] His misquotation reinforces the larger ironic deflation
of heroism in war that the novel undertakes by turning the word of God
into a sword to be swallowed—thus converting the Bible into one of the
"amusements" Crane's father deplored. But the image of stabbing through
the mouth also creates a violent, obscene, and uncanny image that renders the analytic distance of the irony at best uncertain. The effect is rather
to inject a note of horror into the novel's vision of spectacular entertainments, rather than the word of God, being incarnated in those who watch
them. We are not enjoined to draw (much of) a distinction between the
two, but to shudder at the violent spectacle of a film—via Henry's filmic
memories—making the self over in its own distinctly material image.

The same can be said of *Red Badge*'s most famous scene, in which
Henry unexpectedly encounters a corpse in the woods after searching
for signs in nature to justify his decision to flee. He finds the dead soldier
propped against a tree at a place in the woods where "the high, arching
boughs made a chapel," and stares at it in shock "in the religious half-light"
(37). The body is a riot of gruesome and not-quite-believable color—the
blue uniform faded to a "melancholy shade of green," the eyes "changed
to the dull hue to be seen on the side of a dead fish," the red of the mouth
changed to "an appalling yellow," and the skin grey (ibid.). The narrator describes Henry as frozen in place by dead eyes that seem to return his gaze;
the corpse is an inanimate "thing" that turns him "to stone." Of central
importance here is the fact that the corpse occupies the position of Christ
in the natural chapel. Henry's mortification as he looks at it thus ironically
evokes the *imitatio Christi*—a central trope in Puritan theology—whereby

the believer undergoes a transformative experience of the word, aspiring to imitate Christ.[48] The scene derives its power not only from the similarity between the corpse and Christ, however, but from the uncanny and lurid excess of color on the corpse's face.

Mass culture figures significantly here as well. Nicholas Gaskill has recently made the persuasive argument that Crane's much-noted obsession with color derives from his attempts to transfer the coloristic effects of new chromolithographic techniques being used in the mass press into a literary method.[49] Crane's frequent textual invocations of color, as is the case here, are often strangely unlocatable relative to particular perceivers or objects. As Gaskill shows, the colors are often multiplied in such a way as to create a sense of stylized abstraction characteristic of the flat color blocks in late nineteenth-century advertising. The resulting blockage to visualization allows Crane to detach a given color from its object and "magnif[y] it until it becomes the dominant feature of the scene, a quality that floats through forms and events without attaching itself to any one body" (734). Gaskill shows that color in Crane evokes color *qualia*—the feeling of seeing or experiencing a color that is distinct from the physical or material causes of perception in the light and in the structure of the eye. Much as was the case for the philosopher and logician C. S. Peirce, color in Crane's texts is virtual, Gaskill argues. It occupies a hazy place reducible neither to a subject nor an object: "a general entity that has 'real' bearings on the world without being actualized in experience" (ibid.). In the scene above, then, we are invited not only to shudder at the uncanny similarity between the transitional or intermediate self of the Puritan *imitatio Christi* and a decaying corpse in the woods, but also to *experience*, as readers, the difference between the intermediate self and the virtual self solicited, via color, by both Crane and by mass entertainments.

Gaskill's analysis helps us to understand in more historical terms a phenomenon in Crane's texts highlighted by Michael Fried: recurring scenes involving a living gaze at a dead and disfigured face, such as the image of the sword-swallowing hero or the corpse in the natural chapel. In these often unsettling and violent moments, Fried argues, Crane unwittingly allegorizes the material work of his own writing. The face figures the act of putting marks on the page, for Fried, due to the similarity between the size of a face and the size of a sheet of writing paper, as well as the fact that Crane's faces are often pictured in proximity to other, explicitly evoked tools of the writer's trade. Most important, these upturned faces are frequently being disfigured in ways that suggest the movement of a hand or pen. In the chapel scene, a line of ants is crossing the face of the dead soldier; in Crane's short story, "The Upturned Face," the dilemma gruesomely turns on the question of who will place the final shovelful of dirt on the face of a dead soldier being buried. The exchanges between animate and inanimate that structure these scenes, Fried argues, allegorize the act of writing as a disturbing process in which the writer hallucinates real characters and events—referential depth—behind what are in fact only material lines on the page.[50]

Yet, as noted earlier, the idea that the self is mediated by the materiality of language and representation was not news to American writers, schooled in the feeling of the divine word. What *was* new was the uncanny similarity between the promising experience of the "living" word and the sensory thrill of mass cultural amusements. The allegories of writing noted by Fried are best understood in this context. Crane's faces are generally neither white nor blank prior to their disfigurement, as we might tend to expect if they are to be understood as allegorical symbols of the blank page. Instead, they are usually colored, in the virtual sense that Gaskill notes. These revelations about the face's color tend to *precede* the figurations of writing that are such an important part of the scene, and are distinguished from them by being less strongly focalized through the point of view of a character.

For example, in the chapel scene, the narrator first describes the color of the face, and only afterward describes the writing-like movement of the swarming ants, whose image "pursues" the youth as he flees. Earlier in the novel, Henry, marching in a line of soldiers, encounters a corpse. We are told that "the youth could see that the soles of his shoes had been worn to the thinness of writing-paper" (18). But beforehand, we learn that the corpse's "suit" has turned "yellowish brown" (ibid.). In the short story "The Upturned Face," the corpse that the soldiers are trying to bury has a "chalk blue" face that they cannot bear to cover, but finally do.[51] Even in Crane's romances and fiction on non-war topics, the faces are often disfigured by a more "natural" process of coloration in advance of the disfiguring movements that more directly evoke writing for a particular character. "The Monster," a story about an African American servant whose face is destroyed by brightly colored chemicals that pour down from a desktop onto him during a fire, exemplifies this theme via the "natural" disfigurement of race. What Fried compellingly isolates as the "excruciating" work of writing in Crane is in fact a confrontation between two forms of disfigurement: the colored face, whose disfigurement is often temporally unlocatable within the story, or in relation to a particular character's point of view; and a movement of disfigurement that more explicitly figures writing. Color *pre*figures the work of writing, in other words, by means of an originary *dis*figuration that transcends the scene altogether.

The importance of a distinctly virtual experience of color to Crane's allegories of writing suggests that the conflict these faces allegorize involves not "writing as such," in Fried's words, but writing in the wake of mass spectacle and its dangerously ungrounded sensory appeal. In Crane's allegory of the upturned faces, color quite literally takes the place of divine grace as the legitimizing ground for the writer's work. The feeling of color has much in common with the feeling of the divine word; both occupy a different ontological order from the material world but nevertheless act upon it. Yet colors—and by extension the colored action of mass culture and mass spectacle—replicate the feeling of incipience associated with the living word while offering no promise of redemption.[52]

The horror-struck gaze in Crane, mortified in imitation of the dead face and the inert page alike, thus evokes an uncanny similarity between the virtual self solicited by mass entertainments and a prophetic American selfhood that is perpetually in process, "cudgeled" by the good news of its progressive destiny. We can conclude that, although they are often used to deflate hubristic notions of prophetic selfhood, mass entertainments in Crane's texts do not act on the embodied mind in purely material ways, as they do in Howells. Popular amusements in *Red Badge* are instead figured as uncanny sites of self-making and self-undoing that supersede the divinely guaranteed possibility of self-recognition through writing. As such, they indicate Crane's profound and troubling ambivalence about the ways in which the feeling of divine prophecy that sanctioned his writer's mission was increasingly giving way to the dispossessing pleasures of mass spectacle.

The Homeless Machine: War and After

Crane's novels and short stories during and after the Greco–Turkish War of 1897 suggest even more clearly that a conflict between the American literary public sphere and mass cultural spectacles was formative for the metaphors of writing that run throughout his work. After seeing war for the first time as a reporter, in the Greco–Turkish War, Crane was finally able to write authoritatively from experience, portraying not only the life of the soldier on the battlefield but also that of the war correspondent. In highly revealing ways, his portraits of writers at the front often satirize the conventions of sensational reportage at the same time as they celebrate the challenge that was posed by the spectacularization of the news to the ideal of the bourgeois public sphere. In Crane's war romance *Active Service* (1899), for example, the central conflict in what is otherwise a highly conventional marriage plot concerns the opposing forces of sensational journalism and the cultural elite. The novel's hero is Rufus Coleman, who is an editor at the scurrilous *New York Eclipse,* a thinly veiled reference to Hearst's *Journal,* which had employed Crane to report the Greco–Turkish War. Coleman is stymied in his desire to marry his beloved, Marjory Wainright, by her father, a professor who disapproves of Coleman's profession. In the novel's opening pages, Marjory approaches her father to ask for permission to marry, finding him at work in his office:

> There was disclosed an elderly narrow-faced man seated at a large table and surrounded by manuscripts and books. The sunlight flowing through curtains of Turkey red fell sanguinely upon the bust of dead-eyed Pericles on the mantle. A little clock was ticking, hidden somewhere among the countless leaves of writing, the maps and broad heavy tomes that swarmed upon the table.[53]

The Greco–Turkish conflict that will be the subject of the novel's later pages (Marjory and her father will soon be trapped behind battle lines in Turkey, waiting for rescue by Coleman) looms here in the reddened light that falls, "sanguinely," on the bust of Pericles. As in *Red Badge,* a violent threat to life is foreshadowed by color, and in particular by a colored face. But the subject of the bust and its proximity to the professor's desk once again link the perception of color to a conflict related to writing. Redness disfigures the face of the exemplar of reasoned oratory, Pericles, emphasizing not only the unknowability of color—color is different for everyone—but also the impossibility of achieving a truly shared understanding of it through language. What the professor doesn't know, in other words, is that meaning in language, like color, can only be known through its effects. It is thus not surprising to find that prior to being interrupted, he had been trying to write in a very strange and ineffective way:

It was plain to her that he had been writing ... one of his sentences, ponderous, solemn and endless, in which wandered multitudes of homeless and friendless prepositions, adjectives looking for a parent, and quarrelling nouns, sentences which no longer symbolized the language-form of thought but which had about them a quaint aroma from the dens of long-dead scholars. (113)

The professor's "homeless and friendless words," whose symbolic link with thought is broken, threaten any faith he, or we, might have in the transparency of language to intention. The scene suggests, moreover, that Crane credits the loss of this faith to mass culture's threat to the cultural elite and the bourgeois public sphere. For the passage connects the professor's inability to write both to the violation of his privacy and to the announcement that a yellow journalist wants to marry his daughter. The blank bust, disfigured by red light, in other words, emblematizes a problem not just with writing, but with writing in the context of the kind of spectacular journalism that Coleman, and Crane himself, practice.

That Crane's subject here is the critical and contentious relationship between the bourgeois public sphere and an emerging mass public is suggested by the next scene, which takes place in the newspaper office of the professor's now archenemy, Coleman. Unlike the professor's "homeless and friendless" words, Coleman's words always find their mark. In outlining to his staff their roles in producing the Sunday edition, Coleman's "face was lit with something of the self-contained enthusiasm of a general" (130). His staff had long been accustomed to "the precision with which he grasped each obligation of the campaign toward a successful edition" (129). Crane makes clear that truth, in the context of yellow journalism, takes second place to designs that force the audience to pay attention. An illustration of dead seamen in a wreck that strongly evokes the *Maine* disaster doesn't fit in to the layout of the page properly, so Coleman instructs the illustrator to break one of the spars in the drawing and to "work up" the eyes of the dead sailors, who are "grisly and horrible figures." A photograph of a "babe ... born lacking arms" he deems of sufficient interest to readers to be included in the edition by "weighing its value as a morsel to be flung to a ravenous public..." (126). Coleman's arrangement of the Sunday edition overrides considerations of privacy as much as decency, marking a stark contrast to the professor, who passively waits for inspiration and illumination in his private study. Most important, however, while the professor's words attempt, and fail, to describe something "out there" to readers, Coleman's words and images *do* something to them, something violent. Once the public sphere has been invaded by mass culture, with its wealth of appealing colors, Crane suggests, words are cut off from their relationship to transcendence. A professor's daughter can marry whomever she wants. And writing becomes a kind of war.

The opening of *Active Service* thus encapsulates the distinct nature of the problem facing Crane in his struggle to define his own brand of analytic realism. As the martial language used to describe Coleman's work suggests, Crane is no less critical than Howells of mass culture's power over the embodied mind. Coleman's colored supplement takes aim at his readers and viewers in such a way as to suggest a dangerous collapse between the virtual experience of war and the war itself. But at the same time, Crane portrays the decline of the public man of letters, perhaps modeled on his father, or even Howells, with evident relish. *Active Service* thus offers valuable insight into one of the most distinctive aspects of Crane's style. It suggests that the upturned face disfigured by color recurs with such frequency in his work because it allegorizes his ambivalence about the fate of realism in the context of mass culture and mass witnessing, and the particular way in which, in America, the latter entailed a withdrawal of the promise of transcendence from the experience of the word. Viewed in relation to this impasse, Fried's persuasive diagnosis of Crane's metaphorics of writing takes on greater historical contour.

Active Service in fact makes all but explicit the connection between Crane's textual investigation of color and the new uses of color in popular culture during the 1890s. As Coleman waits impatiently for Marjory to appear after another unsuccessful meeting with her father,

> he gazed about at the pictures and the odds and ends of the drawing-room in an attempt to make an interest in them. The great garlanded paper shade over the piano-lamp consoled his impatience in a mild degree because he knew that Marjory had made it. He noted the clusters of cloth violets which she had pinned upon the yellow paper and he dreamed over the fact. He was able to endow this shade with certain qualities of sentiment that caused his stare to become almost a part of an intimacy, a communion. He looked as if he could have unburdened his soul to this shade over the piano-lamp. (134–35)

This scene offers a highly critical allegory of yellow journalism's disorienting sensory appeal. As Coleman "reads" the yellow shade, which is disfigured by the writing-like action of the pin, he is at first to some extent the "author" of the "paper" he also "reads." He is "able to endow" the shade with his sentiment for Marjory, but only in a limited way, projecting "certain qualities" of his feeling onto it while remaining aware that he is doing so. Yet Coleman soon loses this capacity for detachment in the wake of what is here figured as a highly colored newspaper. By the end of the description, Coleman seems to have forgotten that it is he himself who first "made an interest" in the yellow paper. He "endows" the shade with a "sentiment" that becomes the "cause" of his stare's "communion" with its object. At the formal level, it is as if the strangely unlocalizable *qualia* of color causes a confusion over subject and object that spurs the passage to expand its perspective outward. Coleman thus becomes subject to humiliation by way of objectification, a fate that Crane often reserves stylistically for his characters. By the end, we gaze on Coleman from an exterior position, where his will to power and romantic illusions are belittled; we are left with the spectacle of a man ridiculously poised to address an inanimate object as if it were alive.

Although in some ways *Active Service* is derivative of Crane's other war stories, particularly *Red Badge*, what sets it apart is the way the novel addresses the question of mass culture's significance for the writer and journalist. As is so frequently the case in Crane, the main character's experience of war yields solutions to conflicts experienced by the character and his author respectively. Accustomed to a hubristic life of playing general at the newspaper, Coleman, much like Henry Fleming, encounters the shock of battle in Greece and Turkey and must learn to accept that he is a plaything of circumstance. There is no intrinsic meaning to the events of war, and the best one can do, Crane suggests, is take advantage of chance events.[54] Repeating the central conceit of *Red Badge*, in which a knock on the head by a crazed private gets taken as a sign of Henry's courage, Coleman accidentally ends up behind the lines, where he appears to the professor and Marjory as a kind of savior. Like Henry, Coleman is in no hurry to dispel this false image—in fact, he pragmatically uses it to win Marjory's hand. The endings to both books suggest a solution to the allegories of writing that suffuse Crane's texts as well. To write, as well as to fight, is to submit oneself to chance and circumstance, to simply make do in the face of losing any external guarantee that meaning inheres in one's words or actions.

But because this familiar battlefield denouement belongs to a story about a war correspondent rather than a soldier, Crane uses it to comment more directly on the collective acts of meaning-making at work in mass culture, portraying those as chance events as well. Nearing the front, Coleman happens upon a crowd of Greek soldiers watching the burial of a fallen Turkish soldier, and "moved by a strong mysterious impulse," he too goes forward to look at the "clay-colored" corpse's face. Suddenly,

> a snake ran out from a tuft of grass at his feet and wriggled wildly over the sod . . . One of the soldiers put his heel upon the head of the reptile and it flung itself into the agonized knot of death. Then the whole crowd powwowed, turning from the dead man to the dead snake. . . . This incident, this paragraph, had seemed a strange introduction to war. The snake, the dead man, the entire sketch, made him shudder of itself, but more than anything he felt an uncanny symbolism. (168)

Coleman's profession and his description of the event as an incident, paragraph, or a sketch takes up the writing metaphor once again, as does the by now familiar sequence: a compulsion to look at the colored face of the corpse followed by the sight of a disfiguring mark in action—the snake—that is more definitively focalized through the character. The snake's wriggling across the sod resembles the material mark of the written word because it initially does little more than attract attention; like handwriting, or the smoke from one of the recently obsolete battlefield guns mentioned in "Editha," it has no meaning in and of itself. The scene thus offers a commentary on reading and interpretation as a mode of "making an interest" in the intrinsically meaningless—even chance—"marks" of the mass press, much as in the scene of Coleman with the lampshade. As the crowd turns from the Turkish corpse, killed by a Greek, to a snake, also killed by a Greek, Crane suggests that this random event has become, for them, a portentous sign of the impending conflict. They interpret the crushing of the snake as a symbol for what is likely a divinely ordained future defeat of the Turkish Army. The scene therefore has a strongly self-reflexive quality, forecasting the fact that Coleman's "yellow" words and "sketches" will also be interpreted in ways beyond his control, via chance encounters between the mind and the materiality of the newspaper.

Coleman's reflections on the emergence of the symbol suggest that the horror and fascination so often associated in Crane with figures of writing and with color has to do with more than a confusion over subject and object. It also pertains to the difficulty of localizing thought itself. Like Henry Fleming in *Red Badge*, Coleman feels a sense of dread, which the narrator associates with his desire for Marjory. "It was no doubt a mere occurrence; nothing but an occurrence," he tells himself, "but inasmuch as all the detail of this daily life associated itself with Marjory, he felt a different horror." The source of this obscure horror has to do with the capacity of his mind to wander, in a quite literal way:

> He interwove his memory of Marjory with a dead man and with a snake in the throes of the end of life. They crossed, intersected, tangled, these two thoughts. He perceived it clearly, the incongruity of it. He academically reflected upon the mysteries of the human mind, this homeless machine which lives here and then there and often lives in two or three opposing places at the same instant. He decided that the incident of the snake and the dead man had no more meaning than the greater number of the things which happen to us in our daily lives. Nevertheless it bore upon him. (169)

In his horror at discovering his mind's capacity to join any sign to any other sign, Colman describes thinking itself as a continual act of sign-making, turning mind not into an essence but a function inseparable from the workings of language. The emphasis on the mind as a "homeless machine . . . that often lives in two or three opposing places at the same instant," also places the mind outside of the individual, bounded consciousness. Crane again resembles C. S. Peirce, who argued both that thinking is inseparable from language and that the indexical component of language—the material mark on the page—meant that mind is external to persons.[55] Peirce's example of an external location for the mind, however, was that of a nearly outdated medium—the inkstand.[56] Crane's portrayal of the homeless mind suggests that it may live equally in the author's pen and paper and in the scare heads, fonts, and images of the sensational newspaper. Within this radically deterritorialized notion of mind, the only thing that guarantees the arrival of meaning in the scene above is the nationalistic faith that sustains the crowd.

By invoking a material encounter between media and mind as a way to explain the public's enthusiasm for war, this scene suggests significant parallels not only to the ideas of Peirce but also to those of Peirce's colleague, William James.[57] James's letters during this period show him busy applying his own and Peirce's insights about the embodied mind and the "language-form of thought" to observations of the press and public.[58] His public essays reflect concerns about the press obliquely but unmistakably. In "On a Certain Blindness in Human Beings," an essay published the same year as *Active Service*, James begins by noting that "our judgments concerning the worth of things, big or little, depend on the *feelings* the things arouse in us."[59] The essay elaborates the contextual and culturally specific nature of ideals, warning that each person's "peculiar ideality" is unknowable to members of other cultures or classes because it emerges from the "non-thinking level, the level of pure sensorial perception" (631). In perhaps his most direct condemnation of imperialism, "The Moral Equivalent of War," written ten years later, James makes clear that a shared perceptual *media* environment is capable of creating a dangerous blindness toward other idealities, as it did in 1898. Once "our people had read the word 'war' in letters three inches high for three months in every newspaper," he ruefully remarks, "our squalid war with Spain became a necessity."[60] Much as he deplored it, yellow journalism illustrated for James, at least in retrospect, that emotion could not be eradicated from the public sphere.

In linking judgment to feeling, James was beginning to articulate the philosophical tenets of pragmatism and radical empiricism, as based in the idea of virtual experience, or an experience without a subject. It is tempting to wonder whether the virtual experiences of the war news spectacles were a significant influence on the development of this insight.[61] As Nancy Bentley notes, James's pluralism and his emphasis on the neurological basis of cognition meant that literary culture and the bourgeois public sphere could not be the only sites for reasoned exchange; although James never makes the argument explicitly, by his own definition, popular culture and even yellow journalism could be full of significance as well.[62] "Wherever a process of life communicates an eagerness to him who lives it, there the life becomes genuinely significant," he writes in "On a Certain Blindness in Human Beings," noting that a pleasurable quickening and the sense of satisfaction it brings make significance potentially inherent in all human activities, from strenuous physical actions, to flights of imaginative fancy, to the reflective work of philosophy (631). However, while James did not discriminate as far as the kinds of experiences that could be understood as meaningful, he hoped by proclaiming this very fact to bypass a dangerous blindness inherent to the embodied mind—a blindness that his letters suggest he saw being exploited by the press, especially in regard to unjust imperialist wars. James's definition of significance as an embodied process accordingly should be understood as more than an attempt to formulate a philosophy broadly appropriate to postindustrial modernity.[63] It was also a warning about the negative political consequences for any kind of public sphere of the fact that our minds, as *Active Service* also grimly asserts, are not fully our own.

As the snake scene suggests, when Crane portrays the war correspondent's experience at the front, in contrast to when he writes exclusively about soldiers in battle, he explores the way mass culture and mass entertainments can be a source of danger for the "homeless" mind. Other stories about writers at war also take up this theme. The short story "Death and the Child" tells the story of Peza, a student and a newly minted war correspondent who is eager to fight for Greece, his father's country, but who ends up fleeing from the front in humiliation. In the story's final, devastating line, Peza confronts a peasant child who has been viewing the fighting from a distance, and who asks him the devastating question "Are you a man?"[64] This story of hubris punctured by war and shame is familiar from Crane's earlier fiction and short stories; it repeats the narrative of Henry Fleming's struggle with his own fears about courage and manhood in *Red Badge* and that of many other soldier-protagonists. As Fried notes, moreover, there is much to suggest that the materiality of writing is once again a deeper source of fear and horror in the story. At one point, Peza gazes in shock at bloodstained makeshift bandages covered with writing that gets reproduced in the story for no particular reason: "Fig. I.— Fig. 2.— Fig. 7."[65] Viewing the war from afar, the child notices "battle lines writh[ing] . . . in the agony of a sea-creature on the sands."[66] Finally, Peza ultimately flees from the front when he imagines himself being "*drawn and drawn* . . . slowly, firmly down" under the earth by "dead men" (emphasis mine). The uncanniness of the blank page returns as he stares at a corpse with the telltale upturned face whose "two liquid-like eyes were staring into his face."[67]

Yet because "Death and the Child" concerns a war correspondent rather than a soldier, the questions it raises thematically about courage and allegorically about writing more explicitly implicate spectacular entertainments. Casting around for an explanation for why the soldiers he sees behind the lines do not seem afraid,

Peza tried to define them. Perhaps during the fight they had reached the limit of their mental storage, their capacity for excitement, for tragedy, and had then simply come away. Peza remembered his visit to a certain place of pictures, where he had found himself amid heavenly skies and diabolic midnights—the sunshine beating red upon desert sands, nude bodies flung to the shore in the green moon-glow, ghastly and starving men clawing at a wall in darkness, a girl at her bath with screened rays falling upon her pearly shoulders, a dance, a funeral, a review, an execution, all the strength of argus-eyed art; and he had whirled and whirled amid this universe, with cries of woe and joy, sin and beauty, piercing his ears until he had been obliged to simply come away. He remembered that as he had emerged he had lit a cigarette with unction, and advanced promptly to a café. A great hollow quiet seemed to be upon the earth.

This was a different case, but in his thoughts he conceded the same causes to many of these gunless wanderers. They, too, may have dreamed at lightning speed until the capacity for it was overwhelmed. As he watched them he again saw himself walking toward the café, puffing upon his cigarette. As if to reinforce his theory, a soldier stopped him with an eager but polite inquiry for a match.[68]

The analogy Peza draws between his experience at the "place of pictures," which equally evokes a proto-cinematic space and an art gallery, and that of soldiers fighting a war seems at best naïve. Yet, the story ultimately suggests that fighting a war is no different than watching a movie or looking at a painting. Peza's experience of pictures is surprisingly commensurate with war; he will flee from the real in the same way and for the same reason that he flees from pictures. As Bill Brown notes about this scene, the corpse who looks at Peza "with liquid eyes" just before he runs repeats the confusion of opposites he remembers from the picture palace, which, insofar as it evokes film, is also a locale in which the inanimate becomes animate.[69] Visual culture constructs battlefield fantasy, with disastrous consequences. For Brown, then, "Death and the Child" discloses the hidden relationship between "war and play, death and amusement" that Crane could not investigate within an American context.[70]

Yet this scene, and its influence on subsequent events in the story, ultimately has less to do with the porous boundary between real and imitation than with the humiliating subordination of the mind to incommensurate experiences of what James called "eager quickening." Again, as in *Red Badge,* Crane devotes a considerable amount of detail to conveying Peza's strange memory of the pictures, in such a way as to suggest that cognition, rather than embodiment or fantasy, is his subject here. For instance, the passage suggests that the comparison Peza makes between himself and the soldier is not qualitatively different than an act of reasoning. Almost exaggerated care is devoted to specifying that Peza is engaged in careful deliberations as he examines the nonchalant soldiers. First the narrator describes his attempt at definition, then the memory he weighs and extrapolates to cover a "different case," and finally his arrival at a common "cause." Judgments rely on feelings, as James put it; Peza's blindness toward the soldiers' experience of the fight exemplifies the way that incommensurate idealities can emerge from different impressions of images. Death and amusement are on a continuum in this story and throughout Crane's work because of the humiliating vulnerability of the homeless mind, which now must inhabit technologies other than the written word. Much like James, Crane doesn't discriminate among the types of sensory experience that are constitutive of reason, but instead between incommensurate sensory worlds.

One way of understanding James's willingness to see the potentiality for reason as inherent in any experience of "eager quickening" during the age of America's imperial expansion was that he was seeking a way to shore up what he viewed as the public sphere's crucial function of resisting sovereign violence. For Crane, however, the same extension of significance to forms of mass culture at a time of war seemed to signify the opposite—the birth of a "pathological public sphere" in which the only authentic experience left to be communicated is one of violence.[71] Once the word loses its relationship to transcendence, scenes like the previous suggest, the writer's mission is no longer to present representative instances of social life for analysis, per Howells. Nor is it to bear witness to "vital significance" wherever it may be found, as James put it in regard to Whitman.[72] The satisfaction James saw in the eager quickening of poetry is vitiated, for Crane, by the withdrawal of the divine from the experience of the word. This withdrawal has left the mind vulnerable and exterior, living in places its owner doesn't intend and can't predict. The conception of mind as homeless machine is an important reason that Crane has often been understood to allegorize *all* experience, including writing, as one of violent shock. Yet shock does not mean that experience is inaccessible. Instead, Crane embraced a difficult mission: to be true to an experience that is no longer strictly his.

Crane's 1897 short story "The Open Boat," published in *Scribner's* magazine, makes clearest both his similarities to and his divergence from James. As noted previously, it is a story about a shipwrecked war correspondent who is trapped with three other men in a rowboat, trying to reach land in rough seas. In writing it, Crane drew on his own ordeal as a shipwreck survivor just several weeks earlier, after he had secretly procured passage to Cuba on the ill-fated gunrunning vessel *The Commodore*. He had been en route to Cuba in order to take up his first assignment as a correspondent, for the Bacheller publishing syndicate. But Crane had also written up a journalistic account of the incident a mere four days afterward for the *New York Press*, which ran it under the title "Stephen Crane's Own Story." In the few weeks between the initial journalistic treatment and the later literary treatment, Crane became a celebrity as a war correspondent, even though he had not yet reached a war zone. He was able to write "The Open Boat," unlike "Stephen Crane's Own Story," in relative ease, for in the interim William Randolph Hearst had taken him on staff for the *New York Journal* on the basis of the publicity surrounding the shipwreck.[73]

The similarities between "The Open Boat" and "Stephen Crane's Own Story" demonstrate the overlapping and inchoate nature of the distinction between literary culture and the emerging mass public sphere in the 1890s. For instance, it makes little sense to distinguish between Crane's two stories on the basis of fact versus fiction, or "low" journalism versus "high" literature. Both works are "literary" in the sense that they make liberal use of metaphor and figurative language and provide an equally "subjective" and experiential view of events. Both also aspire to accurately represent a real event, as evinced by "The Open Boat"'s subtitle: "A Tale Intended to Be after the Fact: Being the Experience of Four Men from the Sunk Steamer Commodore."[74] Moreover, Crane and his editors seemed to assume that both stories would have the same readers. There are several unexplained details in "The Open Boat," such as a brief mention of others who died in the original wreck, that would only be clear to readers of the original account. In the *New York Press* story Crane in fact invites his newspaper readers to stay tuned for a more elevated treatment later: "The history of life in an open boat for thirty hours would no doubt be very instructive for the young," he notes near the end of "Stephen Crane's Own Story"—anticipating the appearance of "The Open Boat" in countless anthologies in the twentieth century—"but none is to be told here now."[75]

"The Open Boat" is best described instead as a *cultivated* version of "Stephen Crane's Own Story." Like Howells's "Editha," it plucks a representative instance from a widely familiar scenario in the mass press—the dangerous and daring "filibustering" expeditions to Cuba—in order to effect an ironic and "instructive" reversal. Specifically, the pacing and emphasis of the later *Scribner's* story offers a significant contrast to the strong narrative movement of the *New York Press* account. Whereas the latter begins on the docks of Jacksonville and ends on the beach at Daytona, the great majority of "The Open Boat" is devoted to the monotonous and backbreaking experience of rowing, emphasizing the helplessness and immobility of Crane and his comrades as they spend thirty hours trying to signal land before washing up on the shore. "The Open Boat" also ironically undercuts the original story's emphasis on the value of the celebrity reporter's identity and personal experience by differentiating the men not by name but by function—as "cook," "captain," "oiler," and "correspondent."

But perhaps the most important way in which "The Open Boat" invites us to read between the lines of "Stephen Crane's Own Story," and perhaps of other press accounts of the Cuban conflict, is through the emphasis it places on the perception of color. This is made immediately apparent in the famous first lines:

> None of them knew the color of the sky. Their eyes glanced level,
> and were fastened upon the waves that swept toward them. These
> waves were of the hue of slate, save for the tops, which were of
> foaming white, and all of the men knew the colors of the sea.[76]

As in *Red Badge* and *Active Service,* color in these opening lines links a prophecy about the violent end of the characters to the problem of skepticism. The waves' threat to the men is inseparable from the unanswerable question about what the men know and how they know it, which is in turn figured as the problem of color *qualia.* The color in these opening lines is not generated by the physical organs of the men's vision, nor is it fully a property of the waves themselves, for it is heightened, as is often the case in Crane, by its association with water (and here, the dominance of water in the frame of vision), which allows the hue of color to "intensify, to disconnect itself from any particular body, and to spread across the scene."[77] Moreover, the "cause" of the waves' color—the sun, and its particular position at a given moment—cannot be known directly because of the struggle to stay afloat: "The sun swung steadily up the sky, and they knew it was broad day because the color of the sea changed from slate to emerald-green" (886–87). We are left to conclude that the sea figures a real sensory and physiological experience—a "general entity," in Peirce's words—that is irreducible to subjective actualization. This experience nevertheless provides the grounds for the shared social production of meaning, such as the stories that will later be told by the men in the boat, including "Stephen Crane's Own Story." For the story ends not only with the rescue but with the beginning of interpretation, as romantically authorized by the voice of nature itself: "When it came night . . . the wind brought the sound of the great sea's voice to the men on shore, and they felt that they could then be interpreters" (909).

While the four men are united in their struggle to stay alive, "The Open Boat" does not eliminate the differences among them. The three who make their living on the sea are to some extent used to circumstances that the correspondent is facing for the first time. Crane depicts the correspondent as liberated to consider questions of significance by the very fact that he is not habituated to the work they perform, much as James saw the loafer Whitman as liberated in relation to the busy city street. At the story's outset, while the cook bails, the oiler rows, and the captain broods blackly over his lost ship, the correspondent, rowing as well, observes—and wonders. He "watched the waves and wondered why he was there" (885). Midway through the story, dead with fatigue from rowing, he "wonder[s] ingenuously how in the name of all that was sane could there be people who thought it amusing to row a boat" (891). Finally, once the boat has swamped and they are forced to swim for it, the narrator tells us, "There is a certain immovable quality to a shore, and the correspondent wondered at it amid the confusion of the sea" (907). As Philip Fisher notes, wonder has a privileged relation to the border between sensation and thought. The term's capacity to be both a noun and a verb in English joins sensory pleasure, as in the expression "What a wonder," to the cognitive work of scientific inquiry into causes, or first principles, as in "I wonder why."[78] In wondering particularly *as* he rows at how anyone could find rowing amusing, the correspondent contemplates the radical incommensurability of opposed sensory experiences while in the middle of one of those experiences himself.

In the correspondent's wonder, what is often a humiliating unconscious disjunction between worlds in Crane's other fiction becomes instead a fluid relation that can be known in an immanent way. The boatload of men adrift on a sea of color figures the relationship between sensation and thought as a movement or transition that is navigated by the mind, rather than an uncanny resemblance that produces a belated sense of shock or an experience that remains unknown and unintegrated. The story hence suggests, with James and Emerson, that the feeling of thinking itself, and particularly the feeling of reading and writing, is capable of transcending the blindness inherent to embodied cognition. One particular passage is especially suggestive here. Rowing through the night and thinking himself alone while the others sleep, the correspondent "suddenly" recalls a verse that "chime[s] the notes of his emotion" (902). The verse, it turns out, is from a hackneyed sentimental ballad, Caroline Norton's poem "Bingen on the Rhine," first published in 1883. The correspondent's sudden mental image of the solider as he rows helps him to understand the different ideality of a previous generation:

> In his childhood the correspondent had been made acquainted with the fact that a soldier of the Legion lay dying in Algiers, but he had never regarded it as important. . . . It was less to him than the breaking of a pencil's point. Now, however, it quaintly came to him as a human, living thing. It was no longer merely a picture of a few throes in the breast of a poet, meanwhile drinking tea and warming his feet at the grate; it was an actuality—stern, mournful and fine.
>
> The correspondent plainly saw the soldier. He lay on the sand with his feet out straight and still. While his pale left hand was upon his chest in an attempt to thwart the going of his life, the blood came between his fingers. In the far Algerian distance, a city of low square forms was set against a sky that was faint with the last sunset hues. The correspondent, plying the oars and dreaming of the slow and slower movements of the lips of the soldier, was moved by a profound and perfectly impersonal comprehension. He was sorry for the soldier of the Legion who lay dying in Algiers. (902–3)

The irony here, as always in Crane, is that the correspondent's sorrow for the soldier of the Legion who lay dying in Algiers is not and could never be "impersonal," if by *impersonal* we mean that it has no connection to the experience of the perceiver. The correspondent "sees" the solider and feels sorrow for him only because he interprets the poem in relation to his own situation. His self-interested pity would seem to make it impossible that the poet—or perhaps even any writer, including Crane—has the ability to communicate anything (the pencil has thus lost its "point" in another sense). But if by *impersonal* we mean, in Sharon Cameron's sense, an experience of subjective dispossession, something like Emerson's description of his experience of his son's death, then the correspondent's vision *is* impersonal. For in drawing a parallel between "plying the oars" and dreaming of the movements of the soldiers' lips, Crane equates being physically moved by the indifferent, colored waves with being moved by the words of a poem on the page. He hence suggests that writing has a rhythm and movement that might be transmitted to readers, even if other ways of communicating fail.[79]

"The Open Boat" condenses many of the themes that, this chapter has argued, preoccupied Crane, as a realist writer critical of the emerging mass public sphere. As the story of a failed expedition to Cuba, it has a particularly intimate connection to the problem of Crane's experience as a war writer who had not (yet) seen a war. It also marks the first moment at which Crane was writing publicly and self-consciously from within his new role as a correspondent. In particular, it is the product of Crane's effort to reenvision his earlier journalistic treatment of the same incident, and thus to engage with the inchoate critical and analytical difference between the mass public sphere and literary culture. Finally, and most simply, the story places its four characters, named only as the correspondent, the cook, the oiler, and the captain, into the same boat. Their shared plight allows Crane to emphasize what the writer's role might be in overcoming the human "blindness" inherent in the fact of embodied cognition.

For all of these reasons, "The Open Boat" anticipates many of the concerns of the writers I discuss in the following chapters. The story suggests that the experience of language itself might offer a way to save the American writer's mission from being swamped by a rising tide of spectacular entertainments. For the correspondent undergoes a kind of conversion during his thirty hours on the sea. It is not a conversion to the cause of war and militarism, nor to the mission of realist social analysis, but to something altogether more elusive and strange. In emphasizing that the correspondent wonders "*amid* the confusion of the sea" (italics mine) or that he wonders why he was there while watching the waves, or that he dreams while he plies the oars, Crane places wondering in *medias res,* as if it were possible to experience, endure, and even convey through the movement of language the quasi- "origin" of thought within a sea of sensation. The "terrible grace" of the colored waves in the story thus stands in for a kind of cause of cause—the quasi- or virtual cause of meaning's incipience in motor activities and perceptions (886). Of course, the image of a man in a rowboat, struggling to survive, suggests that awareness of this loss of transcendence is almost unbearable, and writing in turn is a profoundly dire exercise. The task then becomes one of determining whether the "profound and perfectly impersonal comprehension" achieved by the correspondent in this strangely peaceful yet terrifying story can be experienced—as others in the pages to come profoundly hoped it could—apart from the violence with which, in Crane's work, it is so deeply entwined.

CHAPTER 2

Realizing *Trilby*

Henry James, George du Maurier, and the Intermedial Scene

I N HIS NOVEL *Author, Author!*, a fictionalized treatment of Henry James's life during the difficult, transitional phase of his career in the mid-1890s, David Lodge tells the story of James's struggle with declining sales and a faltering playwriting career by focusing on his friendship with illustrator and novelist George du Maurier. Du Maurier's sudden, stunning success as the author of the wildly popular novel *Trilby* (1894), which was adapted many times for the stage, fills the James character with jealousy, social and sexual insecurity, and a longing for recognition. Redemption comes only when James learns to impart the principle of scenic presentation from drama into his fiction, which frees him up "to reveal the secret workings of consciousness in all of its dense and delicate detail."[1] James's failure to rival *Trilby*'s success is ultimately redeemed by this act of appropriation, Lodge suggests, as well as by the recognition James himself would posthumously receive as "the master" of the psychological novel.

Lodge's novel draws on the argument of James biographer Leon Edel, based on various claims made by James himself in his notebooks and prefaces, that a quest for psychological depth motivated his turn to scenic construction during the mid- to late 1890s.[2] However, more recent critics have challenged the idea that James's late style should be understood as a psychologically motivated incorporation of drama. In an influential reading, Sharon Cameron has argued that critical functions of consciousness are effectively shared between characters and even come to suffuse the scene itself in James's major late works.[3] Others have argued against the idea that an incorporation of dramatic writing into fiction is the best way to account for the highly and self-consciously mediated nature of James's late style. James's increased use of modal verbs and of lengthy, digressive sentences with multiple subordinate clauses is often seen to be inspired instead by the rise of new media technologies such as the telegraph and the

typewriter, particularly given James's own switch to dictating his novels
and short stories to a typist in 1897.[4] Finally, David Kurnick has recently
questioned the notion that James embraced the novel form itself after his
theatrical failures, seeing instead in James's experiments with dramatic
dialogue a profound challenge to depth psychology, and by extension to
the interiorizing psychological and disciplinary injunctions of the novel
and naturalistic drama alike.[5]

    In what follows, however, this chapter takes seriously Lodge's idea that
du Maurier and the many theatrical incarnations of *Trilby* had an influence
on the development of James's late style. Rather than seeing du Maurier as
the object of James's pathological Oedipal rivalry, as Lodge does, I argue
that he and his work were *aesthetically* significant to James throughout the
1890s as he rethought his approach to fiction. The French-born du Maurier
gazed on the London social scene as something of an outsider, exemplify-
ing in both his life and his illustrations the paradox of the involved, yet
distanced spectator, which would soon come to pervade James's fiction as
well as his autobiographical writing. At the same time, du Maurier's damaged eyesight—he had suffered a detached retina in his youth—evoked for
James a hazy, potential form of perception, in between the analytic insight
and the intuited ideal, much like that later evoked by his own sentences,
with their syntax of suspense and latency.[6] Finally, du Maurier's success
with *Trilby*, a novel about a mesmerized singer, was arguably a stimulus
to James's critical observations of popular culture throughout the remaining years of his career. *Trilby*'s popularity cannot wholly be attributed to
du Maurier's traffic with stereotypes or his dramatization of late-Victorian
obsessions such as mesmerism, the unconscious, and the occult, as cultural historians tend to suggest.[7] After all, such themes were ubiquitous
at the fin de siècle.[8] Instead, I contend, it was *Trilby*'s *citable* quality that
created its "mania." The novel's loose concatenation of illustrations, song
lyrics, and scenic construction allowed part or all of its story to be easily
transposed from one medium to another. *Trilby*'s very generic instability
as a novel offered the public a lure to interpretive actualization valuable
in its own right, a quality that James was later to praise about the theatrical and popular entertainments he recalled from his youth in his memoir
A Small Boy and Others.

    Of course, there is no single explanation for the development of James's
late style during the 1890s. This chapter focuses on James's relationship

with du Maurier not to overdetermine the significance of a biographical detail, but instead as means to investigate the underexamined links between the scenic principle in James's later work and the visual, sonic, and gestural citationality characteristic of late nineteenth-century pictorialism, of which both *Trilby* and Trilby-mania were exemplary. Pictorial practices that emerged in the 1820s and '30s were still very much in use upon the arrival of mass culture in the 1890s. The hallmark of pictorialism—the citation in one medium of a scene or "situation" from another—set in relation to each other media including painting, illustration, drama, and forms of mechanical reproduction from photography to early film. In contrast to studies that have emphasized the influence of a particular medium on James's work, I argue that it was this intermedial quality of early mass culture that inspired James's distinctive grammar of latency, as well as his explorations of the mediated texture of contemporary life. Conversely, I contend that the energies of intermedial, rather than purely linguistic, citation are at the root of James's often-noted utopian social imaginary, within which sexual identity and selfhood are portrayed as irreducible to psychology. As such, it is neither the drama nor the theater that James incorporates into his late style, but rather theatricality, and specifically the theatricality of an emerging mass public sphere, which *Trilby* itself did much to consolidate.

I explore an inherent paradox of mass pictorialism: its exciting transformational energies ceased at the moment they became actualized in commercial products—such as the often flamboyantly sexual products associated with *Trilby*. James's late style appropriated pictorialist practices of intermedial citation in order to turn them against this commercial culture, which had vastly increased over the course of the late nineteenth century, and which he disparagingly called the "hungry, triumphant actual."[9] The reason James drew on pictorialism rather than drama per se for this purpose was that there was something much larger at stake for him in regard to the public than a desire to be recognized by it (although perhaps he would have enjoyed taking "bow after blushing bow" at the footlights, as Lodge puts it).[10] Like many other liberal American intellectuals, writers, and artists in the late nineteenth century, James was concerned about the threat posed to literature and the arts by a burgeoning popular and mass culture. At the heart of this threat lay the accelerated and expanded pictorialism enabled by illustrated print culture, photography, and early film. The ability to cite one theme or form in the medium of another by mechanical means marginalized print, drama, and painting commercially while creating interpretive communities that looked uncannily like those within the traditional bourgeois public sphere. As du Maurier's case dramatically demonstrated, a newly visual and sonic public sphere relegated texts and authors to a lesser status as simply a starting point or script loosely governing an explosion of what were, to James and others, pointless, commercially motivated realizations in a variety of media. At stake in James's appropriation of pictorial energies into his writing, I suggest, was the hope that the experience of a distinctively linguistic potentiality or citationality might help to rescue the literary itself as a site for the cultivation of reason.[11]

The chapter's first section explores the nature of nineteenth-century pictorialism and the transformations it underwent with the rise of mechanical media, as exemplified in the *Trilby* "boom." The second section examines James's writings about du Maurier for the insights they yield into his evolving attitude toward pictorialism, understood in the distinctively intermedial sense mentioned above. In the third section, I discuss James's late style on its own terms, charting the broader links between his stylistic evocation of potentiality and the rise of mass pictorialism, encompassing theater, media, and illustrations. While the idea of potentiality suggests a certain disconnect from the critical or analytical point of view of James's earlier realist phase, James's resolutely depsychologizing move to the potential or virtual, I suggest, in many ways intensified the critical and analytical edge of his prose. Returning to du Maurier in the final section of the chapter, I focus on James's acerbic critical dismissal of Trilby-mania in his 1897 obituary for du Maurier. James uses the much-noted modal quality of his late writing to describe the relationship between words and images and between *Trilby* and its readers as experiences that are always prior to their actualization in particular products and socially scripted forms of desire and identification. James's late stylistic turn to the virtual also allowed him to redeem his own relationship to du Maurier from these social scripts. Du Maurier was an intimate friend who had been inspired to write *Trilby* by James himself. Yet it was only by chance, James suggests, that their relationship—and perhaps its latent homosexual undertones as well—became actualized in the book's publication, and became a source of lucrative profits for the book, theater, and film industry for decades to come.

Trilby and the Art of the Situation

In January 1894, the American magazine *Harper's Monthly* began to serial-
ize a new novel that was to become the publishing sensation of the decade.[12] *Trilby*, written and illustrated by du Maurier, tells the story of an
impoverished artist's model working in the Parisian Latin Quarter, who is
notable for her beautiful feet, her fondness for modeling in the nude, her
statuesque proportions, and her military-style overcoat. Trilby O'Farrall
is surrounded by a bevy of admiring English artists, modeled on acquain-
tances from du Maurier's student days in Paris, each of whom falls in love
with her for her boyishness, among other qualities. "Little Billee" loves
her most of all. But she is whisked away from her friends by Svengali, a
brilliant and sinister Jewish musician-enchanter, who transforms her
into an international singing sensation.[13] Although Trilby has no innate
singing ability, by mesmerizing her, Svengali infuses her with a beautiful
voice and forces her to perform unconsciously to weeping and hysterical
crowds across Europe. After engineering Trilby's rise to fame as a kind of
human phonograph, Svengali suddenly dies of a heart attack in the middle
of a performance. Trilby is reunited with her friends, but her freedom is
only momentary; a photograph of Svengali mysteriously arrives in the
mail, mesmerizing and ultimately killing her with a look from beyond the
grave.[14]

Book historians have helped to shed light on *Trilby's* popularity by citing the coincidence of its publication with the rise of the bestseller system, the popularization of the art book, and the imposition of copyright
on literary imports to the United States in 1891, which enabled the beginning of book marketing of a type and scale more familiar today.[15] This
marketing included, most notably, the use of product tie-ins, evident in
items such as the Trilby hat, the Trilby shoe, a Trilby ice cream cone in the
shape of a foot, and even a Trilby sausage reportedly created by a Boston
butcher, whose advertising tag line was "fills a long felt want."[16] As such,
Trilby-mania provides a vivid example of Jennifer Wicke's contention that
nineteenth-century novel reading was a form of "social reading," conducted
in the dialectical space between novel and advertisement.[17] Literary critics
and cultural historians, however, have shown that the novel itself hardly
needed marketing, for it offered fin-de-siècle readers all of the popular
themes of the era rolled into one, including the racialized enchanter with

the death-dealing gaze, the idealized sphere of artistic production, and the closet drama of male homosexuality.[18] *Trilby's* popularity as both a book and play has also been written up to the fact that the strapping, boyish Trilby and her diminutive English lover, not to mention their domination by Svengali, played to loosening sexual mores and provided an outlet for changing social and sexual roles, particularly for women.[19]

Historical contextualizations of *Trilby*, however, have an uncanny way of reproducing the deterministic logic of visual captivation and domination that the book itself investigates. For they tend to focus on *Trilby's* narrative and thematic content, and to suggest that it mirrored its audience's desires, hence reproducing the inexorable teleology of the story itself. Just as Trilby the character is mesmerized by Svengali, so too does *Trilby* the novel mesmerize the fin-de-siècle public.[20] As critic Brander Matthews put it the year after *Trilby's* publication, in an article praising du Maurier's storytelling abilities, "No sooner did [Trilby] show herself than hundreds of thousands of readers lay prostrate at her incomparable feet."[21] A better way to account for du Maurier's sudden and strange success, as I suggest following, is to look to the novel's formal properties, particularly its use of illustrations. *Trilby* showed herself, and her lovingly rendered feet, at the precise moment in which the nineteenth-century pictorial, or "situational," aesthetic was being revitalized by the rise of mass illustration and film.[22]

As Martin Meisel has shown, painters, dramatists, and writers had initially turned to the device of the scene or tableau in the early nineteenth century in the wake of a massive expansion in audiences for print and pictures.[23] Concrete, everyday situations of ordinary people in private life required a less abstract and conventional style than the standard iconography used for extraordinary and well-known events and figures, such as in history paintings of the Battle of Waterloo, or dramatic portrayals of Hamlet. Art depicting the everyday life of a broader audience strove for "specification, individuation, autonomy of detail" rather than the idealized poses and situations of mythic heroes and aristocrats. Yet these real details still needed to contain "a larger meaningful pattern, appealing to the moral sense and the understanding."[24] The pictorialist mandate was to infuse images and stories from everyday life with timeless meaning. Artists, writers, and dramatists accordingly adopted a set of scenic and situational conventions, such as the stock poses and expressions of melodrama, that were specific to everyday life. Both ideal and real, these conventions could be taken up—or "realized"—in different artistic media. Visual, narrative, and dramatic art became reconceptualized as flexible languages rather than static iconographical systems, capable of being translated into one another—for instance, in dramatizations of Dickens, or in Dickens's own highly theatrical scenes and characterizations in his novels.[25] At the root of these practices of translation between the arts lay the ultimate goal of nineteenth-century pictorialism: "the Realization of the Ideal."[26]

While *Trilby* is often heralded as the "first bestseller," conjuring images of a reading public hanging on every serialized word, in fact the novel was known almost as much through images, music, and performances as it was through words.[27] After its publication, the novel was adapted for theater and film, and references to it appeared in dances, paintings, photography, *tableaux vivants,* private theatricals, fundraisers, consumer products, museum exhibitions, and advertising.[28] As much as *Trilby* was consumed by readers, it was also actively produced by them in a variety of media and performance venues. Songs and illustrations from *Trilby* were reproduced on lecture platforms and in drawing rooms across the United States, clubs were formed to discuss it, the Daughters of the American Revolution were photographed in tableaux taken from the illustrations, and a town in Florida was named after it. Multiple unauthorized parodies and burlesques, some of them done in drag—"Thrillby," "Drilby Reversed," "Frilby: An Operatic Burlesque"—sprang into circulation, spurring Harper and Brothers to flex their newly acquired copyright muscles.[29]

What was most often referenced from the novel in these venues were its situations, such as Svengali's physiognomic inspection of Trilby's throat prior to mesmerizing her, or Trilby's gaze at Svengali's photograph before her death.[30] These highly pictorial scenes were highlighted and conveyed by du Maurier's illustrations. Much as had been the case with earlier novel crazes, such as those surrounding Harriet Beecher Stowe's *Uncle Tom's Cabin,* or, in England, Dickens's *Pickwick Papers,* *Trilby*'s many pictures enabled its scenes to be continually reappropriated and recontextualized and often given a fresh new treatment from a surprising angle.[31] Evidence that the illustrations were important to its popularity can be gleaned from the fact that *Trilby*'s initial publication in England without illustrations, in the traditional three-decker format, went largely unnoticed. Only after the illustrated version was serialized in *Harper's* in the United States, and then published in Britain in one volume did sales pick up and a wave of dramatizations, products, events, and exhibitions follow.[32]

Historical accounts of *Trilby*'s thematic resonance with other 1890s fictions also tend to make us forget the formal and thematic incoherence of the actual storyline. The loose construction of the novel's plot may have also encouraged the immense scope and range of the Trilby scenes found throughout popular culture. Trilby's doomed love affair with Little Billee, her mesmerism by Svengali, and her tragic expiration frequently shade into authorial asides on the artistic sensibilities and moral hypocrisy of the age; musical and song lyrics set off from the text; snatches of untranslated French; and literary tableaux of bohemian life in Paris that are unrelated to the story and seem more properly to belong to a memoir of du Maurier's early days as a painter. *Trilby* lent itself to broad circulation in a variety of media and public events by this quality of fragmentation. It is less a novel than a rambling autobiographical memoir—or perhaps a scrapbook—of Paris in the 1850s, infused with a smattering of *La Bohème* and *Dracula*. Fans of *Trilby* could convene debates about sexual morality or Darwin, beginning where du Maurier and his characters left off, sing songs taken from the novel's pages, or attend a museum exhibition of its drawings.

The rage for *Trilby* illustrates that nineteenth-century pictorialism did not dissipate immediately with the coming of film, as film historians have tended to imply.[33] Instead, one scholar of the *Trilby* boom has described a "technological acceleration" of pictorial practices at the turn of the century, an intensifying drive to "realize" a familiar scene or situation across different media.[34] Rather than dissipating, the emphasis of such realizations shifted. The act of realization itself often became the main source of interest, rather than a means to the larger end of reconciling the ideal and the everyday. The shift is evident in the ways in which *Trilby*'s mesmeric themes were depicted on stage and screen. Unlike the book, vaudeville sketches and films based on *Trilby* showed Svengali using mesmeric powers to turn people into paintings or tableaux, and, in at least one instance, to turn a statue of Trilby into a barefoot dancer. Mesmerizing realizations also took center stage in Herbert Beerbohm Tree's London dramatic adaptation of *Trilby*. In the final scene, Svengali, played by Tree, mesmerizes Trilby (and the audience) by himself assuming the pose of a *tableau vivant*.[35]

Trilby-mania suggests that the new technological reproducibility of nineteenth-century pictorialism transformed the practice of realizing the ideal into that of realizing the virtual. Although the quest to represent ordinary domestic scenes had helped to reconceive the different arts as interrelated languages earlier in the century, that interrelation had been understood as one of *translation*, implying that the arts ultimately shared a common master language.[36] With the beginnings of mass pictorialism, the relationship between the arts and the new mechanical media became instead one of *transposition*, a shift or change in medium authorized by no larger common language.[37] The act of citing a situation from another art or medium was emancipated from fidelity to the ideal and from the quest for unification and Romantic expressivity that it had entailed in an earlier era.[38]

The democratic impulse that had previously governed the quest to "realize the Ideal" via the situation did not vanish with this shift, however. In many ways, it, too, was heightened and accelerated, as evidenced by the way that spectators and audiences began to realize *themselves*, like Tree in his onstage *tableau vivant*, as characters in one of *Trilby*'s scenes—not necessarily strictly taken from the novel. Women dressing as the heroine got the opportunity to wear male clothes, go barefoot, and, as authorized by one London burlesque, to smoke cigarettes.[39] Cross-dressing, foot fetishism, sadomasochism, and same-sex desire were explored via personal and public *Trilby* performances and products. Reading, viewing, and recreating the novel's tableaux created a social space for imaginative acts of transformation, detaching them from the pathological, individualized identities specified by consolidating medical and legal discourses. Precisely because the practice of realization had become emancipated from its moral significance, however, such acts of intermedial citation, and the genius for combination and recontextualization they occasionally revealed, could claim no ultimate reason or motive. As Henry James was later to note in his obituary for du Maurier, Trilby-mania, which James deplored, disclosed an endless vista of commercially driven realizations—a kind of perpetual motion machine of citationality. Nevertheless, du Maurier and his strange success were to prove aesthetically generative for James. For *Trilby*'s intermedial citationality was to stage a return in James's least popular works—now considered masterpieces—under the aegis of a socially and ethically radical literary style.

The Virtual Thing

James's friendship with du Maurier was not lost on the many commentators who wrote about the astonishing publicity for *Trilby*. The close relationship between the two men was in fact often commented upon, for

James had actively encouraged du Maurier to try his hand at the novel.[40] James's involvement with *Trilby*'s birth embodied one of the central concepts in the pervasive pictorialist tradition—the common language shared between artist and novelist. In this case, however, it was the illustrator who wrote the novel, and the outcome was not the realization of a striking artistic effect, but an unexpected outburst of cash and commercial activity. As *The Critic* archly noted in 1895:

> Mr. du Maurier and Mr. James took a walk together, one day, and the artist unfolded to the novelist the plot of "Trilby," suggesting that he should use it in a novel. Mr. James persuaded him to write the story himself. He did so; and what has been the result? Think of the time and skill, the money and material that have been employed in putting the thing in type, preparing its illustrations, printing it as a serial and reprinting it in book-form; in dramatizing it, burlesquing it in books and on the stage, in adapting its songs and illustrations for reproduction on lecture-platforms and in drawing-rooms. . . . It has enriched its author, added to the wealth of its publishers, put money in the purses of playwright and manager and replenished the treasuries of more than one excellent charity. Directly or indirectly, no doubt, it has caused much more than a million dollars to change hands within the past eighteen months. And last but not least, it is responsible for this pamphlet, in which is chronicled the story of its rise and progress.[41]

The joke here has to do with the lack of fit between professional specialties as well as between cause and effect: an illustrator takes up the medium of a novelist, and, instead of failing, earns far more from his work than would have been thought possible, or desirable. A more subtle target of *The Critic*'s mock astonishment here may be the fact that such a popular novel's publication was recommended by a novelist who had such difficulty himself in achieving literary and theatrical success. In contrast to *Trilby*, neither of the James novels that had likely inspired *Trilby*—*The Bostonians* and *The Tragic Muse*—had done well.[42] Further, at the height of the Trilby "boom," with London productions based on du Maurier's novel opening around him to nearly assured success, James was booed at the premiere of his play *Guy Domville*.[43] For *The Critic*, Trilby and Trilby-mania stand revealed as the astonishing offspring of an obscure writer who has no idea how to please the public and a popular illustrator who doesn't know how to write.

Another reason James was associated in the public sphere with the *Trilby* craze was that he had previously been asked on several occasions to comment in the American press on du Maurier's earlier work as an illustrator for *Punch*. These writings suggest that James's involvement with *Trilby*'s success was less unlikely than it might seem. James had long been interested less in du Maurier's ideas about storylines than in his illustrations, and in the scenic principles of pictorialism that they embodied.[44] In his comments in particular about du Maurier's eyesight, James reveals that he understood pictorialism as the realization of a phenomenological experience, rather than of an ideal situation. It was to the literary exploration of this experience that he would increasingly turn after his public rejection and *Trilby*'s stunning success.

As early as 1883, for example, in a profile of du Maurier published in *The Century* magazine, James's interest in the phenomenology of pictorialism is already evident. He begins the piece, entitled "George Du Maurier and London Society," with an extensive description of his own memories of reading *Punch* as a small boy and encountering the illustrations of du Maurier's predecessor, John Leech. Adopting a focus he would later develop more fully in the first volume of his memoir, *A Small Boy and Others*, James emphasizes less the content of the scenes he remembers seeing in the pages of English periodicals than the rapturous experience of looking at them, which is in turn closely tied to his own exclusion from the "society" they depict. James writes of his younger self that "England and London were at that time words of multifarious suggestion to this small American child" because of a promised, but frequently deferred, trip abroad.[45] James "longed so to behold" the world depicted in Leech's 1850s illustrations for *Punch* that "the familiar woodcuts . . . grew at last as real to him as the furniture of his home" (49). English children's picture books had a similar effect. James recalls the characters in one such book "each holding up a tankard of foaming ale [which] seemed somehow to commemorate one's own possible arrival in Old England" (50). This state of imagined anticipation has a curiously retrospective quality, since the characters "commemorate" his imminent arrival. The anticipated retrospection, which is also retrospective anticipation on the part of the older writer, has a phenomenological, almost erotic texture that lends it a value in its own right. The young James, and seemingly the older James as well, cares less for the content of illustrations than for the way they ravish his senses. Describing himself with evident relish as a "perverted young New Yorker," James recalls "[lying] on the hearth-rug inhaling the exotic fragrance of the freshly arrived journal," which brings "the aroma of a richer civilization," and dazzles him with its plates "plastered with blue and pink" (49–50).

When he finally turns his focus to du Maurier, James depicts his friend as distinctly different from the "intensely English" Leech, who seemed intimately familiar with the London society of his drawings (52). Instead, James positions du Maurier as an outside observer, like he himself was as a young American child. In perusing du Maurier's cartoons for *Punch* and his illustrations for fiction: "One may almost fancy that the picture came first and the motive afterward. That is, it looks as if the artist, having seen a group of persons in certain positions, had said to himself: 'They must—or at least they *may*—be saying so and so'; and then had represented these positions and affixed the interpretation" (59). The illustrator's art, James reminds us, is not only visual but verbal, for he must also supply the caption to his scene, thus transforming the picture back into a story. In depicting the French-born du Maurier as an observer of a particular scene who hopes for a certain conversation to be happening, James presents his friend as, like himself as a youth, "perversely" interested less in what is being said than in his own ability to attribute a certain conversation to the figures in the picture. It is as a result unclear whether or not James really likes du Maurier's drawings in this early profile. On the one hand, the article is full of lavish praise; on the other, he attributes to the illustrator a perverse and childish relationship to his subject.

James's praise is also qualified by a series of caveats throughout the piece, in which he blames du Maurier's failing eyesight and the fact that he had originally studied to be a painter for his strangely hypothetical and belated relationship to the scenes he depicts. Both, James implies, make him less successful as an illustrator than he might have been. At stake are the standards of pictorialism in its early nineteenth-century sense. It's clear that, working in an unfamiliar medium, with a physical disability, du Maurier doesn't quite succeed in realizing the larger, meaningful pattern fully in the detail for James; he overburdens the palpable sense of ordinary, domestic scenes with an older, more static iconography better suited to classical heroes and heroines or comedic figures. At their best, James suggests, du Maurier infuses his drawings with "the fatal gift of beauty," which "throws the legend into the shade" (56). Du Maurier's "great passion" is for "loveliness observed in the life and manners around us," which he reproduces "with a generous *desire* to represent it as usual" (italics mine) (54). At their worst—as would be the case with the towering Trilby ten years later—the figures in du Maurier's drawings have a grotesque quality. Beautiful people are depicted as classical goddesses, James jokes, incongruously peopling the drawing room, while ugly ones possess a disconcertingly *total* form of ugliness, displaying "the completeness . . . the perfection, of certain forms of facial queerness" (55). Considered in relation to the kinds of art he might have been making, James thus rules du Maurier's illustrations better than anyone else's, yet "arbitrary and inadequate" (53).

However, it is clear that James also sees great value in the incongruity of du Maurier's painterly drawings. At several points in the essay, James suggests that du Maurier sees not the ideal in the real, as pictorialism dictates, but the *potential*. Discussing the many social gatherings depicted in du Maurier's drawings—in parks and drawing rooms, at concerts, and elsewhere—James notes, "He has indeed a preference for quiet and gradual movements. But it is not in the least because he is not able to make the movement definite. . . . It is not too much to say that the less flagrant the attitude, the more latent its intention, the more successfully he represents it" (59). Du Maurier's illustrations, for James, successfully realize a latent or anticipatory form of sociality, showing social relationships in the process of formation, a matter of subtle gestures, movements, and attitudes. It is as if James is suggesting that du Maurier's detached retina, although disqualifying him from realizing a narrative, allows him to realize something more important—the phenomenological experience of sociality as it emerges. This ultimately gives his art less a reflective than a transformative power for James, as if the strangely nascent quality of the images make it possible to reexperience a child's-eye view and to imagine joining a scene predicated on one's own exclusion.

The way James contrasts du Maurier's work with that of his predecessor Leech gives some insight into James's complex relationship to pictorialism. James praises Leech for making *Punch* an "abundant" and "accurate" source of information about English society, even though his own youthful rapture over Leech's drawings had little to do with their empirical insights. Leech, for James, was a close and highly instructive observer of particular people, capable of realizing their underlying national and racial commonalities and typicalities in a way that was nearly museum-worthy.[46] Because he finds pleasure in classical repose and completeness and "attempts to represent it as usual," du Maurier, by contrast, often overrides the attention to material particulars of dress and deportment required for the exhibition of national and racial types. Readers of *Punch* can learn very little from du Maurier's drawings about real English people, James notes, for "if we were to construct an image of them from the large majority of du Maurier's drawings, we should see before us a people of gods and goddesses" (53). Nevertheless, James emphasizes that du Maurier is a "much deeper observer" than Leech who "attempts discriminations" of which his predecessor never dreamt (53, 55).

In praising the mid-century illustrator Leech for his analytic eye, James in a sense articulates the terms of his own early novels and short stories. Literary realism of the variety endorsed by James's friend William Dean Howells also offered a museum-worthy analysis of social life in the here and now, realizing the *typical,* rather than the ideal, in everyday particulars, and encouraging readers to pick up on subtle social distinctions via irony.[47] James describes the 1850s *Punch,* through the work of its illustrators, as doing very much what he himself was doing in the 1880s in works such as *Washington Square,* which du Maurier illustrated, or *The Portrait of a Lady,* depicting "the smallest details of social habit" through an irony that "has always been discreet, even delicate" (51). In his discussion of du Maurier, by contrast, we find James thinking about an analytic art whose grammar might be more vague but whose construction might thereby allow for a focus on the latent meanings within the social scene and on an eroticized aspiration to belong.

James's short story "The Real Thing," syndicated in American newspapers in 1892 partly to finance his dramatic work, also addresses du Maurier's talent for seeing latent social form.[48] Based on a real event in du Maurier's life, the story concerns an illustrator who is approached by an impoverished society couple seeking work as models. The illustrator initially hopes to "seize . . . their type" in a painted portrait, but the couple have come to offer themselves instead as subjects for illustrations in a particular work of upscale literary fiction by an unappreciated author, the "rarest of the novelists . . . Philip Vincent" (310, 318). This was perhaps a nod to James's *Washington Square,* illustrated by du Maurier in the late 1870s.[49] The aptly named Monarchs assume they will be better at modeling than the narrator's usual working-class models, because they are "the real thing." However, they prove unusable precisely because their zeal to embody the static deportment, carriage, and dress of the upper classes frustrates the illustrator's pictorialist method. Comically—and impossibly—they have effaced all individuating detail and specificity from their appearance. "The hand of time had played over [Mrs. Monarch] freely, but to an effect of elimination," the narrator notes, upon first viewing her "tinted oval mask" of a face; "she was singularly like a bad illustration."[50] Having already realized the ideal in themselves, the Monarchs are ill suited for the work of modeling for an illustrated novel, for they consider it debasing to vary their look according to the different situations that make up the plot. In turn, the illustrator's drawings come out gigantic, because the static, ideal forms the Monarchs embody can only be copied and amplified, not realized anew.

The story emerges as a satire on both the business of illustrating books and the class stratifications of London society. On one level, in something of an inside joke, James archly suggests that du Maurier's gigantic, classical figures might in fact be accurate copies of the stiff, static manner and postures found in everyday upper-class London drawing rooms. On another, broader level, he points up the lack of distinction between such poses and those found in mass pictorialism, particularly advertising, seen less as a series of creative realizations than as an endless reduplication of the same. Examining the Monarchs' over-perfect carriage and mien, born in part out of their expert ability at posing for both *tableaux vivants* and society photographs, the illustrator sardonically remarks, "I could imagine 'We always use it' pinned on their bosoms with the greatest effect" (313).

"The Real Thing" has provoked a tremendous amount of criticism, much of it revolving around the question of the reliability of the illustrator's views as a proxy for James's aesthetic concerns. Leon Edel and F. O. Matthiessen initially read the story as a dramatization of the principles of anti-realism, in which James uses the illustrator—who is also the narrator—as a mouthpiece to forward a theory of art as the transfiguration of a mundane world.[51] More recently, critical suspicion has fallen on the narrator's objectifying gaze and on his denial of the power relations inherent in the expansion of the market economy and the rise of mass media. The narrator's art is often complicit, in these readings, with the persistent inequality of a mass-mediated public sphere, in which "the real thing" is a function only of representation, monetary exchange value, and the often inequitable exchange values of words and images.[52] Central to such

readings is often the fact of James's own professed "jealousy" of illustrations.[53] Recent investigations of the story's publication history have revealed that it was initially published in American newspapers and that it
was itself illustrated, suggesting that James may have designed the story as
an arch commentary on its own immediate context.[54]

There are several moments near the story's end, however, in which
James, once again invoking his friend's failing eyesight and his hypothetical relationship to the social scene, suggests that the "real" might be less a
function of monetary and linguistic exchange in the story than their phenomenological precondition. After the narrator has rejected the Monarchs
as models, he begins to see them in a rather different light. At one point,
Mrs. Monarch decides that the working-class model Miss Churm, who
has taken her place, should be wearing her hair differently:

> "Do you mind my just touching it?" [Mrs. Monarch] went on—a
> question which made me spring up for an instant as with the
> instinctive fear that she might do the young lady a harm. But she
> quieted me with a glance I shall never forget—I confess I should
> like to have been able to paint *that*—and went for a moment to my
> model. . . . She disposed her rough curls, with a few quick passes, in
> such a way as to make Miss Churm's head twice as charming. (344)

With Mrs. Monarch's look, the narrator's distanced point of view shifts,
as he once again imagines her a worthy subject for a hypothetical painting. Initially, the narrator had "seized" her "type" and hoped to render it
on canvas, but now he wants to paint something far different—the relationship *between* himself and Mrs. Monarch, as conveyed by her gaze at
him, much as a portrait in oils might reveal to the viewer a sitter's intimate
relationship to the painter. The knowing, rather commanding gaze seems
to transcend their relative economic positions of employer and employee,
reasserting Mrs. Monarch's superior social position over the narrator's superior economic one. As readers, however, we are shut out from visualizing this moment in the story ourselves by virtue of James's use of the
bare linguistic pointer—*that*. Like the narrator, we are both included in
the scene and excluded from it, enthralled by what we imagine is Mrs.
Monarch's Svengali-like domination of the illustrator, as well as the mesmerizing magic of her "passes" over Miss Churm's hair.

This mysterious relationship between Mrs. Monarch and the narrator has a strangely atemporal quality as well.[55] "That" is invoked via the subjunctive mood—"I confess I *should like* to have been able to paint *that.*" The modal verb "should" suggests that the narrator's desire to be able to paint Mrs. Monarch's gaze at him is hypothetical, full of possibility. At the same time, the infinitive phrase "to have been able to" locks the narrator's ability to paint the look into the past, frustrating that possibility. But James also makes the narrator's ability to paint irreducible to linear time altogether, by locating it grammatically in the zone of potentiality—a past future that has not been able to come to pass. And it is here that perhaps we can understand why this is something that needs to be "confessed," rather than simply stated. For it is the priority or anticipation of the painting that, as with the case of the young James reading *Punch,* or du Maurier's hypothetical captions, is "perversely" valued for its own sake. When we recall du Maurier's own fraught relationship to his original art, we see James again inspired by his friend to consider the ways in which a social and perhaps a sexual liminality might be effectively evoked by an uncompleted act of pictorial realization.

That "The Real Thing" owes a debt to the aesthetic value James saw in du Maurier's frustrations as a painter is made particularly clear in the final interaction between the illustrator and his strange visitors. Not content with simply sitting and watching, the Monarchs are so desperate for money that they are willing to work as servants to the narrator and his working-class models, cleaning his dishes and bringing in tea. Their actions prompt him to an emotional realization that interrupts his work:

> When it came over me, the latent eloquence of what they were
> doing, I confess that my drawing was blurred for a moment—the
> picture swam. . . . They had bowed their heads in bewilderment to
> the perverse and cruel law in virtue of which the real thing could
> be so much less precious than the unreal; but they didn't want to
> starve. If my servants were my models, then my models might be
> my servants. They would reverse the parts—the other would sit for
> the ladies and gentlemen and *they* would do the work. (345)

The propositional and chiasmic structure of the sentence "If my servants were my models, then my models might be my servants" signals the Monarchs' folly. Rather than understanding that they are exchanging *places* with the "servants," they instead see themselves "revers[ing] the parts," as if they were taking part in a social drama of birth and breeding. In fact, those parts are opposed *positions*, established only by the capacity to imitate, and therefore open to anyone. However, there is a further dimension here that is even more important than the "tragedy" of the Monarchs' refusal to accept "their fate," and that is the "latent eloquence" of their heretofore unsuspected ability to act as servants. As was the case in "Du Maurier and London Society," the illustrator's exclusion from the social scene leads to an aesthetic grasp of its potential or latent quality. For he, like du Maurier, can only hypothesize a caption for the scene he witnesses. What they *might* be saying, he thinks, as he watches the Monarchs work, is that "they would reverse the parts—the other would sit for the ladies and gentlemen, and *they* would do the work."

The narrator's aesthetic values thus emerge as a proxy for James's own, but they offer less a challenge to realism than a redefinition of it. The narrator's final experience of the Monarchs redefines the real as the virtual.[56] More specifically, it redefines the real as virtual *experience*, for the illustrator's position as the excluded, yet included observer, is imagined in phenomenological terms. Much as du Maurier's limited eyesight in real life—his *physical* inability to visually distinguish borders and boundaries—leads him somehow to a superior pictorialism, according to James, the narrator's blinding emotion at the end of "The Real Thing" leads him to a vaguer, but truer picture: "My drawing was blurred for a moment—the picture swam." James manages to suggest that seeing the eloquent latency of social form is both superior to and generally *incompatible* with the sharp analytic insight and objectifying distance required for the truly "illustrative" drawing. For the illustrator's realization comes at the expense of his illustration by the end of the story—"My pencil dropped. . . . My sitting was spoiled and I got rid of my sitters" (345).

"The Real Thing" reveals the extent of the tribute James had paid to du Maurier in his earlier profile. For in his nonfictional account of du Maurier's talents as an illustrator, James had credited his friend with achieving something of which his fictional illustrator seems to be incapable. Du Maurier's illustrations actually do "swim" on the page, James suggests, realizing not the ideal—but instead, due to du Maurier's visual impairment—the virtual. Insofar as this achievement also allows du Maurier to link the scene of the social's enactment to those that it excludes, his art has a utopian aspect for James, suggesting the possibility that the social world could be other than it is. Perhaps it is not surprising, then, that James himself begins to emulate the style of du Maurier's illustrations, however grotesque their effect, in the very grammar of his prose.

"Lawless" Pictorialism and the Virtuality of Style

Readers of James interested in his ties to pragmatism, via his brother William James and family friend Ralph Waldo Emerson, have often argued that language and thought are inseparable in his late works, and that consciousness in late James cannot be reduced to individual psychology.[57] Lambert Strether in *The Ambassadors,* Milly Theale in *The Wings of the Dove,* the governess in "The Turn of the Screw," and numerous others in James's mature fiction think of themselves as having distinct identities. But at climactic moments in each story, they experience a failure of distance and distinction between themselves and others, disclosing that consciousness is in fact shared by virtue of the fact that language is shared. In the conversations between characters in such works, as a result, one person's interpretation of the speech or thought of another does not indicate mutual understanding. Instead, interpretation is often a way of *creating* thoughts and attributing them to particular persons. As Sharon Cameron notes of the many scenes of wordless intuition and internal speech in *The Golden Bowl,* "Meanings are not being understood" between James's characters in his late phase, "they are rather being imposed."[58]

In his preface to the New York edition of *Roderick Hudson,* James defines the "art of representation" in terms that recall Emerson. "Around every circle another can be drawn," the latter had written in 1841, describing the way that ideas and actions, much like reference in language, perpetually evolve to exceed their delimiting frames of meaning, including those of the mind itself.[59] Likewise, James sees the problem of the writer as one of how to evoke the perpetually limitless "developments" and "relations" pertinent to his chosen subject, without sacrificing an overarching formal structure:

> Really, universally, relations stop nowhere, and the exquisite
> problem of the artist is eternally but to draw, by a geometry of his
> own, the circle within which they shall happily *appear* to do so. He
> is in the perpetual predicament that the continuity of things is the

whole matter, for him, of comedy and tragedy; that this continuity is never, by the space of an instant or an inch, broken, and that, to do anything at all, he has at once intensely to consult and intensely to ignore it.[60]

James's career can be understood as a series of shifting responses to this fundamental problem. In his realist phase, as exemplified by *Washington Square*, he limited the proliferating associations of words and their meanings by investigating the complex motives of well-delineated and discrete characters, understanding them, much like William Dean Howells, as "types." In later novels like *The Ambassadors* or *The Golden Bowl*, published in 1903 and 1904, the drama of limiting and circumscribing meaning, both by and between persons, becomes *itself* the subject.

Queer theorists, too, have argued that consciousness, by virtue of its location in language, is external to persons in late James. Drawing instead on psychoanalysis and on Foucauldian discourse analysis, they have tended to see in this innovation the seeds of an ethical and social radicalism whose main mode of delivery is James's style.[61] In a recent reading of James's 1903 short story "The Beast in the Jungle," Leo Bersani argues that the main character, John Marcher, who is unable to return the love of a woman, is less a conventionally delimited character type, subject to unconscious wishes, than a representation of unconscious latency itself—the "it" that always precedes the "I." Accordingly, Bersani argues against interpreting Marcher as a moral failure or a repressed homosexual, both of which are suggested by the story's manifest content. Instead, he points out that James's syntax describes Marcher as a *virtual* character, existing, like the Lacanian unconscious, "only in a mode of expectancy."[62] Via a proliferation of modal verbs and subjunctive moods—typical of James's late style—the story suggests that rather than an ethical failure to marry, Marcher's mysterious "fate" is instead "a kind of being, or a form of law, inherently incompatible with the very category of happening."[63]

The challenge to psychological interiority in late James, for queer theorists like Bersani, is inseparable from the question of sexuality, or more particularly of sexual representation. Rather than setting forth a model of social and sexual relations to be either imitated or shunned, "The Beast in the Jungle," Bersani argues, disrupts the reproduction of the psychosexual social order and the realization of the normative social subject.[64] It does so by delineating a protagonist who exists ontologically outside of time, and therefore also outside of, or rather in the transition to, meaning in language. As "pure potential," Marcher's "fate" discloses the unacknowledged potentiality and variability of social and institutional forms dependent on effacing their reliance on language—most centrally among them, marriage. Bersani's reading highlights the way in which morally and ethically questionable interactions between characters in late James are often redeemed by the latent or belated quality of Jamesian syntax, which effectively describes those interactions as irreducible to their own actualization.

While pragmatists and queer theorists have tended to focus on James's ties to philosophy, many historically minded readers have instead credited the derealizing properties of the late Jamesian sentence—and the latent, impersonal consciousness it foregrounds—to the broader influence of late nineteenth-century theater, popular culture, and new media technologies, such as the telegraph and the typewriter. Several critics have noted that while James decries contemporaneous popular culture, he lavishes praise on *mid*-nineteenth-century visual and theatrical culture in his memoirs, particularly in the first volume, *A Small Boy and Others*.[65] In this extraordinarily "besotted" text, as David Kurnick argues, theater stands revealed as an inspiration for James's style, particularly the "world-making" and "self-enhancing energy" of theatrical spectatorship, which "promise[s] an experience of sociality and an apprehension of a world in which it would be durably on offer."[66] Others have noted that the communicative opacity of James's late works evokes some of the unintended effects of new communication technologies in the 1890s. James's late fictions, in Mark Goble's words, "incorporate a phenomenology of mediated experience as the very basis of their aesthetic structure."[67] Much like the strangely knowing yet thoroughly obscure conversations in late James, the typewriter, to which James dictated his late works, arguably also externalizes consciousness, turning thinking into a shared affair in more ways than one.

James's writings about du Maurier, however, suggest that, to him, the aesthetic importance of theater, media, and popular culture had more to do with the *inter*medial relations of mass pictorialism than with the intrinsic qualities of any particular medium. In both "Du Maurier and London Society" and "The Real Thing," James's fascination with his friend's failing eyesight and his intermediate status between painter and illustrator leads to insights about the way identity and consciousness are irreducible to persons. The hypothetical rather than documentary quality of du

Maurier's captions seemed to suggest early on to James that interpretation is less an intuition of the meaning already present in other minds than a way of determining meaning. For James, in other words, du Maurier's hybrid position somewhere in between the different "languages" of the arts made *his* art into a revelation of the subtle and constitutive interrelationships between people, and between the artist and the scenes he illustrates.

James's fictional and nonfictional portraits of his friend also suggest to me that the intermedial citationality of popular culture was formative for the socially, sexually, and ethically radical aspects of his late style identified by queer theorists. The demure Mrs. Monarch's sudden, bold look at the illustrator in "The Real Thing" can be interpreted as at odds with the Monarchs' "true marriage" for the way it invites the illustrator into an obscurely intimate relationship that is never fully explained. At the same time, in the grammar of the illustrator's response—"I confess I should have liked to paint *that*"—the subjunctive "I should have liked to paint" potentializes the unvisualizable *that* relative both to their commercial relationship and the circuits of heterosexual exchange. The illustrator's desire to paint Mrs. Monarch, confessable though it is, emerges as of a different ontological order than that of the world in which her gaze itself is actualized. As Bersani notes, the phenomenology of the look is "de-realized" by being grammatically relegated to a hypothetical and anticipatory state. Alternatively, we can say that James's style functions here as a way "to return potentiality to actualized existence . . . to make manifest the potentiality inherent in actualization," as Kevin Ohi puts it.[68] All of this takes place in the story precisely at the moment that James seeks to describe the illustrator's hypothetical relationship to another medium—painting.

James's discussion of du Maurier, of course, is not unique in disclosing the aesthetic concerns that were beginning to preoccupy him in the 1890s. The origin of those concerns can be accounted for in more detail, and on James's own terms, by consulting his more programmatic statements. The project for the modern novel he outlined in two essays, "The Art of Fiction" and "The Future of the Novel," which I discuss following, provide a particularly helpful introduction to his emerging interest in a poetics of the virtual. Yet his writings about du Maurier and his struggles are valuable for what they reveal about the importance to James of the transformation of earlier nineteenth-century pictorialist practices. James's turn to the virtual was not simply a feature of his late style, or the result of the influence of a particular technological medium; the inspiration he took from du Maurier suggests that mass pictorialism was a formative influence that has gone largely unacknowledged by critics.

Other factors unrelated to du Maurier also point in this direction. For example, in *A Small Boy and Others*, James looks back with fascination at the novelistic adaptations he particularly enjoyed in the theater of his youth. Recalling his rapt attentiveness at the theatrical production of Harriet Beecher Stowe's *Uncle Tom's Cabin*, James writes:

> We lived and moved at that time, with great intensity, in Mrs. Stowe's novel [which was] my first experiment in grown-up fiction. There was, however, I think, for that triumphant work no classified condition; it was for no sort of reader as distinct from any other sort.... It... had above all the extraordinary fortune of finding itself, for an immense number of people, much less a book than a state of vision, of feeling and of consciousness, in which they didn't sit and read and appraise and pass the time, but walked and talked and laughed and cried and, in a manner of which Mrs. Stowe was the irresistible cause, generally conducted themselves.... If the amount of life represented in such a work is measurable by the ease with which representation is taken up and carried further, carried even violently furthest, the fate of Mrs. Stowe's picture was conclusive.[69]

One motivation for James's odd and compelling formulation that he and others "lived and moved ... *in* Mrs. Stowe's novel" (emphasis mine) likely has do with the fact that pictures from the text literally surrounded him, because he "lived and moved" as a child in the cultural environment of mid-nineteenth-century America. What James calls the "life" of Stowe's work would seem here to be inseparable from the many realizations of the novel's affecting scenes in the products, paraphernalia, and theatrical adaptations that circulated after its publication. Yet, although *Uncle Tom's* "life" is *in* these many realizations, it is not *of* them. James ultimately describes the "fate" of Stowe's novel in terms reminiscent of John Marcher's fate in "The Beast in the Jungle." *Uncle Tom*, in James's account, emerges as "a kind of being, or a form of law, inherently incompatible with the very category of happening," in Bersani's words. In other words, James praises Stowe's *Uncle Tom's Cabin*, qua novel, for the way it manages to occupy some other order of being than that of its many realizations.

This description of *Uncle Tom*, surprisingly enough, recalls James's own goals for the modern novel as he initially framed them in "The Art of Fiction" (1884) and "The Future of the Novel" (1899). In the former, James argues that the form of the modern novel cannot be specified in advance as a set of proscriptive rules for writing about experience, because of a fundamental lag time or gap between consciousness and experience. To formalize the novel curtails the temporal unfolding immanent both to writing and to reading, limiting the novelist's ability to write and the reader's ability to think about and discuss what the novelist writes.[70] In the latter essay, James elaborates this definition further by distinguishing between the novel and the book. Whereas the novel is virtual, a continual movement of self-difference and temporal unfolding, the book is actual, a material object that is manufactured and circulates to a given public of readers, for whom it has a purely referential status.[71] That James describes Stowe's "picture" as the kind of novel that he also considered the centerpiece of his mature style suggests that that style may have owed a significant, and largely unacknowledged, debt to the practices of pictorial realization that the *Uncle Tom* mania exemplified in the 1850s, and Trilby-mania rekindled in the 1890s.

That a pictoralist transposition of media, rather than the intrinsic qualities of a particular medium, grounds the "aesthetic structure" of James's late work is also suggested by his novella "In the Cage," which I discuss in the introduction. In this story about a telegraph operator who lives vicariously through a love affair conducted by her aristocratic customers, it is less the medium-specific qualities of the telegraph on which James focuses than on the way the telegraph office—which is also a post office—itself becomes a highly erotic scene of intermedial exchange. As a result, the story becomes another demonstration of the value of the excluded rapt observer, and her capacity to aesthetically grasp the exchangeability of media—and of the identities media mediate—as a beautiful form. Further, the scenes of intermedial transposition in the Victorian post office parallel the scenes of dictation that were beginning around the same time in James's home office. Insofar as dictation can be considered formative for his late style, we can conclude that it was not the typewriter or the voice per se that was formative, but the potentiality inherent in the transposition from one medium to another.

James's choice of Alvin Langdon Coburn's photography for the frontispieces of the New York edition suggests that the practice of pictorial realization continued to be important to him after the 1890s. Rather than being drawn to Coburn's work because he shared—or rejected—photography's modernist and avant-garde aesthetic, as some critics have claimed, I think James favored photography because of the way it gave new life to an older pictorialist aesthetic.[72] Success for a novelist, as he defines it in the preface to the *Golden Bowl*, lies in the ability to convincingly realize an ideal scene or scenario, and in the realizations that novelist thereby inspires in the work of other artists in other media. James notes that he seeks to "reduce one's reader, 'artistically' inclined, to such a state of hallucination by the images one has evoked as doesn't permit him to rest till he has noted or recorded them, set up some semblance of them in his own other medium, by his own other art."[73] Contemporary illustration, by contrast, is a "competitive process" that often produces grotesque forms—"flesh and fish on the same platter"— by trying to imitate the characters and story too closely. In a description that recalls his earlier account of du Maurier's incongruous and incompletely realized images, James cautions that "to my sense . . . to graft or 'grow,' at whatever point, a picture by another hand on my own picture" is "always . . . a lawless incident."[74] Coburn's photographs, however, are in "as different a 'medium' as possible," and hence, James implies, they achieve a dialectical realization that has been largely lost by mass illustration. As James notes, he "welcomes illustration" only so long as it "stand[s] off and on its own feet and thus, in a separate and independent spirit of publication, carr[ies] its text in its spirit, just as that text correspondingly carries the plastic possibility."[75]

As in his discussion of du Maurier, in his account of Coburn's work, James ultimately finds something inherently valuable in the grotesque and "lawless" modern pictorialist practices that he otherwise dismisses. Toward the end of the same paragraph, he personifies the relationship between Coburn's image and his text as erotic and flirtatious, involved with each other, rather than chaste and distancing in pursuit of fidelity to an ideal scene. "The reference of [a series of reproducible subjects] to Novel or Tale," James goes on to specify, "should exactly be *not* competitive and obvious, should on the contrary plead its case with some shyness, that of images always confessing themselves mere optical symbols or echoes, expressions of no particular thing in the text, but only of the type or idea of this or that thing."[76] This discussion of the relationship between Coburn's photographs and his fiction draws our attention much more to the enticing act of realization itself than to its putative content or end point. While the pictorial sentiment is familiar here, the blushing appeal of the image as it pleads and confesses its generality to the text distracts us from the concomitant idea that images and text "stand off" from each other, separate and independent, expressing a common ideal in their different languages. The relation between different media is a flirtatious and fascinating one, perhaps much like that between James and the younger Coburn. As is the case with the illustrator's desire to paint Mrs. Monarch's look, or with the telegraph girl's erotic experience of transcription in "In the Cage," intermedial exchange for James has an aesthetic value in its own right, because it offers a way to potentialize erotic relations—or to eroticize potential relations—that are otherwise socially unacceptable.

These relations, in turn, are also characterized by the pleasures of anticipation and delay. For the project of illustrating the New York edition, James explains, he and Coburn had to search together throughout London to find the scenes that they—or more likely James—wanted to use. The fact that the scenes "awaited us somewhere," in places James coyly refuses to name, is—rather to the detriment of Coburn's photographs—"what was above all interesting" about them.[77] James's emphasis on anticipation here, as in "The Beast in the Jungle," potentializes a stable and reproducible social order founded on marriage. In describing his wanderings with Coburn, James subtly parallels the two of them with the lovers Prince Amerigo and Charlotte Stant of *The Golden Bowl* undertaking the ostensibly innocent task of searching for a wedding present on the eve of Amerigo's marriage to Maggie Verver.[78] It is as if the waiting James shares with Coburn, as they search for a shop like that where the golden bowl was purchased, is of a different order, and of a vastly greater value, than the "happening" of—well, of the photograph itself.

James's description of the search reveals that his choice of Coburn was based on their joint commitment not to the ideal scene, but to the virtual scene. The two men shared, James notes, the "fond idea" that "the aspect of things or the combination of objects . . . might, by a *latent virtue* in it, speak for its connexion with something in the book, and yet at the same time speak enough for its odd or interesting self" (emphasis mine).[79] The distinctive hazy pictorialism of Coburn's photographs here becomes a form of incomplete realization that has much in common with James's own grammar of latency. The "fond ideal" governing the work of both, as the phrase punningly suggests, lies somewhere in between the real and ideal. It thus becomes inseparable not only from the fondness of male artists and writers for their art, but also from their fondness for each another, which in turn, is indistinguishable from the "lawless" realizations of mass pictorialism.

Finally, a "lawless" and ungovernable pictorialism also offers a good description of James's late *expository* writing. Examples abound in *The American Scene,* James's memoir of his 1904–05 tour of the United States. The text has been productively analyzed elsewhere for the way it seeks stylistically to inject a sense of potential and uncertainty into the inexorable growth of industrialization and urbanization in the United States, commonly thought of as divinely ordained and unstoppable.[80] Often noted also is the way in which James virtualizes his own past in this text. Rendering deliberately hazy the distinction between remembrance and re-creation becomes a way for him to oppose the linear, measurable time imposed by the engines of "progress" in Progressive Era America.[81] Much like Henri Bergson, as discussed in the introduction to this volume, James distinguishes throughout *The American Scene* between real time as changes in kind—a creative elaboration from virtual to actual, in which the new is never constituted in advance but evolves unpredictably out of the old— and a false conception of time as changes in degree, in which what is possible has existence simply added to it to make it real. James complains that the forces of American modernity are engaged in a "perpetual repudiation of the past," willfully refusing to grasp the movement of creative elaboration that ties together present and past, and perpetually seeking to make the past a "a victim of supersession."[82]

What has been less noted is the degree to which this text uses figures of pictorialist realization in order to describe—or rather to mimetically *enact*—the relation between present and past that James seeks to recover within American modernity. Musing on the destruction of old Boston neighborhoods, James moves restlessly through a startling number of media metaphors in one short passage alone, as he thinks about the temporal continuity hindered by America's devotion to "the hungry, triumphant actual" (53). He finds in the new Boston, first, "the hundred emendations and retouches of the old picture . . . tending . . . to confound and mislead . . . the lights and shades of remembrance" (ibid.). The retouching of the picture as a figure for a purely additive conception of change then gives way in the next paragraph to writing as a figure for the same thing, as James reflects that "*the will to grow* was everywhere written large, and to grow at no matter what or whose expense" (54). Writing then in turn resolves itself within James's prose into dance. A linear conception of progress can also be described as "the very screeches of the pipe to which humanity is actually dancing" (ibid.). From there, we return quickly to painting—"What would it [the will to progress] ever say no to? Or what would it ever paint thick . . . with sympathy and sanction?" James wonders (ibid.). Finally, at the end of the paragraph, James arrives at the theater, the final resting place for this series of restless tropic substitutions, and the site at which he discovers the "true name" for the "will to grow." It is, in short, "the monstrous form of Democracy" that is "shak[ing] the loose boards of its theatric stage to an inordinate unprecedented rumble" (ibid.). Like du Maurier's classical giants in the drawing room, or the Monarchs serving tea, James ultimately decides that democracy—the exchangeability of everyone—amounts to more than simply a grotesque incongruity to be shunned or avoided. It has a "consistency" and "intensity" that "shines through with its hard light, whatever equivocal gloss may happen momentarily to prevail" (55). In other words, democracy, too, is irreducible to the scene of its own happening. When virtualized in this way, it becomes a fit subject for realization in the figurative language of literature. "As an explication or an implication," James notes, as if considering a short story he might set stateside, "the democratic intensity could always figure" (56).

From picture, to writing, to dance, to the stage, James's metaphors displace one another in this passage in a restless attempt to find an accurate figure for the reduction of potentiality to possibility that he sees everywhere in American life. While the stage, as it often does, ultimately provides that figure, it is the media forms of painting, drama, and illustration, all incessantly displacing each other in James's prose, that embody the movement of his thought, and finally give him, through the master trope of the theater—the "total" art—an ability to imagine the American scene otherwise. Like Emerson in his later essays, James abandons his thought to the movement of linguistic tropes, and "Democracy" becomes the name for this abandonment, and for a latent or virtual form of sociality with a world-making energy.[83] Yet, unlike in Emerson, this movement of thought in James no longer proceeds under the sign of writing. It is instead the lawless incidents of intermedial transposition to which the American self is abandoned, and out of which James in turn draws his queer politics of style.

In light of James's pervasive thematic and stylistic evocation of pictorialism, then, it seems reasonable to conclude that his dealings with the intermedial world of the 1890s, including not only his attempts to write for the theater but also his correspondence and negotiation with editors over publication in illustrated books, magazines, and newspapers, were more important than any particular medium as a formative influence on his late style. Considered from this perspective, the impersonal consciousness that suffuses James's late works looks like a good way to describe the enticing promises of a life lived within a newly multimedia society. In such a world, the caption doesn't fully control the meanings that can be gleaned from an illustration and a film's intertitle offers only one possible interpretation of a suggestive scene. James's extensive, admiring treatment of the analytic art of John Leech, from this perspective, looks like a final fling with the realism he was leaving behind in the face of these developments, while his admiring account of du Maurier's illustrations, by contrast, forecasts the stylistic shifts necessary to formulating a new response. It is thus not difficult to see, in James's meditations on his friend's art, the beginnings of his attempt to work out the terms by which he himself might aspire to transform the "illustrative" mission of the realist novel—so that it, too, might be able to evoke, in what he considered to be the superior medium of writing, the virtual sociality of a multimedia age.

The Two *Trilby*s

In the fall of 1896, three years after the beginning of Trilby-mania and shortly before James began dictating his work, du Maurier died.[84] James was called upon by *Harper's Monthly* to write an obituary for his friend, and what resulted was a piece of writing that is particularly revealing of his complex attitude toward the phenomenon of mass pictorialism. The *Harper's* assignment put James in the awkward position of trying to praise his friend's accomplishments and interpret the meaning of his success without fully countenancing—or further contributing to—the "mania" that he deplored. In trying to walk this line, James dramatically expands his stylistic evocation of virtuality. In so doing, he opens the possibility that style, both his own and that of his friend, might redeem the death of du Maurier, and that of authorship more broadly, at the hands of an interpretive community no longer beholden to the written word.

Aesthetically and socially radical as it is, James's definition of the modern novel as both virtual and "discussable" in "The Art of the Novel" can be understood as voicing a more conservative concern, which he shared

with Matthew Arnold and many other guardians of "high" culture during this period, about the decline of the public sphere and of the public
exercise of critical and disinterested judgment at its heart.[85] This concern
is placed front and center in du Maurier's obituary. What James objects
to above all in the craze for all things "Trilby," for instance, is "an attitude
unfathomable" on the part of the public, which, echoing the content of
the novel itself, he describes as "a mere immensity of sound," a "senseless
hum" whose behavior eludes reason and explanation.[86] Trilby-mania trou-
bles James because it cannot be explained in terms of any known contract
between author and reader, whether that of du Maurier's intention to produce a certain effect; the public's independent pleasure in his creation; or
the strictures guarding du Maurier's private life from scrutiny. The public
has "no mind . . . to reflect on the prodigious keeping up, on one side and
the other, that such terms as these implied," he notes (608). The result of
the novel's ungovernable and wildly proliferating realizations is, for James,
quite literally, the death of the author. Du Maurier simply "turned for ref-
uge to the only quarter where peace is deep" (607).[87]

When, as he can hardly avoid doing, James dutifully takes up the much-
debated question of the origins of *Trilby* and the appeal of its images, his
solution is to suggest that there were two fundamentally different yet in-
terconnected *Trilbys*—the potential and the actual. The potential book is
located in a time and space irreducibly prior to and yet generative of the
actual, the material object that was circulated to a wider public and caused
the craze. James traces the origin of *Trilby* to a series of popular lectures
on illustration that du Maurier gave to the English public. In these talks,
which, James suggests, were devoted largely to making money, du Maurier
had already found his "tone," which "was to resound over the globe; yet
we none of us faintly knew it, least of all the good people who, on the
benches, were all unconscious of their doom" (603). Rather than functioning as a sign of the inevitable coming popularity that, now, at the time
of the writing, has already arrived, du Maurier's "tone" is both absolutely
other to and yet also continuous with its actualization in *Trilby*. For, James
continues, in du Maurier's lectures, "the printed page was actually there,
but the question was to be supremely settled by another application of it.
It is the particular application of the force that, in any case, most makes
the mass (as *we* know the mass) to vibrate" (ibid.). By asserting that the
printed page was "actually there" in the talk, James contests the idea that

the talk was the origin of *Trilby*, as if the novel existed Platonically as an ideal form in du Maurier's speech, only to be copied and disseminated to a vast and uncomprehending audience via writing. Instead, the novel, in du Maurier's lecture, is present as a potentiality. It is both there and not there, best understood as a "question" about its own existence that becomes "settled" in the many physical books, products, and performances of *Trilby*. Among the crowd of listeners, moreover, are some discerning readers and writers—a mysterious sodality of the "we"— who understand *Trilby*'s duality and grasp the fact that the origin of a work is incommensurate with the different "happenings" of its commercial success.

One of the payoffs of such incommensurability is a form of immortality for the writer. In defiance of the contemporaneous biographers and fans who sought to read du Maurier's life into his texts, James specifies that there is in fact nothing to be read, because those texts contain everything: "The author is personally all there [in his texts]. . . . Everything in him, everything one remembers him by and knew him by and most liked him for, is literally, is intensely there" (604). In specifying that *everything* is there in his writing, both literally and intensely, James suggests that even du Maurier's "real" life might have been an actualization of the virtual life found in his books. Since James was beginning around this time to construct a literary style responsive to the notion that consciousness is not contained in individuals, but is shared between people and even objects, then it seems possible that what he has in mind here is the startling idea that du Maurier does indeed live on in his works themselves, virtually present for eternity.[88]

James's turn to style as a redemption from the actualizations of the market becomes clearest in the obituary when he discusses the illustrations for *Trilby*, which, even at the time, were often credited with the novel's success. As in "Du Maurier and London Society" James again emphasizes the precarity of du Maurier's sight as one of the sources of the images' immense appeal. Unlike in that essay, however, James brings his most temporalizing stylistic armature to bear in this discussion. Du Maurier, James notes, "saw, with a creative intensity, every facial and corporeal queerness" in his "musical and vocal types," evident in *Trilby*, with its many scenes of performance (601). Yet, once again, du Maurier's talent lies in the failure of his eyesight, which James here associates with synesthesia, a condition prior to the differentiation and actualization of the senses:[89]

It seemed to me that he almost *saw* the voice, as he saw the features
and limbs, and quite as if this had been but one of the subtler
secrets of his impaired vision. He talked of it ever as if he could
draw it and would particularly like to; as if, certainly, he would
gladly have drawn the wonderful passage ... through which proper
"production" came forth. Did he not, in fact, practically delineate
these irresistible adjuncts to the universal ravage of Trilby? It was at
any rate not for want of intention that he didn't endow her with an
organ that he could have stroked with his pencil as tenderly as you
might have felt it with your hand. (601–2)

James's virtualizing syntax exempts his friend here from the drive to visualize and materialize Trilby's voice, which was a characteristic both of
Svengali's relationship to Trilby the character (see Figure 1), and of the
public's relationship to *Trilby* the novel, via highly sexualized products like
the "Trilby sausage." In his rhetorical question, "Did he not, in fact, practically delineate these irresistible adjuncts to the universal ravage of Trilby?"
James suggests that both novel and illustrations are temporally incommensurate with their actualizations in book form. He does so by evoking
the presence of both the past tense, "Did he not?," and the suggestion of a
possible future tense, "to the universal ravage of Trilby," making causality
impossible to distinguish. The invitation to stroke Trilby's throat in the
images is both a subsequent *addition* to her public "ravage" and the *cause*
of that "ravage." The two *Trilbys* arise, James suggests, because du Maurier
"practically" has the ability to draw, not the voice itself, but the *passage* of
the voice. As such, he creates an enticing sexual lure that is simultaneously
of a different order than its satisfaction. In praising du Maurier for the ability to evoke an ontological realm prior to actualization, and demonstrating
that power in his own sentences' resistance to grammatical time, we can
infer that he is trying to resist interpreting du Maurier's drawings as the
cause of *Trilby*'s success. At the same time he seeks to credit his friend and
implicitly himself with access to a realm of potentiality that is both generative of and incompatible with success.

In his emphasis on the "passage" to production of both voice and
novel, James was elevating the most distinctive quality of the *Trilby* boom
itself—its citationality—to the central principle of his and his friend's art.
James comes closest to acknowledging this incorporation of the mass pictorialism he otherwise rejects in his discussion of du Maurier's prior il-

Figure 1. "Himmel! The Roof of Your Mouth," illustration by George du Maurier for Trilby. *General Research Division; The New York Public Library; Astor, Lenox, and Tilden Foundations.*

"'HIMMEL! THE ROOF OF YOUR MOUTH'"

lustrated novel, the much less successful *Peter Ibbetson*. Perhaps because few had read it, or simply perhaps because it is itself a virtual *Trilby*, James allows his admiration for the citational style of mass pictorialism to shine fully through in his discussion of this novel. *Peter Ibbetson*'s illustrations, he writes,

> are an example of illustration at its happiest; not one's own idea, or somebody else's, of how somebody looked and moved or some image was constituted, but the lovely mysterious fact itself,

precedent to interpretation and independent of it. The text might have been supplied to account for them, and they melt—I speak now of their office in all the books equally—into their place in the extraordinary general form, the form that is to be described as almost anything, almost everything but a written one. (606)

As the "lovely mysterious fact itself," the illustrations would seem to realize a scene that transcends interpretation, a success by traditional pictorialist standards. But James at the same time notes that the union of ideal and real is *precedent* to interpretation. The term precedent implies a form of "lawless" realization, opening the door to the endless interpretations that he decries with regard to *Trilby*. It is as if the very fact of the illustrations' temporal priority also somehow justifies—like a legal decision that relies only on precedent—whatever subsequent interpretation they receive. Really, then, nothing is capable of bringing an event like the *Trilby* boom to an end. There can be no regulative ideal—no ideal scene or story—governing the interpretations that *Peter Ibbetson*, at least, may generate.

Even more remarkably, James notes of *Peter Ibbetson* something that he might well also have said about *Trilby*, and that in fact he *did* say about du Maurier back in 1880—that its text "might" have been supplied to account for the images. *Peter Ibbetson*'s combination of pictures and text not only reverses the text's usual interpretive priority over the image, as James describes it; it also blurs the very distinction between text and image, merging them all into one "extraordinary general form." This form resembles nothing so much as the perpetual movement of citation that constituted the "mania" for all things *Trilby*, and also, a generation earlier, for *Uncle Tom's Cabin*. Du Maurier's "form" is "a string of moods and feelings, of contacts and sights and sounds" that is "talked . . . and sung, joked and smoked, eaten and drunk, dressed and undressed, danced and boxed, loved and loathed, and, as a result of all this, in relation to its matter, made abnormally, triumphantly expressive" (605–6). Far from condemning the practices of visual citation and recontextualization characteristic of the publicity surrounding his friend's novel, James here seems to celebrate the nascent or virtual sociality they disclose.

It is worth remembering, however that it is *James's* writing here that becomes "abnormally, triumphantly expressive" by reclaiming du Maurier's sung, joked, and smoked "general form" for language. The masterful, rhythmic list of paired past tense verbs that slow us down on the approach to their final act of expression recreates the moving experience of "Trilby-mania," much like the series of tropic substitutions of painting, dance, and theater in *The American Scene*. In the temporizing stylistic shift that James embraces in his late work, in other words, it is the moving experience of language alone, rather than the intermedial citations of the mass public sphere, that is at issue. In contrast to the endless citationality of "Trilby-mania," forever driven to new actualizations in the service of the commer-cialized mass public sphere, the multiple interpretations generated by the latency of the Jamesian sentence are governed and constrained by their resistance to actualization. The two *Trilbys*, the virtual and the actual, thus allow James to celebrate the author's authority over his text, the integrity of his inspirational processes, and the bonds between male authors who have in common an epistemologically valuable, because enticingly pain-ful, exclusion from the social, sexual, and literary scene.

A final glance at the references to du Maurier in James's last autobio-graphical writings reveals that, as might have been expected, James did indeed see his own career as closely entwined with that of his friend. In *Notes of a Son and Brother*, the second volume of his memoirs, published in 1914, James describes himself and his brother William as fans of du Maurier because of their own intense desire to become the "new man" of European arts and letters that he embodied. He explains that the brothers first got to know du Maurier through his drawings. By 1862, James writes, du Maurier's illustrations "had already engaged our fondest attention—were they most dawningly in the early *Cornhill*, or in *Punch*, or in *Once a Week*? They glimmer upon me, darkly and richly, as from the pages of the last named."[90] James's abrupt shift of tense from "dawning" images in the past to their present "dark glimmer" in his memory makes it difficult to lo-cate in strict grammatical time exactly when and how du Maurier's draw-ings "fondly" engaged the young Jameses through the illustrated press. The same is true of the interruption of the clear temporal progression of the past perfect—"They had already engaged"—with a question about exactly where it was the images first "dawned." The temporal confusion draws at-tention away from the subject of James's youthful influences and toward the artificiality of memory and the autobiographical enterprise itself. Yet the dawning and darkening of the images also have the quality of growth, maturation, and decline, registering the movement of creative elaboration that equally defines life and the aesthetic process. James's memory, in other words, misses the virtual quality of the image, but his syntax doesn't. By virtualizing du Maurier's images, we can infer that James thereby sought to redeem not only the origin of his friend's commercial success, but also that of his own seemingly less successful career.

James makes the distinction between the time of linguistic predication and the time of life especially clear in his description of the moment he and his brother heard about du Maurier's visual impairment from their worldly friend John Chandler Bancroft, who had lived and worked in Europe in the mid-1860s:

> More touching to me now than I can say, at all events, this recapture of the hour at which Du Maurier, consecrated to much later, to then still far-off intimate affection, became the new man so significantly as to make a great importance of John Bancroft's news of him, which already bore, among many marvels, upon the supreme wonder of his working, as he was all his life bravely to work, under impaired and gravely menaced eyesight. (337)

Henry's and William's reception of news about du Maurier was significantly influenced by the fact that his images had already engaged their "fondest attention." Once they heard Bancroft's story, the impression already made upon them by the illustrator's work transformed du Maurier into the object of intense admiration and identification. Yet the moment of this transformation evades its own capture through a grammar that clearly specifies linear progression. In writing that "Du Maurier *became* the new man so significantly as *to make* a great importance of John Bancroft's news of him" (emphasis mine), James blurs past and future together, and suggests that the temporal point at which du Maurier's drawings inspired the James brothers, via Bancroft's storytelling, is generative, but is nevertheless, in Bersani's words, "incompatible with its own happening."

In setting the scenario of du Maurier's appreciation in the past, in a private circle of male artists and writers, James constructs a grammatical and temporal loop. He imparts a value to the irreducibly generative priority of du Maurier's drawings through the figure of prolepsis, in his parenthetical note that du Maurier was "consecrated" to "far-off intimate affection." The structure crosses a present knowledge with a past ignorance, representing a point of origin that is impossible to express, even as it generates—by "consecrating" du Maurier to later affection—the act of autobiographical recall itself. But such a continuity nevertheless fully *exists*, James wants to

Figure 2.
"Saltram's Seat,"
photogravure by
Alvin Langdon
Coburn. Harry
Ransom Center,
The University of
Texas at Austin.

say, as a generative kernel for the autobiographical enterprise. We might infer as well that this kernel has the potential to germinate—or not—in the diverse acts of interpretation that will be undertaken in future by the many fans of *Trilby* and one of the fans of *Peter Ibbetson*—James himself.

That James is seeking a kind of redemption not only for his long-lost friend but also for himself becomes evident when he notes that his memory of du Maurier's first influence on him through the illustrations is "more touching to me than I can say." He thereby foregrounds the affecting quality of his own memories instead of interpreting the drawings as the inarguable signs of du Maurier's future accolades. Grammatically evoking the way memory feels, James virtualizes the past, opening up the possibility of interpreting what might seem in hindsight like portentous events as instead prefiguring alternate futures—not only that of du Maurier's literary success, but also James's as well. Perhaps he even had his brother's later career in mind, since William had originally wanted to be an artist rather than a philosopher. By the time James had come to write his memoirs, however, it must have seemed that he and du Maurier were most in need of such a rehabilitation. For, twenty years after its publication, the *Trilby* juggernaut they had inadvertently launched together was still going strong.[91]

One of the frontispieces for James's New York edition stands out from the rest for its biographical resonances. The image that waited for Coburn and James to find it for volume 15, which contains short stories about literary life, was of a bench on which James and du Maurier likely rested during their frequent long walks on Hampstead Heath.[92] The title of the image, "Saltram's Seat" (see Figure 2), offers an arch commentary on both du Maurier's and James's relationship to publicity, for Saltram is an intellectual con man in "The Coxon Fund," a story in the volume. The picture also offers an enticing lure to interpretation through what is not there. Like all of Coburn's images for the New York edition, there are no people present; James thus specifically withholds from view the oft-evoked popular image of du Maurier and himself as collaborators in the realization of *Trilby*. As always, however, the scenic principle in late James is not a mode of exclusion but a way of allowing the observer to imagine otherwise. What the empty bench tells us is that the relationship between the popular illustrator and the unpopular novelist was inherently incompatible with its own happening. As a way to commemorate his long-lost long friend, James pictures only the scene of their interaction, as if to say: *that* conversation might have turned out quite differently.

· CHAPTER 3 ·

Syncope Fever

James Weldon Johnson and the Black Phonographic Voice

J AMES WELDON JOHNSON'S 1912 *The Autobiography of an Ex-Colored Man* is commonly read as a modernist novel of black alienation.[1] It chronicles the life of a black ragtime piano player and composer during the so-called nadir of race relations in America who tries and fails to achieve legitimacy for classical music based on black folk songs. "Ex-colored man" is light-skinned enough to "pass," and occasionally does. But over the course of the novel—and particularly when playing ragtime—he is exploited by whites as a kind of human phonograph, in ways he doesn't seem quite to acknowledge. After witnessing a lynching, he abandons his quest to achieve cultural legitimacy for black folk music, and, at the novel's end, admits that he has decided to live the rest of his life more comfortably as white. In a further twist, the novel itself also "passed" at the outset. Via a canny publishing strategy, Johnson initially circulated the fictional *Autobiography* as real, releasing it anonymously on its first publication in 1912.[2]

The first-person voice of the novel is thus highly unreliable, mirroring the generic instability of the book itself, which is called an autobiography but is really a fiction. In a further twist, Johnson, a critic, poet, songwriter, and black civil rights leader as well as a novelist, reused several passages from it in the 1920s and 1930s in his own voice, in prefaces to anthologies of poetry and music and in his essays promoting black cultural achievements. In his 1926 preface to *The Book of American Negro Poetry*, for instance, Johnson had this to say about the purpose of anthologizing black literary and cultural achievements: "A people may become great through many means, but there is only one measure by which its greatness is recognized and acknowledged. The final measure of the greatness of all peoples is the amount and standard of the literature and art they have produced."[3] He goes on to include ragtime as one of the artistic products that might "measure" black achievement and change white America's mind about black inferiority:

> Ragtime has not only influenced American music, it has influenced American life; indeed, it has saturated American life. It has become the popular medium for our national expression musically. And who can say that it does not express the blare and jangle and the surge, too, of our national spirit?
>
> Anyone who doubts that there is a peculiar heel-tickling, smile-provoking, joy-awakening, response-compelling charm in Ragtime needs only to hear a skillful performer play the genuine article, needs only to listen to its bizarre harmonies, its audacious resolutions often consisting of an abrupt jump from one key to another, its intricate rhythms in which the accents fall in the most unexpected places but in which the fundamental beat is never lost in order to be convinced. I believe it has its place as well as the music which draws from us sighs and tears.[4]

From this historical distance, Johnson's argument for ragtime's legitimacy might seem unremarkable. Yet it is both a groundbreaking statement about the value of black cultural achievement and a subtle and complex piece of rhetoric. In declaring both the national expressiveness *and* the black originality of ragtime, Johnson was ahead of his time. Well into the 1920s, the genre was dismissed by many blacks as a highly commercialized form, closely associated with minstrelsy, with a shameful history of appropriation by whites.[5] Further, Johnson's use of the word *peculiar* to qualify the "heel-tickling, smile-provoking, joy-awakening, response-compelling charm" of the music is a fascinating rhetorical move. "Peculiar" suggests the distinctiveness of the "genuine" African American ragtime performer and performance, as if Johnson wanted to draw a contrast between the "real thing" and the derivative popular dances, Broadway shows, college songs, racist sheet music, player piano rolls, and phonograph recordings based on ragtime songs.[6] But "peculiar" also implies the oddity or strangeness of this genuine article *wherever* it is heard—the difficulty of ever finding its "place" or of restoring it to the group of people to whom it truly belongs. Finally, of course, "peculiar" evokes the antebellum South's "peculiar institution" of slavery. By evoking ragtime's "peculiar" charm, Johnson suggests that what is distinctive about the music is its ability to slip the bonds of categorization altogether.

Adding to the "audacity" of this seemingly straightforward, even naïve, passage is the fact that much of it was originally written not in 1926, but in 1912, long before the Harlem Renaissance and the so-called Negro vogue in America. It was not originally published as part of an essay, but instead as part of *The Autobiography of an Ex-Colored Man;* much of this paragraph is taken from the narrator's description of a performance he witnesses.[7] At the time of the novel's publication, black culture as such was barely on the national radar. Instead, cultural gatekeepers were absorbed in a project of national (not racial) uplift that aimed to elevate popular tastes and establish a distinctively American musical culture. In later claiming his "unreliable" narrator's voice, speaking from within a highly "unreliable" autobiography, as his own, Johnson makes us see *The Autobiography of an Ex-Colored Man* not only as anticipating the Harlem Renaissance, but also as more closely engaged with this earlier cultural politics than has generally been assumed. As a result, ex-colored man both is and is not Johnson; he makes an argument Johnson seems to endorse on behalf of both American and African-American cultural uplift, but, throughout the story, remains ignorant of the ways in which his talents and cultural "voice" are exploited and appropriated by whites, in a series of events that demonstrate to the reader the arbitrary, material, and even violent basis of all cultural value. Hovering in between ideal and real, as much as between white and black, the narrator and narrative voice of the *Autobiography* can best be described as virtual.

In this chapter, I suggest that Johnson derives his representational strategy from the "phonographic" art of ragtime itself. I begin by exploring the cultural nationalism of the prewar period in greater detail, focusing specifically on the "ragtime craze" and the controversy it caused for America's Idealist musical establishment. Johnson's postwar work of cultural uplift emerges against this background less as an attempt to measure black achievement by an external standard, I argue, than as an immanent linguistic experiment with the production of cultural value. Johnson's experimental approach has much in common with the pluralism of the prewar pragmatists and owes a direct debt to the ongoing experiment with voice and writing in the black tradition, as exemplified by the work of W. E. B. Du Bois.

The main section of the chapter then offers an extended reading of *The Autobiography of an Ex-Colored Man* in relation to the ragtime controversy. In contrast to the common interpretation of the ragtime-playing narrator's voice as "unreliable," I argue that ex-colored man's narrative, much like the music he plays, is structured by a resonant gap between inscription and voice. This evocation of the virtual can be found both inside the diegesis and outside it, in the virtual experience of reading created by the open, ragged relationship between the fictional text and Johnson's later essays in his "own" voice. The chapter concludes that the "phonographic" voice of the novel should be understood less as an attempt to analyze the experience of race in America than as a crucible for the production of what Johnson called new "mental attitudes" about race. By the novel's end, these have yet to arrive.

My approach is influenced by recent critical reevaluations of the African American literary and musical tradition that have begun to challenge the idea that its central concern is with literacy and with the overcoming of an oral, vernacular culture. Instead, as Alexander G. Weheliye, Brent Hayes Edwards, Nathaniel Mackey, and others have recently argued, the most consistent formal preoccupations of black aesthetics are with the relations *between* literacy and orality, and between media such as literature and music.[8] What frequently distinguishes black literary and musical practice, they argue, is its challenge to Western philosophical and aesthetic conceptions of an originary oral presence, or "voice," that transcends the materiality of the copy, the imitation, or the reproduction. Instead, black writers, musicians, and singers, in forms such as scat, blues poetry, the spirituals, and hip-hop, have historically explored the expressive potential of the zone in between articulate speech or melodic song, on the one hand, and the materiality of rhythm and "pure" sound, on the other. Such edgy "phonographic" sounds bridge and articulate the gap between the *phone* and the *graph*, speech and writing.[9] They can be generated by the body in performance, or "heard" in relation to the marks on the page. They can also be generated by the medium of technology and technological recording—for instance, in the scratching of the record needle in the grooves of the record.[10]

Psychoanalysis, semiotics, and critical theory have attached significant importance to this inarticulate zone between speech and sound—what Julia Kristeva called the "semiotic"—seeing it as central to human development, the functioning of language, and the formation of the social. But the critics mentioned argue that the potentiality of the voice has a particular meaning in the context of African American culture and cultural politics. The "fugitivity" of meaning that is heard there evokes a desire for freedom and flight from the violence of slavery and its legacies.[11] Experiments with sound, sense, and writing evoke a "subjunctive mood," with the capacity to pose sober, open-ended questions about whether black equality and freedom are really on their way.[12] The "telling inarticulacy" of the virtual voice, in Mackey's words, when understood in the context of the history of slavery and its legacies, offers a form of compensation in the linguistic and musical register for the static, imprisoning representational orders of original and imitation that make up the stuff of race prejudice in day-to-day life.[13]

The work of these critics gives us new purchase on understanding why blackness has so often featured in the American national imaginary as a *failure* of speech—an inarticulacy that can't, or won't, "tell." Historically, forces of political and social modernization such as law, new economies of speculative exchange, and new media technologies have wanted to preserve not black voices but the spectacle of black linguistic and gestural excesses and the materiality of the black body.[14] At the heart of this violent, deplorable history lie the contradictory principles of "commandment" and "commencement" that, as Jacques Derrida has argued, secretly inform dominant archival practices.[15] Like the father, the archive commands and institutes, establishing the importance of texts, objects, and voices by forcibly housing or inscribing them in particular and arbitrary material locations, from the courthouse, to the library, to the record groove. But like the mother, the archive overtly claims only to "commence," simply to preserve, house, or "voice" what is intrinsically meaningful. In order to sustain this contradictory act of self-origin and self-naming—or *autopoesis*—the archive must project its internal difference outward, onto the other. At stake in attempts to archive examples of black "inarticulacy" for the purposes of national self-definition, then, is an attempt to sustain the idea of a nation whose cultural origins might be magically and maternally disentangled from the inconvenient political facts of theft and violent dispossession. Black cultural practices have responded by highlighting "sound's refusal to resolve into sense."[16] For, as Bryan Wagner notes, the virtual voice "evinces . . . the identity-forming violence that cannot be admitted to the occasion of self-naming without fracturing the controlling fiction of origin."[17]

Acquiring Soulfulness

There is no better illustration of Wagner's claim than the attitude taken by many defenders of the American classical music establishment toward ragtime. Johnson's early writings and the first publication of *The Autobiography of an Ex-Colored Man* occurred during a period characterized not only by lynching and Jim Crow laws but also by the beginnings of a black-influenced mass culture, in ragtime music and its host of attendant dances.[18] This "ragtime craze" was met with a flurry of articles and speeches by cultural gatekeepers about the need to uplift American musical tastes and to establish an archive of indigenous classical compositions that might ensure America's cultural independence from Europe. Their worries came into high relief during the "ragtime debates" circa 1900, as conservative music journalists who sought to inculcate an appreciation for European classical form confronted apostles of the new who saw in ragtime and the spirituals a home-grown American "folk" tradition.[19] On the one side were the classical music magazines of the era, such as *Etude, Musical Courier, Musician,* and *Musical America,* which, in addition to providing a forum for debates about all things musical, served as a means for advertisers to reach students and teachers of instrumental music, chiefly piano. These journals' contributors deplored ragtime and were deeply engaged in trying to establish institutions that might preserve and house the canon of European classical music on American shores, a mission to elevate popular tastes that had become something of a sacred calling for many by the turn of the century.[20] On the other side were a few prominent American composers, such as Arthur Farwell, and many European ones, such as Antonín Dvořák, who praised the music and were known for introducing African American folk material into their work.[21] They were supported by African American composers and a host of critics (including Johnson himself in later years) who argued in letters to the editors of the music magazines as well as in articles in less conservative venues such as the *New Republic* that, although debased and commercialized, ragtime was a uniquely new expression of the American "spirit."[22]

The stakes of the debate on both sides need to be understood in terms of the formal and historical contradiction black musical expression poses to the nation's story of origins. In the anti-ragtime camp, that story was eloquently told by the German-born conductor of the Boston Symphony, Karl Muck, in a widely cited interview in which he was asked to comment on the precarious state of America's musical development. To cultivate an American style of musical expression, Muck cautions, Americans should look within, not without. Although an education in the European classics is a necessity, he warns American composers to avoid copying Europe because, unlike Europe, the New World has had "no long, slow centuries of simple, primitive existence," where music "wells up out of great love, great joy, great splendid response to nature."[23] Instead, it was born as a full-fledged civilization, founded by "grown up" pilgrims led by ideas, not emotions. "In America," Muck predicts, "you will have for your later day music the *great idea of democracy, of freedom for all the people.*"[24] He concedes in passing that America does have an inspiring "folk" tradition, leaving it unnamed, but cautions immediately that the nation's popular music, including ragtime and the "music machines" on which it is played, do not qualify. They are merely "the expression of a restless desire of the people for excitement, for change, for intoxication."[25] Given the attention accorded to Muck's fellow European, Dvořák, for his argument that American composers should draw on their "sympathetic comprehension of the deep pathos of slave life," the "folk music" to which Muck refers would most likely have included the spirituals.[26] We can account for the short shrift given to them in the essay by the racist commonplace that African American music could never transcend the emotive register. Perhaps just as important, however, is the fact that "this wonderful music of bondage" posed a challenge to the idea that whites founded America with "freedom for all the people" in mind.[27]

By linking folk music to a machinic ragtime, Muck reveals an important fact about the outcry against black-influenced popular culture that characterized this era. Battles over the nation's musical contribution were taking place while the meaning of music itself as an expressive and preservative medium was under threat. The phonograph, along with piano rolls, was making music material, as were new scientific investigations of how sound waves were involuntarily produced and received by the body. As Friedrich Kittler has noted, by 1900 in Muck's homeland—and the American classical music establishment's motherland—acoustical physiology had effected a "historical transition from intervals to frequencies, from a logic to a physics of sound."[28] The work of the widely influential German scientist Hermann von Helmholtz may serve as a case in point. As early as the late 1850s, Helmholtz had revealed the ear to be a "nervous piano" that functioned by being set into "sympathetic vibration by . . .

waves of sound."[29] By 1900, music was no longer an unruly and ethereal vibration that transcended the body to express and preserve the national soul. Instead, music had become a material matter of vibrations and frequencies recorded and played back by the brain, the inner ear, and the voice box.

By keeping black music inadmissible to the cultural origins of America's national expression, those origins were preserved from the taint of slavery. And the idea of origin itself was also preserved from the depredations of scientific materialism. Muck's emphasis on ragtime as the expression of "restless desire . . . for . . . excitement and change" keeps vocal ideality secure for the production of national origins by linking both race and ragtime, through the metonymy of the machine, to the body *in* the voice. His strategy was not an original one. Because of its dual associations with race and with recording machines, ragtime was widely described during this period as a force that was turning American listeners into "nervous pianos" instead of vessels ready to be infused with the democratic spirit. In its presence, listeners became vulnerable to the ubiquitous disease of neurasthenia, for which the only cure was a diet of the classics. Arthur Weld felt the need to reassure his fellow music teachers:

> You should have little difficulty—if you go about it in the right way—in making such a person [a fan of ragtime] learn to regard the "coon" songs with positive abhorrence, and turn to Schubert and Schumann when in search of true melody and that sense of relaxation and comfort which music at its best can bring to the most tired and fevered brains. There is certainly no repose in the stimulating vulgarity of a "rag-time" melody, or the debasing excitation of a "coon" song shouted boisterously by harsh, worn voices.[30]

The diagnosis of neurasthenia had been formulated by the "father of neurasthenia," George M. Beard, in the 1870s and 1880s. Beard argued that a variety of personal and social problems could be ascribed to a surfeit of uncertainly physical "nerve" energy afflicting Americans in particular, which could only be ameliorated by a disciplinary regimen of robust physical activity.[31] Weld's argument is typical of neurasthenia's bodily economics.[32] The classical listener's attention constitutes a reinvestment of bodily energy that leads to future spiritual elevation. The ragtime listener, by contrast, spends his nerve force wastefully and ends up in a state of dissipation. This language echoes the lyrics of so-called coon songs and some ragtime songs, which highlighted illicit, wasteful forms of black expenditure as a contrast to white frugality, as did the stereotypes of minstrel excesses on the covers of the sheet music.[33]

In Weld's rhetoric, therefore, a difference internal to the American archive he seeks to cultivate is pressed outward to differentiate between the classical listener and the racialized popular music enthusiast. The classical melody is maternally relaxing and comforting, conserving a message that transcends the context of its utterance. The shouting, "worn" voice of the nervous ragtime song emerges as nothing more than the sound of a particular body's wear and tear.[34] But the distinction between voice and sonic materiality is clearly also internal to any classical composition. It moreover evokes the uncanniness of a phonograph recording in which the listener hears for the first time the acoustical vibrations that have always already been present in his speech. In what Kittler calls the "discourse network of 1900," the voice's newly perceptible material substrate must be assigned to the neurasthenic ragtime song alone, in order to preserve the notion that voice and melody might fully conserve "true" meaning in sound.[35]

As Weld's emphasis on "true melody" suggests, the primary complaint cultural gatekeepers made against ragtime was that its much-vaunted rhythmic innovation—at its most basic, a regular march tempo in the bass set against a syncopated melodic line in the treble—was not an original musical technique, but was instead a copy of European forms. A host of angry critics anticipated Theodor Adorno's critique of jazz in stridently contesting the idea that syncopation, or "ragged time," was original, noting that European folk music had made use of syncopation for decades.[36] The difference between original European folk syncopation and its imitation by what was sometimes known as "Ethiopian" ragtime rested above all on questions of "motive." In Spanish folk songs, A. J. Goodrich notes, "syncopation served a distinct purpose" and, in capturing it on paper, J. S. Bach and G. F. Handel made it an "inherent part of the music design."[37]

Just as the classical melody must be dissociated from the "worn" ragtime voice, so too must motivated syncopation be distinguished from unmotivated, particularly since the question of syncopation invoked the gestural mimeticism of dance. By rehashing the stereotype of the "imitative Negro," critics sought to preserve a distinction between original and copy under pressure from a rhythm that can pass from one body to the next with no discernable source.[38] Yet the distinction doesn't quite hold. Goodrich argues that "rag-time is merely a common form of syncopation in which the rhythm is distorted in order to produce a more or less ragged, hysterical effect. . . . The rag-time 'compositioners' have undoubtedly found their most direct source of supply in the Hungarian song-dances."[39] The attempt to specify a failed, conscious imitation on the part of "compositioners," who cannot even correctly name themselves, is belied by the earlier reference to hysteria, which suggests an imitation of a wholly different order. Questions of original and copy are displaced by the specter of a mimesis that can take place not between composers but between bodies, and can even erupt within them, in defiance of their owners' conscious control. This aspect of the "dance craze" was reported with as much fascination as disdain. A visitor from idealist Germany seemed to relish his alarming introduction to American popular culture while listening to ragtime:

> Suddenly I discovered that my legs were in a condition of great excitement. They twitched as though charged with electricity and betrayed a considerable and rather dangerous desire to jerk me from my seat. . . . It wasn't that feeling of ease in the joints of the feet and toes which might be caused by a Strauss waltz, no, much more energetic, material, independent as though one encountered a balking horse, which it is absolutely impossible to master.[40]

Claims about ragtime as a black imitation of European folk music compete here with an imitation that bypasses human control altogether, and might be more properly specified as machinic. "Energetic, material, independent"— the body hears and then imitates sounds on a frequency all its own.

In the article "Ragtime: A Pernicious Evil and Enemy of True Art," Leo Oehmler provides an illuminating explanation of the nature of ragtime syncopation's "evil" for the classical music establishment. Like other critics, Oehmler draws on new scientific and medical knowledges, particularly brain physiology and psychophysics. He turns to the etymology of the term syncopation to drive home his dramatic title: "The word syncopation is derived from 'syncope,'" he writes, "a medical term meaning, 'a heart beating unevenly through excessive agitation.'"[41] He then goes on to condemn what he calls the "syncope fever" engulfing America with the advent of ragtime. *Syncopation* does indeed derive from *syncope*, denoting a "failure of the heart's action," but it is more frequently used to designate the loss of consciousness that results.[42] *Syncope* also denotes the loss of letters from within a word, often to fit it into a poem's metrical scheme, as when "never" is reduced to "ne'er," or "even" to "e'en," and the elision is marked with an apostrophe.[43] Because the definition includes both a loss of consciousness and a loss of letters, implicitly associating the two, "syncope fever" suggests the paradoxical idea that the illusion of a lyrical vocal presence conveyed by the syncope as poetic technique might be undone by the very technique itself. In using the phrase to describe the effect of ragtime on classical musical appreciation, Oehmler also implies that, in ragtime, classical musical technique undoes itself in a similar manner. The musical equivalent of poetic metricality is tempo, which in ragtime piano, again at its most basic, is maintained in the left hand. Yet instead of fitting a "singing" melody to that tempo, and thereby drawing attention away from its rhythmic support, the right hand of the ragtime pianist plays the melody off the beat. It is as if the melody, always coming in a little late, were produced rather than simply sustained by its own technique. In ragtime, classical listeners heard the reverse of their credo—voice emanating from writing, the commencement emanating from the commandment.

"Syncope fever" thereby emerges as Derridean "archive fever." Ragtime is a danger to the national musical archive because it reveals that any potential American *classical* compositions might also be syncopated—founded, that is, not on an "idea" of democracy but on an alternating rhythm of inscription and consciousness, writing and voice. And in fact, a "syncope fever" emerges in accounts of classical playing and performance throughout the pages of the music journals, even in articles that are not about ragtime at all. In "Habits of Accuracy," Frank L. Reed holds forth at length on the multiple positionings, alignments, and adjustments of the piano-playing body necessary before the classical musician can make an "attempt to reach the true inwardness of [the emotional elements of a piece]."[44] He marvels:

In simply adjusting the hand to primary position think of the number of acts involved, each governed at first by a conscious thought!—fingers curved, knuckles flat, or slightly depressed, wrist flexible and on a level with the back of the hand and making no break in the line from the knuckles to the inside of elbow joint, thumbs extended, raised and curved towards the palm at first joint. . . . The stroke of a key, whether with the finger alone, or in combination with the hand, forearm or entire arm may be roughly

divided into three elements,—the lift, the preparation, and the
attack; besides these there is the nervous grasp of the key by the
fingers, which endures for a longer or shorter time, and the release
which is equivalent to the lift in the next series of movements.
All these movements must at first be practiced consciously and
rhythmically.[45]

Through its Tayloresque language of workplace efficiency, which would
seem at first far removed from the wasteful expenditure of ragtime technique, Reed's microcosm of the piano-playing body undermines the very
notions of motive and expressivity it seeks to preserve.[46] While robust
physical training is as necessary for the pianist as for the neurasthenic in
warding off nervousness, it turns out that the body is already nervously
responding to stimuli unbeknownst to the player at the level of the finger
that grasps the key. Moreover, while each movement of the arm or hand
may be governed at first by a conscious intent, "true inwardness" is not
a product of consciously motivated bodily technique; it is the effect produced after technique becomes unconscious and habitual. Circa 1900,
even the very classical piano practice necessary to cultivate the nascent
"music of democracy" is subject to "ragged time." Both ragtime and classical music have intimations of the hysterical as well as the deathly: "If technical execution is all that one hears in a composition," the same magazine
cautions its readers in the following issue, "it descends to the level of a
music-box and is as dead as the human body from which the spirit has
winged its flight. The question nearest the heart of a player conscious of
her need is, '*How can I acquire soulfulness?*'"[47]

For many, the answer to this urgent question—which had come to
pervade a wide variety of discourses besides that of music by the turn of
the century—was obvious: ragtime, the "folk music of the American city,"
had "soul" aplenty.[48] Its syncopation was bracing rather than enervating,
invoking not "nervousness" but instead, when performed "authentically,"
a wholly original spirit of freedom and flight that captured the essence of
the nation. One critic defended ragtime syncopation as follows:

As a nation we are conspicuously not slow and steady. But it is
possible for energy to be just as righteous if it is neither of these
things. We move swiftly, stop suddenly and start unexpectedly in

another direction. . . . This may be the true American rhythm, and when it is once recognized and valued it will no longer be travestied, but expressed in music that is popular in the organic sense of the word.[49]

Ragtime enthusiasts hear American freedom and self-making in the music's syncopated rhythms, providing an illustration of Michael Rogin's apt observation that "the forms that transported settlers and immigrants beyond their Old World identities rested on the fixed statuses of those who did not choose to make the journey."[50] The transportation that allowed ragtimers to forget those whose statuses were fixed—that of metaphoric substitution—often took them in the same direction as the music's critics. For example, the influential critic Hiram K. Motherwell vividly evoked automaticity and nervousness in his defense of ragtime. Discussing his experience of listening to the hit song "Waiting for the Robert E. Lee," whose lyrics prominently feature "shufflin'" minstrel figures, Motherwell notes:

> I felt my blood thumping in tune, my muscles twitching to the rhythm. I wanted to paraphrase Shakespeare—
>   "The man who hath no ragtime in his soul,
>   Who is not moved by syncopated sounds"
> and so on. If any musician does not feel in his heart the rhythmic complexities of "The Robert E. Lee" I should not trust him to feel in his heart the rhythmic complexities of Brahms. This ragtime appeals to the primitive love of the dance—a special sort of dance in which the rhythm of the arms and shoulders conflicts with the rhythm of the feet, in which dozens of little needles of energy are deftly controlled in the weaving of the whole.[51]

By invoking the "primitive love of the dance," Motherwell anchors in the other the unsettling evacuation of agency and motive that phonographically engages the white body's twitching nerves and muscles. Yet further substitutions efface this move, as the likeness Motherwell establishes here between Johannes Brahms, Shakespeare, and "The Robert E. Lee" allows him, by the end of the essay, to identify ragtime as a vehicle of national expression to rival those of old Europe:[52]

> As you walk up and down the streets of an American city you
> feel in its jerk and rattle a personality different from that of any
> European capital. This is American. It is in our lives, and it helps to
> form our characters and condition our mode of action. It should
> have expression in art, simply because any people must express
> itself if it is to know itself. No European music can or possibly
> could express this American personality. Ragtime I believe does
> express it. It is to-day the one true American music.[53]

Motherwell casts authentic ragtime as American *autopoesis*, the sound of
a nation hearing and understanding itself speak. By naming its constitutive difference as the sameness of national identity, the "ragged time" of
the syncope is reinvested to preserve American "soul" in the age of the
phonograph.

The Crucible of Form

This brief survey of the context for Johnson's writings about ragtime reveals the challenge he faced in attempting to discuss black music and
cultural production in a way that would cater neither to the idealist attack on the music nor its equally idealist defense. In the former, ragtime
syncopates the expressive voice of classical melody, threatening to reveal
classical music's own parasitical dependence on the material techniques
of rhythm and movement. In the latter, ragtime's rhythms emancipate the
body, but only on condition that the music's "peculiar" past be dissolved
into the master-signifier of Americanness—an act of loving theft, in Eric
Lott's words.[54] What Johnson needed was a way to embrace ragtime's
subversive challenge to idealism while establishing its legitimacy as an
American expressive form, one inseparable from—although not reducible
to—black culture and history.

A possible model for this task could be found in the writings of white
cultural pluralists and radical intellectuals such as Randolph Bourne and
Horace Kallen. Bourne and Kallen, whose mentors were John Dewey and
William James, sought to extend the latters' challenge to idealism to encompass the pressing questions of culture and cultural identity during the
prewar years. Both critics advocated a practical, experiential, and experimental definition of American culture as less a stable essence than a perpetual process of mixing and blending, defining culture, like experience

for James and Dewey, as transitional and processual—a matter of provisional doing rather than essential and established being. Kallen described the nation as a symphony in which "the playing is the writing," and in which different ethnic groups often play dissonant parts. Bourne's more well-known theory of a "transnational America" posited that national identity is not a stable essence but an ongoing practice of "weaving" together immigrant identities. Both visions challenged champions of an assimilative "melting pot," as well as those who embraced what they saw as European cultural superiority, by means of the pragmatic idea that culture is inseparable from its doing and making.[55]

However, both men also sought to distinguish the "transnationalism" they wanted to promote from what they saw as the indiscriminate mixing and blending of a highly commercialized mass and popular culture. "Genuinely" transitional or processual cultural forms were to be rigorously marked off from what Bourne called "the American culture of the cheap newspaper, the 'movies,' the popular song, the ubiquitous automobile."[56] America was to be conceived instead as a mosaic-like federation, in which "self-conscious cultural nuclei," such as the ethnic enclaves beginning to form in urban communities, join together without merging.[57] African American culture was not one of the nuclei that Bourne and Kallen mentioned in their elaboration of this mosaic. Perhaps it was because the violence of slavery and *forced* immigration would seem to vitiate the possibility that blacks could easily become part of a peaceful national "spiritual welding," an America perpetually in process.[58] More likely, however, was the fact that race remained an entrenched, essential category for both men.[59] Racial essentialism can help to explain their rejection of the "movies" and especially the "popular song," which were not only thoroughly commercial but also thoroughly miscegenated cultural forms. These media exposed race as a malleable, rather than a fixed and essential category, even as they often exploited racial stereotypes for commercial gain.

It was ultimately W. E. B. Du Bois's vision of cultural pluralism, which wove the dissonance of slavery into the national song, that had the most significant influence on Johnson. Also influenced by William James, yet trained in Germany, where he absorbed the works of Hegel and German Idealism, Du Bois made the "problem" of African American identity central to the vision of cultural nationalism he espoused in his monumental work *The Souls of Black Folk* (1903).[60] The text fuses sociology, history, and personal narrative into a prophetic call for black uplift, race nationalism, and a vision of whites and blacks "dwell[ing] above" what he famously termed "the Veil" of race.[61] In the final chapter of *Souls*, "The Sorrow Songs," Du Bois directs the weight of his analysis toward the search for cultural identity, arguing that the spirituals are "the singular spiritual heritage of the nation and the greatest gift of the Negro people" (205). Like Johnson's use of "peculiar," both Du Bois's "singular" and his emphasis on the "gift" of the spirituals have an ambivalent tone.[62] So also do Du Bois's descriptions of the "blending" and weaving of the races that, for him, define American identity and the American cultural heritage of the spirituals. "Actively we have woven ourselves with the very warp and woof of this nation—we fought their battles, shared their sorrow, mingled our blood with theirs," Du Bois intones. ". . . Our song, our toil, our cheer, and warning have been given to this nation in blood-brotherhood" (215). The "perpetual weaving" of immigrant cultures envisioned by Randolph Bourne and Horace Kallen takes on a minor key in Du Bois's formulation. Where Bourne and Kellen confidently predict an eventual "spiritual welding," Du Bois "warns" that American identity voices itself only in a dissonant and unfinished mood.

Also important for Johnson were the multiple affective and rhetorical registers used in *Souls*, and particularly its play with the idea of voice. At the beginning of each chapter Du Bois places a bar of music from a spiritual—without identifying information such as a title or lyrics—and a few lines or verses of poetry, mostly by white British or American poets, with the author's name given. At first glance, it seems as if Du Bois seeks to make American whites recognize through this device that "their" literate culture is a secondary and derivative product of a more original and authentic black orality. It is equally possible to interpret Du Bois as expressing his longing here for an equivalent black form of literacy that, with the coming of progress, might eventually leave oral culture behind. The juxtaposition on the page conveys both of these ideas visually, suggesting that black suffering, toil, and violent dispossession are the material preconditions for a transcendent expression of spirit in poetry—one that is currently for whites only, but might one day be accessible to all.

But rather than endorsing orality or literacy alone, Du Bois reveals here his embrace of long-standing African American musical and cultural practices that explore the play between the oral and the literate. The wordless spirituals in Du Bois's epigraphs gesture beyond the dialectic of voice and writing to an experience of the voice as potentiality, halfway to meaningful speech, in which the question of mutual recognition across the divide of race sounds unresolved.[63] In inviting his readers not only to understand but to see and sense the "telling inarticulacy" of the sorrow songs in the writing on the page, Du Bois evokes less a gap between voice and writing than a fracture or edge that itself sounds. The epigraphs to *Souls* refuse to resolve the contradiction between attributed white poetry and wordless, anonymous black music, in order to sound out the linguistic and historical violence inherent in creating an archive of the spirituals.[64] With the black spirituals reduced to unattributed marks on the page, and the white poetry carefully documented and preserved, the epigraphs expose the denied and racially embodied contradiction between writing and voice, commencement and commandment, inherent in American ideals of cultural self-making.

In *The Autobiography of an Ex-Colored Man,* Johnson was profoundly influenced by *Souls,* particularly as regards the work's autobiographical form, generic boundary crossing, and quest narrative.[65] Yet, in both novel and essays, he embraces popular culture—unlike Du Bois, who barely mentions it, and very much unlike Bourne and Kallen, who mention it only to distance their processual vision from it.[66] In fact, Johnson sometimes sounds a bit like champions of ragtime such as Hiram Motherwell, declaring ragtime to be "the popular medium for our national expression musically." One reason for Johnson's positive attitude toward popular culture is that, during the era of the ragtime debates, just before writing *The Autobiography of an Ex-Colored Man* and early in his career, he was a commercially successful lyricist and part of the celebrated black songwriting team of Cole and Johnson Brothers.[67] It is thus perhaps not surprising to find that, like critics in the pro-ragtime camp, Johnson argues for the universal appeal of ragtime's syncopated rhythms. Yet, reflecting both his intimate experience of the music and his political commitment to black equality, he tends to describe those rhythms rather differently. The result is a pragmatic yet peculiarly subversive form of cultural "uplift."

In a 1915 editorial for the *New York Age,* for example, Johnson pens an interesting response to a question that would have implicated him directly as a member of one of the first successful black songwriting teams. He describes an irate letter to a local paper from a white musician, who wants to know why white society people prefer to have black musicians, rather than trained white ones, play ragtime at social gatherings. Rather than associating a "primitive love of the dance" with blackness, Johnson responds by arguing that black musicians create music that cannot be imitated in the medium on which white musicians rely—writing:

> In a way, Mr. De Bueris is right when he says that white musicians can play ragtime as well as Negro musicians; that is, white musicians can play exactly what is put down on the paper. But Negro musicians are able to put into the music something that can't be put on the paper; a certain abandon which seems to enter in the blood of the dancers, and that is the answer to Mr. De Bueris' question, that is the secret, that is why Negro musicians are preferred.[68]

Johnson clearly wants to establish that the ability to transmit "abandon" into the white dancers' bodies is possessed by African American musicians, not white ones. But the nature of that transfer is profoundly ambiguous. The "abandon" of the dance is a "certain" one—both difficult to specify yet undeniable. Like the gestural language of movement in dance, black performance does not happen in a "primitive" part of the brain, nor is it localized in an individual body. Instead, it happens in between the musicians and dancers, and in between the players and the paper on which the music is written down. Johnson, in short, like Du Bois, offers a complex and nuanced conception of the virtual experience of African American musical form, but he also takes up a more open-ended, pragmatic approach reminiscent of Kallen and Bourne. African American culture is for him both a source of moving "inarticulacy," in Mackey's words, and a way of experimenting with the cultural values of a society in transition.

   Johnson's experiment continued after the war, during the flowering of the Harlem Renaissance and the vogue for "the Negro," when an interest in archiving, preserving, and producing black culture was taken up by blacks themselves, albeit within a culture still largely in thrall to racist notions of the "primitive." In the 1920s and '30s, up until his death in 1938, Johnson became a preserver, collector, and privileged interpreter of musical and written texts—a cultural *archon*—who authored groundbreaking prefaces and introductions to collections including *The Book of American Negro Spirituals* and *The Book of American Negro Poetry* mentioned earlier. The essays from this later period productively synthesize his new role with his prewar involvement with popular music to argue for ragtime's value despite the racial essentialism that persisted well into the new era. Johnson's '20s and '30s writings on cultural preservation have been dismissed as elitist, yet it is far from clear that his prefaces should be relegated to a dusty history of what Richard Wright calls "prim and decorous ambassadors who went a-begging to white America."[69] They reveal subtle and sometimes radical notions about how to archive and preserve black vernacular culture from within particular configurations of power and history—notions that may have grown out of his early experience with the disruptive effects of ragtime's "syncope fever."

In many of his postwar essays, Johnson describes an archive of black music and art that could only undermine its own claims to totality, insofar as the popular and vernacular forms he seeks to preserve deform the very distinctions between themselves and the medium that would preserve them. Johnson's discussion of ragtime's "peculiar" ability to defy categorization as either the property of African Americans or a national, even universal, form of expression offers one example. Another can be found in his discussion of the spirituals, whose sentimental appeal had undergirded Dvořák's plea for folk music as American music. Johnson, by contrast, suggests that these songs' persuasive power lies elsewhere than in an appeal to sentiment. Instead, the music renders uncertain the physical and spectatorial distance that enabled whites to consume blackness as either comic or pitiable. "This gift has been regarded as a kind of side show," he writes, "something for occasional exhibition; wherein it is the touchstone, it is the magic thing, it is that by which the Negro can bridge all chasms. No persons, however hostile, can listen to Negroes singing this wonderful music without having their hostility melted down."[70] He describes the spirituals as both the agent of change for white "mental attitudes" and the means or tool by which that change may be measured. The idea of a "touchstone," itself a measurement tool, allows Johnson to stress a tactile quality to the singing voice, and suggests the idea of a voice that does not so much dwell above the bodily and earthly veil, as rub together the sonic textures of white and black. This treatment of the spirituals' elusiveness disassociates hearing from transcendence or transparency to "soul" through the implication of touch, which renders subject and object elusive, fugitive. Such language in turn renders indeterminate the question of who or what it is that the spirituals measure. A touchstone is traditionally used to verify the purity of gold or silver, but here the metaphor would seem to indicate that the spirituals verify a foundational *im*purity or mixture of white and black. While they would seem to measure "the Negro's" worth, enabling him to bridge the color line, as a "touchstone," the singing in fact tests the metal—or mettle—of white listeners.

A similar ambivalence inheres in Johnson's idea that the spirituals should be preserved because they can "melt down" hostility. The sacred songs are a crucible, in which hostility is neither vanquished nor tragically expressed, but severely tested or sounded out through intermixture. Their value is experimental—it lies as much in the way they provoke and expose white racism as in the way they measure black achievement. To put it somewhat differently, the distinctions so necessary to Johnson's ostensible work of cultural preservation—between the thing to be recorded and the recording method itself—go up in smoke. Black "greatness" can only emerge empirically through the *practice* of art and music, and perhaps also the writing of prefaces, not via the spectatorial, distanced appraisal of recognition. It will succeed or fail only through the experiences that Johnson and others were creating through writing, art, and music for white and black alike. As he notes elsewhere of the "art approach" to the problem of white prejudice, "The results of this method seem to carry a high degree of finality, to be the thing itself that was to be demonstrated."[71]

While Johnson eschews discussion of sound reproduction technologies per se in his later nonfiction, therefore, his interest in the cultural work performed by black vernacular and popular music nevertheless can be seen as "phonographic," in the terms that I set out at the beginning of this chapter. Despite his own status as black cultural *archon,* Johnson hears a sonic materiality at work in black music that sounds out the play between the archive's contradictory principles of commencement and commandment. It is especially striking that, even during the drive to anthologize black culture after the war, he does not fully embrace notions of authenticity and originality and reject ragtime in the service of establishing an entirely oppositional black literary and cultural tradition. Instead he values ragtime and the spirituals for the way they sound out the impurities that the keepers of any collection of sacred texts or objects must reject.[72]

The Phonography of an Ex-Colored Man

While Johnson's later nonfiction articulates a logic of black musical form as a kind of crucible for cultural value, the 1912 *Autobiography of an Ex-Colored Man* explores the clash between this form and the ragtime "rage" of the prewar era. The main character is a light-skinned black ragtime musician who, remaining nameless throughout the narrative, passes back and forth over the "color line" as he travels around America and Europe. As described earlier, after witnessing a lynching in the American South, he decides to pass for good, giving up his goal of composing classical symphonies based on ragtime and the spirituals. Despite its characteristically prewar preoccupation with national expression, the work has received a great deal of critical attention that has tended to erase the historical and musical context of its first publication.[73] Drawing on its second publication in 1927—under Johnson's name and at the height of the Harlem Renaissance—critics have frequently analyzed it as a prescient literary investigation into the visual logics of racism, passing, and narrative unreliability.[74] But contextualizing the work in relation to the pervasive sense of crisis about the national musical archive of the prewar era permits a reading more attuned to black identity's aural than its visual dimensions.

Within the story, as in the music journalism of the time, ragtime is closely associated with problems of inscription and playback, motive and automaticity, that characterized the neurasthenic body. The narrator first encounters the music in a context typical of both neurasthenia and "coon songs": the "gas-light life" of gambling, illicit sexuality, and immoral spending he leads after losing his tuition money for Atlanta University (83). Eventually, though, he finds work as an expert ragtime player, which opens doors to the houses of wealthy white patrons. These ambiguous figures are much like the white consumers of the music who were undergoing a "craze" for it within the novel's larger cultural and historical moment. In one passage, the narrator paints a vivid picture of a white audience at a private dinner party where he has been hired as the entertainment:

According to a suggestion from the host, I began with classic music. During the first number there was absolute quiet and appreciative attention, and when I had finished, I was given a round of generous applause. . . . When dinner was served, the piano was moved and the door left open, so that the company might hear the music while eating. At a word from the host I struck up one of my liveliest ragtime pieces. The effect was surprising, perhaps even to the host; the ragtime music came very near spoiling the party so far as eating the dinner was concerned. As soon as I began, the conversation suddenly stopped. It was a pleasure to me to watch the expression of astonishment and delight that grew on the faces of everybody. These were people—and they represented a large class —who were ever expecting to find happiness in novelty, each day restlessly exploring and exhausting every resource of this great city that might possibly furnish a new sensation or awaken a fresh emotion, and who were always grateful to anyone who aided them in their quest. . . . When the guests arose, I struck up my ragtime transcription of Mendelssohn's "Wedding March," playing it with terrific chromatic octave runs in the bass. This raised everybody's spirits to the highest point of gaiety, and the whole company in-voluntarily and unconsciously did an impromptu cake-walk. From that time on until the time of leaving they kept me so busy that my arms ached. (86–87)

The narrator describes the white slummers' automatic movements in terms that, within the cultural imaginary by 1912, often betrayed anxieties about mechanistic forms of cultural expression that seemed to insert a lag-time between the body and consciousness. On the one hand the scene would seem to bend Muck's critique of the "restless desires" indulged by popular music to an antiracist cause, pointing out that such music's racial associations are exploited to satiate frivolous *white* desires "for excitement, for change, for intoxication." At the same time, it seems to condemn rag-time's appropriation and adulteration, because attitudes that anticipate critics such as Motherwell come into play in the admiration ex-colored man professes for more authentic forms of ragtime elsewhere in the book.[75]

However, by having the white socialites perform a "cakewalk," Johnson goes a step further than Motherwell to link both white appropriation and black performance to slavery.[76] A closer look at the language in this pas-sage reveals that it indicts both sides of the ragtime debates, exposing the "identity forming violence" of the American "national" archive itself. Ex-colored man describes the "impromptu cakewalk" as an unconscious performance by the white audience, emphasizing an opposition between the listeners' involuntary response to his ragtime skills and their restrained and controlled response to his classical ones. But a "cakewalk" evokes the basic material attributes of a "Wedding March." The difference that seems to exist between them is in fact more properly described as the effaced difference *internal* to the "Wedding March."[77] Felix Mendelssohn's piece seeks to make the listener forget one of its constitutive parts—its rhythm, or, as Derrida would put it, its writing—in order to sustain the impression of a transcendent melodic line. Yet ex-colored man, a master of technique, lays bare the music's hidden sonic and rhythmic substrate. His "rag" reduces the melodic metaphor to the metonymy on which it depends, reducing the "Wedding March" to nothing more than a "cakewalk." In setting bodies into motion, the form of "The Wedding March Rag" sounds out an impure zone of potentiality in between inscription and consciousness, writing and voice, that its performers seem wholly to forget.

Another way to describe what happens when ex-colored man plays music for his white patrons, therefore, is to say that he becomes a phonograph.[78] They interact with him in much the same paradoxical way that people interacted with the recording phonograph toward the end of the nineteenth century, for example, in response to Thomas Alva Edison's "Library of Voices." Edison sought to demonstrate that his new machine could immortalize the dead by recording their voices for posterity, yet although audiences were compelled by this fantasy of transcending time and mortality, they found that the phonograph unsettlingly materialized the voice.[79] Ex-colored man's ragtime playing embodies similar contradictions for the white socialites. His performance seems to promise them not only a novel form of entertainment but also the elusive possibility of arresting and storing time. He notes of himself in relation to his main patron that "I was his chief means of disposing of the thing which seemed to sum up all in life that he dreaded—time. As I remember him now, I can see that time was what he was always endeavoring to escape, to bridge over, to blot out; and it is not strange that some years later he did escape it forever, by leaping into eternity" (104). As Best and others note, Edison also described the phonograph's archival capacities in a language that evoked slavery. His immortalizing machine worked by means of "the captivity of all manner of sound-waves heretofore designated as 'fugitive.'"[80] Similar overtones of slavery sound throughout the "Wedding March" scene.

As a cure for national soullessness, in short, machinic ragtime proves to be a curse for ex-colored man; it demands something very like his own perpetual captivity. Insofar as whites' desire to listen is sustained by the perpetual projection of an internal difference outward—onto a fascinating figure who is both man and machine, both fugitive and captive—it can never be satisfied. "The man's powers of endurance in listening often exceeded mine in performing," ex-colored man writes of his patron in another scene. He continues: "This man sitting there so mysteriously silent, almost hid in a cloud of heavy-scented smoke, filled me with a sort of unearthly terror. He seemed to be some grim, mute, but relentless tyrant, possessing over me a supernatural power which he used to drive me on mercilessly to exhaustion" (88). The description echoes the racialized dispossession endemic to many accounts of mechanized popular culture in the teens. But Johnson allows the full resonances of this dispossession with slavery to sound, in order to show that the fugitive ragtime dance he knew so well had become the elusive object of the nation's newfound archive fever.

The magnitude of Johnson's achievement here in the years before the "Negro vogue" becomes evident when we consider an earlier narrative of mechanical and racialized enslavement, one that was still circulating far more widely at the turn of the century—George du Maurier's *Trilby*, discussed in chapter 2. Du Maurier's wildly popular 1894 novel about a white woman who is turned into a singing machine by a Jewish hypnotist conductor is referenced both in the Frédéric Chopin compositions ex-colored man plays throughout the novel (one of Trilby's most popular and mesmerizing songs is a Chopin impromptu) and in the trancelike states induced in white listeners by his "ragging" of classical compositions. Svengali's stereotypically rapacious Jewishness and Trilby's helpless feminine body embody the idealist fears evident in the ragtime debates about the materialization of the voice and the violence perpetrated on the body by a psychophysics of music. By invoking *Trilby*, Johnson would seem to be suggesting, against du Maurier, that it is in fact white people from the dominant culture who force other races to mechanically "sing" against their will, not the other way around. In the *Autobiography*, the production and often violent maintenance of categories of race and racial difference are a means to project elsewhere the white body's uncertain agency in the context of mechanical reproduction.[81]

The significance of *Trilby*, however, cannot be fully understood without reference to Johnson's romantic narrator. He is portrayed as deeply invested in the dualisms that underpin the classical musical establishment's idealist aesthetics, making *Trilby* just the kind of story he would have enjoyed. Accordingly, it is no surprise that in his account of his childhood piano practice, the narrator reveals how deeply attached he was to the notion that a melodic line conserves meaning through the voice. Drawing a distinction worthy of the *Etude* writers, the narrator notes, "I [did not] depend upon mere brilliancy of technique, a trick by which children often surprise their listeners; but I always tried to interpret a piece of music; I always played with feeling" (18). As if quoting from the music magazines of the day, he is at pains to distinguish his highly expressive classical playing from soulless imitation. He also shores up his ideas of musical expressivity by turning to the metaphor of the voice, noting, "Very early I acquired that knack of using the pedals, which makes the piano a sympathetic, singing instrument" (ibid.).

However, the narrator's performances occasionally founder because his inspiration comes from the voice of his mother. He becomes a youthful prodigy at classical piano playing, but he credits his skills to the fact that "I did not begin to learn the piano by counting out exercises, but by trying to reproduce the quaint songs which my mother used to sing, with all their pathetic turns and cadences" (ibid.). These unnamed "quaint" songs, as in Karl Muck's account, are most likely the spirituals. The narrator's mother, unbeknownst to him as a young child, is black and of southern origin; his father is a white aristocrat, probably from a former slaveholding family. As in the ragtime scene quoted earlier, when the young ex-colored man plays the spirituals, the racial repressed returns in the contemporaneous language of nervous automatism. "Often while playing" the narrator notes, "I could not keep the tears which formed in my eyes from rolling down my cheeks. Sometimes at the end, or even in the midst of a composition, as big a boy as I was, I would jump from the piano, and throw myself sobbing into my mother's arms. She, by her caresses and often her tears, only encouraged these fits of sentimental hysteria" (ibid.). By describing his mother's complicity with his loss of emotional control—he notes, "I should have been out playing ball or in swimming with other boys of my age; but my mother didn't know that" (19)—the narrator implies that, as a man, his identification with her is inappropriate; he seeks to distinguish himself from her feminized position and also to distinguish his adult point of view from the childish feelings and behavior he is portraying. However, because his inarticulate sobs seem to result from playing the spirituals, his identification with her seems wholly appropriate; it is based on their unacknowledged shared status as, historically, the material property of an absent white father.[82] Because the spirituals are in turn the true inspiration for his *classical* performances, the narrator's inarticulate sobs sound out the logic of the American musical archive as an irresolvable dissonance between the voice that commences and the inscription that commands.

Drawing on the spirituals to cultivate just the sort of musical repertoire that many cultural gatekeepers advocated, the young narrator's fraught and emotional playing dramatizes the way in which, at the turn of the century, America's history of slavery and miscegenation can be heard only as an inarticulate sound.

Not only is ex-colored man likened to a phonograph within the text, the "voice" of the "autobiography" is also itself "phonographic," in the sense that it too is structured by a resonant gap between inscription and consciousness. In what the narrator notes as the most important moment of his childhood, a schoolteacher cruelly and publicly reveals his race: "In the life of everyone there is a limited number of unhappy experiences which are not written upon the memory, but stamped there with a die; and in long years after, they can be called up in detail, and every emotion that was stirred by them can be lived through anew; these are the tragedies of life" (13). The reliability of ex-colored man's understanding of his past experiences is thrown into question by the material ways he describes his memories. He uses a distinction between "stamped" and "written" in order to emphasize the "high fidelity" of his recall. Yet the very distinction itself implies that racialization is incompatible with the ability to remember by casting it as the bodily registration of a trace or inscription that necessarily occurs in the absence of consciousness.[83] In making this distinction, the narrator heightens the reader's sense of a gap between the time of the telling and the time of the event itself that is a denied structural component of all autobiography.[84] Because it implies a discontinuity between consciousness and memory—racialization as shock—the narrator's perfect recall turns into its opposite, suggesting that in retelling the events of his life, he cannot help but invent or embellish his experiences.

The novel's phonographic logic, however, does not preclude the possibility of getting at the truth of ex-colored man's life story. Instead, inspired by the space in between inscription and voice, Johnson is able to suggest both that the narrator is missing something *and* that he is faithfully recording events. The novel's tropes of writing and inscription tell us that the narrator is "unreliable," in other words, precisely *because* the "real" of his experiences is being recorded and captured. Other pivotal moments in the narrative suggest similar discontinuities between present and past. Just as it does at the home of his millionaire patron, the narrator's performance of ragtime in a Tenderloin club attracts the attention of white women. In one scene, he is drawn to a particularly attractive one, with eyes (in another nod to du Maurier) like "Trilby's 'twin gray stars'" (79). But when her black lover arrives and shoots her in a fit of jealous rage, ex-colored man flees the club. As he rides away in a taxi, he describes his shock: "The cool air somewhat calmed my nerves and I lay back and closed my eyes; but still I could see that beautiful white throat with the ugly wound. The jet of blood pulsing from it had placed an indelible red stain on my memory" (91). As with the notion of the memory "stamped with a die," the narrator's drive to literalize and visualize memory, to stress its inscription within him as a way to emphasize the impossibility of erasure, at the same stroke suggests a syncope in memory. A psychic static interrupts the narrator's otherwise lucid autobiographical voice at these moments. He "registered" the events, but did not process them at the time, opening the possibility that he misrepresents or embellishes them as he writes. His failed performance of Chopin as a child also sounds here in the fatal throat wound, which suggests a breakdown of the voice's symbolic guarantee of presence more broadly, and, by extension, the loss of the *Autobiography*'s own claim to authoritative recall.

Arguably the most important syncope in ex-colored man's narrative occurs near the end of the novel, when he witnesses a lynching in the midst of his quest through the South to gather black folk material for his musical compositions. He notes of the victim, who is about to be burned at the stake, "There he stood, a man only in form and stature, every sign of degeneracy stamped upon his countenance" (136). In attempting to account for racialization and racial violence, the narrator once again evokes two kinds of writing, yet the distinction that he tries to make between written transparency—here, a "sign" that represents "degeneracy"—and the violent imposition of a mark or brand collapses. The "sign" of race is also a "stamp," both read and imposed by the narrator's description. The narrative static increases as ex-colored man writes the law of race onto the body of the other, a process to which he has unknowingly borne witness throughout the novel.

Just as the distinction between literal and figurative writing collapses here, so too does another distinction ex-colored man seeks to draw—between the present-day rule of law and a primitive and violent pursuit of the "outlaw." The narrator presents lynching as an occasion for national shame because it besmirches America's identity as "the great example of democracy to the world" (137). He describes it as a form of arrested development: "The Southern whites are not yet living quite in the present age;

many of their general ideas hark back to a former century, some of them to the Dark Ages" (138). Yet his idealism once again emerges as complicit with the very structures he seeks to criticize. Because the "sign of degeneracy" is also a "stamp," what the black countenance signifies is the denied internal difference of the law's *autopoesis.* The novel's emphasis on race as inscription reveals that the law constructs the outlaw in order to ratify its own authority.[85]

While this internal difference cannot be "read" on the countenance, it can be heard. Although throughout the book the narrator has described his own memory in terms of a visual inscription, suggesting at the same time a syncope of both memory and consciousness, in this scene memory survives as a function of the aural: "Fuel was brought from everywhere, oil, the torch; the flames crouched for an instant as though to gather strength, then leaped up as high as their victim's head. He squirmed, he writhed, strained at his chains, then gave out cries and groans that I shall always hear" (136). The victim's "cries and groans" echo the evocative and inarticulate sounds of the "sorrow songs," serving as a testimony to the racial cost of both the narrator's and white America's archive fever. This scene is of particular importance, we discover at the end of the book, because it has led the narrator to abandon his work of transcribing and collecting folk songs, to abandon his race, and finally to write the "autobiography" itself in order to "divulge" this "great secret of my life" (1). It is therefore not so much the fact of the lynching itself as its "telling inarticulacy" that should be understood as the "origin" of ex-colored man's narrative voice.

In turn, to understand that voice's widely debated ambiguity, we should attend not to the visual but to the friction between the aural and visual. The *Autobiography* has been interpreted in divergent ways over the course of its critical history precisely because the significance of its phonographic quality has been overlooked. Commentators have tended to bifurcate into two camps, both of which have emphasized the literariness of the work and its visual logic, arguing either that the novel exposes black identity and all identity as a fiction, or that it portrays a character who is insufficiently true to his identity.[86] Yet the work suggests that both of these options are true at once by replacing the dual optic of narrative transparency or opacity offered by the era of the book with a narrative inspired by the virtuality of black artistic practices in the age of mechanical reproduction. Narrative "unreliability" evaporates along with ex-colored man's "secret" in a novel that records not only what its narrator intends to say but also the noise he doesn't know he makes.

Ragged Time

I have been examining how the narrator functions phonographically both thematically and formally within the narrative, but the playback of the *Autobiography* for the listening reader, as John Durham Peters and Eric W. Rothenbuhler note of the phonograph record, itself "audiblizes two histories: one of recording and one of the record."[87] On the one hand, the recording—ex-colored man's narrative voice—is disembodied, anonymous, and speaks uncannily from nowhere, gaining the authority of the "real" much like a phonograph record. This is especially true because the book "passed" as an anonymous autobiography for several years. On the other hand, the record—the book itself—speaks simultaneously in a voice that, unlike ex-colored man's, achieved a belated sense of recognition when Johnson eventually claimed authorship of it as a work of literary realism. In addition to its fictional passages, we can hear someone else talking in the *Autobiography* who exhibits an uncanny degree of fidelity to Johnson in his later essays and prefaces. Passages like the lynching scene, in which the clarity of the narrator's retelling is riven with psychic static, are now and then interrupted by ones nearly identical to those Johnson published later under his own name. As I noted in the introduction to the chapter, ex-colored man uses almost the same words as Johnson will use ten years later to argue that American musicians should not dismiss ragtime, but should instead pay attention to its universal appeal. As another example, when the narrator records his experience listening to a singer at a southern revival meeting, his description is similar to a childhood memory Johnson will later cite in his preface to the *Book of American Negro Spirituals*.[88] Furthermore, the novel pauses during this scene to give readers the words of "Swing Low, Sweet Chariot" and "Steal Away to Jesus," reprinting and offsetting the same lyrics that appear later in the *Spirituals* preface, as if the *Autobiography* at this point were merely a faithful recording executed in a notebook by ex-colored man or by Johnson himself.[89]

Yet, in a move that mirrors what until recently has been the larger critical dismissal of Johnson's nonfiction, passages from the novel that he reused under his own name in his later essays and prefaces have largely been ignored, understood as mistakes, or even occasionally cited by critics as evidence of the narrator's fatal cross-identification with the white gaze.[90] What does it mean to listen to Johnson's voice in the text? It is to recognize that the novel itself bears a relationship of "ragged time" to Johnson's later essays, which retroactively mobilize a black aesthetics of formal experimentation within the earlier "unreliable" voice. It is also to recognize that the *Autobiography* in fact gathers together fictional narration, sociology, history, and even in places "real" autobiography, and that to draw the boundaries of literary fiction around it risks invoking the "archive fever" whose racialized consequences are the subject of the text itself. Finally, and most important, it is to miss what listening meant *to* Johnson in his later political work of "uplift." The *Autobiography*'s limits are porous, open, "ragged," archiving black performances in a way that preserves their energy and originality, yet allows their discrepant forms to invade and transform the voice that seeks to contain them. The work as a whole therefore can best be understood to function formally less as literature or history, dramatic monologue or sociological document, than as a crucible that dissolves and tests the purity of its many different readings. Much like the crackle and hiss of a phonograph record, the form of the work itself sounds. In assembling ex-colored man's flawed perspective together with his own experiences and views, Johnson inaugurates black modernism with the "telling inarticulacy" of a deconstructed archive—a record of missed moments, a virtual voice.

CHAPTER 4

Wonder and Decay

Djuna Barnes's New York

To the ever-repeated sensations with which the daily press serves its public he opposes the eternally fresh "news" of the history of creation: the eternally renewed, the uninterrupted lament.

—Walter Benjamin, "Karl Kraus"

ALTHOUGH THERE WERE MANY former journalists among the crowd of expatriate American women writers living in Paris during the storied 1920s and 1930s, by the time she arrived in 1921, Djuna Barnes, the author of the much-acclaimed modernist novel *Nightwood* (1936), had had a particularly dramatic career. Like several of her contemporaries, Barnes had written for magazines such as *Vanity Fair, Theater Guild,* and the *New Yorker* before leaving the United States and continued to do so from abroad. However, in contrast to her often more genteel contemporaries on the left bank, she had also written for nearly every newspaper in New York City. Beginning in 1913, Barnes had supported herself, her newly divorced mother, and her younger brothers by publishing more than a hundred articles and interviews, in addition to dramas and short stories, in the daily papers.[1] Entertainment was the mandate of much of this work. Barnes was frequently engaged in publicizing lower-class amusements, such as the circus and the Coney Island freak show, as "safe" for middle-class audiences. The period's rage for "slumming tours" and for the emerging leisure-time activity of tourism is also evident in much of her writing. She provided firsthand accounts of trips into mysterious ethnic locales in New York, wrote a series exposing her own neighborhood of "bohemian" Greenwich Village to curious uptown eyes, and produced short articles on "local color" in and around Manhattan, Brooklyn, and the Bronx.

However, Barnes's glamorous later life as a Parisian expatriate and an experimental modernist writer between the wars has tended to make us forget that she also contributed to social problem journalism.[2] While her articles between 1913 and 1921 often profiled artists, writers, and performers, she also wrote about the unjust sentencing of criminals, including a mother stealing bread for her children; the lives of down-and-out squatters near Coney Island; a suffrage rally and a "suffrage school" for women; the closing of the Arbuckle, a floating residence hotel for impoverished working women; and a meeting of the Industrial Workers of the World. There was also a reform angle to her pieces publicizing entertainments for middle-class audiences; the "cleaning up" of public culture was a priority of the vice commissions that had been established in many American cities, including New York, by the early years of Barnes's career. Their mandate was to shine a light not only on "sexual slavery," or prostitution, but also "sexual perversion," generally meaning homosexuality.[3]

There is a compelling tension between the commercial function of Barnes's journalism and its reformist bent. Reform itself could be fun to watch—even sexy—a fact that becomes particularly evident in her "stunt" work. Perhaps the most striking articles Barnes wrote were the ones where she became a female stunt journalist, in the tradition of Nellie Bly, for Joseph Pulitzer's sensational *New York World*. Documented in photographs, she underwent force-feeding to publicize the plight of hunger-striking suffragists, "interviewed" a large gorilla at the Bronx Zoo, attended a boxing match, and was "rescued" from an apartment building by firefighters in training. Putting her body on display, Barnes engaged in a type of personal and embodied reporting indebted to the conventions of newspaper reform journalism by women but updated for the emerging mass market. Providing a so-called women's angle on pressing social issues, she not only reported on the news but herself *became* the news, by selling her own alluring persona and image.

Critical approaches to Barnes's work have tended to focus not on her journalism but instead on her later "major" works, particularly *Nightwood*. In this chapter, I argue that the most striking aspect of her later work— her "baroque" style—owes its origin to the social problem journalism she wrote in her youth. The 1936 *Nightwood*, as many have noted, flaunts its opacity and revels in its artificiality, drawing more attention to the surface of language than to what language has to say. The novel is filled with digressive, ornamental flourishes; obscure comparisons; epigrams;

and unexpected and unusual juxtapositions, all of which declare their allegiance less to plot, character development, or even to the novel's own thematic preoccupation with irrationality, perverse sexual desire, loss, and degradation, than to the figurality of language itself. As Monika Kaup has recently argued, this style is aptly described as "neo-baroque."[4] Its excessive, hyperbolic quality—and particularly the use of open-ended, proliferating metaphors—has significant parallels to the baroque trope of the *horror vacui*, or "fear of the empty space," in which an artist fills in with detail all of the blank space within the frame, both hiding and reaffirming the void underneath. Likewise, Barnes places a frequent emphasis in her later work on a perpetual and deforming tension between opposites, which is similar to the dynamic movement of baroque art in its challenge to the static, stable, and hierarchical structures of classicism. Finally, Kaup shows that the definition of the baroque as an epochal and epistemic border, rather than strictly an art-historical period, formulated most influentially by historian Michel Foucault and philosopher Gilles Deleuze, is also very relevant to Barnes's writing. In *Nightwood, Ladies Almanack, Ryder,* and *The Antiphon,* Kaup shows, Barnes uses twentieth-century ideas about the corrupting force of power and unconscious desire to actively subvert nineteenth-century ideals of liberalism and social progress. Yet her true feelings about the latter remain unclear because of her hyperbolis and excessive style. In this, she is similar to baroque philosophers and theorists, who did not so much reject the triumph of Enlightenment reason over the sacred cosmology of medieval and Renaissance culture as attempt to slow down its arrival by "proliferat[ing] indefinitely the process of naming things."[5] The baroque offers the best way to understand Barnes's true ambivalence toward the loss of nineteenth-century ideals. Her twentieth-century neobaroque writing seeks to keep "Some Thing . . . rather than nothing," in Deleuze's words, by means of style.[6]

In the pages that follow, I show that Barnes's neobaroque style, credited by Kaup and others to the influences she absorbed as an expatriate between the wars, was in fact forged in response to the shifting episteme between reform and entertainment, progressivism and consumer culture, that characterized pre–World War I New York. I trace Barnes's baroque aesthetics to this tension at the heart of many of her early pieces. In particular, I suggest, Barnes frequently turns to the baroque's favorite device—allegory, and the arbitrary relationship at its heart between the sign and what it represents—as a way to avoid having to portray her subjects in static, unchanging ways:

either as poor and downtrodden in the dark heart of the city, or as glamorous objects of desire, fixed, like herself, in the unblinking, camera-like eye
of a consolidating entertainment industry. Baroque allegory and baroque
style allow her instead to potentialize or virtualize the subjects of her articles, capturing their, and thereby her own, capacity to become something
entirely—even obscenely—other. Barnes's early journalism thus reveals
the unexpected significance of the American Reform Era to this radical expatriate modernist at a formative moment in her career.

While Barnes's New York journalism makes less extensive use of her
typically neobaroque stylistic devices, it has much of what Victoria L.
Smith calls the "thickly brocaded" quality of her later work, offering less
a description of who, what, when, and where than an exfoliation of metaphors and linguistic associations that refuse to offer up a clear picture.[7]
Listen, for instance, to Barnes describing, for publicity purposes, the "typical" New York woman often seen in summer at one of the city's many
roof gardens: "[She] is languid, impressive, wears long, lassitudinous side
curls, and strings the contour of her face to the sharp-pitched key of a
large expanse of white forehead and a sudden, downward wave of well-
ordered hair. She is essentially crepe; she moves in long, pathetic lines."[8]
This strange portrait illustrates Alan Singer's argument about *Nightwood*
that Barnes's metaphors serve as "points of departure rather than reser-
voirs of accumulated meaning."[9] The metaphor here seems to be of a string
stretched taut, but its purpose is not to elucidate the woman's appearance
or personality—as, for example, attractively "high strung." Instead, Barnes
compares the face, the tenor of the metaphor, to a vehicle for which there
is no unifying ground—a "sharp-pitched key" of a "white expanse." It
becomes impossible to establish the nature of the resemblance between
literal and figural because the metaphor refuses to illuminate its subject;
it is open-ended and indefinitely extending, infused with the energy and
dynamism that are the hallmark of the baroque style Barnes loved.[10]

Moreover, Barnes's commentary on the sights and sounds of New York
often evokes the baroque's theological sense of loss and guilt. As I discuss
following, Manhattan, Brooklyn, and the Bronx, as Barnes depicts them in
the 'teens, are postlapsarian worlds, in which experience exists in a perpetual tension between opposed poles of salvation and damnation. Although
Barnes's melancholy, dualistic, and vertically oriented cosmological vision
is less extensive in her early reporting than in her later writing, it is already
significant—and striking enough to make one pause in trying to discern

her attitude toward her subjects. Sometimes her emphasis on verticality seems to be satirical, as in the roof garden denizen's "sudden, downward wave of well-ordered hair," or in this description of watching a fashion show: "The styles have got us by the throat—we laugh as they hurl us to the ground. We exult as we sink into that deep peace, gently lulled into stupefaction by the burden of duchess lace upon our minds, tulle upon our hearts, and gossamer upon our senses" (208). Sometimes, the effect is frankly eschatological, as in her description of a boatload of soldiers heading out to fight in World War I, their voices "a strange cry, a happy cry, an exultant cry, proclaiming doom and death" (289).

This tone of theological and eschatological doom is often missed by Barnes's feminist, queer, and new historicist readers, who have in recent years considerably, and valuably, expanded the Barnes canon to include her early journalism.[11] Reacting to Barnes's first critics, like T. S. Eliot, who focused only on *Nightwood* as a token female-authored example of "high" modernist form, such readers have focused instead on her writing's politically subversive aspects.[12] Critical accounts of her early journalism, as a result, have deemphasized style in favor of historical and thematic content, examining the way her pieces—especially her stunt journalism—reflect larger cultural shifts in prewar New York, particularly in regard to film, theater, performance, and the conventions governing the image of the female body in popular culture.[13] But I argue that Barnes's vertical cosmology, which represents even the most mundane events of everyday life as perched on the abyss, calls into question the historical critique that she is often assumed to be making.[14] For it redefines history itself as secondary and unreal, the product of a debasing fall into duality that is the occasion for a melancholy experienced less on an individual or social scale than on a world-historical one. A sense of "planetary defeatism" suffuses Barnes's journalism, as Walter Benjamin described the work of Viennese newspaper satirist Karl Kraus, making it into a "strange interplay between reactionary theory and revolutionary practice."[15]

In order to more fully capture the sense of this interplay, my approach to Barnes's early work focuses on the connections between style and history. The first part of the chapter explores in more detail how Barnes's newspaper journalism shines a light on the conflict between reform and entertainment. On one side of this conflict was a renewed voluntarism during the period, whose proponents enjoined "good works" on the public via exposés in the illustrated periodical press. On the other

side, I argue, was the public passivity fostered by the rise of mass entertainments. The second and third parts of the chapter draw on Walter
Benjamin's theory of the baroque to delve more deeply into the development of Barnes's *neo*baroque style. I argue that many of her articles' most
intriguing stylistic features, in recalling the baroque, embrace the artificiality and theatricality of mass culture and mass entertainments without
relinquishing nineteenth-century ideals. Through recourse to the obscene; through extreme, vertical contrasts; and finally, through the (dis)
organizing principles of assemblage, Barnes seeks to rescue her subjects
from equally untenable options: the sanctimonious "salvation" of reform,
whose true satisfaction lies in the hereafter, or "damnation" to a fully creaturely existence in a world dominated by mass culture, whose rewards go
no further than the entertaining image in the here and now. Emerging on
the scene at the confluence of Progressive Era reform and mass entertainment, Barnes, I argue, fashioned her literary identity as the self-appointed
allegorist of a fallen world.

The Rogues' Gallery

It might seem surprising to consider Barnes's writing as indebted in any
way—other than by a gesture of rejection—to a reformist impulse. She
had come of age during the greatest wave of reform journalism in the
United States, the years from 1903 to 1910, during which novels, sermons,
newspaper articles, and especially magazine exposés sought to take action
against political corruption, illegal trust activities, child labor, and slum
conditions, as well as mismanagement, fraud, waste, and abuse at institutions from police departments to mental homes.[16] These urban "muckraking" crusades were preoccupied with the instrumental reason of the scientific "expert" or "specialist" and were often accompanied by a focus on
sexual morality. It would not have been lost on the bisexual Barnes, who
had many gay friends among her circle of artists and writers in Greenwich
Village, that the saloons, social clubs, and dance halls of New York's vi-
brant working-class gay subculture on the Bowery and the Lower East
Side were frequently infiltrated by journalists, raided by the police, and
patrolled by undercover detectives.

But there were significant philosophical quandaries at stake in reform
that could not so easily be solved by outright rejection. The most important of these was progressivism's challenge to the passivity of both religious

and secular idealism.[17] Many American religious leaders had historically followed a Calvinist line of thinking that dictated that social status should be understood as a portent of salvation. Secular thought from the 1870s onward had done much the same by linking the ideologies of social evolution and the free market, arguing that any unwanted effects of industrialization were a part of the cycle of natural selection. By the 1890s, these "ideologies of noninterference" had come to seem, for many, merely a convenient way to avoid responsibility for the poverty and suffering produced by industrialization.[18] Reform-minded thinkers and writers began to argue instead that poverty, suffering, and crime had social causes, that predestinarianism was a tool for maintaining social privilege, and, most important, that individual agency was a valid way to deal with social problems. The result, as Gregory Jackson has recently argued, was that the formerly "heretical" idea of salvation through "good works" came to prominence, unifying religious and secular authorities, as well as different forms of print and popular culture, by the end of the century.[19] The goal of stimulating readers and institutions to take action cut across widely different genres, including journalistic exposés, Social Gospel tracts, realist novels, and self-help literature.

The explosion of images in the periodical press; the advent of print journalism, especially magazines, as a true "mass" medium by 1900; and the beginnings of film also fuelled the voluntarism of the 1890s and the wave of reform journalism that followed in the next decade.[20] In a sense, it was the reliance on advertising revenue that made effective public exposés possible, because advertising made magazines cheap to print and to buy and thus expanded readership to a truly national scale.[21] The photomechanical reproduction of line drawings and photographs, in turn, helped to draw in growing numbers of readers and potential consumers. But images, including those of early film, or film-like experiences such as Jacob Riis's magic lantern shows, also provided a means to more effectively strip the gilding off the so-called Gilded Age, exposing the visual and verifiable facts of poverty, abuse, and suffering on which its wealth was founded.

It has often been assumed that Progressive Era images of poverty and neglect were designed to keep middle-class onlookers at a safe distance from their working-class subjects. The simultaneous growth of advertising suggests that such images, far from being a stimulus to reform, were being passively consumed as a way to affirm class difference. Jackson, however, shows that Riis and other reformers understood spectatorship as an *interactive* experience, in line with the larger voluntaristic ethos mentioned previously.[22] Photography, illustration, slides, and early films bearing witness to slum life were considered to function less as documentary evidence than as interactive simulations. Often by encouraging audiences to interpret the images via biblical allegory, reformers sought via new technologies to produce a vivid experience that could effectively substitute for the real thing.[23]

The involved, interactive, spiritual experience supposed to be stimulated by journalistic exposés, or slide lectures like Riis's, had much to do with the material fact that media and theater were inextricable from each other in the late nineteenth century. Theatrical mass "attractions" united the fascinating realism, mechanism, and voyeurism of the filmic image with active, involved spectators, co-present to each other and to the image, staged as a kind of performance. Media spectacles in late nineteenth-century America, such as those of the Spanish-American War, discussed in chapter 1, were supposed to reinforce the prophetic meaning already associated with the experience of the word and the image in American Protestant theology and nationalist self-understanding. This is one reason that the period was awash with vitalistic claims about the progressive power of images, such as those of Riis, which often had the effect of spiritualizing American modernity itself, as I discuss in the introduction to this book.

Yet by the time Djuna Barnes had become an urban journalist, in 1913, the idea of spectatorship as an interactive virtual experience with an implicit or explicit spiritual meaning had become closely bound up with the consolidation of the profit-seeking film industry. Specifically, film's popular draw and more commercially lucrative potential during the decade from 1915 to 1925 in New York City were coloring much of the reform agenda in regard to public culture.[24] Live performances were vanishing, and at the decreasing numbers of venues that remained—vaudeville, dance halls, the circus, the theaters, and Coney Island—owners and managers were trying to make the live event itself more like a mass cultural spectacle. Under the guise of reform, but really for the sake of revenue, they sought to eliminate interactions between audience and performers, to censor socially transgressive behavior on the part of performers, and to turn unruly crowds into homogenous, silent, and disciplined masses of spectators, like those we associate with film today.[25] Interactive audience responses to the simulation of the real were being pacified, in other words, in order to construct a more commercially viable form of entertainment that could be more easily controlled and distributed. Barnes, as Laura

Winkiel has shown, often satirized such attempts to control the public in her journalism, and bemoaned the disappearance of live, interactive entertainment. Yet she was also very much a publicist and promoter of this brand of entertainment "reform."[26]

Coincidentally with the beginnings of national production and distribution networks for film and the decline in local, participatory entertainments like vaudeville, the war in Europe and the rise of government-sponsored propaganda were leading intellectuals to question the nature of the muckraking exposé's appeal to the public. Theories of suggestion and the "crowd mind" produced in the 1890s were beginning to be taken seriously in the United States one or two decades later as a way to explain the appeal of media spectacles.[27] For instance, in *The Crowd: A Study of the Popular Mind*, French sociologist Gustave Le Bon argued that seemingly independent individuals could be merged into a single mind, their conviction compelled like "the button of an electric bell," by a persuasive speaker or by ideas presented in "very absolute, uncompromising, and simple shape [that is] . . . in the guise of images."[28] As a result of the dominance of this highly suggestible and primitive crowd mind in modern life, Le Bon claimed, the press evokes automatic, instinctive responses rather than stimulating conscious thought or reason.[29] After WWI, as a result of theories like these, influential press commentators like Walter Lippmann, whom I discuss in chapter 5, would abandon their belief in a rational public sphere altogether, embracing instead the idea that media compelled conviction by mental persuasion from centralized sites.[30]

For a gloomy young devotee of Burton's *Anatomy of Melancholy* like Barnes, then, to become a female stunt journalist and illustrator in the New York of the 'teens was to occupy two incommensurable positions at once—the characteristic posture of the baroque. On the one hand, Barnes was subjected to the quasi-theological mandate to do good work, which meant representing urban life symbolically and encouraging active acts of empathetic identification and involvement with the downtrodden by setting an example herself.[31] On the other hand, she was confronted with the simultaneous and often overlapping mandate to popularize increasingly homogenous—and therefore, increasingly "reformed"—sites of entertainment to readers and viewers whose minds were conceptualized as essentially passive. Thinkers like Le Bon argued against the very possibility of empathetic identification, or the idea that the image could offer a mode of affective training for saviors of the poor and downtrodden. Instead, emotional responses to symbolism were passive, unconscious, and inevitable, especially for certain segments of the population.[32] This amounted to a melancholy conclusion indeed for proponents of Progressive Era voluntarism, suggesting a return to the fatalism before religious or natural law that had characterized an earlier generation. Crowd theorists implied that it was a waste of time to try to raise public awareness, because the public mind was governed by immutable laws and was therefore impervious to real change in the here and now.

Two remarkable back-to-back interviews Barnes did with police officials in the spring of 1918 suggests that she saw in these developments a deplorable, covert return to Calvinism's attitude toward social problems, and, on a far grander scale, to the injunction of the Protestant Reformation itself: salvation by *sola fides,* or "faith alone." Yet they also make clear that she was equally unwilling to embrace the nineteenth-century belief in the "good works" of the institutions of press, police, and government that still provided the justification for many of her own assignments. In the first, a profile for the *New York Sun Magazine,* Barnes interviews New York Police Commissioner Richard E. Enright. The piece is designed to showcase improvements in the New York Police Department, which had been one of the most corrupt in America until it was reorganized by Theodore Roosevelt in 1896.[33] The title, "Commissioner Enright and M. Voltaire," positions Enright as a reformer by drawing attention to his love of the writing of the primary representative of Enlightenment reason. Enright's main claim to fame is also emphasized by Barnes in the interview: the Rogues' Gallery. His department had recently adopted and popularized a collection of 43,000 identifying photographs of criminals, collected by Enright's predecessor Thomas Byrnes. Such collections were ostensibly designed for the purposes of identifying those known to have already committed crimes. But the collocation of images was also used as a form of "evidence" by proponents of hereditary theories of criminality, who believed that criminal "types" could be discerned by experts schooled in the science of physiognomy.[34]

Rather than showcasing the ideals of enlightened policing, Barnes instead uses the interview to explore her own struggle as an interviewer to find a justification or higher meaning in Enright's work. Throughout the piece, she peppers the police commissioner with questions about the nature of crime and the possibility of reconciling free will and determinism. "Some of the nicest people I know are either potential or real criminals," she tells Enright, invoking the commonly held Progressive view that environment is the cause of crime (301). Enright responds by asserting that he "emphatically" believes "the stars make us what we are" (302). Barnes then evinces her horror at this denial of free will: "This is quite frightful; this puts us beyond the reach of ourselves. If we are good, it is the stars; if we are bad, they also are to blame" (ibid.). Enright, however, affirms his belief in the soul and in the idea that "this life is only a preparation for the next" (ibid.). At another point, Barnes asks Enright how he can claim to have lived a happy life, given his exposure to crime and suffering. Enright affirms that his life has been happy because he is convinced that "there must be some purpose behind it all, some divine power that will set the wrong right" (303).

Enright's claim that the "stars make us what we are" would have had a distinctly outdated sound to many of Barnes's readers, despite his supposedly up-to-date methods. For his attitude—as likely embellished by Barnes—recalls both the Calvinist notion of social status as exemplary of salvation, and its close partner in crime, free-market evolutionism. The tendency to default to theology and natural law in response to social problems had been under attack for several decades by the time Barnes wrote this piece, perhaps nowhere more vehemently than in the context of print culture itself. Thus her Leibnizian preoccupation with free will would have brought to mind the question of meaningful action and human volition recently raised by the Social Gospel, temperance, and reform movements, as well as by many journalists, especially female journalists. Barnes's comment about the "potential criminal," however, also illustrates that she sees an even more archaic attitude in Enright's approach, and in the decline of voluntarism that it portends. As an in-between figure, the potential criminal evokes the baroque preoccupation with forms adequate to representing tension or movement in a vertical cosmos. In flourishing this figure in front of Enright, Barnes suggests that Enright's "enlightened" form of policing represents the dawn of a new and repressive classical age against which she seeks some form of countermeasure.

Barnes ends the interview on a revealing note. Following up on Enright's affirmation that things will be better in the next world, Barnes asks, "But in the meantime?" He responds:

"In the meantime, we must do the best we can for those who come nearest us. For me it is crime, for you—"

"Ah, and for me also, perhaps."

He looked at me, puzzled.

"You see," I continued, "I have a lot of friends, as I before said, who are either potential criminals or criminals in action; and these somehow one likes—why?"

"Why? Well, you see, we all love the specialist," he answered and broke out into laughter. (303–4)

Barnes contests Enright's deterministic views on criminality as fated by the "stars" by emphasizing the affection and desire the criminal incites. Much like Andy Warhol a half-century later in his silkscreen of the NYPD's "Thirteen Most Wanted Men," she associates the photographs of the wanted "rogues" with a series of glamour shots more characteristic of celebrities or film stars.[35] By specifying that, as a young and attractive female journalist, she "likes" the compelling star power of the criminals in Enright's gallery, Barnes suggests that Enright's enlightened tactics have more in common with a new order of mass-reproduced entertainment than an old order of progressive reform. She responds to the images on Enright's wall like an enthralled female film spectator, for whom the criminal's image connotes consumerism and stimulates only illicit desire.

As Enright's joke acknowledges, there is a further dimension at play in the fact that the criminal mirrors Enright himself and especially his predecessor, the specialist Byrnes, who had popularized the Rogues' Gallery via a published version entitled *Professional Criminals of America*. The idea of a "professional criminal" brings to mind the dynamic interplay between the opposed poles of detective and the criminal in the detective story. Another reason why Barnes emphasizes the police commissioner's love of Voltaire thus emerges. Voltaire's story of Zadig demonstrates that the detective—as a "specialist in crime" or a "professional"—can easily be mistaken for the criminal, and vice versa. Barnes generalizes this quality in noting that some of her "best friends" are potential criminals. It is as if Barnes wants to suggest that all experience to some extent occupies this dynamic and tense middle position, leaving the essential question for enlightened policing—Who is the real criminal?—radically uncertain.

An illuminating contrast to the Enright interview can be found in its companion piece Barnes published a week later, also in the *New York Sun Magazine*, entitled "Woman Police Deputy Is Writer of Poetry." Here the interviewee is Deputy Police Commissioner Ellen O'Grady, an advocate

for women who had been appointed by Enright to showcase his dedication
to rooting out corruption in the police force.[36] O'Grady, Barnes reveals,
has very different views on the question of crime, and "potential criminals," from those of her boss. When Barnes notes, in a repetition of her
question to the latter, "any one of us might commit a murder," O'Grady responds, "It has been said quite truly that we are all potential criminals. It is
true that environment makes most of us what we are; then we must change
the environment . . . by education: education of the senses and of the mind
. . . [and] of the heart" (312). By posing the same question to both, Barnes
draws an implicit comparison, suggesting that the Irish Catholic O'Grady
acts to remedy social injustice, whereas the dour Enright simply has faith
that criminals get what they deserve. It is clear where her sympathies lie
despite the fact that O'Grady is a champion of sexual morality with whom
she might otherwise have little in common. In a significant contrast in
tone with the previous week, the two companionably discuss O'Grady's
work in rooting out prostitution; prison reform; psychoanalysis (O'Grady
is not a fan of Freud); the possibility of a life "beyond good and evil"; the
meaning of criminality; O'Grady's Irish background and family; and, as
the title promises, her poetry.

Appropriately for this latter interview, at the outset Barnes deftly
makes use of the allegorical symbolism characteristic of reformist literature. While "Commissioner Enright and M. Voltaire" neglected to describe Barnes's trip to Enright's office, "Woman Police Deputy Is Writer of
Poetry" opens by taking readers on a tour of the street where both Enright
and O'Grady work:

> Imagine a day on Centre Street, overcast and threatening rain; a
> day through which shuffle flickering tramps like wicks that are
> dying. . . . Imagine the cries of someone in a vacant lot raised high
> above the multitude on a soapbox with wide, imploring, heed-
> less arms. . . . Then imagine the long, cold corridors of Police
> Headquarters, the uniformed men with their badges winking
> sleepily above their hearts. . . . Imagine all this, and you have the
> environs and the person of Mrs. Ellen O'Grady, Fifth Deputy
> Police Commissioner. (305)

In calling on readers to imagine the urban environment and denizens of
Centre St., Barnes conjures up the damned landscape and souls in Dante's

Inferno. In so doing, she reflects the distinctly homiletic mode of texts such as Riis's *How the Other Half Lives* or Benjamin Flower's *Civilization's Inferno, Or Studies in the Social Cellar,* which evoked the city as both a literal and a metaphysical landscape in need of earthly and spiritual redemption.[37] The muscular response to social problems that O'Grady enjoins on Barnes, in other words, mirrors that which Barnes also enjoins on her readers via images that are designed to provide them with a virtual experience of poverty and suffering. Her opener suggests that her objections to Enright the previous week are a function of her own commitment to reform.

Despite her greater sympathy for O'Grady's approach, however, Barnes's skepticism about her methods is also evident throughout the interview. The deputy police commissioner's poetic turns of phrase, for instance, raise some red flags. As befitting a poet, O'Grady describes the potential criminal in highly symbolic terms. Although she does not believe in "Freudism," she does believe in what she calls the "psychological moment": "Take a person at the edge, just before he goes over—a person with the knife lifted, one with the poison to his lips, he who is about to shoot—and you have a chance for redemption such as you will never have again and which you could not have had before. One always saves and loses the most at the edge of things" (310–11). The mission of the police department and the court system, for O'Grady, is to determine guilt or innocence by gentle and intuitive acts of contextual judgment particular to each case, not, Barnes implies, by merely consulting an abstract gallery of photographs. Yet the faith that intentions can be read in a momentary flash of wordless and mysterious insight—as this overly artful and melodramatic image suggests—makes the potential criminal at the same time into a dubiously romantic symbol, perhaps of the kind that O'Grady herself employs in her after-hours poetry.

Barnes's skepticism emerges as well in more direct ways. She asks O'Grady, for instance, whether or not she believes that poverty is the cause of most crime. O'Grady says that "poverty is the greatest of all evils," but she then adds, "because people do not understand how to be poor. Poverty drives the children into the street, we all know that, and from there to the saloons; but why? Because their own homes are not only poor but dirty" (309). Admonished by Barnes that "soap costs money, Mrs. O'Grady," the latter then responds that it is better to starve to death than to succumb to the degradation of dirt or crime: "I know, I know, but some there are who have proved their divine ability, some who reach heaven little but skin and bones; but this kind He loves best" (309). Mrs. O'Grady's contextual view of crime, Barnes wants us to realize, is no more tenable than the secular determinism of Enright's gallery of rogues. For O'Grady spiritualizes the potential criminal, via the image of the child poised between salvation and damnation. Sympathetic to O'Grady's approach, Barnes nevertheless parts ways with her use of this common trope of the Reform Era. In her revealing double portrait of Enright and O'Grady, Barnes thus suggests that her own task as a female journalist is to navigate between the incommensurate demands that each represents—on the one hand, to publicize the cinematic rogues of an emerging consumer culture and, on the other, to defend the vulnerable children of an urban-industrial underworld.

American Mourning Play: Barnes, Benjamin, and the Baroque

Barnes's baroque dilemma thereby emerges in the interplay between "Woman Police Deputy Is Writer of Poetry" and "Commissioner Enright and M. Voltaire." She finds herself forced to choose between a vitalistic progressivism that conceals an untenable Christian notion of redemption at its heart, and the return, by other means, of a mechanistic conception of social evolution that sees suffering only in terms of fate. The drama of this dilemma further emerges when the interviews are considered alongside the work of Walter Benjamin, the twentieth-century theorist of the baroque with whom Barnes has the most in common.[38] For Benjamin also returned to the baroque, and specifically to the distinctive mode of signification characteristic of baroque theater, in order to confront the waning of nineteenth-century ideals on religious and metaphysical grounds. In his 1925 *Habilitationsschrift*, *The Origin of German Tragic Drama (Ursprung des deutschen Trauerspiels)*, Benjamin examined the long-forgotten German baroque tragedies—literally "mourning plays"—of the seventeenth century, finding in them an aesthetic response to modernity that was to inform his understanding of expressionism and his later analyses of the poetry of Baudelaire, the Parisian urban landscape, and new media technologies, including photography, and, most influentially, film.[39] Distinguishing the baroque mourning play from the genre of tragedy with which it was often associated, Benjamin argues that the former's characteristics—court intrigue and the tyranny of the sovereign's power, hyperbolic lamentation and sorrow, physical suffering and spiritual torment, fragmented scenes, lack of character motivation, and an emphasis above all on an allegorical and theatrical display of the space of the stage and the properties that occupy it ("the profane world of things")—were a response to a religious and metaphysical crisis caused by the rise of Protestantism.[40] The idea of *sola fides*, or "faith alone"— the Lutheran doctrine that individuals should encounter God individually through the mediation of scripture, rather than together, via liturgical ritual—created, he argues, a "religious aspiration" deprived of a "religious fulfillment."[41] Lutheranism, and later Calvinism, left behind a sense of the guilt inherent in creation, but deprived the faithful of access to meaningful human action—via the mediation of church and state institutions—that could bring redemption from their "creaturely" fate. The mourning plays, in contrast to the medieval passion plays that preceded them, thus lament this creaturely state, according to Benjamin, and take a fully historical and "fallen" existence, rather than a Christian eschatology, as their exclusive subject. They also put on display a crisis of sovereign authority that Benjamin saw as typical of the German Reformation, as evinced by the violent yet martyred despots that people their stages. In the wake of the injunction to "faith alone," Benjamin notes, the divinely justified acts performed by the law and the sovereign were coming under suspicion, as arbitrary, unsanctioned instruments for the execution of justice (65–74).

Barnes's responses to Enright evoke a similar crisis over the loss of good works. In her updated, early twentieth-century American version of the history Benjamin evokes, it is Enright's Rogues' Gallery that provides the scripture in which the guilty are enjoined to have faith, and the salvation by good works that gets lost is that of the Progressive reformer, O'Grady. Enright, via the Rogues' Gallery, enjoins us to read each criminal face as the product of heredity and an overarching criminal "type," placing the guilty beyond the reach of the "education of the heart" O'Grady advocates. Nothing can be done for the purposes of the fallen's salvation, as Barnes emphasizes through her mock-horror—guilt is already established, and for the guilty, a profane, temporal, and creaturely fate is all that remains. But the Rogues' Gallery also thereby subsumes the particularity of each face into a larger system of differences, making the faces into signifiers and evoking the specter of arbitrariness. This visual language of criminality thus also banishes meaningful acts of individual redemption, but in a different way. The faces now gain meaning only from the differences with each other, not from the presence or absence in each person of a transcendent divinity or typicality. Barnes essentially makes the New York police commissioner and proprietor of this collection into something of a baroque sovereign. Enright's outlandish insistence on "the stars" as a justification for his own exercise of power makes him seem arbitrary and dangerous. Yet, again like the baroque sovereign, Enright is represented as a man martyred to events beyond his control and reduced to a vain hope that, in regard to the suffering he witnesses, "there must be some purpose behind it all."

In both interviews, the image of the "potential criminal" recalls the heightened theatrical allegory that Benjamin saw at the heart of the baroque *trauerspiel*. With its pile-up of clauses and lilting, exaggerated list of lurid crimes, O'Grady's evocation of the "person with the knife lifted, one with the poison to his lips, he who is about to shoot," emerges more as a theatrical pose or gesture, reminiscent of an allegory on stage, than a symbol of innocence or documentation of degeneracy. Benjamin emphasizes that, in contrast to the symbol—a mystical, instantaneous fusion of representation and idea—allegory is a temporal progression of symbols, a collection of fragments which points to meaning according to conventional rules, and thus only in an incomplete way (159–74).[42] The baroque plays, according to Benjamin, explicitly bring out this "antimony" between convention and expression at the heart of allegory. Because of its temporal, historical quality, the allegorical mode always threatens to suggest that "any person, any object, any relationship can mean absolutely anything else" (175). As Weber notes, in his interpretation of Benjamin's theory of the baroque:

> Whatever is represented allegorically has no being apart from its being represented. Above all, its essence is inaccessible to good works, or to work of any kind. In the absence of the possibility of meaningful action, what emerges is mourning and melancholy as eminently theatrical attitudes. In this sense, allegory is eminently theatrical, since the being of what it represents can be determined only by virtue of its being placed before (*vorgestellt*) someone else: for instance, before a spectator.[43]

Barnes's provocative, playful statement to Enright, "Some of the nicest people I know are potential criminals, or criminals in action," takes up a mournful, theatrical attitude toward the potential criminal, stripping this image of its symbolic relationship to transcendence. Particularly through her joke about the criminal's attractiveness, Barnes ultimately suggests that whether "a person at the edge, just before he goes over" is about to be saved or damned depends only on whom he is placed before.[44] Insofar as anyone might be one, the potential criminal's meaning comes to derive from theatrical display, and not from a language-like system of images, from fate, or Christian grace.

The Enright interview itself is perhaps best described as a play of masks that takes its meaning only from the theatrical staging that Barnes gives it. Enright is a strange figure who "strokes" his "very nice white and curling hair" as he smiles at her. Barnes's questions to him, moreover, are comically incommensurate and prolix, given the subject matter. Imparting a highly artificial, mock philosophical tone to the proceedings, they might best be described as *staging* the subject of enlightened policing, institutional reform, and the new systematic methods for fighting crime. Finally, Barnes is herself, as always, the attractive young female reporter, for whom reporting the news cannot be separated from becoming the news. In that sense, Barnes's "being" is derived from her position in front of a spectator, like the being of the criminal himself.

Ultimately, then, Barnes harps on the "potential criminal" in these two interviews in order to find a way out of the conflict between faith and good works altogether. Baroque theatricality is more than merely a lament for the loss of a relation to transcendence, for Benjamin and Barnes. Allegory has a dialectical tension at its heart by virtue of its temporal quality, which allows the allegorist, according to Benjamin, also to *redeem* a world condemned to inhabit a profane, "creaturely" state. On the one hand, the German baroque stage, according to Benjamin, devalues the profane world of temporal progression and historical change as incomplete and incapable of signifying a path to salvation. On the other hand, insofar as the allegorical symbols that appear on its manifestly material and earthly boards can be interpreted as incomplete precisely *because* of their profane nature, Benjamin suggests that they are redeemed by their very *in*ability to point to or indicate the divine on their own. Even though "any person, any object, any relationship can mean absolutely anything else" in allegory, Benjamin notes, "All of the things which are used to signify derive, from the very fact of their pointing to something else, a power which makes them appear no longer commensurable with profane things, which raises them onto a higher plane, and which can, indeed, sanctify them. Considered in allegorical terms, then, the profane world is both elevated and devalued" (175). Allegory, in other words, can be a means of preserving the possibility of a relation to transcendence via the *potentiality* of signification. The potential to signify keeps open a route toward transcendence—keeping it "in play," in more than one sense. The Reformation's challenge to meaningful good works, then, is effectively neither accepted nor refused by the mourning play, according to Benjamin. Meaningful action is instead redeemed by being put on display.[45]

"Commissioner Enright and M. Voltaire" is thus best understood as an attempt to "save" a symbolic mode of representation—here the "civic melodrama" of social reformers—by potentializing it rather than rejecting it outright.[46] Opposing Enright, in other words, is a way to keep silent faith with O'Grady down the hall. Although Barnes cannot endorse O'Grady's Christian pieties, she doesn't have to reject them either. For by insisting to Enright on the potentiality of criminality, or more specifically on the potentiality of the criminal *act,* Barnes "saves" the "person on the edge" from the creaturely fate of becoming defined by heredity or by an arbitrary system of signification. If Barnes's best friends are both criminals and *not* criminals—that is, if they are truly potential criminals—then there is no way to take the measure of their crimes. Their actions are still in the midst of "coming to pass." Barnes thus virtualizes the fatalistic methods of classification with which Enright seeks to map out the world.

Barnes's writing itself, finally, has something in common not only with the baroque mourning plays, but also with the fragmentary mode of organization that Benjamin embraced in trying to account for them. *The Origin of German Tragic Drama* refuses to subsume the phenomena that make up its subject under a general class or an abstract temporal progression of genres and styles. To the frustration of many readers, Benjamin never gives us a classification of baroque drama—for example, delineating, as Aristotle did for tragedy, its formal or generic characteristics, or even providing a clear idea of its origins. Instead he establishes a constellation of issues within which the mourning plays move: the broad theological justification behind the Protestant Reformation, the particulars of contemporaneous emblem books, the psychology of melancholia, the figures of the sovereign and the intriguer. Instead of "describing" the objects of his inquiry (*beschreiben*) Benjamin thus "circumscribes" (*umschreiben*) them. In baroque fashion, he delimits their edges and boundaries in order to preserve a sense of their variability and historical becoming—both the impossibility of their repetition and the fact that they could have been other than they were.[47]

Barnes also weaves a set of veils around her objects of inquiry in order to avoid fixing in place their essential nature. In "Commissioner Enright and M. Voltaire" she never gives us a description of the Rogues' Gallery, the NYPD's crowning achievement, and barely offers a profile of Enright himself. The assemblage of description, arcana, and philosophical speculation we are given in both this article and "Woman Police Deputy Is Writer of Poetry" imparts a sense that the phenomena that make up the ostensible subject at hand might not in fact have taken place at all. This quality of Barnes's early work is not an inevitable result of its ephemeral, fragmentary nature as journalism or juvenilia. Instead it is a result of Barnes's emerging interest in the baroque. For only the baroque allowed her to stay true to the spirit of O'Grady's wise insight, "One always saves and loses the most at the edges of things."

Resisting Arrest

There is one final reason why Barnes, like Benjamin, might have begun to revive baroque styles and forms at the beginning of the twentieth century. The beginnings of mass distribution systems for images, particularly film and photography, may have been influential for both in this regard. For the fragmentary, unfinished character of baroque theatrical "pieces" offers a good way to capture what both perceived to be the broader fragmentation and anatomization of modern experience with which film in particular was closely implicated.[48] As noted previously, the years of Barnes's journalistic apprenticeship were characterized by the consolidation of the film industry, which meant film's increasing independence from spectators' everyday experience in particular performance or exhibition venues. As numerous film scholars have shown, moreover, with the growth of narrative cinema, filmmakers were also pursuing ever more sophisticated formal techniques for cultivating individual, rather than communal or public, forms of reception.[49] The rise of film spectatorship thus seems to have delivered a familiar and melancholy message from the deep past to both Benjamin and Barnes about the ineffectiveness of the nineteenth century's worldly institutions and organizations and the resulting condemnation of twentieth-century humanity to a fully and futilely "creaturely" existence.[50]

It is thus hardly surprising to find that Barnes also takes up the sav-

ing, potentializing tools of baroque style when she describes the dimin-
ishing landscape of New York City's live entertainments in the 'teens. In
contexts far removed from the criminal justice system, Barnes often sees
sovereign power, criminality, and degradation in New York street life and
in its public culture and entertainments and conveys them via a theatricalized mode of literary allegory. For instance, in "Twingeless Twitchell and
His Tantalizing Tweezers," one of her very first articles for the *Brooklyn
Daily Eagle* in July 1913, Barnes describes a crowd mesmerized by the public extraction of a man's tooth, as performed by a charismatic street-corner
dentist eager to demonstrate his painless technique. One can imagine this
article, written by someone else, as a light-hearted snapshot of Brooklyn
life with reformist sympathies; Twingeless Twitchell, like Frank Norris's
MacTeague, was probably a member of the vanishing breed of unaccred-
ited dentists. Barnes's charge was likely to paint an entertaining picture of
a populist do-gooder who challenges the arbitrary decrees of the professional classes but who also might pose a real danger in need of regulation.

However, such is not quite what we find. The piece, first of all, focuses
not on the dentist but on the rather disturbing absorption of the crowd.
Twitchell's snappy speech—he tells his audience at one point, "I'm here
to collar the dollars"—reveals his persuasive power over what many critics of the sensationalist press were beginning to call the "crowd mind."
His description of the agony of aching teeth acts on the assembled onlookers with an immediacy that is like the push of a button: "groans rise
from the crowd as each one remembers a sleepless night and a swollen
face. . . . He holds them with his glittering instruments" (23). Twitchell
wields a dangerous fascination in his theater of dentistry, as the motions
of his spectators reveal. The crowd gathers not for the promise of a painless extraction but rather because they have ceded their individual identity
to an act of group identification, producing a general excitement whose
strings "Twitchell" is adept at twitching: "A thrill of anticipation ran
through the crowd. People in the el trains twenty feet above leaned out
of the windows, entranced at the sight. A taxi went chugging by and then
suddenly stopped. . . . A chic French maid came tumbling forth from a
nearby millinery shop" (23–24).

Twitchell compares himself to a preacher: "There are two hundred thousand paid persons in this country to tell you how to take care of your souls,
but . . . I am the only man who tells you how to take care of your teeth. Yet
there is as much brimstone contained in an aching tooth as there is in all the

hereafter put together" (22–23). His rhetoric contains highly incongruous juxtapositions, including the comparison of tooth decay to eternal "brimstone," and dentistry to ministry. Instead of a similarity, these metaphors emphasize a tension between irreconcilable, vertical dualities, characteristic of an irredeemably postlapsarian state. The redemption that Twitchell promises from cavities and damnation alike is highly suspect, conveyed by analogy to preachers who are also "paid persons," and to an unbridgeable gap between the external, phenomenal world of bodily decay and the internal feeling of faith necessary to saving the soul. Ultimately, the unmotivated, gratuitously artificial nature of the metaphors in Twingeless Twitchell's speech validates the very connection between the two realms that these metaphors challenge. Incongruously yoking rotting teeth to rotting souls, this mesmerizing speaker suggests the insufficiency of language to capture the "hereafter" in any form.

Barnes's highly theatrical depiction of the actual tooth-pulling casts the unlicensed dentist as an actor playing the lead role in a street-corner theater of cruelty. Twitchell's "platform" is a stage filled with illuminated props—"medicine bottles and instruments that shone wickedly in the light of a flickering acetylene torch that sputtered vain protests at the darkness" (22). His performance is highly interactive, as befits the unreformed nature of the service—and the entertainment—he provides. He finds a willing "victim" in the crowd and bids him mount the stage, where, "with all the finesse of a skilled surgeon performing for an academy of the world's best physicians he eliminated the aching tooth. The unknown arose with a dazed look in his eyes" (24). By imitating the "finesse" of the highly skilled, Twitchell seems to be putting on an act. But that act's imitative nature is belied by the fact that the result *does* in fact seem to have been painless, given the volunteer's hypnotic daze. At the same time, in a final turn of the screw, that very daze evokes, again, the mental state of a crowd-member with no capacity for responsiveness on his own behalf. A volunteer in name only, his "eyes [are] fixed on the glaring lights, like a rabbit . . . charmed by the bead in the python's eye" (24).

The story of "Twingeless Twitchell" is ornately framed. Barnes inserts two characters who witness the scene and are highly disturbed by its transgression of public and private boundaries—"just like washing one's linen in public." They also wonder, as befitting an unlicensed demonstration, if what they have witnessed was actually painless (25). The highly philosophical meditations of both Twitchell and these onlookers give all of them something of the quality of ventriloquist dummies. The reader cannot help but wonder if Barnes really saw what she saw, or if this startling portrait of public dentistry has only been a front for her own confusing platitudes about the "hereafter." Like the highly theatricalized figures populating Benjamin's baroque mourning plays, Twitchell, his volunteer, and the crowd itself are placed "at the edge," in states of ambiguous tension that hold at bay both the promise of reform and the fully creaturely fate of the enthralled and manipulated spectator. "Twingeless Twitchell" ultimately neither entertains us like a crowd at a film nor spurs us to carefully interpret the particulars of the scene and advocate for better-certified dentists. Instead it juggles reality and representation to virtualize and thereby "save" the wandering street-corner theater of dentistry from either fate.

Throughout Barnes's journalism we find the antinomies of the baroque functioning in a similar way in the service of a distinctly modern problematic of spectacle and mass witnessing. For instance, her many pieces on Coney Island—probably written in the service of the amusement park's attempt to attract a more genteel clientele—provide an impressionistic survey of her experience of the tourists, the food vendors, the roller coaster, and the freak shows.[51] Of particular interest are her descriptions of Coney's many performers—from the exhibition dancers to the street children hawking questionable wares—whom she portrays as hovering in states of violent suspense or tension between materiality and transcendence.[52] Visiting a sideshow in 1917, Barnes presumably has her choice of what "freaks" she might describe to her readers. The one she chooses to feature is a former miner who was impaled by a pick in an industrial accident, reflecting the period's preoccupation with the need to ameliorate corporate exploitation and neglect.[53] The demonstrator vividly realizes the story of the man's misfortune for the crowd while turning him around before them:

"An explosion in the mine, a falling of stones and coal, a man pitching forward in the darkness, a stumbling foot, a prayer to God, and then a pick through the body—you see." He gives the young man another twist, tapping him upon the stomach. "Here is where the pick entered." He turns him again, this time tapping him on the back. "And here is where the pick thrust its head out." He smiles, rubbing his hands. The young man turns again, a fixed look upon his face, neither pleasant nor otherwise—a cool, self-possessed

stare—a little uncertain, perhaps, whether to be proud or sorry for
the accident that has made him of interest to the gaping throng.
(279)

On the one hand, the "gaping" crowd's drive to gaze at the impaled gaping body again invokes the growing explanatory appeal of crowd theory's
specular logic. Imagistic words replicate themselves within suggestible
minds, merging those minds into a single group under the sway of one
charismatic figure. From this perspective, the young victim of the mining
company, now exploited for commercial gain to satiate the crowd's mor-
bid fascination, would seem to put the final nail in the coffin of reform-era
faith in the display of victimized body as a means toward ameliorative action. But on the other hand, Barnes's account downplays the persuasive
language of the demonstrator and emphasizes instead the way he fascinates the crowd by making the damaged, incomplete body on display
seem both present and absent at the same time. Turning the man and tapping him on the stomach, he eerily imitates the action of the pick, both
pointing at the body and puncturing it. The demonstration concludes
with a particularly startling *trompe l'oeil* effect in which the demonstrator
blows smoke through the man's body.

As this scene illustrates, Barnes sought a way to respond to the simultaneous demand to energize the volition of her audiences through images
of suffering, and to entertain them by means of those same images. Her
solution is to display them instead as what might justly be called melancholy emblems, suspended somewhere between salvation and damnation.
The freak hovers halfway between an irredeemable bodily existence in
the here and now of the ogling crowd and an unknowable "hereafter" in
which the crimes against his person might find some sort of redress. What
O'Grady would call the right "psychological moment" when the "chance"
of redemption is greatest becomes frozen into place instead as a kind of
memento mori. In the hands of the demonstrator the freak thus becomes an
object not of revulsion or prurience, but instead of strange and disturbing
wonder.

The links between Barnes's emerging neobaroque style and the decline of Reform Era voluntarism are especially clear in the piece she
wrote for the *World* in 1914, mentioned earlier, "My Sisters and I at a New
York Prizefight." Barnes attends a fight in Far Rockaway in order to document the novel presence of women in the crowd and to explore her own

responses as a woman supposedly attending one for the first time. The presence of female spectators at the fight suggests a new and improved venue, one that has been made "safe" for New York women, whose increasing independence and mobility were leading them into public spaces in ever greater numbers, primarily as consumers. The article's subheading promises that it will collapse reform and entertainment together in the service of picturing these desiring female spectators—chiefly, the author herself: "Following the Example of Their French and English Cousins, New York Women Have Begun to Flock to the Ringside—Here Is an Impressionistic Picture of a Boxing Bout before a Mixed Audience by a Woman Who Had Never Seen One."[54] However, Barnes, the "woman who had never seen one," refuses to comply with this mandate. Instead of women enthralled by the spectacle of male bodies in the ring, she paints a picture of women caught in the characteristic pose of the baroque, suspended between high and low:

> After a sudden, uneasy stir, the crowd settles down to watch. Some lean forward with hands, palms outward, thrust between their knees. Others lean back, with arm extended over another's chair. But the women who dared the ringside and the girls further back sit rigidly upright, balanced between wonder and apprehension, their faces . . . set in a fixed smile, as of a man beheaded while a joke still hovered in his throat. (170–71)

The women's "rigid" posture again evokes O'Grady's "psychological moment" of tension between salvation and damnation. Yet their "wonder" at the boxers suggests that they appreciate the performance not for its erotic charge alone but as an artificial spectacle or show, which promises a rather different form of redemption for their threatened souls. Moreover, instead of inviting us, as O'Grady might, to a gentle act of interpretation as to these women's ultimate chances for salvation, Barnes puts their spectatorship itself on display, highlighting its artificiality and theatricality by way of a highly curious metaphor. A beheaded man evoking John the Baptist at the moment of his beheading by Salomé replaces the image we might expect—that of Salomé herself, with her sinuous dance. Yet Salomé hovers in the background nevertheless. The female spectators hang in a kind of suspended animation between these two figures, their rigid, balanced posture resisting the pull toward either.[55] All we can say for sure about this metaphor is that it is unreadable in terms of the prevailing erotic narrative of why women like boxing, even as it manages to suggest that there is something decidedly wrong with liking to watch.

Barnes's boxing report ultimately saves boxing from being understood either as a sport for men or one for women by virtualizing gender itself. Near the end, she delivers a preliminary assessment about women's motivation for attending, based on what she has overheard around her. Not surprisingly, she initially concludes that women are driven by desire and a feminine interest in appearance, in contrast to men: "All the men are aware from the beginning that Bloom has the best of it; somehow they know the things that count in the game, and their interest is proportionate to their knowledge. But the woman's interest lies not in strength but in beauty. She is on the side of the boxer who has a certain trick of the head, a certain curve of the chin, a certain line from throat to brow" (6). Yet shortly thereafter, Barnes closes the piece quite differently, by suggesting that knowledge and desire have only an arbitrary relationship to gender:

> In the blank pause that followed the finish, a man suddenly struck a match. It illumined a face drawn, paler than it had been, with eyes more heavily lidded. The match went out, and I was left to puzzle and question.
>
> Was it, after all, the men in the audience who had been careless and indifferent to pain? Was it the sound of a snapping fan that I had heard? Was it a woman's voice that had murmured, "He has fine eyes?" A woman's hand that had gripped my arm in the dark? A woman's breath that had ceased so suddenly?
>
> And whose voice was it who had cried out just before the finish, "Go to it and show us that you're men?" (173)

There is no knowing how men and women react differently. Men may watch out of fear, and women may be experts at assessing the boxers' skills. As befitting the idea of a single "crowd mind" hungry for sensation, all attempts to interpret gender difference while the fight is in process are doomed to failure, at least until the lights come up. The relationship between gender and desire thus emerges as either arbitrary or simply unknowable in its essence.[56] As far as the all-important question of why women watch boxing, then—all bets are off.

Barnes's journalistic assignments were not confined to official or unofficial sites of entertainment. She frequently put on display the very land-scape of New York itself, turning it into a theatrical scene across which progresses a series of uninterpretable and ominous allegorical signs and figures. In a 1917 assignment for the *World*, "The Hem of Manhattan," Barnes circled the island on a boat to experience Manhattan from the per-spective of a tourist.[57] When she boards, she finds an upper deck filled with "stiff-backed, Middle West school teachers" who are interested only in the "educational parts" of the New York and New Jersey skylines (288, 290). Barnes, alone among them, sees what is really at the edge of the water—prisons, hospitals, a home for "incurables," and the boatload of soldiers mentioned previously, with their "exultant" cries "proclaiming doom and death" (292, 289). This "hem" of Manhattan becomes the real subject of the article, as if to make up for the schoolteachers' refusal to look. For three and a half hours, Barnes mockingly and hyperbolically declares, she suffers "despair" as, like an allegorical procession, "misery, poverty, death, old age, and insanity" pass "in review" before her (288, 286).

Manhattan's "hem," as Barnes describes it, is a place filled with "per-sons at the edge" in a variety of senses. At the water's edge, men pick over trash "like carrion birds" for materials to be reused in mills and paper fac-tories, so that someone can "mak[e] a million upon this terrible resurrec-tion" (291). Then there is human trash, in the form of a home for the "in-sane" and for the elderly who, unlike the physical refuse, have been wholly abandoned. In the tradition of reform journalism, Barnes invites her read-ers to "look for yourselves and see"—and presumably to *do* something, such as redressing the adjacency of the homes for the insane to a garbage barge, or lending a hand to the "gray figures bent like hooks" traversing the lawn of an old men's home. Yet she simultaneously emphasizes the impos-sibility of salvation (291). The incurables and the insane are condemned to their creaturely state. "It was from the water's edge that we crawled in the days of our oblivion . . . and it is to the water's edge that we are brought back again in the end, the great, wet tomb that dries all tears" she intones (ibid.). We can conclude that Barnes's larger point in depicting the people at the "hem" is to stress the impossibility *either* of ameliorating their con-ditions or of finding them entertaining. The very extremity of the language of doom, death, and decay flamboyantly draws attention to its own artifi-ciality. Manhattan's hem is a "great wet tomb" that "dries all tears," a yoking of incommensurable opposites that shatters the contextual ground of the figure itself and denies us a clear picture of what Barnes actually sees from the boat. All we can really conclude about the shoreline is that it is caught between a debased materiality and a transcendent "hereafter," pointing or gesturing toward an unspecifiable beyond.

Eschatological and obscure turns of phase litter this article, as if gazing at the shoreline "in review" has intensified Barnes's tendency to embrace baroque modes of representation. She concludes the piece with a disparaging comment about tourist postcards: "Someone was yawning at my side and buying postal cards, thirty-five views for a quarter, and I had a thousand for nothing! And yet the city gave out only a faint sound of fabric being rent: one-half of the mass pulling one way and the other half in an opposing direction" (294). The faint sound of rending fabric suggests social and psychic destruction. But the open-endedness of the metaphor makes it impossible to attach this meaning, for Barnes gives us no unifying ground or likeness under which to subsume the city and the fabric. Violent, and vividly material, the "rending" that somehow characterizes Manhattan's hem cannot be captured in the image on a tourist's postcard, but nor, Barnes wants to suggest, can it be captured in *any* image—not even that proffered by herself, the allegorist of the ruined cityscape that passes "in review" before her.

The rending fabric in "The Hem of Manhattan" is representative of a larger emphasis throughout many of Barnes's articles on the violent sonic release of obscure, unstated tensions, often via the laugh. The police commissioner's laugh "breaks" out at the joke about the "potential criminal." During backstage antics with Piccadilly chorus girls who are visiting New York for a season, Barnes inserts an obscure epigram: "It is night which has been shattered into laughter; it is also laughter with the restraint of night."[58] Attending a fashion show, Barnes comments, as noted previously, that "the styles have got us by the throat—we laugh as they hurl us to the ground" (208). In these unsettling resolutions, in which nothing is resolved, laughter is unmotivated by character or action, or even by the larger object of Barnes's satire. It functions primarily as an interruption of meaningful speech, forming an accompaniment to Barnes's exaggeratedly artificial metaphors of New York life. We are left to conclude that the laugh and the digressive metaphor gain their meaning from their opposition to the symbolic representation of an imperiled city and its denizens.

Barnes invoked the baroque thematic of a dualistic, melancholy existence with an especial vehemence in her "tour" pieces, like "The Hem of Manhattan," perhaps because of their formal similarity to allegorical processions. Another article of this ilk, published in the *Brooklyn Daily Eagle*, profiled a nighttime outing to Chinatown. The piece offers a particularly clear illustration of the extent to which the declining fortunes of Progressive Era voluntarism influenced the development of Barnes's neobaroque style. For Barnes's piece replicates in a satirical vein the genre of the simulated slum tour, like that of Riis's magic lantern lecture, which encouraged audiences to read allegorical meanings of "awakening, atonement, redemption, nativity, hell's harrowing, and, above all, pilgrimage" into images of tenement life, in order "to emblematize the social rewards of charitable intervention timely met."[59] Such tours can be understood, with reference to O'Grady, as an attempt to spur audiences into action by means of images of "people at the edge, just before they go over."

In "Chinatown's Glories Crumbled to Dust," as in "The Hem of Manhattan," Barnes is critical of the blend of reform and entertainment that characterizes her particular historical moment. She opens by admitting that she and her crew are in search of entertainment. Playing off of readers' familiarity with sensational literature about Chinatown during this period—the neighborhood was popularly associated with gang wars, opium smuggling, and prostitution—Barnes humorously contrasts their expectations with the reality of the slum they discover.[60] "We expected," she reports, "to eat chop suey as the mildest thing we could do, and we expected to taper it off with a tong war" (124). By contrast, her small crowd finds that "there is no Chinatown." The area around Mott Street has been cleaned up and consists mainly of grocery stores, restaurants, Christian missions, poverty, "Yankee" slummers, and crowds. She goes in search of thrills and finds only redemption:, "We . . . were disappointed to find that no nation can so run the gamut of evil . . . that in the end redemption does not put out a claiming hand" (129). Barnes pretends to be disappointed that she doesn't get to experience the evils of Chinatown, thus exposing the hypocrisy of the allegorical tour narrative promulgated by reformers. Both Chinatown's "evil" and its "redemption" are constructions, she suggests, designed simply to titillate white New Yorkers.

However, alongside the satire, Barnes turns to a hyperbolic language of death and decay throughout the article to suggest that the "dust" into which "Chinatown's Glories" have tumbled does indeed place its residents at risk of damnation. Barnes reports that describing Chinatown is difficult, for "in death it is appalling," a statement whose extremity belies the jocular refusal to engage with social realities that marks much of the article. This

strand of gloom continues with her description of a highly theatrical beg-
gar "with wide, lamenting gestures . . . a bitter, staggering, broken, crooked
body wending its way through a broken, crooked street" (127). Further,
the landscape of Chinatown is strewn with mysterious and unreadable
signs—that is, signs that are written in Chinese, and hence unreadable to
her. They are for that reason, portentous: "high, slim boards lettered in tea-
packet alphabets," "weather-beaten signs banging in the wind," "prayers
. . . entangled in the edges of a spiked language" (123–24, 124, 130). There
are also melancholy objects encountered in the course of the tour that
gain significance because of their incompleteness: "odd edibles"; handle-
less, broken china cups; and tables "wherefrom all the pearl inlay has been
pried by tourists" (124, 129). At the center of this urban theater of ruin,
Barnes suggests that there is more, or rather less, in her statement "There
is no Chinatown" than meets the eye. Evoking the baroque *horror vacui,*
she shows Chinatown existing under the pall of a metaphysical void, thus
erasing its inhabitants' individuality and subjectivity to a far greater degree
than any tourist. "For leagues the sky runs in dark blue, dotted by the stars,
until it reaches that space that looks down upon Mott and Pell Streets," she
reports. "Here the sky goes out and the stars die, and there is only a black,
impenetrable, overhead abyss, a black, gaping hole up in eternity" (127).
Barnes's eschatological tone departs most fully here from the arch and satirical reversal of expectations that prevails elsewhere in the article. There
is more going on than a satire on the eradication of local color and culture
by tourism and reform; irony itself quails here before the abyss.

The article, then, does not entirely jettison the allegorical language of
reform. As with Barnes's other forays into the depiction of social problems, the very extremity of the thematic of salvation and damnation, along
with her ornate figures of speech, holds competing narratives in tension.
In the face of demands that she provide either a call to action or an equally
mortifying entertainment on her journey into the depths, Barnes offers up
to her crowd of readers instead the wonder of her startling—and, in this
case, startlingly primitivist—baroque lament.

Perhaps the most important object Barnes seeks to save through her
thematic and formal preoccupation with baroque theatricality is herself.
The tension in her pieces between active reformist spectatorship and paci-
fying entertainment; between criminal transgression and the lure of the
spectacle; and between the enlightened public and the eager, often mesmerized crowd implicated her directly in a way that it never did Walter

Benjamin—or, for that matter, Karl Kraus. As many critics have noted, Barnes was in a highly paradoxical position as a female reporter, charged as she was with investigating the city and its denizens while also putting on a highly entertaining show. All four of her "stunt" pieces for the *New York World* confront this paradox head-on, most famously "How It Feels to Be Forcibly Fed," which exposes the brutal tactics of the opponents of women's suffrage.[61] Barnes often portrays herself in these stunts as a version of the exhibition demonstrator, as featured in her sketches of the Coney Island freak show and the Brooklyn street-corner dentist. This creates a kind of *mise-en-abyme* effect as she appears as her own master of ceremonies or carnival barker, putting her own body on display with a theatrical flourish that at the same time evokes a generalized sense of approaching doom.

Of all Barnes's stunts, the most illuminating in this regard is "My Adventures Being Rescued," published in the *New York World Magazine* in 1914. Discussing the New York City Fire Department's new methods for rescuing people from burning buildings, the piece's overt intention is to publicize urban reform and thereby to cultivate an informed citizenry. Accompanying Barnes's description of the various techniques—involving ropes, ladders, and the like—is a series of photographs of herself (and, in one instance, a fireman), trying out each technique while suspended outside a third-story window. Along with being instructive, of course, the stunt and its accompanying images have entertainment value and, like the boxing match piece, mix titillation and gender subversion. Although the title suggests the sensational rescue of a woman by a man, the photographs in fact show Barnes seeming to rescue the fireman, and then herself. In the first picture, a black-clad Barnes appears with the fireman on the rope, suspended upright with her legs nonchalantly crossed, while he is supine as if reclining in her arms. She appears less the vulnerable girl in need of rescue than the classic "cinema vamp."[62] In the other photographs Barnes is alone, sitting in the rope swing looking at the camera, scaling a wall on a tiny ladder, and staring into the camera with an iron rescue loop dangling from her waist.

Throughout the article, however, Barnes focuses less on the gendered dynamics of her rescue than on the contradictions within the idea of "rescue" itself, given its material and spiritual connotations. She opens the piece with an extended discussion of the larger philosophical paradox that her stunt can be taken to represent—the aspiration to engineer one's own salvation:

"Three times that morning I was saved, and each time I had wished it onto myself. When you get into a fix by the act and workings of providence you are looking for salvation in the natural course of events. It is a different matter to get into danger for the express purpose of making providence practical."[63] Barnes here frames her own stunt as a form of potentially hubristic voluntarism, bringing a cosmic perspective to bear on the larger business of progressive reform itself. Reformers, after all, seek precisely to take a "practical" attitude toward events—like tenement fires—once seen as inevitable. By deliberately placing herself in danger, Barnes suggests that she is tempting fate. Commissioner Enright might well agree.

That philosophical justifications for reform are on Barnes's mind becomes particularly apparent during her description of this stunt's most frightening moment—when she swings out of the very first window. She describes the watching crowd below as a personification of the conflict between reform and entertainment. Her own position on the rope becomes a precarious balancing act in more ways than one:

> Out on the other side of the wall the world had stopped to look on. An auto slowed down. A flock of school children and a couple of "white wings" all stood with heads upturned skyward. A man with a screaming white apron tied about a conscienceless girth, who had been cutting perishable merchandise, grinned in the glare of light shining and dancing upon his cleaver. A drowsy expectancy lay along Sixty-Eighth Street and touched the spectators with a sort of awesome wonder.
>
> I was a "movie," flashing transient pictures upon a receptive sky. (186–87)

The quotations around "movie" remind us that film was not yet a medium in its own right in 1914. Going to the "movies" could still mean encountering an unpredictable lineup of short films and newsreels interspersed with vaudeville routines or educational lectures and demonstrations. Barnes wants us to understand that she is a "movie" here, in other words, because she is putting on an entertaining show. Yet narrative film was also beginning to make its ascendancy as a more lucrative and homogenous form of mass entertainment. This development is reflected in the two groups of spectators. On the one hand, the "conscienceless" butcher with his gleaming knife places Barnes in the position of the threatened and

threatening female bearer of the look, as codified by the emerging gendered representational codes of narrative film.[64] On the other, the school-
children and street sweepers who also gaze skyward remind us of the vanishing educational and hygienic value that reformers hoped movies and
images could provide to the public at large.

Viewed in this context, Barnes's description of her own mysterious,
emblematic appearance overhead draws attention to the insufficiency of
either the worldly narrative of gendered desire associated with the codes
of entertainment and mass spectacle or the theological framework of social reform. Both fail, she suggests, as ways of imbuing her image with
meaning. In their place, the obscure metaphor, "I was a 'movie'" arrogates
the power of meaning-making to Barnes herself. She does not compare
herself to elements within the frame of the "movie," since she describes
herself as the one doing the "flashing" and thereby separates herself from
the images and the screen. But neither does she liken herself to the apparatus of the camera, the mechanism for the production of illusion via
movement and light. The obscure relation between metaphoric tenor and
ground instead virtualizes her presence in the sky, and perhaps also the images of her suspended body that she knew the article's photographs were
going to provide. For it suggests that her body is both there and not there,
both material and immaterial, or "transient." This impression is reinforced
by the "wonder" she attributes to her spectators; they are drawn to watch
not out of a revivified sense of conscience or a destructive, worldly desire,
but instead out of fascination at seeing a trick being performed. Barnes's
movie metaphor conjures up an impossible image of a virtual body in
order to ward off the demand for a spectacle of imperiled femininity that
will arouse either conscience or desire. Rather than a woman about to fall,
Barnes becomes the allegorist of an already "fallen" world.

Because "*all* meaning has ceased to be self-evident" in the allegorical
worldview, as Richard Wolin notes, "the allegorist alone is sovereign. He
is responsible for bestowing meaning in an inverted world."[65] From the
street-corner dentist to the slum tour, the freak to the female boxing fan,
the master "demonstrator" throughout Barnes's New York journalism during the war years is always Barnes herself. As if "turning" a freak on display,
she fascinates through her startling rhetorical turns from figural to literal
and back again. In part these turns are metaphoric, as in the strangely proliferating and groundless descriptions of the New York shoreline in "The

Hem of Manhattan." But they are also prosopoetic, as in "Twingeless Twitchell," where she ventriloquizes the people about whom she writes, imbuing them with bizarrely elevated philosophical language. Above all, they are theatrical and allegorical, as in the unreadable, decaying signs that pervade her accounts of various tourist and slumming sites. The point of Barnes's ornate tropes, ventriloquist technique, and obscure allegorical tours, I have been suggesting, is that they are incompatible with either the older story of the good works performed by institutions such as the mass press and the police, or the newer story of the crowd's destructive desire for images. They suspend both, by displacing the emphasis away from the crowd altogether and onto the demonstrator herself, who always holds the cards. Barnes's "pieces" thereby pursue a cosmic goal—to save history itself from condemnation to a progression of abstract epochs, ideas, or technological innovations, and to restore a sense of phenomenological becoming through the potentiality of language. In this she succeeds, for her baroque staging of New York life suspends her *readers* in between the vanishing hope for social salvation and the unmistakable glare of the publicity era to come.

CHAPTER 5

Gertrude Stein Talking

Dᴜʀɪɴɢ ᴛʜᴇ ꜰᴀʟʟ ᴏꜰ 1934, Gertrude Stein returned to America from Paris for the first time in thirty-one years in order to undertake a publicity tour promoting her work. Stein had long been notorious, particularly in the American press, for her obscure writing, but the popularity of *The Autobiography of Alice B. Toklas* took her celebrity to a new level. Her brooding profile had appeared on the cover of *Time* the previous year, with a quotation taken from *Toklas* as a caption: "My sentences do get under their skin."[1] Twelve front-page columns and copious photographs in New York's daily newspapers announced her arrival in New York aboard the liner *SS Champlain*. Interviews began on board ship even before she disembarked and continued to be published in splashy formats in the front pages of nearly every town she and Toklas visited.[2] By the end of her tour, Americans were encountering Stein's name, along with quotations from or parodies of her writing, in ever more diverse places, from musical revues and phonograph records to courts of law. Courtesy of the relatively new technology of talking film, they could even hear and see her in a Pathé newsreel, reading aloud an excerpt from her successful opera, *Four Saints in Three Acts*, which had recently debuted on Broadway.[3] A testament to Stein's ubiquity in media and popular culture during these years can be found in the Warner Brothers film *Top Hat*, starring Ginger Rogers and Fred Astaire. At one point, Rogers receives a garbled telegram and simply comments in passing, "Sounds like Gertrude Stein!"[4]

Stein had written a series of lectures to deliver on her tour that purported to explain to the public for the first time at any length the philosophy behind her notoriously difficult experimental writing. She also published, en route, a number of magazine and newspaper articles detailing her opinions and impressions of American life, which appeared in venues such as *Cosmopolitan*, *Vanity Fair*, the *New York Herald Tribune*, and the *Saturday Evening Post*. The lectures—"What Is English Literature," "Pictures," "Plays," "The Gradual Making of the Making of Americans,"

"Portraits and Repetition," "Poetry and Grammar," and "Narration"— summarize the different phases of Stein's writing and explain the influences of other forms of literature and art on her work. The articles and interviews, by contrast, capitalize on her celebrity status to comment freely on a variety of issues pertaining to contemporary life in America, from education, to crime, to newspapers, to publicity, to cuisine, to the New Deal. Most strikingly, both her lectures and her articles depart significantly from the difficulty and obscurity of her experimental style, as many reporters noted throughout her tour.[5] "Why don't you write like you talk?" was one of the first questions put to her in New York.[6]

In the pages that follow, I argue that Stein's writings in the 1930s, and the aesthetic principles they affirmed, were a direct response to her experience of her own growing celebrity and to the increasingly mediated nature of American life that it disclosed. The argument bridges two distinct critical approaches to Stein's work—those of pragmatism and historicism. Studies of Stein's relationship to pragmatist philosophy have largely neglected to discuss the more popular magazine and newspaper writings she produced during this period.[7] Much has been made, by contrast, of her lectures, and of the fact that, in them, Stein credits her influences to a distinctively American tradition of writers and thinkers, including Walt Whitman, Ralph Waldo Emerson, Henry James, and, more ambivalently, her former teacher William James. What is often understood to tie Stein to these particular writers and thinkers—and to others she did not acknowledge, such as Wallace Stevens, George Santayana, and Robert Frost—is her radical understanding of language as a force or action that creates meaning rather than reflecting it. Often termed either "pragmatist," or "radical empiricist," after different phases of William James's philosophy, it stands in studied opposition to the idea that language is supposed to reflect static ideals, inherited traditions, or a priori frameworks of meaning. By contrast, historicist literary critics have devoted significant attention to historically contextualizing Stein's aesthetics in relationship to the views and attitudes about American life expressed in her magazine articles and letters. In examining her reactions to aspects of the larger cultural landscape of the Great Depression, including its new culture of celebrity, its media technologies, and its progressive politics, they often find in Stein a devotion to precisely the opposite set of principles.[8]

In fact, such divergent formal and historical approaches have led to strikingly different, and often starkly opposed, convictions about the fun-

damental ideas informing Stein's work as a whole. For critics attentive to
her language's significant debts to the tradition of American modernist
and pragmatist poetics, Stein is a champion of novelty, uncertainty, and
experimentation; a celebrant of the inseparability of reason and feeling;
and an advocate for the impossibility of a stable and centered self, placing
her in the tradition of Emerson and William James. For critics interested
in the *content* of her writing, particularly her convictions about the United
States in the 1930s, by contrast, Stein is a champion of common sense,
certainty, and authority; a celebrant of abstraction and *dis*embodiment;
and a defiant advocate of individualism and autonomy who more properly should be classed with figures such as Ayn Rand and Otto Weininger.[9]
Perhaps no other writer has engendered such incommensurate critical
conclusions about the core tenets of her aesthetic program.[10]

   In examining Stein's writing only on its own terms, and using the lectures as a guide or blueprint, we miss the ways in which the radical poetics
she enshrined in the modernist canon in the mid-1930s was a response to
shifts in the intellectual landscape during the interwar period. Conversely,
in reading Stein's more popular writings only for their historical content,
we miss the ways in which Stein was actually experimenting not just with
language but with the very medium of her publicity itself in the 1930s.
Instead of explaining Stein's aesthetic program as either a manifestation of
the Emersonian literary tradition or as a symptomatic reaction to changes
in material culture, this chapter argues that Stein's articulation of her pragmatist aesthetics in the mid-1930s is instead *addressed* to the conditions of
her fame in America.

   My main focus in this chapter, however, is not the lectures themselves,
but instead the articles in the popular press and other lesser-known writings from this period. What these writings reveal, I argue, is that the radical American literary lineage that Stein officially claimed in her lectures
was not simply a recitation of what she had always been doing. Instead,
emphasizing language as action rather than reflection allowed Stein to
issue a challenge to mass culture and mass communications technologies—and especially to the interwar notion of communication itself as a
mirroring of minds—from within their very forms. Paradoxically, however,
as I show through a reading of her work *Four in America*, Stein's conception of American literature's force or vitality is modeled on her own mass-
mediated celebrity itself, with its power to bring a public sphere into being.

   The first section of the chapter examines the hallmark of Stein's celebrity—a nearly continual debate about whether or not she "communicates." I connect this debate to a profound ambivalence about the centralized message control increasingly being exercised by the expanding and consolidating culture industry that helps to explain the fascination with both Stein's personality and her writing.[11] The second section turns to *Four in America* and to a series of articles Stein wrote for the *New York Herald Tribune*. I argue that Stein shared with progressive thinkers like John Dewey an idea of communication as partaking or sharing and a belief in the social importance of this activity. However, Stein's interest in a revitalized public sphere is coupled with her well-known antipathy toward the progressive institutions of government, press, and education. The dance of pronouns and grammatical shifters in her sentences and paragraphs, I suggest, is designed to rival such institutions by allowing any member of the public to feel him- or herself being addressed—in much the same way as the celebrity's image potentially appeals to each and every fan.

Communicative Labor and Star Turns: Stein in 1930s America

As several recent studies of Stein's American celebrity have made clear, her fame in the 1930s was not in fact new. *The Autobiography of Alice B. Toklas* did not catapult Stein out of obscurity overnight, as critics—led by Stein's own declarations to this effect—have tended to assert. Instead, the book became a bestseller because Stein was already well known, and had been ever since the 1913 Armory Show of avant-garde art.[12] Nor was Stein's celebrity unique when compared to the treatment received by many of her peers. Recent studies of modernism and celebrity have revealed that modernist authors received a surprising amount of often thoughtful publicity during the interwar period in both the United States and Britain. In part, this was because distinctions between elite and popular readerships and publics that are now commonplace were then still in the process of formation.[13] James Joyce's *Ulysses*, for instance, was published in the United States while Stein was on tour and was reviewed favorably on the front pages of many newspapers. Joyce himself appeared on the cover of *Time* the year after Stein did (and again in 1939, with the publication of *Finnegans Wake*), and he, too, was parodied widely for his incomprehensible style.[14] Moreover—just like Stein—Joyce, Fitzgerald, Eliot, Pound, Lewis, Dos Passos, and others actively fashioned *themselves* into celebrity authors, as Aaron Jaffe has shown.[15] Drawing on such studies, Jonathan

Goldman has recently suggested that the modernist "cult" of the author—in which the author is understood both to transcend and to be dependent upon audience recognition—helped to create the phenomenon of twentieth-century celebrity itself. Modernism and celebrity are thus "mutually constitutive, two sides of the same cultural coin."[16]

These recent accounts from the new field of "celebrity studies" have done much to further uncover the close links between elite modernist writers and the popular or mass audiences they supposedly rejected, a project that has been underway for some time.[17] Yet in emphasizing celebrity as an interpretive paradigm or cultural logic, celebrity studies has tended to downplay the broader cultural debates that celebrities often help to mediate. The historical roots of celebrity suggest that the phenomenon is itself inseparable from the public sphere, as critics writing in the *Publications of the Modern Language Association*'s recent special issue on the topic have argued.[18] Joseph Boone and Nancy Vickers note in their introduction that, because celebrities are "created by and subject to the vagaries of public opinion," they are at the same time "the very substance of a public discourse through which communities negotiate mores, values, and politics."[19] As such, however, celebrities mediate a debate and discussion that is infused with "private" feeling, and hence far from the disinterested public exercise of reason through print celebrated in Jürgen Habermas's influential definition of the public sphere.[20]

Stein in the 1930s offers an example of the way that celebrities, despite and even because of the emotion they engender, can become the "substance" of a public discourse with wider significance. The discourse in question regarding Stein had to do with communication, a topic with no small relevance in a mass society in a time of economic depression and social unrest. As I noted earlier, and discuss in more detail in the second half of this chapter, much was made on Stein's arrival of the unexpected clarity of her speech and writing, which had resulted from changes she made to her style during and after the writing of *The Autobiography of Alice B. Toklas*. This shift provided a useful "hook" for articles; throughout Stein's tour, editors called on scholars, critics, and other "experts"—including psychiatrists—to revisit their earlier opinions about her. During and after the Armory show and the publication of Stein's *Tender Buttons,* many of them had condemned her more repetitive patterning of words and sentences as difficult, obscure, or a hoax, and her personality as decadent or mentally ill. Fifteen years later, the experts refused to raise their opinion of her, despite the changes in her style. Stein, they now argued, was unable to "communicate." Whereas in her earlier style she had been unintelligible or mad, in her later style, they claimed, she was simply unwilling or unable to use language as a vehicle for conveying a meaning to a reader.

For instance, a critic for the *Washington Post* wrote that Stein's "cardinal sin" was "neglecting her reader" and failing to "communicate directly, clearly and with efficiency," for "writers will be first and necessarily judged on the amperage, the current, of their communication."[21] So envisioned, communication was a form of labor or work that Stein was too lazy to undertake, or too incapable. "It is simply a natural aversion to work that explains Gertrude Stein's shorthand English," another critic notes, in a debate about Stein staged in the *Golden Book* magazine in January 1935.[22] Even the behaviorist psychologist B. F. Skinner inveighed against Stein's inability to communicate. In a widely cited article in the *Atlantic Monthly*, Skinner defined her earlier, more experimental work as automatic, unconscious writing by a "second self," a phenomenon Stein had studied when working in the Harvard psychology laboratory as a student. The more recent work, Skinner argued, was simply a conscious attempt to communicate that was unable to fully shake off the automatic behavior. Despite Skinner's specialty in behavior, not meaning, he bizarrely condemns those aspects of Stein's writing that he sees as pure behavior for their lack of meaning. When Stein writes only "what her arm [writes]," Skinner notes, "it is an arm that has very little to say."[23]

While Stein's writing was condemned for not communicating, her personal presentation was much more accessible and friendly than many had expected. As Kirk Curnutt has noted, Stein's greater accessibility in person fit well into the common trope of the celebrity's public and private self in the 1930s.[24] Much like the celebrities Stein met on her tour, such as Charlie Chaplin or Mary Pickford, her public and media appearances seemed to reveal an authentic self beneath or behind her popular image. A headline in a society column about Stein's appearance at a charity fundraiser, also in New York, proclaims "Captures Audience by Her Frankness," while the article notes her "humor and total lack of artificiality. . . . She talked to everyone just as if they were intimate friends."[25] "Her pleasant and rich voice has been heard on the radio," notes another critic for the *Washington Post* in December 1934, "but still, I believe, the average person yet thinks of her as, in the *New Masses'* phrase, the apostle of gibberish."[26] Seen behind the closed doors of a society function, or heard in the supposedly greater intimacy of the radio, Stein's real self was disclosed, in distinction from the image that others had of her.[27]

Despite the accusations that Stein's work had no social value, the duality between the candid author and her celebrity image was a way for many to claim that Stein, behind the scenes, *was* "working" at communication. Reporting for the *New York Herald* on one of Stein's first lectures, at Columbia, Joseph Alsop noted that Stein's personality impressed the assembled experts more than her writing, but he also declared that Stein and Toklas were "dressed for hard work" when they arrived and that Stein pronounced her words "without a trace of affectation."[28] In an article about Stein's address to "society leaders" and Museum of Modern Art members at the Colony Club in her very first lecture, the *Times* emphasized her simplicity, not complexity. "The speaker's dress, almost like a nun's, forms contrast with brilliance of the audience," the subheading notes, while the article contrasts Stein's dress with her listeners' gowns and the "crimson damask hangings of the white walled ballroom."[29] Bantering easily and engagingly with reporters, reading her writing aloud and creating what Alsop called "a feeling of warm attention in the air, as if the people present were half catching what was being said and liking the speaker," the "real" Stein, these reports tell us, somehow makes her point—but not by conveying her ideas to an audience.

Although Stein was not the only literary author given front-page coverage, nor was she unique in being recognized as a "real person" beneath her public image, there was one compelling paradox that made her celebrity in the 1930s distinctive. Evidently she communicated somehow by *not* communicating, at least not in the sense of sending a message. Stein's perplexing duality is the subject of numerous headlines—"Gertrude Stein Arrives but 'Parks' Stutter," for instance, or "Gertrude Stein Arrives and Baffles Reporters by Making Herself Clear . . . Declines to Be Abstruse in Explaining Why Most of Her Writings Are."[30] It unites the many seemingly unrelated instances in which Stein's name is cited in passing, from Ginger Rogers's garbled telegram in *Top Hat* to a news report about the discovery of the neutrino.[31] Finally, as noted previously, it was recognized as her calling card to fame. Reporting on why various "Matinee Idols Find Spotlight Is Boring," for instance, the *Washington Post* notes of Stein, "She is certainly an attractive old lady, and if she is actually the world's greatest literary hoax she manages to produce an extraordinary effect of sincerity, though nobody knows quite what she is talking about."[32] Stein takes her place in the pantheon of celebrities, in other words, not because she doesn't make sense, but because in some mysterious way she does, frustrating the experts and delighting everyone else.

One of the major reasons Stein became the "substance" of a public discourse about communication, I argue, pertains to technological changes in the news media.[33] For the media of Stein's publicity, like her speech and writing, had also recently become surprisingly clear. The 1930s were notable for a general increase in the size of news photographs, a greater emphasis on contrasts in scale, more close-ups with tighter cropping, the use of captions for photographs, and the invention of the action photo layout, showing successive images of an extended action.[34] Writing of Margaret Bourke-White's photography for *Life,* founded in 1936, John Tagg argues that the hallmark of American press photography by the 1930s "is not that it inscribes an act of seeing, but that it constructs a legible message: a pictorial summation from which the arbitrariness of chance and the excess of particularity that afflict photography are strangely drained."[35] More accurate forms of photomechanical reproduction, in other words, frequently brought with them an aspiration to expunge all traces of subjective viewpoint or rhetorical persuasion from the image.

This new age of communicative transparency finds a resonant metaphor in the advent of talking film, in 1927. The coming of sound had been accomplished over a lengthy process of trying to clear static and noise and to make the voice audible, within recent memory of Stein's visit.[36] In a similar way, captions had begun to be used to provide an explanatory "voice" to the events depicted in the newspaper or magazine image. It is possible even to speak of a broader drive for technological and corporate synchronization in the 1930s, in which executives, politicians, and business leaders pursued communicative clarity on a national and societal scale by attempting to control and disseminate meaning from central sites, through the mass production of radios, the rise of radio broadcasting, the consolidation of sound engineering companies with the motion picture industry, the beginnings of television, and the changes in photojournalism mentioned previously.[37] Even the expert voices available to discuss Stein in the news can be understood as a part of this wider cultural preoccupation with efficiently conveying meaning. A new ideal of press "objectivity" had come to the fore that called explicitly for both specialist reporters and the input of experts, in order to filter out excess information that might overwhelm the public.[38]

The media and media technologies through which the public encountered Stein, however, suffered from the same paradox as her speech. In both cases a surprising new communicative clarity was inseparable from the irrational semantic noise of emotion, intimacy, and desire. Stimulating consumers to buy products was the main goal of the extensive emphasis on legibility and message control in the news and entertainment media, and across the consolidation of the media industry more generally. These products very much included celebrities themselves. For the celebrity's face to inspire love and adoration, that face must be seen with as much clarity as possible.[39] Using close-ups, action layouts, and extensive captioning, the visual look of Stein's coverage was no exception. Images of Stein and Toklas getting into airplanes, riding in Fords, and greeting reporters testified as much to the widespread preoccupation with communicative clarity as they did to the cult of the celebrity.

A critical discourse about communication may have come into being through Stein's celebrity, therefore, because the very form of that celebrity highlighted an irreconcilable gap between the communicative clarity advocated by experts and the kind Stein herself seemed to be providing. One of the most striking aspects of any perusal of Stein's press coverage is encountering her language, in all its semantic multiplicity, in the form of headlines, captions, and pull quotes—all forms devoted, as Stein's critic cited earlier puts it, to "communicat[ing] directly, clearly and with efficiency." One article's coverage of Stein's onboard interview in New York Harbor exemplifies the jarring results, laid out as it is in the *Saturday Review of Literature* like a filmstrip, a caption under each still (see Figure 3).[40] The editor synchronizes Stein's voice with her face at the moment that she seems to be proclaiming that her writing is in fact clear—"I think I write as I talk." But is Stein saying she writes in the same style as she talks? Or, is she staying that she writes at the same *time* as she talks? Perhaps this second interpretation has occurred to the photo editor as well, for, in the middle frame, the camera has captured Stein with one hand on the arm of a deck chair, making it look as if she is writing at that very moment. Stein undermines even this attempt to clarify her meaning through the synchronization of voice and image, however.[41] For she then apparently tells the serious circle of grey-suited men looking at her intently, "You can hear better than you can see."

The debate about whether or not Stein communicated, moreover, was a popular and public version of what had become a ubiquitous topic in

4|3|3 4   THE SATURDAY REVIE

Exile's Retui

Saturday Review N

Interviewers meet Gertrude Stein on board the Champlain, as she returns for a visit after thirty-one years abroad. "Why don't you write as you talk?"

"I write as words come up naturally to me. I think I write as I talk. . . . I do talk as I write, but you can hear better than you can see."

"I like to talk to people. I am always wandering about the streets having conversations with people. I like single human contacts. . . ."

Figure 3. Clipping from "Exile's Return, and Other Celebrations," Saturday Review of Literature, November 3, 1934. Gertrude Stein and Alice B. Toklas Papers. Yale Collection of American Literature, Beinecke Rare Book and Manuscript Library, Yale University.

philosophy and social thought during the 1920s and 1930s. As John Durham Peters has shown, "communication" had at least three different connotations during the post–World War I period, the first of which, I find, was particularly in evidence in criticisms of Stein: the accurate sharing of consciousness.[42] Sounding like the Cambridge critics C. K. Ogden and I. A. Richards in *The Meaning of Meaning* (1923), Stein's critics castigated her for her inaccuracy as a speaker, accusing her of failing to work hard enough to replicate her intentions in other minds. The tone of moral outrage evident in such claims is closely connected to a perception also shared by Ogden and Richards that such a failure was a barrier to rational social organization and functioning, especially given the distractions available in other communications media.[43] Motivating those accounts may well also have been the second—closely related—definition of communication Peters notes: the propagandistic manufacture of consent. With hundreds clamoring to get in through the door to her lectures, Stein might well have been viewed as propagandistic, in the sense that she was charming people with her personality and disseminating symbols that worked primarily by playing on the emotions (since they evidently didn't work any other way). If so, it could not have helped matters that in her celebrity coverage she was often described in militaristic terms, her hair close-cut like a "general," "crossing swords" with reporters.[44] This second definition of communication as the manufacture of consent was central to empirical communications research, which was also a product of the interwar period in the United States.[45] As Peters shows, the mentalism of both definitions of communication, in which meanings are found not in words but in minds and in references to objects, meant that communication always entails the "specter of miscommunication."[46] Communications theorists aspire to a utopic "concourse of consciousness," but perpetually fear society might become a "maze of isolated souls" vulnerable to propagandistic control.[47]

I see a third definition of communication also noted by Peters— communication as partaking—at play, more subtly, in the descriptions offered of Stein's "hard work" and of the "warm attention" she elicited when she spoke. As propounded by Martin Heidegger and John Dewey, communication as partaking, Peters points out, is closer to the term's etymological root as imparting, sharing, or making common.[48] For Heidegger, writing in 1927, human sociality and the constitution of the self in language are fundamental givens, not goals to be achieved; communication therefore entails the interpretation and recognition of this "thrownness" into the world.[49] John Dewey, writing the same year in a more practical and democratically minded vein in *The Public and Its Problems*, makes a similar point that "there is no sense in asking how individuals come to be associated. They exist and operate in association."[50] Language is a "transaction," not a mirroring of minds—a way of participating in the social world that enables the participants to recognize the primary facts of their relationality, not a way to bring that relationality into being (13). While Stein often played in her interviews with the paradox of whether or not she communicated in the mind-to-mind sense, she herself also highlighted the idea on her tour that her language was a form of sharing or partaking. She parries reporters' questions in the filmstrip sequence noted earlier, for example, by simply saying, "I like to talk to people. I am always wandering about the streets, having conversations with people."

Had he taken note of it, Dewey might have seen in Stein's language a version of communicative partaking, and in her celebrity a kind of public sphere in the making. For Dewey put forward a compatible definition of the public as communicative partaking during his own debate with the media critic Walter Lippmann, a proponent of the propaganda theory of communication. In response to Lippmann's claim that the public's vulnerability to emotional persuasion made rational public debate and an informed public into a fantasy, Dewey argued in *The Public and Its Problems* that the public sphere was instead merely temporarily "eclipsed," and capable, under the right conditions, of return.[51] Agreeing that the public was in crisis, Dewey identified the problem not as one of fantasy but of too many publics that were diffused, scattered, and inchoate (110–42).[52] The public, in short, was an inchoate potentiality, not a fantasy—a virtual experience in need of the right conditions to be actualized, and best understood, in any case, as perpetually experimental and in process:

> The local face-to-face community has been invaded by forces so vast, so remote in initiation, so far-reaching in scope and so complexly indirect in operation, that they are, from the standpoint of the members of local social units, unknown. . . . At present, many consequences are felt rather than perceived; they are suffered, but they cannot be said to be known, for they are not, by those who experience them, referred to their origins. It goes, then, without saying that agencies are not established which canalize the streams of social action and thereby regulate them. Hence the publics are amorphous and unarticulated. (131)

For Dewey, the problem was losing touch with the relations between thought and world, not the mirroring between inside and outside that constituted what Lippmann called "the pictures in our heads." He condemned "advertising, propaganda . . . the 'featuring' . . . of passing incidents" not for manipulating minds but for "violat[ing] all the moving logic of continuity" (168). Relations between, rather than within, individual minds were what mattered, Dewey claimed. Thoughts were not internal to persons and their habits, but instead, by virtue of thought's grounding in shared language and experience, "secreted in the interstices of habits" (160).

Dewey's solution for a diverse, scattered, and distracted populace lay not in a cadre of experts, as Lippmann proposed, but in better "agencies" of education, press, and government, able to channel the impersonal movement of thought toward better habits, selves, and publics. In other words, Dewey did not advocate for the press to apply scientific techniques to itself, nor for more scientists to write for a broader public, nor for intelligence workers to replace the public. Instead, mass media should be reconceived as a perpetual experiment in helping people to recognize the fundamental human relationality denied or occluded by the distracting and antidemocratic forces of a mass consumer society. This entailed that art and science must somehow fuse together within the practices of mass communication itself. In Dewey's words, "the highest and most difficult kind of inquiry and a subtle, delicate, vivid and responsive art of communication must take possession of the physical machinery of transmission and circulation and breathe life into it" (184). He urged the mass press to strive for what he paradoxically called the "application" of science "*in* life."[53] When contrasted to this obscure and optimistic vision, Lippmann's crisp and skeptical argument for relying more on expert opinion in reporting the news and running the government would have far more influence in the decades to come.[54]

In surveying the media of the interwar period and finding it devoid of the immanent forms of inquiry and the communicative practices necessary to produce and nurture a democratic public, Dewey might be forgiven for overlooking Stein's celebrity coverage and the appearance in the press of her experimental writing. Gazing at the celebrity visage would perhaps count for Dewey among the habits inimical to nurturing a dynamic and interactive public sphere. Yet, under the very noses of the experts, Stein's celebrity and her art were bringing into being an inchoate public debate, infused with feelings not yet recognized, about the issues at stake in Dewey's disagreement with Lippmann.[55] Moreover, as I discuss in the next section, Stein saw her public appearances and her writing for the mass press as precisely a way to "breathe life" into the press's "physical machinery of transmission and circulation." Through her celebrity and her writing, Stein sought to help her audiences recognize the primacy of their relations to each other—but also to turn that recognition itself against the very progressivism Dewey espoused.

The Force of a Caress: Celebrity, Writing, and the Virtual Public Sphere

The year before her lecture tour, as Stein was already basking in the celebrity brought by the success of *Toklas*, she was also completing work on one of her stranger literary pieces. *Four in America* styles itself as a study of four representative Americans—Wilbur Wright, George Washington,

Henry James, and Ulysses S. Grant. But it is not a study of their characters, the historical events in which they participated, or their significance for literature or history. Instead, the subject is what each of them would have done had he pursued a different occupation. Four questions printed on the first page of the book, under the title, establish its aims: "If Ulysses S. Grant had been a religious leader who was to become a saint what would he have done. If the Wright brothers had been artists that is painters what would they have done. If Henry James had been a general what would he have had to do. If General Washington had been a writer that is a novelist what would he do."[56] Among these questions, the latter two would seem to hold especial relevance for the author herself. Stein had claimed in *Toklas* that she had recently begun to consider Henry James to be "her forerunner . . . the only nineteenth century writer who being an american felt the method of the twentieth century."[57] In the "George Washington" section of *Four in America*, moreover, Stein makes clear that she identifies with the father of her country as much as she does with James, noting, "George Washington was fairly famous because he wrote what he saw and he saw what he said. And this is what I do" (168). We can infer that Stein's hypothetical questions, particularly about what would have happened if the novelist had been a famous general and the famous general a novelist, might have something to do with her celebrity, the new phase of her success in America, and the project she was about to undertake to retool her image as a distinctively American writer.

As Sean McGann has recently pointed out, Stein compared her work as a writer with that of the leadership of American presidents throughout the 1930s, setting herself up as a rival to Progressive reform and its institutions of press, schools, and the state.[58] McCann notes that Stein repeatedly described herself, particularly during the Depression years, as a representative American, dedicated to freedom from government control and to an aggressively laissez-faire economic policy. Seeking to displace the influence of presidential rhetoric, the state, educational institutions, and the press, Stein, on her tour, frequently "cast her own public expression as an inspiring and educational force that promised to issue in democratic renewal."[59] *Four in America* is exemplary in this regard. For instance, in "George Washington," Stein explicitly condemns Democratic Party leaders, including Woodrow Wilson and Franklin Delano Roosevelt, whom she sees as guilty of "seduction," presumably because of their oratorical prowess. Elsewhere Stein described the interest in "organization" that began at the end of the nineteenth century—likely meaning progressivism—as "a passion for being enslaved."[60]

While much of the content of *Four in America* is accurately described by McCann as conveying a message of "radically antisocial individualism,"[61] the James and Washington sections focus, paradoxically, on a certain kind of writing that could only with extreme difficulty be described as individualistic. The Henry James section describes a discovery Stein claims to have recently made while struggling to translate a poem by her friend George Hugnet. Translating uncovered for Stein the existence of two seemingly incommensurate ways of writing: "There is the way when you write what you are writing and the way when you write what you are going to be writing or what some other one would have written if they had been writing" (127). Henry James, Stein asserts, "is a combination of the two ways of writing and that makes him a general a general who does something" (137). James is Stein's "forerunner," she suggests here, because he combines these two ways. He works hard to plan what he will say, which allows him to merge minds with his audience—he can write exactly what "some other one would have written if they had been writing." At the same time, however, James is absorbed in the immediate experience of putting words on the page, forgetting his audience and simply writing "what" he is writing. Stein also implies that this is true of George Washington. He "wrote what he saw," she tells us, suggesting that he efficiently transported his own mental pictures—say, of Valley Forge or the Delaware—into others' minds. But he also "saw what he said," experiencing the words themselves, in all of their sensory immediacy, emerging from quill to parchment.

The two ways of writing recall Stein's lifelong aspiration to make her writing capable of providing both "knowledge about" the world—conceptual, reflective, and distanced—and "acquaintance" with it—a more fundamental, direct, sensory knowing that precedes reflection. As many critics have noted, Stein sought for writing what her teacher William James, with his development of radical empiricism, sought for philosophy.[62] In her early portrait phase, for example, by varying the sounds and rhythms of her clauses and sentences, Stein tried to make her writing into a literal extension of the senses, sounds, and rhythms of the person she was writing "about." That way she could provide both an immediate, precognitive, and sensory experience of "acquaintance" with the person, and at the same time a reflection, copy, or description, or "knowledge about."[63] In 1923, for instance, Stein had been working on a series of individual portraits of artists and others she knew, in which she repeated a single word with variations for several lines, toward the same goal of capturing both "acquaintance" and "knowledge about." "If I Told Him," a portrait of Picasso, sounds very different than *Four in America:* "Shutters shut and open so do queens. Shutters shut and shutters and so shutters shut and shutters and so and so shutters and so shutters shut and so shutters shut and shutters and so. And so shutters shut and so and also. And also and so and so and also."[64] Seeking to capture the rhythm of Picasso's living presence in her "portrait" phase, Stein focuses closely on the changing rhythms of her writing on the page, concentrating on minute variations of sound, rhythm, and look. She thus aspires to extend the changing rhythms that make up the essence of Picasso into her writing. But we also learn something "about" Picasso at the same time. Stein strongly implies that he is a diminutive tyrant by invoking Napoleon ("If Napoleon if I told him if I told him if Napoleon" [ibid.]). She is perhaps offering herself as the alternative reigning modernist—a "queen" of formal innovation to rival the Cubist master.

Throughout her lectures, she describes the development of her style in terms that recall this duality, grounding the two ways of writing in a distinctively American tradition of which she and Henry James are the latest exemplars. In "The Gradual Making of the Making of Americans," for instance, she describes moving away from *The Making of Americans,* with its project to provide a "complete description" of every class or kind of person, and embracing instead the more poetry-like portraits of people in order to focus more directly on "a whole human being felt at one and the same time, in other words while in the act of feeling that person."[65] In "Plays," Stein condemns conventional theater for the "syncopation" it induces in the spectator, who must cope with the immediate acquaintance with the body on stage, while trying to remember the names of the characters and to follow the plot. Finally, in "What Is English Literature," Henry James appears again as a herald of Stein's coming because of his two ways of writing. In prophetic language, Stein describes how James and his predecessors Hawthorne, Emerson, and Washington Irving feel their way toward the full flowering of the American literary tradition in the twentieth century (and the arrival of Stein herself). Contrasting James's writing to that of the English Edwardians, Stein notes, "The others all stayed where they were, it was where they had come but Henry James knew he was on his way. That is because this did connect with the American way. And so although they did in a way the same thing, his had a future feeling and theirs an ending. It was very interesting."[66] The difference between Henry James and the Edwardians and between American and English literature more broadly, Stein suggests, is that American writers pay attention to the feeling of writing as it is being written, not just to the concepts they are trying to convey to "future" readers. As a result, reading James or Stein or American writing in general, she often suggests, makes it possible to both feel the living rhythms of the subject at hand and to know something about that subject at the same time.

In *Four in America*, then, written the year before her tour, we might read Stein as simply trying out her central claim for American writing for the first time. She has always been Henry James or George Washington, she announces, both writing what she sees and seeing what she writes. However, *Four in America* uses these figures to explore the problem of communication itself in a more direct way than the lectures do. Just as her contemporaneous critics noted, Stein, in her newly accessible post–*Toklas* mode, sounds in this work as if she is grappling with the problem of how to transfer a meaning to someone else's mind.[67] Washington and James, as she depicts them, confront a stark choice that sounds a lot like the one plaguing communications theorists in the 1920s and 1930s, between what John Durham Peters calls a "dream of instantaneous access" between minds, completely safe from coercion or persuasion, and "a labyrinth of solitude" that leaves them vulnerable to it.[68] They manage somehow to have it both ways, solipsistically absorbed in present immediacy of their own writing— "writing what you are writing"—while telepathically writing exactly what is in their audience's mind, or "what some other one would have written." That Stein has contemporaneous debates about communication on *her* mind in setting up this strange thought experiment is suggested by what she has to say about the question of clarity. Citing the founder of RCA and NBC, who was a confidant of Woodrow Wilson and other U.S. presidents, Stein declares in "Henry James": "Mr. Owen Young made a mistake, he said the only thing he wished his son to have was the power of clearly expressing his ideas. Not at all. It is not clarity that is desirable but force" (127).

While we might expect "force" to be linked with coercion, throughout *Four in America*, it is "clarity"—both of presidential rhetoric and the consolidating media industry—that Stein describes as coercive. "What is an audience," Stein writes in "Henry James," "Everybody listen. That is not an audience because will everybody listen. Is it an audience because will anybody listen" (121). Audiences may not even exist when "everybody" is clearly commanded to listen, Stein suggests, for insofar as a particular audience understands "Everybody listen!" to be addressed to itself, it can refuse to do so. Neither, however, does an audience exist if no one is addressed; then, no one listens, either. Audiences come into being only when the writer or speaker leaves open the question as to whether anybody at all, rather than "everybody" in a particular group, will listen. To write with "force" in other words, is to write in such a way as to raise the question, "Will anybody listen?"

While Stein sets up the problem of communication on Lippmann's or Odgen and Richards's terms, then, she ultimately offers a solution in terms that more closely recall Dewey. For we are led to conclude that the "force" or "vitality" of the combined ways of writing achieved by George Washington and Henry James cannot be reduced to one individual's intention-driven, effortful transfer of meaning between minds. George Washington, Stein tells us, had an audience, but not because—as one might expect, being a general—he commanded people to listen. Instead, Stein states, it was because he wrote out of habit. "Anybody who has the habit can write a novel and George Washington had the habit of novel writing," she writes. "And it is touching a habit is touching if any one listens to it as a habit" (175). In place of the coercion of "everybody listen," Stein imagines a way of speaking or communicating that allows habits to "listen" to one another in the absence of subjects who fully possess or are defined by those habits.[69] This way of speaking or communicating can be reduced neither to the solipsistic nor to the telepathic. It can be "a caress" but— since it also embodies a kind of force—"it can not be tenderness" (127).

Stein's notion of communicative force, since it does not originate in conscious agents or their intentions, suggests that she, like Dewey, sees communication in nondualistic and anti-foundationalist terms, and that she understands such terms to offer an alternative way to imagine the creation of publics and to achieve rational forms of social organization. Rather than working hard to replicate her intentions in the minds of her hearers, Stein promises to help her audience make a habit out of listening to language in such a way that they can recognize what underlies or allows for linguistic habits, and also for the coercive habits of thought she sees being fostered by mass consumer society. By "habits" she evidently means, with Dewey, conventional forms of language and communication, such as the novel that Washington "might" have been writing, or the radio dramas and advertising that Owen Young and RCA did bring into being. For Dewey, however, the agencies that help audiences—or students, or publics—recognize and re-form their habits are flexible and experimental institutions, whether art institutions, educational institutions, or the state. Stein thus is offering her own writing in *Four in America* as a replacement for such institutions, and as an experimental practice that, in Dewey's words, can "canalize the streams of social action and thereby regulate them."

Of necessity, Stein and Dewey have disparate views of exactly what it is that is imparted, shared, or made common in the act of communication. Dewey can hear in the "interstices" of communicative habits a form of authentic human community and shared experience that is vital to the functioning of democracy. Stein, by contrast, hears in the interstices of such habits only the shared experience of the potentiality of reference. What the force or vitality of George Washington's and Henry James's writing, as well as her own, allows audiences to hear is the question "Will anybody listen?" What is held in common, therefore, is not authentic human community for Stein, still less the potential for democracy or any other form of governance, but instead a shared capacity for meaning—the potential "generality" of language.[70]

Four in America's George Washington and Henry James are not just forceful; they are also celebrities. Their status as such is conveyed both by Stein's preoccupation with Washington's fame and James's audience and by the challenge they both present to theories of communication as mental transfer—which was exactly the same challenge Stein's new style was beginning to pose to the experts. Stein also suggests that James and Washington have a form of visibility particularly characteristic of the theatrical celebrity—a visibility she was about to assume in her many public lectures—a live, asymmetrical, and one-to-many relationship with an audience.[71] "Come often to see me is not said by a general," Stein writes, evidently imagining a general, very unlike Mae West, standing at the head of her army, "but any one can see a general indeed yes any one. Henry James was a general" (154). Here, in contrast to John Dewey, Stein links the experimental practice of democracy with the charisma of the celebrity, in her potential address to each of her many fans.[72]

During her lecture tour, Stein deployed both her celebrity and her writing to address more specific concerns in regard to communication in a series she wrote for the *New York Herald Tribune* that took up some of the hot-button topics of the day. Throughout this series, which addressed, among other topics, the press, education, and politics, Stein subtly suggested that her own writing could function as a better "agency" for addressing "the public and its problems" than many of the currently existing ones. In the article "American Newspapers," Stein took up Dewey's concern, shared with many others, about the loss of face-to-face communication characteristic of small-town life and criticized newspaper reporting for its inability to replicate it. For Stein, as for Dewey, what was lost in the shift to a mass medium is not a species of mental communion; instead, change, variation, and the emergence of the new has been foreclosed, obviating the possibility of recognizing a common and communal immersion in temporal becoming. Every time the paper "mentions anybody or anything it has to say the same thing using the same words," Stein notes, "otherwise it would be a shock to the newspaper reader who has gotten used to this formula about this thing, think of Will Rogers, or the comic strips or what they say about me."[73] Instead of reinforcing habits and formulas, it should be the job of newspapers, she argues, to give readers the "feeling" that "what happened the day before . . . happened on that day the same day and not on the day before" (89).

To "feel" that the things that happened yesterday happened today is not to enter a timeless, ideal realm, for Stein is here working once again with the distinction between "acquaintance"—a more immediate, preconscious knowledge—and "description"—or conceptual knowledge. What Stein wants the daily paper to do for the American reader, then, is to enable a conceptual knowledge of time as becoming, by uniting what they know about the quantitative difference between yesterday and today with an awareness of time as something very similar to the Bergsonian *durée*—an unquantifiable, indivisible continuum between past and present.[74] Stein argues that this awareness of becoming can be established through text and type that has a varying rhythm and look on the page. The real problem with the contemporary paper, then, is that it subordinates its own varying rhythm to a single pattern, thus yielding only "knowledge about." It follows a law: "You must not change the tone nor the words that succeed each other." By contrast, newspapermen of the past could modify the look of the type and images to their hearts' content even as they proclaimed the news of the day:

The yellow press that is really the American press then had in every
way by headlines by scare lines, by short lines and by long lines,
by making all the noise and sound they could with their words
and lines tried to . . . mak[e] it be as if the news that had happened
on one day had happened not on that one day but on the day the
newspaper day. And they did and they did do it they almost did
do it and they almost make it come to be that what happened six
hours earlier was what happened six hours later. (89)

The yellow papers' "writing" achieves a variability of visual emphasis, with
the result that readers gain not only the feeling but also, almost, the conceptual knowledge of a continuity between present and past. But the way
Stein writes this passage makes clear that she can do an even better job at
enabling this recognition—and, in fact, she *is* doing a better job, since this
article is itself appearing in the newspaper. Both repetition and variation,
quantitative and qualitative difference are to be found in the line "and they
did and they did do it they almost did do it," as the repetition of "and they
did" varies its look and rhythm over the course of the line. Stein, too, is experimenting with "words and lines" as she writes these sentences, in order
to produce both knowledge about and acquaintance with the medium of
the newspaper.

This is nowhere clearer than in the article's opening paragraph, which
both describes the temporal problem that newspapers present, and,
through its experiments with grammar, suggests that Stein's writing can
provide a solution within the very medium in which she writes. The article
opens quite differently than by stating who, when, where, and what—the
staple of reporting designed for maximum transparency: "What do they
want to know in the newspapers that is what does anybody want to know
just anybody and do they want to know what they do want to know or
do they only think so only think they want to know what they do want
to know from the newspaper because if they do if they only think so then
they do get what they want" (89). In her unanswered question about
newspaper readers and what "they" want, "they" has no clear referent.
Although the pronoun would seem to refer to those who read newspapers,
the shift from "they" to "anybody" in the same line potentializes this act of
reference, undercutting the idea that Stein is referring to newspaper readers as a distinct class or kind. The same movement characterizes Stein's

prepositions. Readers want to know something not *about* the papers, but *in* them, and then, a few lines later, *from* them. Knowing is something that first happens, Stein suggests, within the newspapers, as if newspapers are themselves subjects who know things. Only afterward does this knowledge immanent to the paper become functionalized, becoming something that "they" or "anybody" possesses and takes away from the experience of reading. The play with pronouns and prepositions in the opening paragraph and throughout "American Newspapers" allows readers to recognize that the paper itself in some sense has a mind, given the qualitative nature of time and the fact that thoughts and things do not inhabit different ontological orders. In thus "breathing life" into the daily paper, Stein's writing synchronizes the sender, receiver, and message more effectively than the editors of her piece could hope to do.

In the same article, however, Stein also credits contemporary celebrities with the same power as her prose (and the yellow newspapers of her youth) to impart a knowledge of qualitative change. The big city newspaper's one hope of replicating the face-to-face interaction of small town life without doing anything differently lies in the celebrity, Stein suggests. Figures such as John Dillinger and Charles Lindbergh—as well as, implicitly, herself— are intrinsically "exciting," she claims, quite apart from any story about them. For that reason "what happens to them yesterday is still what happens to them to-day . . . and so any day any newspaper tells anything about them it makes it like to-day and so be exciting" (90–91). Celebrity here has a vitality or force that enlivens the paper and unsettles habits of perception in the same ways that Stein's grammatical variations do, perhaps because they, too, are only potentially addressing their audiences.

In another *Herald Tribune* essay, on the question of why American capitals are never major cities, Stein suggests that the kind of writing she proposes and provides for the daily paper might obviate the need for government altogether. Americans "tucked . . . their capitals away . . . so that they need not have them unless they need them," she concludes (74). By locating their capitals in unnoticed and unimportant places, Stein argues, Americans ensure that government does not become a habit. Besides evoking the familiar specter of big government—doubtless a part of Stein's opposition to the WPA (Works Progress Administration)—throughout the article the repeated emphasis on "capital" suggests a double meaning.[75] Just as Americans "tuck their capitals away," so too does Stein, in her distrust of nouns and proper names and her emphasis on linguistic shifters. While Dewey hoped that governmental agencies could organize feelings into symbols with an organic connection to experience, Stein suggests that her language can do this for readers of the *Herald Tribune* by minimizing names and titles—the habitual stopping places for thought—or discarding them altogether. A good example of the way Stein "put[s] the capital away" leaving it "where nobody would notice it unless they happened to be looking for it" (74) occurs at the beginning of the article. Stein states there of the topic at hand, "Now if anybody begins to think about it what does anybody say. They may say this. I may say this" (ibid.). The opener refuses to name particular people who think one thing or another, and hence to capitalize proper nouns. It moreover suggests that "anybody's knowledge" about American capitals emerges from the indexical experience of language—the "this." The experience of the bare linguistic address is democratic in a different way than that of the agencies of government located in American state capitals. Unlike those agencies, Stein implies, the capacity for speech is always shared in common, and it can never become a bad habit.

Stein's antipathy toward the progressive institutions of the Depression is particularly palpable in this series of articles. Yet the fact that her challenge was coming from a perspective similar to that of the progressive Dewey's—arousing a sense of rivalry—is suggested in a remarkable moment in which Dewey's name surfaces in one of her articles. In "American Education and Colleges" Stein begins by describing education in America as the very Deweyan project of integrating doing and thinking: "Education is thought about and as it is thought about it is being done it is being done in the way it is thought about, which is not true of almost anything" (94). But then, Stein states flatly, "Very likely education does not make very much difference" (94), because

> after all who are the ones who are going to do educating and be educated it is just as well to think about that. After all how much does any one want any one to be different from any other one, one lot of them to be different from any other lot of them. In a great many educations in a great many countries they want one lot of them to be a very different lot from the other lot. Do we. I wonder. Do we. (95)

By saying "Education does not make very much difference" Stein implies that educational institutions are likely to fix or arrest qualitative change and variation—including their own—encouraging the formation of oppressive habits of thought, such as class distinctions. That is, educational environments might not enable recognition of a shared immersion in temporal becoming and democratic community, as Dewey hoped, but instead lead to conformity and habit as they do in "other countries." But Stein's skeptical question about the self-interested power of the "ones who are going to do educating" ends with a pun on Dewey's name that drives home her point in a way that is rather different than this liberal or libertarian paraphrase of her position might suggest. "Do we" evokes Dewey's philosophy that group identity—the "we"—is always a product of activity, or "doing." Stein's pun asks whether institutions such as public and private schools should be the place, in America, where the "we" is produced. But in the variation between the name of Dewey, and the question "Do we," she provides a startling answer to the question of what will produce the knowledge for which he and she both seemed to hope. Writing will produce that knowledge—and more precisely, her writing. Surprisingly enough, Stein is in fact offering her own writing here, in place of schools, as a solution to the ills of the Depression. The article itself becomes a form of experimental communications research that yields not quantitative data on who is persuaded by what, but instead a public—not fully distinguishable from Stein's public of fans—that recognizes the potentiality of reference in language as the common ground of its existence.

Perhaps the reason Stein was imagining herself and her writing in such terms during her American lecture tour was due to the firsthand experience she was getting of the ways in which celebrities could become the substance of a public debate that mixed emotion and reason, challenging the mentalistic theories of public discourse that had risen to prominence, especially in the 1930s. This power was still on her mind in her late novel *Ida* (1941), which she described as a novel about the "Hollywood cinema kind of publicity."[76] The potential address of the celebrity also offers a good description of Stein's style in this work, which tells the story of its eponymous main character, who seems to be known by all, by using complete sentences and a semblance of linear progression: "On the way, just at the end of the city she saw a woman carrying a large bundle of wash. This woman stopped and she was looking at a photograph, Ida stopped too and it was astonishing, the woman was looking at the photograph, she had it in her hand, of Ida's dog Love. This was astonishing."[77] Stein's prose retains an interest in exploring an internal rhythm that extends and embodies the living rhythm of the scene itself, as was the case with "If I Told Him"—in the repetition, for instance, of "the woman stopped . . . Ida stopped," or of "she was looking . . .the woman was looking." But she also gives her readers a scene they can picture, with characters and a sense of dramatic tension. The result is a feeling of potential reference and potential address; Stein *seems* to be telling us something but we cannot really be sure. After all, we do not discover how the woman came to possess the photograph, or much else about this scene. Stein is only potentially communicating, incorporating the dialectic of celebrity itself to explore the uncertain and enticing distance—or the mediated "love"—between the celebrity and her fans.

The fact that the woman is gazing at a photo of Ida's dog "Love," moreover, suggests Stein's awareness that her celebrity brings into being a public discussion about the nature of communication itself. The stranger's interest suggests the emotional draw and asymmetrical address of the celebrity; Ida encounters her in a public place, much as Stein reportedly encountered strangers who knew her on the streets of New York, and she holds and gazes at an image that evokes Stein's and Toklas's private life, as if perusing *Life* magazine.[78] In addition, leaving "Love" aside for a moment, Stein's writings in the 1930s frequently reverted to the figure of the dog as a metaphor for the disturbing ways in which identity can be conceived as an act of mental transfer. "I am I because my little dog knows me," she writes in "The Geographical History of America," the year after her tour, following it up with a series of questions about the impossible quandaries that such acts of identification create for identity itself: "Which is he./No which is he./Say it with tears, no which is he./I am I why./So there./I am I where."[79] In gazing at a photo of her dog, Ida's fan thus also contemplates the problems of knowledge, identity, and communication that Stein's writing raised for many. Stein's own celebrity is figured here as a kind of metacelebrity, as if Stein is imagining herself, *qua* celebrity, as able to put the very terms on which she is herself consumed by her public up for debate.

Although couched in liberal and even libertarian terms, then, Stein's bid to rival the institutions of Progressive Era America through her writing invokes a "force" and "vitality" that is not equivalent to rugged individualism, despite what many historical treatments of Stein's work in the 1930s have suggested. Nor, however, can we equate Stein's writing and views on literature entirely with Dewey's views on habit and communicative partaking, and with the pragmatist and radically empiricist tradition of American experimental writing and experimental selfhood to which he belonged, which stretched back through William James, Henry James, Emerson, and even earlier. For, while Stein herself was eager to affirm her membership in this sodality of American writers and thinkers, *Four in America* and her *Herald Tribune* series show that her conception of linguistic force is borrowed from the charismatic power of the celebrity—and more particularly, from *her* charismatic power, as a celebrity who communicates in ways irreducible to mentalistic transfer. Perhaps Stein imagined that this power, with its ability to bring a public sphere into being, could offer a counterweight to Wilson's and FDR's rhetoric, to Mr. Owen Young's control of the airwaves, to Dewey, and to the "experts" who were everywhere being mobilized to interpret the news and Stein herself. A libertarian as far as politics, but a communitarian with regard to grammar, Stein implies that the only agency Americans need is American writing, or more specifically, the writing of America's newest and most American author yet.

Acknowledgments

THIS BOOK MIGHT HAVE REMAINED virtual forever were it not for the support and encouragement of many people. For their insightful suggestions for revision and their enthusiasm for the project at various stages along the way, I thank in particular Ann Ardis, Jonathan Culler, Mark Essig, Jason Frank, Mark Goble, Eric Hayot, Dana Luciano, Michael Millner, Chris Nealon, Doug Mao, and Kate Thomas. Certain colleagues and friends also gave me something even more important in the past year. For their permission to consider the book done, I am grateful to Kevin Ohi, Peter Coviello, and Pam Thurschwell.

Although it was born somewhere between the University of Chicago, Cornell University, and Columbia University, this book materialized only at Columbia, thanks to some of the most supportive and engaged colleagues I could wish for. I thank especially Rachel Adams, Jenny Davidson, Ann Douglas, Sarah Cole, Sharon Marcus, Julie Peters, and Ross Posnock for their careful and generous readings of my work. Many others at Columbia sustained me intellectually and emotionally when I needed it most, especially Amanda Claybaugh, Julie Crawford, Eleanor Johnson, Edward Mendelson, and Martin Puchner.

I owe a great deal to Stephen Best and to the editorial board at *Representations* for meticulous and extensive comments on chapter 3, which first appeared in *Representations* 96, no. 1 (2006): 99–125. I am grateful for permission to reprint that essay here. Anonymous readers of the manuscript from the University of Minnesota Press and NYU Press also helped me immeasurably in reconceiving the book's aims and structure. A postdoctoral fellowship from the Andrew W. Mellon Foundation from 2006 to 2008, which provided both valuable time and stimulating interlocutors, allowed me to expand the project into book form. Finally, I am grateful to my teachers at Cornell, who long ago launched me on this path, little knowing where it might take me: Mark Seltzer, Molly Hite, Tim Murray, and Amy Villarejo.

ACKNOWLEDGMENTS

I have been very lucky to have Richard Morrison as my editor at the University of Minnesota Press. I thank him for his enthusiastic support of this book, his kindness and intellectual friendship, and his patience with me over the years. I also much appreciate the help of Mike Stoffel, Pam Suwinsky, Erin Warholm-Wohlenhaus, Chris McKeen, and Emily Shortslef in the preparation of the manuscript for publication.

Friends, colleagues, and others in Chicago, Ithaca, and New York City reminded me that there are things that matter in the world besides scholarship and contributed to making writing a less lonely task. They include Michael Allan, Zarena Aslami, Elizabeth Braswell, Japonica Brown-Saracino, Stuart Davis, Amy Foerster, Laurie Fuller, Becky Givan, Nicole Lassahn, Ferdinand, Christopher Love, Philip Lorenz, Jenny Mann, Lida Maxwell, Erica Meiners, Michael Phillips, Cornelia Reiner, Bethany Schneider, Laura Sedlock, Boris Thomas, and Rebecca Zorach. For helping me to understand the joys of the actual, I owe more than I can say to Hattie Myers. I am also grateful to my parents, Jane and Bill Biers, for their support, as well as to Mary Soyer, Jerry Hurwitz, Arnie Lieber, and Elizabeth White.

It is to Katherine Lieber that I owe the most profound debt of all. Without her love and support, this book and this life would be incomplete.

Notes

Introduction

Epigraph from Giorgio Agamben, "On Potentiality," in *Potentialities: Collected Essays in Philosophy,* trans. Daniel Heller-Roazen (Stanford, Calif.: Stanford University Press, 1999), 182.

1. Henry James, "In the Cage," *Eight Tales from the Major Phase: In the Cage and Others* (New York: Norton, 1969), 183. Cited hereafter parenthetically in the text.

2. Marie-Laure Ryan, *Narrative as Virtual Reality: Immersion and Interactivity in Literature and Electronic Media* (Baltimore: Johns Hopkins University Press, 2001), 25–47.

3. Ibid., 27.

4. As Brian Massumi has emphasized in regard to Gilles Deleuze's use of the term, "All arts and technologies . . . envelop the virtual in one way or another." See *Parables for the Virtual: Movement, Affect, Sensation* (Durham, N.C.: Duke University Press, 2002), 137. Anne Friedberg has made a similar point in her history of the virtual visual image, *The Virtual Window: From Alberti to Microsoft* (Cambridge, Mass.: MIT Press, 2006), 10–11. See also Elizabeth Grosz, "Cyberspace, Virtuality, and the Real: Some Architectural Reflections," in *Architecture from the Outside: Essays on Virtual and Real Space* (Cambridge, Mass.: MIT Press, 2001).

5. Ryan, *Narrative as Virtual Reality,* 25–26.

6. Katherine Hayles, "The Condition of Virtuality," in *The Digital Dialectic: New Essays on New Media,* ed. Peter Lunenfeld (Cambridge, Mass.: MIT Press, 1999), 69. Ryan situates the virtual-as-digital somewhere between the first two definitions, depending on a commentator's negative or positive view of digital technologies. See Ryan, *Narrative as Virtual Reality.*

7. A version of this book might well have proceeded more explicitly by way of Deleuze's philosophy of difference, particularly because he has elaborated that philosophy by way of Proust and Bergson. I have decided not to do so because both Deleuze's and Guattari's aspirations to create a semiotics of social systems and Deleuze's Bergsonist account of cinema have no account of experience, and are incapable, in particular, of accounting for the technological alienation that was often a subject of concern for the writers I track in the following pages. On the

limitations of Deleuzean difference for thinking about such questions, see Mark B. N. Hansen, *Embodying Technesis: Technology beyond Writing* (Ann Arbor: University of Michigan Press, 2000), 189. On the limitations of Deleuze's formalist appropriation of Bergson for a theory of cinema, see also Hansen, *New Philosophy for New Media* (Cambridge, Mass.: MIT Press, 2004), 6–8. Much of my inspiration for this book, however, has come from Brian Massumi's use of Bergson, Deleuze, and William James to rethink contemporary critical analyses of culture, media, and politics. See introduction to Massumi, *Parables*.

8. I am deeply indebted for this understanding, and throughout this introduction, to Martin Jay's account of experience in Jamesian pragmatism as well as to his comprehensive survey of the category of experience in Western philosophy and critical theory. See Martin Jay, *Songs of Experience: Modern American and European Variations on a Universal Theme* (Berkeley: University of California Press, 2005), 265.

9. See especially James Livingston, *Pragmatism and the Political Economy of Cultural Revolution, 1850–1940* (Chapel Hill: University of North Carolina Press, 1994), and Nancy Bentley, *Frantic Panoramas: American Literature and Mass Culture, 1870–1920* (Philadelphia: University of Pennsylvania Press, 2009), 247–87.

10. A sampling of this large field includes Mark Goble, *Beautiful Circuits: Modernism and the Mediated Life* (New York: Columbia University Press, 2010); Lisa Gitelman, *Scripts, Grooves, and Writing Machines: Representing Technology in the Edison Era* (Stanford, Calif.: Stanford University Press, 1999); Friedrich A. Kittler, *Discourse Networks 1800/1900*, trans. Michael Metteer, with Chris Cullens; foreword by David E. Wellbery (Stanford, Calif.: Stanford University Press, 1990); Friedrich Kittler, *Gramophone, Film, Typewriter*, trans. with an introduction by Geoffrey Winthrop-Young and Michael Wutz (Stanford, Calif.: Stanford University Press, 1999); Julian Murphet, *Multimedia Modernism: Literature and the Anglo-American Avant-Garde* (Cambridge: Cambridge University Press, 2009); Julian Murphet and Lydia Rainford, eds., *Literature and Visual Technologies: Writing after Cinema* (New York: Palgrave Macmillan, 2003); Michael North, *Camera Works: Photography and the Twentieth-Century Word* (Oxford: Oxford University Press, 2005); Mark Seltzer, *Bodies and Machines* (New York: Routledge, 1992); and Mark Wollaeger, *Modernism, Media, and Propaganda: British Narrative from 1900 to 1945* (Princeton, N.J.: Princeton University Press, 2006).

11. See sources cited in nn. 79–80, following.

12. See Andreas Huyssen, *After the Great Divide: Modernism, Mass Culture, Postmodernism* (Bloomington: Indiana University Press, 1986).

13. See, for example, Kevin J. H. Dettmar and Stephen Watt, eds., *Marketing Modernisms: Self-Promotion, Canonization, Rereading* (Ann Arbor: University of Michigan Press, 1996); Lawrence Rainey, *Institutions of Modernism: Literary Elites and Public Culture* (New Haven: Yale University Press, 1998); Mark Morrisson,

The Public Face of Modernism: Little Magazines, Audiences, and Reception, 1905–1920 (Madison: University of Wisconsin Press, 2001); and recent work on modernism and celebrity discussed in chapter 5.

14. With the rise of a world "fashioned by mass media," Habermas argues, a vast expansion of the market for consumer goods eroded the distinction between the public exercise of reason and the pursuit of private economic, social, familial, and sexual interests. A zone of domesticity formerly considered off-limits to the public gaze was "pried open" by a public now engaged more with the pursuit of sensation, money, and status than with reasoned debate, while the "integrity" of rational-critical debate in the print public sphere was in turn breached by commercial interests. See Jürgen Habermas, *The Structural Transformation of the Public Sphere: An Inquiry into a Category of Bourgeois Society* (Cambridge, Mass.: MIT Press, 1991), 171–72. For challenges to Habermas that stress the idea of multiple publics or counterpublics, see, among others, Rita Felski, *Beyond Feminist Aesthetics: Feminist Literature and Social Change* (Cambridge, Mass.: Harvard University Press, 1989); Bruce Robbins, ed., *The Phantom Public Sphere* (Minneapolis: University of Minnesota Press, 1993); Miriam Hansen, *Babel and Babylon: Spectatorship in American Silent Film* (Cambridge, Mass.: Harvard University Press, 1991), and Michael Warner, *Publics and Counterpublics* (New York: Zone Books, 2002).

15. See Bentley, *Frantic Panoramas*.

16. Ibid., 5.

17. Given the broad synthesis that this book undertakes, I necessarily sidestep many debates about how "mass culture" should be defined. Richard Ohmann has provided a helpful and concise definition on which I rely. Mass culture, for Ohmann, includes "voluntary experiences, produced by a relatively small number of specialists, for millions across the nation to share, in similar or identical form, either simultaneously or nearly so; with dependable frequency; mass culture shapes habitual audiences, around common needs or interests, and it is made for profit." See Ohmann, *Selling Culture: Magazines, Markets and Class at the Turn of the Century* (New York: Verso, 1996), 14.

18. Ralph Waldo Emerson, "The American Scholar," in *Select Essays and Addresses, including "The American Scholar"* (New York: MacMillan, 1922), 195.

19. On the "Bergsonist vocation" of digital technologies, see Hansen, *New Philosophy for New Media*.

20. Jay notes that, for example, what James would call "pure experience," Georges Bataille and Michel Foucault would later call "inner" or "limit" experiences. See Jay, *Songs of Experience*, 361–401.

21. On the Bergsonism of Cather and Stevens, see Tom Quirk, *Bergson and American Culture: The Worlds of Willa Cather and Wallace Stevens* (Chapel Hill: University of North Carolina Press, 1990). On Henry Adams and virtual

experience, see Bentley, *Frantic Panoramas*, 249–60. On Chopin's neurological aesthetics, see Jane F. Thrailkill, *Affecting Fictions: Mind, Body, and Emotion in American Literary Realism* (Cambridge, Mass.: Harvard University Press, 2007), 155–200.

22. On this transatlantic search for a *via media*, see James Kloppenberg, *Uncertain Victory: Social Democracy and Progressivism in European and American Thought, 1870–1920* (Oxford: Oxford University Press, 1986).

23. William James, *Pragmatism*, ed. Bruce Kuklick (Indianapolis: Hackett, 1981), 11–12. (Originally published 1907)

24. Kloppenberg, *Uncertain Victory*, 4.

25. Jay, *Songs of Experience*, 264. See also Giorgio Agamben, *Infancy and History: The Destruction of Experience*, trans. Liz Heron (New York: Verso, 1993).

26. On the "proto-phenomenology" of Brentano, Mach, and the early James, see Judith Ryan, *The Vanishing Subject: Early Psychology and Literary Modernism* (Chicago: University of Chicago Press, 1991). Jonathan Crary provides a help-ful, wider context, documenting a "generalized crisis in perception" in the 1880s and 1890s in response both to new knowledge about perception and to the disci-plinary organization of mass consumption. See Crary, *Suspensions of Perception: Attention, Spectacle, and Modern Culture* (Cambridge, Mass.: MIT Press, 1999), 2. On the search for a more scientific psychology, which was inseparable from these developments, see Edward S. Reed, *From Soul to Mind: The Emergence of Psychol-ogy, from Erasmus Darwin to William James* (New Haven, Conn.: Yale University Press, 1997), and Lorraine Daston, "The Theory of Will versus the Science of Mind," in *The Problematic Science: Psychology in Nineteenth-Century Thought*, ed. William Ray Woodward and Mitchell G. Ash (New York: Praeger, 1982).

27. Friedrich Nietzsche, "On Truth and Lies in a Nonmoral Sense," in *Philoso-phy and Truth: Selections from Nietzsche's Notebooks of the Early 1870's*, ed. Daniel Breazeale (Atlantic Highlands, N.J.: Humanities Press, 1990), 80.

28. Ryan, *The Vanishing Subject*, 11.

29. Crary, *Suspensions of Perception*, 3. As Crary also notes, vision thereby became "only one part of a body capable of evading institutional capture and of inventing new forms, affects, and intensities" (ibid.).

30. See Kittler, *Discourse Networks 1800/1900*, 206–64.

31. As Jay notes of both the pragmatists and twentieth-century thinkers such as Heidegger, the quest to get beyond "the fatal split between subject and object" resulted in the paradox of "a still impassioned defense of experience without a strong notion of the subject who is its purported bearer." Jay, *Songs of Experience*, 265.

32. I do not mean to reduce pragmatism and radical empiricism to vitalism per se. Because of my interest in the relationship among philosophy, psychology, and the virtual "turn," I emphasize here less those aspects of pragmatism that are quintessentially American than those that are part of a broader set of intellectual

responses to modernity. In this I follow especially Kloppenberg, *Uncertain Victory*, as well as Jay, *Songs of Experience*, Bentley, *Frantic Panoramas*, and Livingston, *Pragmatism*. On vitalism, see Frederick Burwick and Paul Douglass, eds., *The Crisis in Modernism: Bergson and the Vitalist Controversy* (Cambridge: Cambridge University Press, 1992).

33. To speak of philosophy "drawing" on psychology is, however, somewhat misleading, because the two were very closely connected. On the history of psychology's separation as a discipline from philosophy and greater specialization as a science, see sources cited in n. 26.

34. The "vanishing subject" is perhaps the fundamental assumption underlying modernist formal experimentation, for, as Ryan notes, "if there is no subject in the conventional sense, there can be no conventional language; similarly, if there is no self, there can be no traditional plot, no familiar character development." See Ryan, *The Vanishing Subject*, 3. On the close ties between modernism and early psychology see also Mark S. Micale, ed., *The Mind of Modernism: Medicine, Psychology, and the Cultural Arts in Europe and America, 1880–1940* (Stanford, Calif.: Stanford University Press, 2004).

35. James drew on the accounts of perception and consciousness he had elaborated in his textbook, *The Principles of Psychology*, and on the transatlantic discussions with philosophers and social theorists mentioned earlier. But he was also indebted to Ralph Waldo Emerson's conception of experience as fluid and transitional, and to his colleague, the logician and semiotician C. S. Peirce, and his application of the scientific method to epistemology (James would have drawn his use of the term "virtual," elaborated above, both from Bergson and from Peirce; the latter had written the definition of "the virtual" for James Mark Baldwin's *Dictionary of Philosophy and Psychology* in 1901). In marked contrast to James, Bergson was initially inspired by distinctions made in mathematics regarding changes of degree and changes of kind. On the influences of Emerson and Peirce on James, see Louis Menand, *The Metaphysical Club: A Story of Ideas in America* (New York: Farrar, Straus and Giroux, 2001) and Ralph Barton Perry, *The Thought and Character of William James*, 2 vols. (Boston: Little, Brown, 1935). On Peirce's influence specifically, see W. J. Gavin, *William James and the Reinstatement of the Vague* (Philadelphia: Temple University Press, 1992); Charles William Morris, *The Pragmatic Movement in American Philosophy* (New York: G. Braziller, 1970); and David C. Lamberth, *William James and the Metaphysics of Experience* (Cambridge: Cambridge University Press, 1999). On Bergson's debts to mathematics see Gilles Deleuze, *Bergsonism*, trans. Hugh Tomlinson and Barbara Habberjam (New York: Zone Books, 1988), 38–40 and Keith Ansell Pearson, *Philosophy and the Adventure of the Virtual: Bergson and the Time of Life* (London: Routledge, 2002). Bergson's and James's correspondence and mutual influence have been well documented.

36. Although James explicitly claimed the title of "radical empiricist," it is generally forgotten that Bergson was also received as a radical or renegade empiricist in his lifetime. Deleuze, for instance, has described Spinoza, Nietzsche, and Bergson as producing a "superior empiricism." See Pearson, *Philosophy and the Adventure of the Virtual*, 11–12.

37. In particular, for James, radical empiricism was an attempt to accommodate two different kinds of knowledge often posited by philosophy: conceptual knowledge, or "knowledge about"; and a more fundamental and direct, precognitive or prereflective knowledge, "knowledge by acquaintance," that lacks the distance and objectivity of conceptual thought.

38. William James, *Essays in Radical Empiricism* (Mineola, N.Y.: Dover, 2003),

39. (Originally published 1912) Hereafter cited parenthetically in the text.

39. Jonathan Levin, *The Poetics of Transition: Emerson, Pragmatism, and American Literary Modernism* (Durham, N.C.: Duke University Press, 1999), 47.

40. Bergson likened the intellect to a film camera in *Creative Evolution*. See Henri Bergson, *Creative Evolution*, trans. Arthur Mitchell, ed. Keith Ansell Pearson, Michael Kolkman, and Michael Vaughan (New York: Palgrave Macmillan, 2007).

41. As Elizabeth Grosz succinctly puts it, for Bergson, "duration is the subsistence of the past in the present and the capacity of this reimbued present to generate an unexpected future beyond that of imminent action." See Elizabeth Grosz, *The Nick of Time: Politics, Evolution, and the Untimely* (Durham, N.C.: Duke University Press, 2004), 186. I am indebted to her lucid explanation of Bergson's concept of duration throughout this section.

42. Although grounded in the new science of experimental psychology, Bergson and James's attempt to elaborate a notion of "virtual experience" was also a return to a very old problem in philosophy, that of how to conceptualize potentiality. Aristotle discussed potentiality in a variety of works, including the *Physics*, *The Metaphysics*, and *On the Soul*, which treat, respectively, the potentiality of movement, of being, and of soul or mind. For a lucid summary of Bergson's treatment of Aristotle's Zeno's paradox in *Creative Evolution* and its significance for cultural criticism and theory, see Massumi, *Parables*, 5–13.

43. Even though Bergson is a thinker of the "virtual-as-potential," his metaphors here are optical, drawn from the pole of the virtual most closely connected to the simulacral, or the "fake." On the "conversion" that gives rise to the mental image, he writes, "it would be necessary, not to throw more light on the object, but, on the contrary, to obscure some of its aspects, to diminish it by the greater part of itself, so that the remainder, instead of being encased in its surroundings as a *thing*, should detach itself from them as a *picture*." The virtual mental image for Bergson in this text is thus perhaps best described as a simulacrum of potentiality. See Henri Bergson, *Matter and Memory*, trans. N. M. Paul and W. S. Palmer (New York: Zone Books, 1991), 36.

44. Ibid.

45. On Bergson's modifications of Darwinism and his challenge to Social Darwinism, particularly the "preformism" of both mechanistic and finalistic explanations of evolution, see Grosz, *The Nick of Time*, 200–203.

46. Here I follow Deleuze's transformative rereading of Bergson as fundamentally preoccupied with the distinction between differences in degree, which are "discontinuous and actual" and differences in kind, which are "virtual and continuous." I also incorporate here Deleuze's later extrapolation of this difference into his own philosophical distinction between the possible and the real, on the one hand, and the virtual and the actual, on the other. See, respectively, Deleuze, *Bergsonism*, 38, and *Difference and Repetition*, trans. Paul Patton (New York: Columbia University Press, 1994), 208–14.

47. James's choice of Memorial Hall, a Civil War memorial, as an example with which to critique idealist notions of objective reference may be no accident. On the significance of the Civil War for the formation of pragmatism's theory of truth, see Menand, *The Metaphysical Club*.

48. The payoff of defining the mental image in this way for James was not so much the promise of a philosophical elaboration of time and the new as it was for Bergson. Instead it was the promise of establishing what he called "the coterminousness of different minds" against the Berkeleyan notion that physical objects are illusions and only one's own mind (and the mind of God) can be taken to exist. See James, *Essays in Radical Empiricism*, 40.

49. In one of the most influential philosophical formulations for literary modernism, James had emphasized in *The Principles of Psychology* that the conjunctive elements of language could grant access to the conjunctive relations of experience, noting that "there is not a conjunction or a preposition, and hardly an adverbial phrase, a syntactic form, or inflection of voice, in human speech, that does not express some shading or other of relation which we at some moment actually feel to exist between the larger objects of our thought." Experiencing the transitional components of language, James thought, made it possible for a mind shut in by habits and by the functional nature of subjectivity to intuit or make contact with the world outside. See James, *The Principles of Psychology*, Vol. 1 (New York: Henry Holt and Co., 1890), 245.

50. See Giorgio Agamben, *"Pardes*: The Writing of Potentiality," in *Potentialities*, 205–19. For a lucid explanation of Agamben's argument, see Daniel Heller-Roazen, "Editor's Introduction" to the same volume.

51. A number of commentators have made this point about both James and Bergson. Literary critics too numerous to cite have established the limitations of William James's philosophical language and have understood those ideas to be put to work more effectively in modernist literature, including that of his brother Henry. One of the most influential criticisms of Bergson's metaphysical language can be

found in Jacques Derrida, *Margins of Philosophy*, trans. Alan Bass (Chicago: University of Chicago Press, 1982), 57–59. For a similar critique in regard to Deleuze, see C. V. Boundas, "Deleuze-Bergson: An Ontology of the Virtual," in Paul Patton, ed., *Deleuze: A Critical Reader* (Oxford: Blackwell, 1996), 81–106. For a response to both, see Jeffrey A. Bell, *Philosophy at the Edge of Chaos: Gilles Deleuze and the Philosophy of Difference* (Toronto: University of Toronto Press, 2006), 167–68.

52. Bergson, *Matter and Memory*, 49.

53. Ibid., 45.

54. See Sharon Cameron, "Representing Grief: Emerson's 'Experience,'" in *Impersonality: Seven Essays* (Chicago: University of Chicago Press, 2007), 53–78.

55. See C. S. Peirce, *Collected Papers*, Vol. 5, ed. Charles Hartshorne and Paul Weiss (Cambridge, Mass.: Belknap Press, 1960), para. 371.

56. James was well aware of these objections, which he paraphrases on page 37 in "A World of Pure Experience" and to which he attempts to respond in "The Thing and Its Relations." See James, *Essays in Radical Empiricism*.

57. The vitalist moment in the United States was due in part to James's own prominence as a public intellectual, to his celebration of Bergson in *A Pluralistic Universe: Hibbert Lectures at Manchester College on the Present Situation in Philosophy* (New York: Longmans, Green, and Co., 1909), to the translation of Bergson's *Creative Evolution* in 1911, and finally to Bergson's subsequent visit to America in 1913. On James's influence, and on the various contexts in which Bergsonism took hold, see Quirk, *Bergson and American Culture*, 52–96. On Nietzsche's popularity in America, see Jennifer Ratner-Rosenhagen, *American Nietzsche: A History of an Icon and His Ideas* (Chicago: University of Chicago Press, 2012).

58. Lyman Abbott, "Henri Bergson: The Philosophy of Progress," *Outlook* (February 22, 1913): 388–91, 391.

59. Gerald Stanley Lee, *Crowds: A Moving Picture of Democracy* (Garden City, NY: Doubleday, 1913), 65. For a discussion of Lee's prosthetic logic, see Tim Armstrong, *Modernism, Technology and the Body: A Cultural History* (Cambridge: Cambridge University Press, 1998).

60. As Quirk has noted, "The greatest influence of Bergsonism resided not in the assimilation of it as a body of thought so much as in the application of selected Bergsonian principles to preexisting, progressive concerns and impulses." Quirk, *Bergson and American Culture*, 62.

61. I have not included John Dewey among the theorists of "virtual experience" discussed here because to a greater degree than James and Bergson he refused all attempts to ground philosophy in fundamentals. For a discussion of the evolution of Dewey's instrumentalism and experimentation, see Steven C. Rockefeller, *John Dewey: Religious Faith and Democratic Humanism* (New York: Columbia University Press, 1991). For a discussion of Dewey's theory of communication as partaking, see chapter 5.

62. For a discussion of the radical democratic vision of Randolph Bourne and other members of the so-called Young Americans, see Casey Nelson Blake, *Beloved Community: The Cultural Criticism of Randolph Bourne, Van Wyck Brooks, Waldo Frank, and Lewis Mumford* (Chapel Hill: University of North Carolina Press, 1990).

63. Walter Lippmann, *A Preface to Politics* (New York: Mitchell Kennerley, 1914), 200. For a discussion of Lippmann's debts to Nietzsche, see Ratner-Rosenhagen, *American Nietzsche*, 177–78.

64. Walter Benjamin, "On Some Motifs in Baudelaire," in *Walter Benjamin: Selected Writings*, Vol. 4, ed. Howard Eiland and Michael W. Jennings, trans. Edmund Jephcott and others (Cambridge, Mass.: Harvard University Press, 2003), 314. Hereafter cited parenthetically in the text.

65. Benjamin, "On the Concept of History," *Walter Benjamin: Selected Writings*, Vol. 4, 390. Hereafter cited parenthetically in the text.

66. Bergson's contention that the past is always in existence, whether or not it is remembered, thus becomes in Benjamin a claim about history. On the ontological status of the past in Bergson, see Grosz, who argues that the Bergsonian *durée* thereby gains a political relevance all on its own (*The Nick of Time*, 178).

67. I am indebted for this reading of Benjamin to Samuel Weber, *Benjamin's -abilities* (Cambridge, Mass.: Harvard University Press, 2008), as well as to Giorgio Agamben, "Language and History," in *Potentialities*, 48–61. As Agamben notes, Benjamin's turn to the potentiality or capacity of language to redeem history puts into question the function of the name, because names are inseparable from historical descent.

68. For a different reading of the parallels between James and the Benjamin of "On Some Motifs in Baudelaire," focusing on James as the urban *flaneur*, see Ross Posnock, *The Trial of Curiosity: Henry James, William James, and the Challenge of Modernity* (New York: Oxford University Press, 1991), 141–66.

69. Katherine Hayles has made a case for understanding "In the Cage" as an anticipation of contemporary digital culture. She finds "intimations of an information regime" in the story that will be the hallmark of twentieth-century literature and a fully "virtual" information-based society, but notes that in the late Victorian period, "the dream of information" cannot yet "offer a real space in which to live" (64, 70). See Hayles, *My Mother Was a Computer: Digital Subjects and Literary Texts* (Chicago: University of Chicago Press, 2005).

70. Richard Menke points out that the telegraph girl's fantasies are couched in the idiom of soundless or wordless communication, which he shows was characteristic of the paper-based telegraph in *mid*-Victorian romances, in contrast with the sounding telegraph of the late nineteenth century. On the ways in which subjectivity and intimacy are irreducibly mediated by the apparatus of the telegraph in the story, see Menke, "Telegraphic Realism: Henry James's 'In the Cage,'"

Publications of the Modern Language Association 115:5 (2000): 983, and Pamela Thurschwell, "Henry James and Theodora Bosanquet: On the Typewriter, *In the Cage*, at the Ouija Board," *Textual Practice* 13:1 (Fall 1999): 5–23.

71. Earlier commentators tended to construe the clear parallels between James and the isolated, excluded telegraph girl as evidence of James's romantic embrace of aesthetic judgment as disinterested and universalizing. More recent commentators have focused instead on the affective and erotic dimension of aesthetic isolation in James, and hence on the social, sexual, and ethical radicalism of the telegraph girl's relationship to her customers, especially when considered in relation to contemporary events of the 1890s, such as the Wilde scandal. More recent examinations of the aesthetic politics of "In the Cage" include Nicola Nixon, "The Reading Gaol of Henry James's 'In the Cage,'" *ELH* 66:1 (1999): 179–201; Eric Savoy, "'In the Cage' and the Queer Effects of Gay History," *Novel: A Forum on Fiction* 28:3 (Spring 1995): 284–307; and Kate Thomas, *Postal Pleasures: Sex, Scandal, and Victorian Letters* (Oxford: Oxford University Press, 2012), 208–23.

72. James's characters, as Kristin Boudreau has shown, often shuttle back and forth between the polarities of idealism and empiricism. For a broader discussion of the influence of this philosophical debate on James's fiction, see Boudreau, *Henry James' Narrative Technique: Consciousness, Perception, and Cognition* (New York: Palgrave Macmillan, 2010).

73. See Charles Darwin, *The Descent of Man, and Selection in Relation to Sex* (London: J. Murray, 1871).

74. As such, she exemplifies the awkward position of many female secretaries and typists made privy to confidential information in contemporaneous fictional and autobiographical portraits in the 1890s and 1900s, including one produced by one of James's own later typists, Theodora Bosanquet. As Pamela Thurschwell has recently pointed out, the secretary's knowledge "threatens any concept of unmediating mediumship." See Thurschwell, "Supple Minds and Automatic Hands: Secretarial Agency in Early Twentieth-Century Literature," *Forum for Modern Language Studies* 37:2 (2001): 157.

75. Henry James, *The Art of the Novel* (London: Charles Scribner's Sons, 1934), 157.

76. Another reason for the strategy of delay is that her fiancé, Mudge, reduces the protagonist's life to empty, homogenous time. When visible across from her in the Mayfair shop, he was like a pendulum clock, she recalls, "mov[ing] to and fro before her as on the small sanded floor of their contracted future" (175). With his departure, at the story's outset, she is able to understand past and future as differentiated from one another. "She was conscious now of the improvement of not having to take her present and her future at once," we are told, "They were about as much as she could manage when taken separate" (175–76). That depar-

ture also makes the time of the entire story one of delay. For throughout the story Mudge wants her to put in for a transfer to where *he* works—as well as, of course, to marry him.

77. The telegraphist feels her experience to be "substitutional" even as she has it, to paraphrase William. See William James, *Essays in Radical Empiricism*, 35.

78. See Stanley Cavell, *Emerson's Transcendental Etudes* (Stanford, Calif.: Stanford University Press, 2003).

79. Such critics include Richard Poirier, *Poetry and Pragmatism* (Cambridge, Mass.: Harvard University Press, 1992); Jonathan Levin, *The Poetics of Transition: Emerson, Pragmatism, and American Literary Modernism* (Durham, N.C., and London: Duke University Press, 1999); Joan Richardson, *A Natural History of Pragmatism: The Fact of Feeling from Jonathan Edwards to Gertrude Stein* (Cambridge: Cambridge University Press, 2007); Steven Meyer, *Irresistible Dictation: Gertrude Stein and the Correlations of Writing and Science* (Stanford, Calif.: Stanford University Press, 2001); Andrew Taylor and Áine Kelly, eds., *Stanley Cavell, Literature, and Film: The Idea of America* (New York: Routledge, 2012); and Paul Grimstad, *Experience and Experimental Writing: Literary Pragmatism from Emerson to the Jameses* (Oxford: Oxford University Press, 2013).

80. Cavellian readings of Emerson and the American Renaissance include George Kateb, *Emerson and Self-Reliance* (Thousand Oaks, Calif.: Sage Publications, 1995); Sharon Cameron, *The Corporeal Self: Allegories of the Body in Melville and Hawthorne* (Baltimore: Johns Hopkins University Press, 1981); Branka Arsić, *On Leaving: A Reading in Emerson* (Cambridge, Mass.: Harvard University Press, 2010), *Passive Constitutions or 7½ Times Bartleby* (Stanford, Calif.: Stanford University Press, 2007), and *Magical Life: Mourning and Vitalism in Thoreau* (forthcoming).

81. See Friedrich A. Kittler, *Discourse Networks 1800/1900* and *Gramophone, Film, Typewriter*. Among those media studies scholars influenced by Kittler who take communicative "noise" as the condition of modernist writing in James and others, see Goble, *Beautiful Circuits*; Mark Seltzer, *Bodies and Machines*; Mark Seltzer, "The Postal Unconscious," *Henry James Review* 21:3 (2000): 197–206; Juan A. Suárez, "T. S. Eliot's *The Waste Land*, the Gramophone, and the Modernist Discourse Network," *New Literary History* 32:3 (Summer 2001): 747–68; and Pamela Thurschwell, *Literature, Technology and Magical Thinking, 1880–1920* (Cambridge: Cambridge University Press, 2001). It's important to note that many of these critics are quite critical of Kittler's totalizing claims about interpretation. For a recent set of critical reengagements with Kittler along these lines, see *Kittler Now*, ed. Stephen Sale and Laura Salisbury (Cambridge, England: Polity Press (forthcoming).

82. Kittler's work represents a synthesis of Foucault, Derrida, Lacan, and McLuhan. For an excellent summary of this synthesis and its significance for the

poststructuralist "presupposition of exteriority," see David Wellbury, introduction to Kittler, *Discourse Networks*, xiii.

83. Poirier, *Poetry and Pragmatism*, 39.

84. See Richardson, *A Natural History of Pragmatism*, ix.

1. Stephen Crane's Abilities

1. See *Stephen Crane: The Contemporary Reviews*, ed. George Monteiro (Cambridge: Cambridge University Press, 2009).

2. William Dean Howells, in *Stephen Crane: The Critical Heritage*, ed. Richard M. Weatherford (London: Routledge, 1973), 62.

3. Stephen Crane, *The University of Virginia Edition of the Works of Stephen Crane: Vol. IX, Reports of War*, ed. Fredson Bowers (Charlottesville: University of Virginia Press, 1971), 451.

4. In an analysis to which this chapter is deeply indebted, Brown has shown that the formal and thematic influence of material culture in Crane's texts more broadly discloses sets of continuities between opposed realms in late nineteenth-century America, such as leisure and work. See Bill Brown, *The Material Unconscious: American Amusement, Stephen Crane, and the Economies of Play* (Cambridge, Mass.: Harvard University Press, 1996), 138.

5. See Amy Kaplan, "The Spectacle of War in Crane's Revision of History," in *New Essays on the Red Badge of Courage*, ed. Lee Clark Mitchell (Cambridge: Cambridge University Press, 1986), 77–108.

6. See Michael Fried, *Realism, Writing, Disfiguration: On Thomas Eakins and Stephen Crane* (Chicago: University of Chicago Press, 1987).

7. See Linda H. Davis, *Badge of Courage: The Life of Stephen Crane* (Boston: Houghton Mifflin, 1998).

8. On Crane's debts to this tradition, see sources cited in nn. 17 and 20 following. For a broader overview of the Puritan roots of American selfhood conceived "as an identity in progress," see Sacvan Bercovitch, *The Puritan Origins of the American Self* (New Haven, Conn.: Yale University Press, 1975), 143. It is important to note, however, that Bercovitch's idea that this is the foundational "myth" of the nation, legitimating American individualism, free enterprise, and exceptionalism, has been contested on a number of fronts. Bercovitch himself and more recent scholars in American studies have understood the American story of instability and continual change to be more anxiety ridden—because inseparable, for example, from economic pressures—and hence best analyzed less as myth, *qua* myth, than as ideology or rhetoric. For an overview of this shift, see especially Philip Fisher, introduction to *The New American Studies: Essays from Representations* (Berkeley: University of California Press, 1991), and essays therein. For an alternative account, focusing on the feeling and affective life of the Puritan pro-

cessual self, see Andrew Delbanco, *The Puritan Ordeal*. Cambridge, Mass: Harvard University Press, 1989. For a challenge to Bercovitch's account of Emerson, stressing process and change as philosophical concepts enjoining a tolerance of the self's passivity and receptiveness, see Branka Arsić, *On Leaving*, 248–50, 337 n. 25 and 366 n. 2.

9. Perry Miller initially pointed out the significance of Locke for Edwards in "Jonathan Edwards on 'The Sense of the Heart,'" *Harvard Theological Review* 41 (1948): 123–45. Recent confirmation for Miller's argument can be found in Joan Richardson, *A Natural History of Pragmatism*, and Ann Taves, *Fits, Trances and Visions: Experiencing Religion and Explaining Experience from Wesley to James* (Princeton, N.J.: Princeton University Press, 1999). I am indebted to Richardson as well as to Sharon Cameron for this understanding of Edwards. See Cameron, "What Counts as Love: Jonathan Edwards's *True Virtue*," in *Impersonality: Seven Essays*, 21–52.

10. See sources cited in the introduction, nn. 79–80.

11. See James B. Colvert, introduction to *The University of Virginia Edition of the Works of Stephen Crane: Vol. VI, Tales of War*.

12. Crane moved to the Bowery to finish writing *Maggie* at the advice of Hamlin Garland. For details of the court case, see Davis, *Badge of Courage*.

13. Even "The Open Boat" arguably anticipates future events. The story's focus on the strong bond of fellowship forged among the war correspondent, the captain, and the sailors shows Crane thinking forward to his coming exploits as a reporter embedded with the Army as much as reflecting backward on his recent lucky rescue. On similarities between "The Open Boat" and an earlier story, "The Reluctant Voyagers," see David Halliburton, *The Color of the Sky: A Study of Stephen Crane* (Cambridge: Cambridge University Press, 1989), 3.

14. Christopher Benfey, *The Double Life of Stephen Crane* (New York: Knopf, 1992), 5.

15. On the analytic aspirations of American realist writers, particularly Howells, who sought to cultivate distance on the social world, see Bentley, *Frantic Panoramas*, 22–68.

16. Thomas Beer reports that Crane consulted the firsthand accounts of soldiers and generals collected in *Battles and Leaders of the Civil War* (1884) for *Red Badge*. See Beer, *Stephen Crane: A Study in American Letters* (Garden City, N.J.: Garden City Publishing, 1923), 97–98.

17. See Larzer Ziff, *The American 1890s: Life and Times of a Lost Generation* (New York: Viking, 1966), 186. See also Halliburton, *The Color of the Sky*, 3–4.

18. Halliburton and Benfey have noted the links between Crane's typological imagination and Protestantism's figural typology. See Halliburton, *The Color of the Sky*, and Benfey, *The Double Life of Stephen Crane*.

19. On the rise in evangelical voluntarism in the late nineteenth century and its ties to the secular tradition of self-help, see Gregory S. Jackson, *The Word and Its*

Witness: The Spiritualization of American Realism (Chicago: University of Chicago Press, 2009).

20. On the parallels between Crane's social sympathy and his father's, see Jamin Rowan, "Stephen Crane and Methodism's Realism: Translating Spiritual Sympathy into Urban Experience," *Studies in American Fiction* 36: 2 (Autumn 2008): 133–54, and Bill Brown, *The Material Unconscious*, 27–71. Andrew Delbanco has described Crane's early writings as "a stylistic incarnation of his father's social criticism" and has noted that "his fiction, despite all its gestures of irreverence toward naive notions of heroism, is cast in the mode of lamentation for a bygone day of moral clarity." See Delbanco, "The American Stephen Crane: The Context of The Red Badge of Courage," in Mitchell, ed., *New Essays on The Red Badge of Courage*, 66, 57.

21. The two typologies were related. As Jackson points out, "American homiletic realism mediates between the spiritual and the empirical in ways that mirror secular realism's movement between the typological and the specific." See Jackson, *The Word and Its Witness*, 6.

22. Although many historians have made this claim, the argument is particularly prevalent in studies of Spanish–American War journalism, including John Tebbel, *America's Great Patriotic War with Spain: Mixed Motives, Lies, and Racism in Cuba and the Philippines, 1898–1915* (Manchester Center, Vt.: Marshall Jones, 1996); Joyce Milton, *The Yellow Kids: Foreign Correspondents in the Heyday of Yellow Journalism* (New York: Harper and Row, 1989); and Charles H. Brown, *The Correspondents' War: Journalists in the Spanish–American War* (New York: Charles Scribner's Sons, 1967). Counterarguments that the McKinley government simply used press fervor as a convenient excuse for territorial expansion can be found in Louis A. Pérez Jr., *The War of 1898: The United States and Cuba in History and Historiography* (Chapel Hill: University of North Carolina Press, 1998); W. Joseph Campbell, *Yellow Journalism: Puncturing the Myths, Defining the Legacies* (Westport, Conn: Praeger, 2003); and Bonnie M. Miller, *From Liberation to Conquest: The Visual and Popular Cultures of the Spanish–American War of 1898* (Amherst: University of Massachusetts Press, 2011). For a more comprehensive survey, including historians who subscribe to the theory of a powerful press influence, see Miller, *From Liberation to Conquest*, 267–68, nn. 13–15.

23. See Phillip Knightley, *The First Casualty: The War Correspondent as Hero and Myth-Maker from the Crimea to Iraq* (Baltimore and London: Johns Hopkins University Press, 2004) 83–120.

24. As Miller notes, the realist school of political thought in the 1950s, exemplified by George Kennan, sought explicitly to distinguish Cold War U.S. foreign policy from the events of 1898. See Miller, *From Liberation to Conquest*, 13.

25. Miller, *From Liberation to Conquest,* 11.

26. The Spanish–American War films are exemplary of early film more gener-

ally, which, as film scholar Tom Gunning has argued, functioned in ways more akin to an exhibition or theatrical show than to an artistic medium with its own internal rules. Gunning tends to play down the way in which theater often worked in tandem with film during this period, however. See Gunning, "The Cinema of Attractions: Early Film, Its Spectator, and the Avant-Garde," *Wide Angle* 8 (1986): 63–70. On the mutually constitutive relations between theater and film in the late nineteenth century, see Ben Brewster and Lea Jacobs, *Theatre to Cinema: Stage Pictorialism and the Early Feature Film* (New York: Oxford University Press, 1997). For a history of these early war films see Anthony Slide, *The Big V: A History of the Vitagraph Company* (Metuchen, N.J. : Scarecrow Press, 1976) and Charles Musser, *The Emergence of Cinema: The American Screen to 1907* (New York: Scribner, 1990).

27. See Amy Kaplan, *The Anarchy of Empire in the Making of U.S. Culture* (Cambridge, Mass.: Harvard University Press, 2002), 149.

28. Miller, *From Liberation to Conquest,* 81–82.

29. See Bentley, *Frantic Panoramas,* 3.

30. For weeks before the staged re-creation of the *Maine's* explosion, the papers had featured gruesome illustrations and photographs of the bodies of the 238 U.S. soldiers who died. See Miller, *From Liberation to Conquest,* 68–69.

31. Miller, *From Liberation to Conquest,* 92–94. Appropriately enough, the "real" Battle of Manila was also put on for show (ibid., 138–39).

32. Ibid., 94.

33. Ibid., 111.

34. Studies of the racial and sexual iconography of the war in the American press include Kaplan, *The Anarchy of Empire;* Miller, *From Liberation to Conquest;* David Brody, *Visualizing American Empire: Orientalism and Imperialism in the Philippines* (Chicago: University of Chicago Press, 2010); and Meg Wesling, *Empire's Proxy: American Literature and U.S. Imperialism in the Philippines* (New York: New York University Press, 2011).

35. On the short-lived anti-imperialist movement, see Robert L. Beisner, *Twelve against Empire: The Anti-Imperialists, 1898–1900* (New York: McGraw-Hill, 1968), and Cynthia Wachtell, *War No More: The Antiwar Impulse in American Literature 1861–1914* (Baton Rouge: Louisiana State University, 2010), which includes further discussion of Howells's "Editha."

36. One example is worth quoting in full—a newspaper ad by the R. S. Crutcher Furniture Company of Atlanta, which printed a large drawing of the *Maine* next to the following text: "The terrible explosion of the U.S. Man of War *Maine . . .* is causing a great deal of excitement among the American people, but for the next 30 days we are going to have an 'explosion of prices' on Furniture, Carpets and Baby Carriages that will startle the entire population of Georgia." Cited in Miller, *From Liberation to Conquest,* 75.

37. William Dean Howells, "Editha," *Harper's Monthly* 110 (January 1905), 214–24: 214. Subsequent references are cited parenthetically in the text.

38. Miller, *From Liberation to Conquest*, 14.

39. See E. L. Godkin, "Excitability," *The Nation* 66:170S (1898), 160.

40. See Wachtell, *War No More*, 118–19.

41. See *Stephen Crane: The Critical Heritage*, 62.

42. See *Stephen Crane: The Contemporary Reviews*, 42, 50.

43. Stephen Crane, *The Red Badge of Courage: An Episode of the American Civil War*, ed. Henry Binder (New York: Norton, 1982), 3. Subsequent references are cited parenthetically in the text.

44. Many critics have noted the pervasive parallels between writing and industrial labor in the novel. On the ways in which *Red Badge of Courage* exhibits a "body machine complex" characteristic of late nineteenth-century industrial culture more broadly, see Mark Seltzer, *Bodies and Machines*. On Crane's revision of the popular image of the war, see Amy Kaplan, "The Spectacle of War in Crane's Revision of History," in Mitchell, ed., *New Essays on the Red Badge of Courage*, 77–108.

45. This is one of many anachronistic touches in Crane's novel about the Civil War. See Brown, *The Material Unconscious*, 125–66.

46. See Alan Trachtenberg, *Reading American Photographs: Images as History—Matthew Brady to Walker Evans* (New York: Hill and Wang, 1989), 78.

47. *The Holy Bible*, Revised Standard Edition, Revelation 19:15.

48. On the Puritan trope of the *imitatio Christi*, see Sacvan Bercovitch, *American Jeremiad* (Madison: University of Wisconsin Press, 1978), 3–31. On the revival of the trope by the Social Gospel movement as a way of advocating for a new voluntarism, see Jackson, *The Word and Its Witness*.

49. See Nicholas Gaskill, "Red Cars with Red Lights and Red Drivers: Color, Crane, and Qualia," *American Literature* 81: 4 (December 2009): 719–45. Hereafter cited parenthetically in the text.

50. See Fried, *Realism, Writing, Disfiguration*.

51. Stephen Crane, "The Upturned Face," in *The University of Virginia Edition of the Works of Stephen Crane: Vol. VI, Tales of War*, 297.

52. Gaskill notes that the "virtual" status of color in Crane was a means by which he sought to explore the specifically textual production of color. If color *qualia* are virtual, it is possible to generate the feeling of perceiving a color in the absence of that color itself, such as is the case for readers of Crane's novels.

53. Stephen Crane, *Active Service*, in *The University of Virginia Edition of the Works of Stephen Crane: Vol. III, The Third Violet and Active Service*, 113. Subsequent references are cited parenthetically in the text.

54. Chance is tremendously significant to Crane as a new force displacing various nineteenth-century determinisms, as it was for Howells and for many others.

On Crane and chance see Jason Puskar, *Accident Society: Fiction, Collectivity, and the Production of Chance* (Stanford, Calif.: Stanford University Press, 2012), and Seltzer, *Bodies and Machines*. For a broader overview of the rise of discourses of chance in the late nineteenth century, see Ian Hacking, *The Taming of Chance* (Cambridge: Cambridge University Press, 1990).

55. On the index, see Peirce, "What Is a Sign?" in *The Essential Peirce: Selected Philosophical Writings*, Vol. 2, ed. Nathan Houser and Christian Kloesel (Bloomington: Indiana University Press, 1998).

56. See Peirce, *CP* 7, para. 366. See also Peter Skagestad, "Peirce's Inkstand as an External Embodiment of Mind," *Transactions of the Charles S. Peirce Society* 35:3 (Summer 1999): 551–61. The inkstand may be a particularly reassuring example. Friedrich Kittler has suggested that handwriting in the nineteenth century allowed literary elites to imagine an imaginary and unbroken circuit of meaning and intention between mind and word. See Kittler, *Discourse Networks 1800/1900*, 25–70.

57. For a broader discussion of the parallels between Crane's work and Jamesian pragmatism see Patrick K. Dooley, *The Pluralistic Philosophy of Stephen Crane* (Urbana: University of Illinois Press, 1993).

58. There is considerable evidence that James moved away from academic psychology toward pragmatist philosophy and radical empiricism in response to contemporaneous political events, which included not only the Spanish–American War and the Venezuelan conflict that preceded it, but also the Dreyfus Affair and especially the American invasion of the Philippines in 1899. On James's anti-imperialism and his political affiliations more generally, see Deborah J. Coon, "'One Moment in the World's Salvation': Anarchism and the Radicalization of William James," *Journal of American History* 83:1 (June 1996): 70–99; George Cotkin, *William James, Public Philosopher* (Baltimore: Johns Hopkins University Press, 1990); Gerald E. Myers, *William James: His Life and Thought* (New Haven, Conn.: Yale University Press, 1986); and Ralph Barton Perry, *The Thought and Character of William James*, 2 vols. (Boston: Little, Brown & Co., 1935).

59. William James, "On a Certain Blindness in Human Beings," in *The Writings of William James: A Comprehensive Edition*, ed. John J. McDermott (New York: Random House, 1967), 629. Hereafter cited parenthetically in the text.

60. William James, "The Moral Equivalent of War," in *The Writings of William James*, 662.

61. Given the significance of the Civil War for James's intellectual development, as Louis Menand has shown, it is not farfetched to imagine that the press's role in the American wars of expansion at the turn of the century might have been an influence on the development of pragmatism. However, as Menand notes, James's commitment to pluralism also predated his criticisms of American imperialism. See Menand, *The Metaphysical Club*, 379.

62. See Bentley, *Frantic Panoramas*, 260–75.

63. Following James Livingstone, Bentley sees this essay, and pragmatism more generally, as part of a cultural revolution in which the "moral contours of selfhood" were refashioned in response to the rise of a consumer economy and the devaluation of productive labor. See also Livingston, *Pragmatism and the Political Economy of Cultural Revolution, 1850–1940* (Chapel Hill and London: University of North Carolina Press, 1994).

64. Stephen Crane, "Death and the Child," in *The University of Virginia Edition of the Works of Stephen Crane: Vol. V, Tales of Adventure*, 141.

65. Ibid., 125.

66. Ibid., 128.

67. Ibid., 139.

68. Ibid., 130.

69. Brown describes this strange "place of pictures" as "oneiric magic-lantern show, protocinematic and vaudevillian—a phantasmagoria of protosurrealist excess where the horrific and the pornographic are as inseparable as 'woe' and 'joy.'" It is worth noting, however, that the place of pictures might well also be an art gallery. James Nagel has noted that several of the pictures recall specific works of Impressionism by Degas and Manet. The understanding of art and film as equally expressive media, as I suggest in chapter 2, is typical of the pictorialist aesthetic of this period. See Brown, *The Material Unconscious*, 166, and James Nagel, *Stephen Crane and Literary Impressionism* (University Park: The Pennsylvania State University Press, 1980), 74–75.

70. See Brown, *The Material Unconscious*, 165–66.

71. Mark Seltzer has coined this term in order to emphasize the ways in which, beginning in the late nineteenth century, "the very idea of 'the public' has become inseparable from spectacles of bodily and mass violence." For Seltzer, "the spectacular public representation of violated bodies" has "come to function as a way of imagining and situating our notions of public, social, and collective identity." On the "pathological public sphere," see *Serial Killers: Death and Life in America's Wound Culture* (New York: Routledge, 1998), 21. See also Michael Warner, "The Mass Public and the Mass Subject," in *Habermas and the Public Sphere*, ed. Craig Calhoun (Cambridge, Mass.: MIT Press, 1992), 377–400.

72. Although the association James made between reason and pleasurable quickening left him open to viewing audiences for mass and popular culture as legitimate publics, he encouraged his listeners to turn to novelists, poets, and literary essayists as the makers of culture best suited to overcoming the barriers between different "idealities." "To be rapt with satisfied attention, like Whitman, to the mere spectacle of the world's presence," James proclaims, "is one way, and the most fundamental way, of confessing one's sense of its unfathomable significance and importance." See James, "On a Certain Blindness," 640.

73. For details of Crane's assignments, see Davis, *Badge of Courage*, and Stanley Wertheim, "Two Yellow Kids: Frank Norris and Stephen Crane," *Frank Norris Studies* 27 (Spring 1999): 2–8.

74. I am indebted to Michael Robertson for many of these observations. On Crane and the fact–fiction discourse of late nineteenth-century journalism, see Robertson, *Stephen Crane, Journalism, and the Making of Modern American Literature* (New York: Columbia University Press, 1997).

75. Stephen Crane, "Stephen Crane's Own Story," in *The University of Virginia Edition of the Works of Stephen Crane: Vol. IX, Reports of War*, 94.

76. Stephen Crane, "The Open Boat," in *Stephen Crane: Prose and Poetry* (New York: Library of America, 1984), 885. Subsequent references are cited parenthetically in the text.

77. Gaskill, "Red Cars," 730.

78. Although wonder requires a moment of pure sensation, and hence disorientation, Fisher argues that, unlike the sublime, it is not traditionally associated with the irrational. See Philip Fisher, *Wonder, the Rainbow, and the Aesthetics of Rare Experiences* (Cambridge, Mass.: Harvard University Press, 1998).

79. This rhythm and movement "finds and founds the self," as Stanley Cavell puts it. See Cavell, "Finding as Founding: Taking Steps in Emerson's 'Experience,'" in *Emerson's Transcendental Etudes*.

2. Realizing *Trilby*

1. David Lodge, *Author, Author!* (New York: Penguin, 2004), 283.

2. See Leon Edel, *Henry James, a Life* (New York: Harper & Row, 1985).

3. Sharon Cameron, *Thinking in Henry James* (Chicago: University of Chicago Press, 1989).

4. Examples include Thurschwell, *Literature, Technology and Magical Thinking, 1880–1920,* and Goble, *Beautiful Circuits: Modernism and the Mediated Life.*

5. See Kurnick, *Empty Houses: Theatrical Failure and the Novel* (Princeton, N.J.: Princeton University Press, 2012), 105–52.

6. I am indebted for these biographical details about du Maurier to Leonée Ormond, *George Du Maurier* (Pittsburgh: University of Pittsburgh Press, 1969).

7. See, for example, Daniel Pick, *Svengali's Web: The Alien Enchanter in Modern Culture* (New Haven, Conn.: Yale University Press, 2000).

8. See Elaine Showalter, Introduction to *Trilby* (Oxford: Oxford University Press, 1998), and Donald Hartman, "Hypnotic and Mesmeric Themes and Motifs in Selected English-Language Novels, Short Stories, Plays and Poems, 1820–1983," *Bulletin of Bibliography* 44:3 (1987): 156–66.

9. Henry James, *The American Scene* (New York: Charles Scribner's Sons, 1946), 53.

10. Lodge, *Author, Author!*, 109.

11. On the critical objections of many of James's contemporaries to the rise of the mass public sphere, and their tacit recognition of its competition with the literary public sphere, see Bentley, *Frantic Panoramas*. On James's centrality to the formation of the idea of the aesthetic vocation or "profession," see Michael Anesko, *"Friction with the Market": Henry James and the Profession of Authorship* (New York: Oxford University Press, 1986), and Jonathan Freedman, *Professions of Taste: Henry James, British Aestheticism, and Commodity Culture* (Stanford, Calif.: Stanford University Press, 1990).

12. When it appeared in serial form, *Trilby* was reported to have increased *Harper's* circulation by 100,000 by its second installment. Advance orders for the book, published in the United States in a single illustrated volume, were so great that *Harper's* had to continually revise its order upward, from 6,500 initially, to, by some reports, 90,000. As many as half a million copies may have sold by 1900, sales figures equaled by few other books at the turn of the century. See Emily Jenkins, *"Trilby:* Fads, Photographers, and 'Over-Perfect Feet,'" *Book History* 1:1 (1998): 221–67.

13. Although it has largely been forgotten, du Maurier's once wildly popular novel lives on today in the enduring cultural figure of "the Svengali," who controls and manipulates the star and her audience from behind the scenes. See Pick, *Svengali's Web*.

14. Like many other so-called mesmeric romances from the late nineteenth century, *Trilby's* plot was steeped in the psychological concept of suggestion. The term had initially designated the means by which ideas lead to one another in the mind, but by the 1890s had come to designate the process whereby an external physical stimulus produces actions in an individual without her knowledge. On the cultural influence of suggestion in both Europe and America during this period see Micale, ed., *The Mind of Modernism*, 2004. On the relationship between the imitation-suggestion paradigm and psychoanalysis, see Léon Chertok and Isabelle Stengers, *A Critique of Psychoanalytic Reason: Hypnosis as a Scientific Problem from Lavoisier to Lacan*, trans. Martha Noel Evans (Stanford, Calif.: Stanford University Press, 1992).

15. See Jenkins, *"Trilby"*; Edward Purcell, "Trilby and Trilby-Mania: The Beginning of the Bestseller System," *Journal of Popular Culture* 11:1 (Summer 1977): 62–76; and Frank Luther Mott, *Golden Multitudes: The Story of Best Sellers in the United States* (New York: Macmillan, 1947).

16. These and other products are documented in Joseph Benson Gilder and Jeannette Leonard Gilder, *Trilbyana: The Rise and Progress of a Popular Novel* (New York: The Critic Co., 1895). http://www.gutenberg.org /files/32887/32887-h/32887-h.htm.

17. See Jennifer Wicke, *Advertising Fictions: Literature, Advertisement, and Social Reading* (New York: Columbia University Press, 1988).

18. See Pick, *Svengali's Web*, and Showalter, "Introduction" to *Trilby*. On *Trilby*'s relationship to the "newly emerging incoherencies between minoritizing and universalizing understandings of male sexual definition," see Eve Kosofsky Sedgwick, *Epistemology of the Closet* (Berkeley: University of California Press, 1990), 194.

19. See Mary J. Russo, *The Female Grotesque: Risk, Excess, and Modernity* (New York and London: Routledge, 1995), and George Taylor, "Svengali: Mesmerist and Aesthete," in *British Theatre in the 1890s: Essays on Drama and the Stage*, ed. Richard Foulkes (Cambridge: Cambridge University Press, 1992), 93–110.

20. Adam Phillips notes this paradox in regard to critical readings of *Trilby*, and points out that what often gets lost is the degree to which the novel itself provides a critical perspective on its own publicity. See Phillips, *Equals* (London: Faber and Faber, 2002).

21. Brander Matthews, "The Gift of Story-Telling," *Harper's New Monthly Magazine* 91 (October 1895), 717–22, 717.

22. On the changes in the visual iconography of the periodical press during this period, which, in tandem with the rise of advertising, helped to exponentially increase circulation, see John Tebbel and Mary Ellen Zuckerman, *The Magazine in America 1741–1990* (New York: Oxford University Press, 1991).

23. Technological advances in dissemination, along with circulating libraries, helped to expand audiences beyond private collections and the expensive three-decker novel. See Martin Meisel, *Realizations: Narrative, Pictorial, and Theatrical Arts in Nineteenth-Century England* (Princeton, N.J.: Princeton University Press, 1983), 4.

24. Ibid.

25. Ibid., 11. As Meisel notes, Gotthold Ephraim Lessing's influential categorical distinction between the arts of time and of space began to give way as practitioners of each art adopted this scenic style. Nineteenth-century novels and plays took on a static, scenic quality, while painting aspired to tell a story. See ibid., 18–19.

26. Ibid., 13.

27. As Kaveh Askari notes, the reception of *Trilby* was as much pictorial as it was discursive. See "Trilby's Community of Sensation," in *Visual Delights Two: Exhibition and Reception*, ed. Vanessa Toulmin and Simon Popple (Eastleigh, England: John Libbey, 2005, 60–72.

28. See Gilder and Gilder, *Trilbyana*.

29. Ibid. For details of these suits, see Purcell, "Trilby and Trilby-Mania," 70–71. Jenkins reports that in productions of *A Trilby Triflet*, performed in

London in the mid-1890s, the parts of Little Billee and Trilby were done in drag. See Jenkins, "*Trilby*," 267 n. 85.

30. As Askari notes, the many theatrical productions were often based on *tableau vivant* performances previously adapted from the novel. See "Trilby's Community of Sensation," 63. Jenkins has credited the novel's success to its illustrations, noting that in 1894 *Trilby* was "almost unique" as a novel for adults with illustrations by its author. See Jenkins, "*Trilby*," 230.

31. On the *Pickwick* craze, see Wicke, *Advertising Fictions*, 26–36. On the many products, theatricals, parodies, and other adaptations of Stowe's *Uncle Tom's Cabin*, see Stephen Railton, *Uncle Tom's Cabin in American Culture: A Multimedia Archive* (Charlottesville: University of Virginia, 2009). http://utc.iath.virginia.edu.

32. See Purcell, "Trilby and Trilby-mania," 64.

33. For an account of the extensive ties between pictorialism in theater and early film, along with a critique of film studies' neglect of same, see Ben Brewster and Lea Jacobs, *Theatre to Cinema: Stage Pictorialism and the Early Feature Film* (New York: Oxford University Press, 1997).

34. Askari, "Trilby's Community of Sensation," 60.

35. Cited in ibid., 67. Askari points out that these visual tricks drew on a trope common to early cinema, which a man makes mesmeric passes over posters, causing women posing as images to step out of their frames and walk away.

36. Meisel, *Realizations*, 95.

37. On the move from linguistic translation to medial transposition brought about by mechanical media, see Kittler, *Discourse Networks*, 265.

38. For one of the most influential formulations of the dialectical relationship between the sister arts, see Richard Wagner, "The Art-Work of the Future," in *The Art-Work of the Future and Other Works*, trans. William Ashton Ellis (Lincoln: University of Nebraska Press, 1993).

39. In William Muskerry's *Thrillby: A Shocker in One Scene and Several Spasms*, performed on May 11, 1896, at the Theatre Royal in Richmond, Trilby introduces herself by saying, "Everybody ought to recognize me by this time. Goodness knows I've been sketched, photographed and engraved often enough. If you have any doubts on the subject, give me a light and I'll realize the poster," a reference to a du Maurier drawing showing her smoking. See Muskerry, "Thrillby" (London: Samuel French, 1896), 1–5. Cited in Jenkins, "*Trilby*," 240.

40. James recorded in his notebook entry for March 2, 1889, that on one of his frequent walks with du Maurier on Hampstead Heath in London, he encouraged his friend to write up his idea about "a servant girl [and a] little foreign Jew who has mesmeric power," noting that "the want of musical knowledge would hinder *me* somewhat in handling it." See Henry James, F. O. Matthiessen, and Kenneth Ballard Murdock, *The Notebooks of Henry James* (New York: Oxford University Press, 1961), 97.

41. Joseph Benson Gilder and Jeannette Leonard Gilder, "Miscellanea," in *Trilbyana: The Rise and Progress of a Popular Novel* (New York: The Critic Co., 1895). http://www.gutenberg.org/files/32887/32887-h/32887-h.htm.

42. In the former, Verena Tarrant, the mesmeric trance speaker, is hypnotized by her vampiric father to perform for enthralled socialists and feminists in Boston and New York. In the latter, the Jewish actress Miriam Rooth cannily manipulates the press and public in order to ascend to greatness on the English stage, after which she immediately marries her business manager and breaks the heart of the stalwart British diplomat who first helped her to succeed. It is easy to see a remix and reissue of both heroines in the figures of Trilby, the Jew Svengali, and the very British young men who are so united in hopeless devotion to her. Leon Edel has chronicled James's struggles with sales in *Henry James: A Life*, 363.

43. Ibid., 423–29.

44. On James's pictorial aesthetic more broadly, see Marianna Torgovnick, *The Visual Arts, Pictorialism, and the Novel: James, Lawrence, and Woolf* (Princeton, N.J.: Princeton University Press, 1985), and Viola Hopkins Winner, *Henry James and the Visual Arts* (Charlottesville: University of Virginia Press, 1970). On the often-overlooked importance of magazine illustrations to James and the transformations they brought in late nineteenth-century culture more broadly, see Amy Tucker, *The Illustration of the Master: Henry James and the Magazine Revolution* (Stanford, Calif.: Stanford University Press, 2010).

45. Henry James, "Du Maurier and London Society," *Century* 26 (May 1883): 48–64, 49. Subsequent references are cited parenthetically in the text. This essay was later revised, retitled "George Du Maurier," and published in the collection *Partial Portraits*, in 1888, along with the seminal essay "The Art of Fiction."

46. Leech's portraits of Frenchmen, for example, are identical to "the Frenchman whom the Exhibition of 1851 revealed to the people of London" (52).

47. See Bentley, *Frantic Panoramas*, 22–68.

48. Charles Johanningsmeier, "How Real American Readers Originally Experienced James's 'The Real Thing,'" *Henry James Review* 27:1 (Winter 2006): 79.

49. James and du Maurier had first become friends through this event, although James was to imply later that he was not happy with the illustrations. See Ormond, *George Du Maurier*, 393.

50. Henry James, "The Real Thing," in *The Novels and Tales of Henry James: New York Edition, Vol. XVIII* (New York: Charles Scribner's Sons, 1937), 308, 312. Hereafter cited parenthetically in the text.

51. See Matthiessen and Murdock in *The Notebooks of Henry James*, 105, and Leon Edel, *Henry James*, Vol. 4 (Philadelphia: J. P. Lippincott, 1967), 23.

52. Rather than showing James's disdain for "the real thing," as Stuart Burrows puts it, "what the story ultimately demonstrates is the impossibility of clearly

distinguishing between the real thing and its representation—for the simple reason that the real thing is always a matter of representation" (81). As a story about
the artificiality of realism, "The Real Thing" thus becomes an allegory of its own
creation. See Burrows, *A Familiar Strangeness: American Fiction and the Language
of Photography: 1839–1945* (Athens: University of Georgia Press, 2008); Catherine
Vieilledent, "Representation and Reproduction: A Reading of Henry James's
'The Real Thing,'" in *Interface: Essays on History, Myth and Art in American Literature,* ed. D. Royot (Montpellier, France: Université Paul Valéry, 1985), 31–49;
Bruce Henriksen, "'The Real Thing': Criticism and the Ethical Turn," *Papers on
Language and Literature* 27:4 (1991): 473–95; Martha Banta, "Artists, Models, Real
Things, and Recognizable Types," *Studies in the Literary Imagination* 16:2 (1983):
7–34; and Joseph Wiesenfarth, "Metafiction as the Real Thing," in Joseph Dewey
and Brooke Horvath, eds., *'The Finer Thread, The Tighter Weave': Essays on the
Short Fiction of Henry James* (West Lafayette, Ind.: Purdue University Press, 2001),
232–51.

53. James's dislike of illustrations has been remarked by many critics and has
been attributed to a variety of sources, including the publication delays they
entailed, the competition between a visual mass culture and the visual techniques
of realism, and James's evolving anti-mimetic theory of literary form. On the frustrations James experienced working with illustrators, see Leon Edel, *Henry James:
The Middle Years, 1882–1895* (New York: Avon, 1978). On James's jealousy of illustration, see Ralph Bogardus, *Pictures and Texts: Henry James, A. L. Coburn, and
New Ways of Seeing in Literary Culture* (Ann Arbor: University of Michigan Press,
1984); Wendy Graham, "Pictures for Texts," *Henry James Review* 24:1 (2003): 1–26;
and J. Hillis Miller, "The 'Grafted' Image: James on Illustration" in *Henry James's
New York Edition: The Construction of Authorship,* ed. David McWhirter (Stanford,
Calif.: Stanford University Press, 1995), 138–41.

54. See Johanningsmeier, "Real American Readers," and Adam Sonstegard,
"'Singularly Like a Bad Illustration': The Appearance of Henry James's 'The Real
Thing' in the Pot-Boiler Press," *Texas Studies in Literature and Language* 45:2
(2003): 173–200.

55. The inaccessibility of the glance's meaning suggests, as Whitsitt notes, that
the experience itself "was never quite present," and was filled out by its subsequent interpretation. See Sam Whitsitt, "A Lesson in Reading: Henry James's
'The Real Thing,'" *Henry James Review* 16:3 (1995): 304–14, 312.

56. In contrast to poststructuralist critics mentioned in n. 52, who chart the
impossibility of separating the real from the representation in the story, those
influenced by the pragmatist or phenomenological tradition argue that the narrator's experience of his models in moments such as these *is* "the real thing." My
reading mediates between these two positions, emphasizing that, by the end of
the story, the "real" thing becomes the virtual thing. For pragmatist readings of the

story, see Sämi Ludwig, *Pragmatist Realism: The Cognitive Paradigm in American Realist Texts* (Madison: University of Wisconsin Press, 2002); George Monteiro, "Realization in Henry James' 'The Real Thing,'" *American Literary Realism* 36:1 (Fall 2003): 40-50; Whitsitt, "A Lesson in Reading"; Virginia Llewellyn Smith, *Henry James and the Real Thing: A Modern Reader's Guide* (New York: St. Martin's Press, 1994); and Richard Hocks, *Henry James and Pragmatistic Thought* (Chapel Hill: University of North Carolina Press, 1974).

57. Earlier pragmatist readers of James have tended to argue that his exploration of the impersonal nature of consciousness is opposed to William James's psychology. See Dorothea Krook-Gilead, *The Ordeal of Consciousness in Henry James* (Cambridge: Cambridge University Press, 1962), and Cameron, *Thinking in Henry James*. More recent accounts attuned to the anti-individualistic thrust of William's philosophy of radical empiricism have seen more of a continuity between them, as well as between Henry and other pragmatist philosophers like John Dewey and George Santayana. See, for example, Levin, *The Poetics of Transition*, and Richardson, *A Natural History of Pragmatism*.

58. Cameron, *Thinking in Henry James*, 108.

59. See Ralph Waldo Emerson, *Essays and English Traits*, Vol. 5 (New York: P. F. Collier and Son, 1909), 155. For a fuller discussion of the significance of the figure of the circle in Emerson as it relates to Emerson's material model of mind, see Arsić, *On Leaving*, 170–75.

60. Henry James, *The Art of the Novel* (London: Charles Scribner's Sons, 1935), 5.

61. The criticism cited here builds on the paradigm-shifting queer theoretical work on James's late style by Eve Kosofsky Sedgwick in *Epistemology of the Closet* and *Touching Feeling* (Durham, N.C.: Duke University Press, 2003), as well as Michael Moon, *A Small Boy and Others: Imitation and Initiation in American Culture from Henry James to Andy Warhol*, Series Q (Durham, N.C.: Duke University Press, 1998).

62. See Leo Bersani and Adam Phillips, *Intimacies* (Chicago: University of Chicago Press, 2008), 24. Bersani is by no means the only one to have noted the way James's sentences confuse the progress of linear temporality. On temporal and grammatical disjunction in James's late style more generally, see David McWhirter, "'A Provision Full of Responsibilities': Senses of the Past in Henry James's Fourth Phase," in *Enacting History in Henry James: Narrative, Power and Ethics*, ed. Gert Buelens (Cambridge: Cambridge University Press, 1997), 148–65, and Peter Rawlings, "Grammars of Time in Late James," *Modern Language Review* 98:2 (April 2003): 273–84.

63. Bersani and Phillips, *Intimacies*, 20.

64. On the queerness of literary language's challenge to the reproduction of normative social relations, see Lee Edelman, *No Future: Queer Theory and the Death Drive* (Durham, N.C.: Duke University Press, 2004). On the ways in which

James's style embodies this challenge by refusing mimeticism and potentializing experience, see Kevin Ohi, *Henry James and the Queerness of Style* (Minneapolis: University of Minnesota Press, 2011).

65. See David Kurnick, *Empty Houses;* Mark Goble, "Delirious Henry James: A Small Boy and New York," *Modern Fiction Studies* 50:2 (2004): 351–84; and Kendall Johnson, "Visual Culture," in *Henry James in Context,* ed. David McWhirter (Cambridge: Cambridge University Press, 2010), 364–77. On theatricality more generally in *A Small Boy,* and its links to a queer aesthetic of embarrassment, see Joseph Litvak, *Caught in the Act: Theatricality in the Nineteenth-Century English Novel* (Berkeley: University of California Press, 1992).

66. The young boy's theatrical witnessing is closely related to the older novelist's style, for Kurnick, because of the effect of co-presence created by the excessive hypotaxis of the Jamesian sentence, which "replicates precisely the situation of the young James whose overwhelmed perception it describes." See Kurnick, *Empty Houses,* 107, 109.

67. See Goble, *Beautiful Circuits,* 81.

68. Ohi, *Henry James and the Queerness of Style,* 19.

69. Henry James, *A Small Boy and Others* (New York: Criterion Books, 1956), 92.

70. Henry James, "The Art of Fiction," in *Henry James: Literary Criticism:* Vol. 1, *Essays on Literature, American Writers, English Writers,* ed. Leon Edel and Mark Wilson (New York: Library of America, 1984), 44–65.

71. Henry James, "The Future of the Novel," in *Henry James: Literary Criticism,* 100–110. I am indebted for this account to Kevin Ohi's insightful reading of these two essays. Ohi notes that James's autobiographical writings describe the writer's life as unrepresentable and unobjectifiable in the same way that he had earlier described the "life" of "fiction" and the "novel." See Ohi, *Henry James and the Queerness of Style,* 3–17, 115–16.

72. As Wendy Graham notes, "Discussions of Henry James's views on illustration often focus on the question of whether he understood and appreciated photography." See sources cited in Graham, "Pictures for Texts," 1.

73. James, *The Art of the Novel,* 332.

74. Ibid., 331–32. *Graft* and *graphic,* as J. Hillis Miller notes, have a common root in the Greek *graphein,* "to write." The metaphor suggests that James's overt resistance here to illustration is grounded in idealism, since the imitative illustration stands in relation to James's text much as writing does to speech for Plato. Metaphors of grafting, for instance, are found in The *Phaedrus,* where they serve to emphasize the corrupting force of rhetoric and writing. See Miller, "The 'Grafted' Image," 140. On writing as a "dangerous supplement" to speech in the Platonic tradition, see Jacques Derrida's discussion of Rousseau in *Of Grammatology* (Baltimore: Johns Hopkins University Press, 1976), 141–65.

75. James, *The Art of the Novel,* 332–33.

76. Ibid., 333.

77. Ibid., 335, 333.

78. Stuart Burrows has discussed the way in which a metaphorics of "retraced steps" unites James and Coburn both with the Prince and Charlotte and with James's own work of revision. He has also pointed out the way that James's conception of photography unites the typical with the concrete. See Burrows, *A Familiar Strangeness*, 108–14.

79. James, *The Art of the Novel*, 333.

80. Ross Posnock has provided the most extensive discussion of this aspect of *The American Scene*, arguing that James uncovers the "plasticity" inherent in "systems of power" and exploits them to forge a "politics of nonidentity" in the context of American modernity more broadly. See Posnock, *The Trial of Curiosity*, 284.

81. See, in particular, McWhirter, "A Provision Full of Responsibilities," and Rawlings, "Grammars of Time in Late James."

82. Henry James, *The American Scene: Together with Three Essays from "Portraits of Places,"* ed. W. H. Auden (New York: Charles Scribner's Sons, 1946), 53. Hereafter cited parenthetically in the text.

83. On thinking as linguistic troping in Emerson, see Cavell, *Emerson's Transcendental Etudes*.

84. Thurschwell discusses James's various amanuenses, who typed his works and sometimes also his letters, in *Literature, Technology and Magical Thinking*, 86–115.

85. On James's evolving concerns about the decline of the public sphere and the rise of modern publicity, see Richard Salmon, *Henry James and the Culture of Publicity* (Cambridge: Cambridge University Press, 1997).

86. Henry James, "George Du Maurier," *Harper's New Monthly Magazine* 95 (September 1897): 594–608, 607. Hereafter cited parenthetically in the text.

87. As in James's short stories about literary publicity, the author's death here is synonymous with a commercialized public sphere's ability to undermine his authority over his text. In both the "Death of the Lion" (1894) and "The Next Time" (1895), for instance, a literary public sphere that is largely run by women leads the narrator's intimate friend to his demise by attempting to promote his brilliant work to a popular audience. Du Maurier's biographer endorses James's view that the pressures of becoming a sought-after novelist contributed to du Maurier's death. See Ormond, *George Du Maurier*, 488–98.

88. Here James anticipates the sentiments of his elliptical late essay, "Is There a Life after Death?" (1909), in which he speculates about whether the expansion of consciousness beyond physicality obviates an author's mortality. See James, "Is There a Life after Death?" in *Henry James on Culture: Collected Essays on Politics and the American Social Scene*, ed. Pierre A. Walker (Lincoln: University

of Nebraska Press, 1999). I am indebted here to Sharon Cameron's discussion of this essay in relation to *The Wings of the Dove*. See *Thinking in Henry James*, 155–57.

89. The infantile state involves no separation of the senses, as Francis Galton and others had revealed as early as the 1880s. See Francis Galton, *Inquiries into Human Faculty and Its Development* (New York: E. P. Dutton, 1908).

90. Henry James, *Notes of a Son and Brother* (New York: Scribner, 1914), 336. Subsequent references are cited parenthetically in the text.

91. Trilby-mania did not stop at the end of the century. Film versions of the novel were made in 1914, 1915, 1923, and 1931.

92. Ormond, *George Du Maurier*, 399. Ormond cites James's obituary of du Maurier for this information, which makes no mention of a bench. However, given James's frequent walks with du Maurier on the Heath, and du Maurier's frequent use of the environs in his illustrations, it seems likely that Coburn's photograph commemorates a location they both knew well. As J. Hillis Miller writes of this photograph, "It is as though Coburn had . . . photographed the empty stage set, in this case an outdoor bench, before, or after, some determining meeting between two characters takes place, or has taken place, there." See Miller, *Literature as Conduct: Speech Acts in Henry James* (New York: Fordham University Press, 2005), 125.

3. Syncope Fever

1. See sources cited in nn. 74 and 86 following.

2. Johnson chose to publish his novel anonymously in 1912 with the white "job printer" of Sherman, French & Co. to gain both black and white audiences for the book; to use the publisher's marginality to enhance the realism of his character's anonymity; and to maintain the fiction that the book was really written by a black man passing for white. See Jacqueline Goldsby, "Keeping the 'Secret of Authorship': A Critical Look at the 1912 Publication of James Weldon Johnson's *Autobiography of an Ex-Colored Man*," in *Print Culture in a Diverse America*, ed. James P. Danky and Wayne A. Wiegand (Urbana: University of Illinois Press, 1998), 244. Goldsby has argued that it is important to place the novel in its original context in order to understand the "complexity of Johnson's efforts to conceive a narrative form and to cultivate a reading public" during a period in which there was almost no public interest in his "culture and voice" (246).

3. James Weldon Johnson, "Preface to *The Book of American Negro Poetry*," in *James Weldon Johnson: Writings* (New York: Library of America, 2004), 688.

4. Ibid., 694.

5. For Johnson, writing during and after World War I, "ragtime" would have signified a number of different things. A syncopated piano style had first emerged

in the mid-1890s, performed by itinerant black male piano players in southern saloons and taverns. By 1900 and just afterward, ragtime songs were being appropriated, composed, and recorded by white and a few black musicians. At this point, the term began to designate a variety of different kinds of syncopated music, including: (1) the vocal "coon song," whose lyrics and sheet-music covers reveled in the stereotypes of minstrelsy; (2) the more elevated "ragtime" song, sometimes shorn of racial references, which was heard in the genteel parlor and the ballroom and often performed by marching bands and instrumental groups; and (3) "classic," nonvocal piano rags whose composers, such as Scott Joplin, sought elite acceptance. See Edward Berlin, *Ragtime: A Musical and Cultural History* (Berkeley: University of California Press, 1980), 5–20. As Eileen Southern notes, most of the money made from ragtime in these years went to whites. On ragtime appropriation, see Southern, *Music of Black Americans: A History* (New York: Norton, 1997), 313; 331–32; and William J. Schafer and Johannes Riedel, *Art of Ragtime: Form and Meaning of an Original Black American Art* (New York: Da Capo Press, 1977), 3–23.

6. The phonograph and player piano aided in the music's appropriation and dissemination and also helped to inaugurate a homogenous mass culture in which nationwide trends such as the so-called ragtime craze could take off (Berlin, *Ragtime*, 32). Lisa Gitelman has elaborated the ways in which recorded "coon songs" transformed the visual form of minstrelsy as "white-constructed 'blackness'" into a matter of "sounding 'black,'" which in turn enabled their metamorphosis into middle-class entertainments. See *Scripts, Grooves, and Writing Machines: Representing Technology in the Edison Era* (Stanford, Calif.: Stanford University Press, 1999), 134.

7. See, for comparison, James Weldon Johnson, *The Autobiography of an Ex-Colored Man*, ed. William L. Andrews (New York: Penguin, 1990), 72–74. Subsequent references are cited parenthetically in the text.

8. See Alexander G. Weheliye, *Phonographies: Grooves in Sonic Afro-Modernity* (Durham, N.C.: Duke University Press, 2005); Brent Hayes Edwards, "The Seemingly Eclipsed Window of Form: James Weldon Johnson's Prefaces," in *The Jazz Cadence of American Culture*, ed. Robert G. O'Meally (New York: Columbia University Press, 1998), 580–601; Edwards, "Louis Armstrong and the Syntax of Scat," *Critical Inquiry* 28:3 (Spring 2002): 618–49; Edwards, "The Literary Ellington," *Representations* 77:1 (Winter 2002): 1–29; Nathaniel Mackey, *Discrepant Engagement: Dissonance, Cross-Culturality, and Experimental Writing* (Cambridge: Cambridge University Press, 1993); Fred Moten, *In the Break: The Aesthetics of the Black Radical Tradition* (Minneapolis: University of Minnesota Press, 2003); and Aldon Lynn Nielsen, *Black Chant: Languages of African-American Postmodernism* (New York: Cambridge University Press, 1997). As will become evident later in the chapter, I am particularly indebted to Edwards, "The Seemingly Eclipsed

Window of Form," for his reevaluation of the role of orality in Johnson's essays on aesthetics.

9. As Jacques Derrida has argued, in the Western philosophical tradition, the domain of the *phone* is that of pure transparency, of a meaning borne on the breath. That of the *graph* is the material substitution for the spoken or sung word. On writing as a "dangerous supplement" to voice and song, see Derrida, *Of Grammatology*, trans. Gayatri Chakravorty Spivak (Baltimore: Johns Hopkins University Press, 1997), 141–268. For a critique of Derrida's failure to fully consider improvisation and sonic materiality in his deconstruction of Western metaphysics, see, respectively, Moten, *In the Break*, 74–77; and Weheliye, *Phonographies*, 30–36.

10. For an analysis of the reciprocal relationship between sound technologies and black cultural practices, see Weheliye, *Phonographies*.

11. On "fugitivity," see Mackey, "Other: From Noun to Verb," in *Discrepant Engagement*.

12. This is Edwards's description of the "mood" of Duke Ellington's literary projects, and of his explicitly socially and racially themed compositions. See Edwards, "The Literary Ellington," 24.

13. See Mackey, *Discrepant Engagement*, 252–53.

14. Stephen M. Best has argued that the "profligate significations" of blackness and minstrelsy served as occasions for institutional self-definition in the late nineteenth century, as, for example, the "symptomatic externalization of the speculative economy's subjective effect" and "the defining, nonteleological, nonpurposive antithesis to early cinema's narrative progression." See Best, *The Fugitive's Properties: Law and the Poetics of Possession* (Chicago: University of Chicago Press, 2004), 187, 197, 265. Bryan Wagner has recently traced the way in which, through their erasure of the outlaw legend Bras-Coupé, both nineteenth-century ethnography and the liberal nationalist tendencies of jazz historiography have made the interimplication of state violence and black culture unavailable to representation except as "the inner distance from speech to noise, from grievance to groan." See Wagner, "Disarmed and Dangerous: The Strange Career of Bras-Coupé," *Representations* 92:1 (Fall 2005): 117–51, 130–31. Finally, in *A Spectacular Secret: Lynching in American Life and Literature* (Chicago: University of Chicago Press, 2006), Jacqueline Goldsby shows that the display of the lynched black body via photographs allowed white Americans to master anxieties about modernity's increasingly indistinct boundaries between original and copy, individual and mass.

15. Jacques Derrida, *Archive Fever: A Freudian Impression*, trans. Eric Prenowitz (Chicago: University of Chicago Press, 1996), 2.

16. Wagner, "Disarmed and Dangerous," 130.

17. Ibid.

18. These included the cakewalk, the two-step, and the march (Berlin, *Ragtime*, 14).

19. Neil Leonard, "The Reactions to Ragtime," in *Ragtime: Its History, Composers, and Music*, ed. John Edward Hasse (New York: Schirmer Books, 1985), 103.

20. See Lawrence Levine, *Highbrow/Lowbrow: The Emergence of Cultural Hierarchy in America* (Cambridge, Mass.: Harvard University Press, 1988).

21. Gunther Schuller, "Rags, the Classics, and Jazz," in Hasse, *Ragtime*, 81.

22. On the first generation of post-slavery black composers, who often incorporated traditional African American performance styles into their work, see Southern, *The Music of Black Americans*.

23. Karl Muck, "The Music of Democracy," *Craftsman* 29:3 (December 1915): 270.

24. Ibid., 271.

25. Ibid., 277.

26. See Antonín Dvořák, "Music in America," *Harper's New Monthly Magazine* 90 (February 1895), 433.

27. The phrase is Thomas P. Fenner's, musical director of the Hampton Institute and arranger of spirituals. Quoted in Eric J. Sundquist, *The Hammers of Creation: Folk Culture in Modern African-American Fiction* (Athens: University of Georgia Press, 1992), 28.

28. See Kittler, *Gramophone, Film, Typewriter*, 24. Kittler credits the phonograph with stimulating new discoveries not only in the field of acoustics but also in the sciences of memory, brain physiology, and psychophysics.

29. Hermann von Helmholtz, quoted in John M. Picker, *Victorian Soundscapes* (New York: Oxford University Press, 2003), 87.

30. Arthur Weld, "The Invasion of Vulgarity in Music," *Etude* 17:2 (February 1899): 52. "Ragtime" and "coon song" were often used interchangeably because they made use of the same syncopated rhythm. On the differences between the two, see n. 5.

31. See George Miller Beard, *American Nervousness: Its Causes and Consequences* (New York: G. P. Putnam's Sons, 1881).

32. On the links between neurasthenia and economic change in turn-of-the-century America, see Tom Lutz, *American Nervousness, 1903: An Anecdotal History* (Ithaca, N.Y.: Cornell University Press, 1991), 1–38.

33. Stereotypes of blacks as chicken stealers, for example, might be the subject of the lyrics and the picture (Lutz, *American Nervousness*, 270). On the degrading lyrics and sheet-music covers of "coon songs," see Schafer and Riedel, *Art of Ragtime*, 24–32; and Berlin, *Ragtime*, 32–38.

34. Ragtime renders audible what Roland Barthes would call the "grain of the voice." See Roland Barthes, "The Grain of the Voice," in *Image, Music, Text*, trans. Stephen Heath (New York: Hill and Wang, 1977). For a critique of the "silencing

invocation" of black difference in Barthesian *signifiance*, see Moten, *In the Break*, 203.

35. Kittler's useful term, in John Johnston's lucid summary, designates "the archive of what is inscribed by a culture at a particular moment in time. The notion of the discourse network points to the fact that at any given cross-sectional moment in the life of a culture, only certain data (and no other) are selected stored, processed, transmitted or calculated, all else being 'noise.'"See John Johnston, "Friedrich Kittler: Media Theory After Poststructuralism," in the introduction to Friedrich A. Kittler, *Literature, Media, Information Systems: Essays*, ed. Johnston (Amsterdam: GB Arts International, 1997), 9.

36. See Theodor Adorno, "Perennial Fashion—Jazz," in *Prisms*, trans. Samuel and Shierry Weber (Cambridge, Mass.: MIT, 1983), 123.

37. A. J. Goodrich, "Syncopated Rhythm vs. Rag-Time," *Musician* 6 (November 1901): 336.

38. In his study of "graphomania" in Bram Stoker's *Dracula*, Mark Seltzer notes that "maladies of energy, motive and agency were in effect understood, around 1900, as maladies of mimesis, representation, and writing." See Mark Seltzer, *Serial Killers: Death and Life in America's Wound Culture* (New York, Routledge, 1998), 74.

39. Goodrich, "Syncopated Rhythm vs. 'Rag-Time,'" 336.

40. Quoted in Neil Leonard, "The Reactions to Ragtime," in *Ragtime: Its History, Composers, and Music* (New York: Schirmer Books, 1985), 109.

41. Leo Oehmler, "Ragtime: A Pernicious Evil and Enemy of True Art," *Musical Observer* 11 (September 1914): 14.

42. *Oxford English Dictionary Online*, s.v. "Syncope." http://dictionary.oed .com.

43. Ibid.

44. Frank L. Reed, "Habits of Accuracy," *Musician* 4 (October 1901): 277.

45. Ibid.

46. See Frederick Winslow Taylor, *Principles of Scientific Management* (New York: Harper and Brothers, 1911).

47. Herbert G. Patton. "Acquiring Soulfulness," *Musician* 5 (January 1902): 276.

48. Hiram K. Motherwell, "Ragtime," *New Republic* (October 16, 1915), 285. Discussing the cinematic experiments of Etienne-Jules Marey and Eadweard Muybridge, Mary Ann Doane has noted a preoccupation with the question of "lost time" at the turn of the century very similar to the problem of the gap between inscription and consciousness I focus on here. See Doane, *The Emergence of Cinematic Time: Modernity, Contingency, The Archive* (Cambridge, Mass.: Harvard University Press, 2002). In an argument that also applies to the white ragtime enthusiasts of an earlier era, Joel Dinerstein has recently claimed that the appeal of African American dances in the big-band era was that they helped to amelio-

rate alienation with machine culture by integrating "the speed, drive, precision, and rhythmic flow of factory work and modern cites into a nationally (and internationally) unifying cultural form." See Dinerstein, *Swinging the Machine: Modernity, Technology, and African American Culture between the World Wars* (Amherst: University of Massachusetts Press, 2003), 5.

49. Cited in "The Crime of Ragtime: Those in Favor," *Musical Courier* (January 20, 1916): 21.

50. Michael Rogin, "The Two Declarations of American Independence," *Representations* 55 (Summer 1996): 13–14.

51. Motherwell, "Ragtime," 285.

52. Motherwell may be alluding here to the Ziegfeld Follies hit, "That Shakespearian Rag." If so, he appears to forget that the song in fact "rags" Shakespeare. It was first published the same year as *The Autobiography of an Ex-Colored Man* (1912), by Joseph W. Stern & Company, and makes a famous appearance in T. S. Eliot's "The Waste Land." Music and lyrics are reprinted in full in Michael North, ed., *The Waste Land: Authoritative Text, Contexts, Criticism* (New York, Norton, 2001), 51–54.

53. Motherwell, "Ragtime," 286.

54. On the dialectic of celebration and repression in blackface minstrelsy, see Eric Lott, *Love and Theft: Blackface Minstrelsy and the American Working Class* (New York: Oxford University Press, 1993).

55. See, respectively, Randolph Bourne, "Trans-national America," *Atlantic Monthly* 118 (July 1916), 86–97, and Horace M. Kallen, "Democracy Versus the Melting-Pot: A Study of American Nationality," *The Nation* (February 25, 1915). On the origins of Bourne's cultural criticism and that of the Young American movement to which he belonged, see Blake, *Beloved Community*. On Kallen's ties to William James and the origins of his thinking about ethnic identity, particularly Jewish identity, see Menand, *The Metaphysical Club*.

56. Bourne, "Trans-national America," 90.

57. Ibid.

58. Ibid., 97.

59. On similarities and differences across Kallen, Bourne, W. E. B. Du Bois, and Alain Locke in this regard, see Menand, *The Metaphysical Club*, 388–408.

60. On Du Bois's pragmatist and pluralist leanings, which became more pronounced throughout his career, see Ross Posnock, *Color and Culture: Black Writers and the Making of the Modern Intellectual* (Cambridge, Mass.: Harvard University Press, 1998). On the ways in which pragmatism and Hegelianism "mutually revised one another" in *Souls*, see also Posnock, "Going Astray, Going Forward: Du Boisian Pragmatism and Its Lineage," in *The Revival of Pragmatism: New Essays on Social Thought, Law, and Culture*, ed. Morris Dickstein (Durham, N.C.: Duke University Press, 1998), 176–89, 181.

61. W. E. B. Du Bois, *The Souls of Black Folk* (New York: Penguin, 1996), 90. (Originally published 1903.) Hereafter cited parenthetically in the text.

62. As Ronald Radano notes, "gift" may be read etymologically, and via its German meaning, as evoking poison, especially in Du Bois's earlier assertion that "the Negro is gifted with second-sight" (Du Bois, 5). See Radano, *Lying Up a Nation: Race and Black Music* (Chicago: University of Chicago Press, 2003), 279.

63. As Eric Sundquist has argued in a searching and extensive discussion of the use of music in *Souls*, "By incorporating the spirituals into the fabric of his text, Du Bois turned sociological commentary into a sensate, vocalized text—radically crossing generic boundaries, employing the languages of silence and implication to carry significant communicative burdens, and dwelling in the most profound autobiographical way in the spiritual resources of his texts." See Sundquist, *To Wake the Nations: Race in the Making of American Literature* (Cambridge, Mass.: Harvard University Press, 1993), 469. On Du Bois's sonic "mixing," see also Weheliye, *Phonographies*.

64. As Sundquist notes, Du Bois's identification of the spirituals as the foundation of black culture was also aimed at white cultural critics and ethnographers who, in seeking in them original expressions of folk culture, often misunderstood their value. See Sundquist, *To Wake the Nations,* 465.

65. Many critics have explored the *Autobiography*'s formal debts to *Souls*. See, for example, Robert B. Stepto, "Lost in a Quest: James Weldon Johnson's *Autobiography of an Ex-Colored Man,*" in *Critical Essays on James Weldon Johnson,* ed. Kenneth M. Price and Lawrence J. Oliver (New York: G.K. Hall, 1997).

66. Du Bois did note at one point that "caricature has sought again to spoil the quaint beauty of the music, and has filled the air with many debased melodies which vulgar ears scarce know from the real." Despite his subversive play with writing and voice, Du Bois, drawing on Hegel, Schopenhauer, and Wagner, often also implies that the spirituals' power is inseparable from the music's transparency to the soul and to the divine. See *Souls,* 206.

67. See Levy, *James Weldon Johnson: Black Leader, Black Voice* (Chicago: University of Chicago Press, 1973), 75–98, and Robert M. Dowling, "A Marginal Man in Black Bohemia: James Weldon Johnson in the New York Tenderloin," in *Post-Bellum, Pre-Harlem: African American Literature and Culture, 1877–1919,* ed. Barbara McCaskill and Caroline Gebhard (New York: New York University Press, 2006), 117–33.

68. James Weldon Johnson, "The Poor White Musician" (1915), in *Selected Writings of James Weldon Johnson,* Vol. 1, ed. Sondra Wilson (New York: Oxford University Press, 1995), 286.

69. On Wright's critique of an earlier generation of black writers, see "Blueprint for Negro Writing," in *The Richard Wright Reader,* ed. Ellen Wright and Michael Fabre (New York: Harper & Row 1978), 37. On Johnson's critics, and on

the ambivalence in Johnson's class consciousness and its links to the wider "New Negro" movement, see David Levering Lewis, *When Harlem Was in Vogue* (New York: Penguin, 1997), 147–48.

70. Johnson, preface to *Book of American Negro Poetry* (New York: Harcourt, Brace, and Co., 1922), 19. Johnson recalls Frederick Douglass, who noted, "I have sometimes thought that the mere hearing of those songs would do more to impress some minds with the horrible character of slavery, than the reading of whole volumes of philosophy on the subject could do." See *Frederick Douglass: The Narrative and Selected Writings,* ed. Michael Meyer (New York: Modern Library, 1984), 28.

71. "Race Prejudice and the Negro Artist," in *The Selected Writings of James Weldon Johnson,* Vol. II, 398.

72. My discussion throughout this section is indebted to Edwards's account of the way black anthology-making and practices of translation helped to create a black internationalism during the interwar period. In Johnson's prefaces, "the frame . . . ends by undoing itself" as Johnson situates African American culture both internal to and excessive to the nation, and celebrates not only literate achievement but also popular and vernacular forms of black culture. See Brent Hayes Edwards, *The Practice of Diaspora: Literature, Translation, and the Rise of Black Internationalism* (Cambridge, Mass.: Harvard University Press, 2003), 49.

73. See Goldsby, "Keeping the Secret of Authorship," 244.

74. On the *Autobiography* as a literary exploration of the problematic nature of racial, sexual, and gender identity, see Kimberly W. Benston, "Facing Tradition: Revisionary Scenes in African American Literature," *Publications of the Modern Language Association* 105:1 (January 1990): 98–109; Cheryl Clarke, "Race, Homosocial Desire, and 'Mammon' in *Autobiography of an Ex-Colored Man,*" in *Professions of Desire: Lesbian and Gay Studies in Literature,* eds. George E. Haggerty and Bonnie Zimmerman (New York, Modern Language Association, 1995), 84–97; Phillip Brian Harper, *Are We Not Men? Masculine Anxiety and the Problem of African-American Identity* (New York: Oxford University Press 1996), 108–13; Siobhan B. Somerville, *Queering the Color Line: Race and the Invention of Homosexuality in American Culture* (Durham, N.C.: Duke University Press, 2000), 111–30; Darieck Scott, *Extravagant Abjection: Blackness, Power, and Sexuality in the African American Literary Imagination* (New York: New York University Press, 2010).

75. See Johnson, *Autobiography,* 74, in which ex-colored man encounters a talented black ragtime player who composes all his songs by ear. To Johnson's contemporaries, the narrator's ragtime transcription of the "Wedding March" would have sounded familiar. It was in fact a real tune published by the leading white popularizer of ragtime, Axel Christensen, in 1902. See Sundquist, *Hammers of Creation,* 22–23.

76. On the cakewalk, see Berlin, *Ragtime,* 14. Originally a high-kicking dance

performed on the plantation by slave couples competing for a cake as a prize, it had become linked to minstrelsy, to vaudeville, and then to the first stirrings of the ragtime craze by 1900 (Southern, *Music of Black Americans,* 273, 314). On the cakewalk as both a parody of white mannerisms and "a matter of physicality become semiotics" in which "the echo . . . is of the slave economy itself," see Best, *Fugitive's Properties,* 141.

77. The phrase "impromptu cakewalk," especially given ex-colored man's earlier fondness for Chopin, itself suggests an irresolvable impurity between classical forms and the black vernacular.

78. Mark Goble has also pointed out that ex-colored man functions as a phonograph in this scene, in a broader survey of black music's association with mechanization and mediation in turn-of-the-century America. See Goble, *Beautiful Circuits.*

79. Media theorists have elaborated the ways in which Edison's project to record and "immortalize" the voices of famous authors and other luminaries came at the expense of banishing ideality from the voice, not preserving it so much as embalming it. On the phonograph's deathly associations in the late nineteenth century, see Picker, *Victorian Soundscapes;* Jonathan Sterne, *The Audible Past: Cultural Origins of Sound Reproduction* (Durham, N.C.: Duke University Press, 2003); Steven Connor, *Dumbstruck: A Cultural History of Ventriloquism* (New York: Oxford University Press, 2000); and Kittler, *Gramophone, Film, Typewriter.*

80. Thomas Alva Edison, "The Phonograph and Its Future," *North American Review* 126 (June 1878): 530. Best notes that Edison's language of slavery and dispossession also pervaded legal debates about sound reproduction's protection under copyright law in the late nineteenth century. See Best, *Fugitive's Properties,* 29–98.

81. Another intriguing possibility is that Johnson, planning to publish the text anonymously, sought to follow in *Trilby*'s footsteps and make the *Autobiography* itself something of an *outré* bestseller. There is more to *Trilby,* after all, than its anti-Semitism; it offers a clever satire on the production and consumption of musical "stars" in the marketplace, and, like *Ex-Colored Man,* it offers the occasional essayistic digression on social problems.

82. As Hortense Spillers has argued, slavery gives mothers and sons a potential axis of identification unacknowledged by traditional theories of Oedipal triangulation. See Spillers, "Mama's Baby, Papa's Maybe: An American Grammar Book," *Diacritics* 17:2 (Summer 1987). Considering the question of ex-colored man's identification as property with his mother should also give us pause in interpreting the narrator's feminization and homosexual overtones as simply authorial condemnations of his racial apostasy. For an example of such a reading, see Harper, *Are We Not Men?* On further cross-connections between racialization, feminization,

homosexuality, homophobia, and the Oedipal logic of the gaze in the novel, see sources cited in n. 74.

83. Goldsby has argued that we can also read these scenes as having a photogenic quality: ex-colored man figures his perception in terms of a photographic camera, while the narrative itself, insofar as it comes into being after the lynching, develops like a photographic exposure. Borrowing a term from Bill Brown, Goldsby points out that the term "intermediality" would apply well to the *Autobiography*. I am suggesting that the novel's relation to its musical context makes phonography another of the work's "intermedial" effects. See Goldsby, *A Spectacular Secret*. On intermediality, see Brown, *The Material Unconscious*, 143.

84. See Paul de Man, "Autobiography as De-Facement," in *The Rhetoric of Romanticism* (New York: Columbia University Press 1984), 67–81.

85. On the outlaw as a figure for the law's self-naming, see Wagner, "Disarmed and Dangerous."

86. While more recent accounts emphasize the way the narrator's gaze renders notions of an authentic black male identity problematic (see sources cited in n. 75), an older critical debate about the degree of structural irony present in the novel understood the work to conserve a notion of racial identity. For samples of these earlier arguments, see Price and Oliver, eds., *Critical Essays on James Weldon Johnson*.

87. See John Durham Peters and Eric W. Rothenbuhler, "Defining Phonography: An Experiment in Theory," *Musical Quarterly* 81:2 (Summer 1997): 255.

88. See Johnson, *Autobiography*, 129–30, and *Book of American Negro Spirituals*, 22.

89. See *Autobiography*, 130–31, and *Book of American Negro Spirituals*, 26. More recent approaches to Johnson's novel have begun to examine the ways that its influences might be musical as well as literary and have taken note, as I do here, of the moments in which Johnson's own voice can be heard in the work. See Cristina L. Ruotolo, "James Weldon Johnson and the Autobiography of an Ex-Colored Musician," *American Literature* 72:2 (June 2000); and Salim Washington, "Of Black Bards, Known and Unknown: Music as Racial Metaphor in James Weldon Johnson's *The Autobiography of an Ex-Colored Man*," *Callaloo* 25:1 (2002). However, because they assume the predominance of the oral in Johnson's aesthetics, these valuable historical contextualizations largely disregard the question of narrative "unreliability" in the text, and take most of ex-colored man's idealist statements about music to be Johnson's own.

90. On Johnson's nonfiction "missteps" see Richard Yarborough, "The First-Person in Afro-American Fiction," in *Afro-American Literary Study in the 1990s*, ed. Houston A. Baker and P. Redmond (Chicago: University of Chicago Press, 1989), 118. On these passages as further evidence of narrative unreliability, see Stepto, "Lost in a Quest: James Weldon Johnson's *Autobiography of an Ex-Colored Man*,"

63–64; and Martin Japtok, "Between 'Race' as Construct and 'Race' as Essence: *The Autobiography of an Ex-Colored Man*," *Southern Literary Journal* 28:2 (Spring 1996): 39. On the novel's generic instability and voice as a product of Johnson's need to portray his narrator as both anti-hero and "race man," see Heather Russell Andrade, "Revising Critical Judgments of *The Autobiography of an Ex-Colored Man*," *African American Review* 40:2 (Summer 2006). On Johnson's combination of ethnography and narrative in *The Autobiography*, see Daphne Lamothe, *Inventing the New Negro: Narrative, Culture, and Ethnography* (Philadelphia: University of Pennsylvania Press, 2008), 69–91. In addition to these sources, Sundquist has provided one of the few joint treatments of the convergence of literary and anthropological or social scientific perspectives in the novel. I am indebted to his description of the relationship between the novel and later essays as one of "ragged time." He concludes that "the challenge is to identify and estimate the curious mixture of sincerity, parodic undercurrent, and unconscious revelation manifest in the narrator's voicing of opinions so much like Johnson's own, but in a novelistic context so loaded with ironies and contradictions." See Sundquist, *Hammers of Creation*, 25.

4. Wonder and Decay

1. For details of Barnes's early life and her many assignments, see Phillip Herring, *Djuna: The Life and Work of Djuna Barnes* (New York: Viking, 1995).

2. Barnes would have known the ins and outs of reform well even before she began to write for the newspapers, because her grandmother Zadel Barnes was herself a journalist who had moved in reformist circles in Boston. Djuna Barnes also told friends she had been named after a character in one of the novels of Eugène Sue, a writer in the sensational "city mysteries" genre that had helped to sensationalize as well as publicize urban corruption and exploitation. For details of Zadel's career, see Herring, *Djuna*, 1–23. On the origins of Barnes's name, see ibid., 319 n. 24. On the popularity of "mysteries of the city" fiction in America in the mid-nineteenth century, see Karen Halttunen, *Murder Most Foul: The Killer and the American Gothic Imagination* (Cambridge, Mass.: Harvard University Press, 1998).

3. George Chauncey, *Gay New York* (New York: Basic Books, 1994), 138.

4. Other evidence of Barnes's neobaroque style besides that listed here includes the drawings and illustrations that adorn both Barnes's parodic queer hagiography of Natalie Barney's Paris salon, *The Ladies Almanack*, and her autobiographical novel, *Ryder*. There is also the "quality of horror and doom very nearly related to that of Elizabethan tragedy" that Eliot observed hanging over *Nightwood* (T. S. Eliot, introduction to *Nightwood* [New York: Harcourt, Brace

& Co., 1937], viii), and that also shadows *Ryder* as well as Barnes's three-act verse drama *The Antiphon*. For Kaup, as for myself, however, the neobaroque is less interesting as a stylistic influence than in how it helps to address the divide between formal and historical readings of Barnes's work. See Monika Kaup, "The Neobaroque in Djuna Barnes," *Modernism/Modernity* 12:1 (2005): 85–110.

5. This proliferation of the naming process characterizes Dr. O'Connor's disjointed philosophical monologue in *Nightwood*, as Kaup notes, and can also be seen as the (dis)organizing principle behind the lesbian saints' biographies in *Ladies Almanack*. See Kaup, "The Neobaroque," 101–2.

6. Quoted in ibid., 89.

7. Victoria L. Smith, "A Story beside(s) Itself: The Language of Loss in Djuna Barnes's *Nightwood*," *Publications of the Modern Language Association* 114:2 (March 1999): 194–206, 194.

8. "Come Into the Roof Garden, Maud," in Djuna Barnes, *New York*, ed. Alyce Barry with drawings by Djuna Barnes (Los Angeles: Sun & Moon Classics, 1989), 155. Subsequent references to newspaper articles by Barnes are to this collection, unless noted otherwise, and are cited parenthetically in the text.

9. Alan Singer, "The Horse Who Knew Too Much: Metaphor and the Narrative of Discontinuity in *Nightwood*," *Contemporary Literature* 25:1 (1984): 78.

10. Barnes's biographers and her letters affirm her interest in the literature of the English baroque in particular. She declared her admiration for Robert Burton's *Anatomy of Melancholy* (1621) and Thomas Browne's *Religio Medici* (1642) on more than one occasion.

11. For second-wave feminist readings of Barnes, see the essays collected in *Silence and Power: A Reevaluation of Djuna Barnes,* ed. Mary Lynn Broe (Carbondale: Southern Illinois University Press, 1991). New historicist and queer readers include Dianne Chisholm, "Obscene Modernism: *Eros Noir* and the Profane Illumination of Djuna Barnes," *American Literature* 69:1 (March 1997): 167–206, and Mary E. Galvin, *Queer Poetics: Five Modernist Women Writers* (Westport, Conn.: Greenwood Press, 1999).

12. See Eliot, Introduction to *Nightwood*, and Joseph Frank, *The Widening Gyre: Crisis and Mastery in Modern Literature* (Bloomington: Indiana University Press, 1963).

13. On Barnes and the broader prewar culture of New York, see Nancy J. Levine, "'Bringing Milkshakes to Bulldogs': The Early Journalism of Djuna Barnes," in Broe, *Silence and Power*; Laura Winkiel, "Circuses and Spectacles: Public Culture in *Nightwood*," *Journal of Modern Literature* 21:1 (1997): 7–28; Katherine Biers, "Djuna Barnes Makes a Specialty of Crime: Violence and the Visual in Her Early Journalism," in *Women's Experience of Modernity: 1875–1945,* ed. Ann L. Ardis and Leslie W. Lewis (Baltimore: Johns Hopkins University Press, 2003); and sections

on Barnes's journalism in Tim Armstrong, *Modernism, Technology, and the Body: A Cultural History* (New York: Cambridge University Press, 1998); and in Scott Herring, *Queering the Underworld: Slumming, Literature, and the Undoing of Lesbian and Gay History* (Chicago: University of Chicago Press, 2007). On the female body in particular in Barnes, see Margaret Bockting, "Performers and the Erotic in Four Interviews by Djuna Barnes," *Centennial Review* 41:1 (1997): 183–95; Deborah L. Parsons, "Women in the Circus of Modernity: Djuna Barnes and *Nightwood*," *Women: A Cultural Review* 9:3 (1998): 266–77; Diane Warren, *Djuna Barnes's Consuming Fictions* (New York: Ashgate, 2008); and sections on Barnes's journalism in Barbara Green, *Spectacular Confessions: Autobiography, Performative Activism, and the Sites of Suffrage* (New York: St. Martin's Press, 1997), and Jean Marie Lutes, *Front Page Girls: Women Journalists in American Culture and Fiction, 1880–1930* (Ithaca, N.Y.: Cornell University Press, 2006).

14. An exception to the tendency to ignore the style of Barnes's early paid work and its links to *Nightwood* can be found in Carl Herzig, "Roots of Night: Emerging Style and Vision in the Early Journalism of Djuna Barnes," *Centennial Review* 31:3 (Summer 1987): 255–69. For a valuable discussion of the *visual* style of Barnes's early journalism in its original context, see Rebecca Loncraine, "Voix-de-Ville: Djuna Barnes's Stunt Journalism, Harry Houdini and the Birth of Cinema," *Women: A Cultural Review* 19:2 (2008): 156–71.

15. Walter Benjamin, "Karl Kraus," in *Reflections*, ed. Peter Demetz, trans. Edmund Jephcott (New York: Schocken, 1978), 247.

16. As a movement muckraking was largely a phenomenon of the magazines, which by the early 1890s had gained a truly national audience for the first time. For an overview of the muckrakers, see Frank Luther Mott, *A History of American Magazines*, Vol. 5 (Cambridge, Mass.: Harvard University Press, 1938), and Louis Filler, *The Muckrakers* (Stanford, Calif.: Stanford University Press, 1993). Social histories of muckraking and of the "magazine revolution" that enabled it include Matthew Schneirov, *The Dream of a New Social Order: Popular Magazines in America 1893–1914* (New York: Columbia University Press, 1994), and Ohmann, *Selling Culture*, 1996.

17. On the period's critique of legal and ethical formalisms, see Eldon J. Eisenach, *The Lost Promise of Progressivism* (Lawrence: University Press of Kansas, 1994); Nancy Cohen, *The Reconstruction of American Liberalism, 1865–1914* (Chapel Hill: University of North Carolina Press, 2002); J. Michael Hogan, ed., *Rhetoric and Reform in the Progressive Era* (East Lansing: Michigan State University Press, 2003); Kloppenberg, *Uncertain Victory*; and Morton White, *Social Thought in America: The Revolt against Formalism* (Boston: Beacon Press, 1957).

18. See Jackson, *The Word and Its Witness*, 249.

19. Ibid., 250.

20. Richard Ohmann has dated the beginnings of mass culture to roughly 1893,

when *Munsey's* magazine reduced its price to 10 cents. See Ohmann, *Selling Culture*, 29. For his helpful definition of "mass culture" see introduction n. 17.

21. On magazine illustrations, see John William Tebbel and Mary Ellen Zuckerman, *The Magazine in America, 1741–1990* (New York: Oxford University Press, 1991), and Schneirov, *Dream of a New Social Order*, 67–72 and 233–34. Illustrations were a major factor in expanding audiences not only for magazines but also for newspapers. On the importance of illustrations to the growth in newspaper circulation during this period, see Michael Schudson, *Discovering the News: A Social History of American Newspapers* (New York: Basic Books, 1978), 95–98. On the technological advances that made it possible to print photographs on the same press as type, see Beaumont Newhall, *The History of Photography*, rev. ed. (New York: Museum of Modern Art, 1982), 249–66. On the "iconographical revolution" that this brought to everyday life, see Neil Harris, *Cultural Excursions: Marketing Appetites and Cultural Tastes in Modern America* (Chicago: University of Chicago Press, 1990), 304–17.

22. Responding to critics of realism such as Alan Trachtenberg, Russ Castronovo, and June Howard, Jackson points out that an experience-based Protestant homiletic pedagogy, stretching back to Jonathan Edwards (and forward to Evangelical theme parks and eschatological video games), informed many of the works of the Social Gospel. Instead of distancing audiences from their subjects, the aim was to motivate "an active engagement with urban social problems." See Jackson, *The Word and Its Witness*, 220. For a classic statement of the counterargument, see Richard Hofstadter, *The Age of Reform* (New York: Knopf, 1955), 196–213.

23. Jackson describes such images as offering a "virtual experience" of the tenements intended to give audiences empathy, rather than a distancing sympathy, toward those they sought to save. See Jackson, *The Word and Its Witness*, 224.

24. See Winkiel, "Circuses and Spectacles," 8.

25. Simultaneously, film itself was leaving behind its original exhibition contexts and becoming its own self-contained language. On the pacification of the film audience, see Hansen, *Babel and Babylon: Spectatorship in American Silent Film*. On the distinctive ontology of early film, see Tom Gunning, "The Cinema of Attractions: Early Film, Its Spectators and the Avant-Garde," *Wide Angle* 8:3–4 (1986).

26. See Winkiel, "Circuses and Spectacles," 7–18.

27. As Czitrom notes, European sociologists and criminologists had been promulgating such notions since the late nineteenth century, as had American psychologists such as Boris Sidis and William James. However, before the war, suggestion was not closely connected with ideas about communications media. *The Crowd*, discussed following, was translated into English shortly after its publication in 1895, but was popularized in England and America by Wilfred Trotter in *Instincts of the Herd in Peace and War* (1908, 1916) and later by Sigmund Freud

in *Group Psychology and the Analysis of the Ego,* in 1921. On Le Bon's influence, see Robert Nye, introduction to Gustave Le Bon, *The Crowd* (Rutgers, N.J.: Transaction, 1995). On the effects of the war on media theory and communications theory, see Daniel J. Czitrom, *Media and the American Mind: From Morse to McLuhan* (Chapel Hill: University of North Carolina Press, 1982). On the darkening cultural mood of Manhattan during and after World War I, see Ann Douglas, *Terrible Honesty: Mongrel Manhattan in the 1920s* (New York: Farrar, Straus and Giroux, 1995).

28. Gustave Le Bon, *The Crowd: A Study of the Popular Mind* (New York: Macmillan Company, 1897), 97, 47. Le Bon uses "image" as an analogue for simple words and formulas—for example, in political propaganda—because he understands actual images to be a more primitive and direct mode of communication. He notes of persuasive and contagious ideas, for instance, that they "are not connected by any logical bond of analogy or success, and may take each other's place like the slides of a magic-lantern." Ibid.

29. Le Bon, *The Crowd,* 172–3.

30. On Lippmann's and others' shifts in thinking about the role of the press in wartime, see Czitrom, *Media and the American Mind.*

31. On the special role of female reporters in the Reform Era—who, unlike men, were charged with reporting their own emotive responses to the news events they reported—see Lutes, *Front Page Girls.* See also Brooke Kroeger, *Nellie Bly: Daredevil, Reporter, Feminist* (New York: Times Books, 1994).

32. Le Bon reassuringly emphasized that these were most likely to be women and "primitive beings" such as "educated Hindoos." See *The Crowd,* 47.

33. On Roosevelt's reforms, see George Edwin Mowry, *Theodore Roosevelt and the Progressive Movement* (New York: Hill and Wang, 1946).

34. The Rogues' Gallery evokes both the method of composite portraiture invented by the eugenicist Francis Galton and the system of criminal identification created by the Paris police official Alphonse Bertillon. As Alan Sekula has noted, when photography was adopted as a policing tactic in the late nineteenth century, it borrowed its function from medical and anatomical illustration, thus coming to define "both the *generalized look*—the typology—and the *contingent instance* of deviance and social pathology." See Sekula, "The Body and the Archive," *October* 39 (Winter 1986): 3–64, 7.

35. For a discussion of this controversial piece, and its connection to Warhol's screen tests, see Richard Meyer, "Warhol's Clones," in *Negotiating Lesbian and Gay Subjects,* ed. Monica Dorenkamp and Richard Henke (New York: Routledge, 1995), 105–6.

36. O'Grady's duties, according to a *Times* article from several months earlier, were the "investigation and elimination of the white slave traffic" and of "men who annoy women on the streets, in the subways, and on the elevated."

"Widow Is Named a Police Deputy: Force Is Warned," *New York Times,* January 29, 1918, 11.

37. On the Social Gospel trope of the urban descent into the "Inferno," see Jackson, *The Word and Its Witness,* 231–49.

38. Benjamin's first thinking about the baroque, as George Steiner notes, emerged in 1916, around the same time that Barnes was learning the ropes as a reporter. Of all the twentieth-century theorists of the neobaroque cited by Kaup, Benjamin's cultural coordinates were the most similar to Barnes's during her mature literary career in the 1920s in Europe. As Diane Chisholm has noted in a different context, Benjamin was also a denizen of Berlin and Paris, and was well acquainted, as was Barnes, with surrealism and the French avant-garde. See Steiner, introduction to Walter Benjamin, *The Origin of German Tragic Drama,* trans. John Osborne (London: Verso, 1998), 8, and Chisholm, "Obscene Modernism," 172.

39. As Asja Lacis described Benjamin's account of his project, his "investigation was not merely academic but directly related to current problems of contemporary literature. In his work he designated the baroque drama's search for a formal language as an analogous manifestation to expressionism." Quoted in Samuel Weber, "Storming the Work: Allegory and Theatricality in Benjamin's 'Origin of the German Mourning Play,'" in Weber, *Theatricality as Medium* (New York: Fordham University Press, 2004), 161. On Benjamin's "baroque modernity" more generally, see Rainer Nägele, *Theater, Theory, Speculation: Walter Benjamin and the Scenes of Modernity* (Baltimore: Johns Hopkins University Press, 1991), and Christine Buci-Glucksmann, *Baroque Reason: The Aesthetics of Modernity,* trans. Patrick Camiller (London: SAGE, 1994).

40. Benjamin, *The Origin of German Tragic Drama,* 57–158; 133. Hereafter cited parenthetically in the text.

41. "Religious aspirations did not lose their importance" with the Reformation, Benjamin notes, "it was just that this century denied them a religious fulfillment, demanding of them, or imposing upon them, a secular solution instead" (79). As Weber puts it in his reading of Benjamin, the Reformation "exalt[ed] the situation of the individual while subjecting that individual to an uncertain destiny . . . unable to influence the future by action, dependent upon a faith whose status remains fundamentally opaque." See Weber, "Storming the Work," 170.

42. On allegory's distinctive relationship to temporality, in contrast to the symbol, see Paul De Man, "The Rhetoric of Temporality," in *Blindness and Insight: Essays in the Rhetoric of Contemporary Criticism,* 2nd ed. (Minneapolis: University of Minnesota Press, 1983).

43. Weber, *Benjamin's –abilities,* 154–55.

44. The intimations of the obscene in Barnes's attraction to criminality also reflect the "offensive, the provocative quality of the gesture" that Benjamin saw

at work in German baroque theater. "If it is to hold its own against the tendency to absorption," Benjamin remarks, "the allegorical must constantly unfold in new and surprising ways. The symbol, on the other hand . . . remains persistently the same" (183).

45. For Weber, "the German baroque mourning play seeks to respond to [a 'fallen' creation] by bringing it on stage and exposing it to the view of those caught up in it. In so doing, the hope seems to be that, qua allegory, such staging will either contain the temporal push toward oblivion or at least slow it down by displaying it." Weber, "Storming the Work," 174.

46. The term "civic melodrama" is Cecilia Tichi's. On muckraking's debts to melodrama, see Tichi, *Exposés and Excess: Muckraking in America, 1900/2000* (Philadelphia: University of Pennsylvania Press, 2004), 76–83.

47. On the difference between circumscribing and describing, see Weber, *Benjamin's –abilities*, 9.

48. On the theatrical medium as a "paradigm for the modern situation," and on the fragmentary quality of theater in Germany, which—like the United States—had no national theater tradition, see Weber, "Storming the Work," 175.

49. On the shift from early to classical cinema, see David Bordwell, Janet Staiger, and Kristin Thompson, *The Classical Hollywood Cinema: Film Style and Mode of Production to 1960* (New York: Columbia University Press, 1985).

50. As Benjamin notes of Baudelaire, whatever is deprived of the "aura"—film's paradigmatic gesture as regards objects and people alike—comes to inhabit the "state of nature." See Benjamin, "On Some Motifs in Baudelaire," 185. That Barnes embraced baroque theatricality as a response to film is perhaps most evident in her ornately illustrated column for *Theatre Guild* magazine in the 1930s, "The Playgoer's Almanac," later "The Wanton Player." See the selection reprinted in Antonia Lant, ed., *The Red Velvet Seat: Women's Writings on the First Fifty Years of Cinema* (New York: Verso, 2006).

51. On the cleaning up of working-class entertainments during this period, see Kathy Lee Peiss, *Cheap Amusements: Working Women and Leisure in Turn-of-the-Century New York* (Philadelphia: Temple University Press, 1986). For an analysis of the complex cultural work performed by the American freak show and the literary and visual representations it inspired, see Rachel Adams, *Sideshow U.S.A.: Freaks and the American Cultural Imagination.* (Chicago and London: University of Chicago Press, 2001).

52. Barnes's portrait of exhibition dances notes the women "pinned" like butterflies to their male partners and celebrates "the catch in the music that makes the feet move." Her description of a child hawking photos to the passing crowd tells us, "There is something incomplete in her great horrifying completeness." See, respectively, "The Tingling, Tangling Tango as 'Tis Tripped at Coney Isle," 44–45, and "Surcease in Hurry and Whirl—On the Restless Surf at Coney," 280.

53. For a reading of this scene as a protest against the commodification of the freak, and for a broader discussion of Barnes's interest in freaks as sources of "visceral experience rooted in pre-verbal understanding," see Nancy Bombaci, *Freaks in Late Modernist American Culture: Nathanael West, Djuna Barnes, Tod Browning, and Carson McCullers* (New York: Peter Lang, 2006), 60.

54. Djuna Barnes, "My Sisters and I at a New York Prizefight," *New York World Magazine*, August 23, 1914, 6.

55. The double meaning of "apprehension" here also evokes suspense, insofar as it suggests both fear and understanding. It thus becomes impossible to decide if we are witnessing an arousing spectacle of female vulnerability or merely women considering the odds on the fight.

56. As Armstrong notes, in his reading of Barnes's relationship to physical culture and the Dadaist fascination with boxing, the question of why women watch resolves into a "game of desire." See Armstrong, *Modernism, Technology, and the Body*, 128.

57. Tourism was becoming a form of middle-class recreation during this period, as many of Barnes's pieces indicate. On the invention of recreation, and its connection to a newly visual mass press, see Brown, *The Material Unconscious*.

58. Barnes, "Futuristic Impressions of the Picadilly Chorus Girls in 'To-Night's the Night,'" *New York Press,* January 31, 1915, Pt. 4, p. 6.

59. See Jackson, *The Word and Its Witness*, 218. On Barnes's critique of the slumming tour, see Herring, *Queering the Underworld*.

60. Alyce Barry, introduction to "Chinatown's Glories Crumbled to Dust," in Barnes, *New York*, 123.

61. On Barnes's critique of the spectacular tactics of the suffragists in this piece, see Barbara Green, *Spectacular Confessions*, 169–85. This surprisingly political stunt by Barnes, who generally treated suffragists with a striking condescension and reportedly greatly feared doctors, may have appealed to her because of its overtones of martyrdom.

62. On Barnes's relationship to this cultural figure in her journalism more generally and in *Nightwood*, see Nancy Levine, "'I've Always Suffered from Sirens': The Cinema Vamp and Djuna Barnes's *Nightwood*," *Women's Studies* 16:3/4 (1989): 271–81.

63. All quotations are taken from page 6 of the *New York World Magazine* for November 15, 1914, in which Barnes's piece first appeared.

64. On the female vamp as the threatened and threatening female bearer of "to-be-looked-at-ness" in narrative film, see Mary Ann Doane, *Femmes Fatales: Feminism, Film Theory, and Psychoanalysis* (New York: Routledge, 1991).

65. Richard Wolin, *Walter Benjamin: An Aesthetic of Redemption* (Berkeley: University of California Press, 1994), 67.

5. Gertrude Stein Talking

1. *Time: The Weekly News Magazine*, 22:11 (September 11, 1933). http://www
.time.com/time/covers/0,16641,19330911,00.html.

2. Ample evidence of Stein's outsized media personality is provided by her
clippings file, which is housed in the Yale Collection of American Literature,
Beinecke Rare Book and Manuscript Library, at Yale University. Additionally,
searches of the online *New York Times* and *Washington Post* archives show that
nonlocal papers also continued to follow her as she traveled. Her name appeared
at least every two weeks in both the *Times* and the *Post* from October 1934 to May
1935. See http://query.nytimes.com/search/query?srchst=p# and http://pqasb
.pqarchiver.com/washingtonpost/search.html.

3. For these and further details about Stein's publicity on her tour, see John
Malcolm Brinnin, *The Third Rose: Gertrude Stein and Her World* (Boston: Little,
Brown and Company, 1959), 334–48. For a broad sampling of the critical and pop-
ular attention Stein received throughout her career, see *The Critical Response to
Gertrude Stein*, ed. Kirk Curnutt (Westport, Conn.: Greenwood, 2000).

4. *Top Hat*. Dir. Mark Sandrich. Perf. Fred Astaire, Ginger Rogers, and
Edward Everett Horton. 1935. Turner Home Entertainment. DVD.

5. Stein nevertheless continued to hone her more writerly style elsewhere,
in more repetitive, associative, and highly patterned prose-poetry works such as
"Stanzas in Meditation" and "The Geographical History of America."

6. See "Exile's Return," *Saturday Review of Literature*, November 3, 1934, in
Yale Collection of American Literature, Beinecke Rare Book and Manuscript
Library, Yale University.

7. A representative sample of the many studies of Stein's relationship to pragmatism would include, on the one hand, those critics working in the tradition
of Stanley Cavell, who see in Stein a species of creative and affirmative linguistic
skepticism; and, on the other, those who focus instead on Stein's preoccupations
with the Jamesian formulations of habit, attention, experience, and consciousness. For examples of the former, see sections on Stein in Richard Poirier, *Poetry
and Pragmatism* (Cambridge, Mass.: Harvard University Press, 1992); Levin, *The
Poetics of Transition*; and Liesl Olson, *Modernism and the Ordinary* (New York:
Oxford University Press, 2009). Among the many examples of the latter, see Pris-
cilla Wald, *Constituting Americans: Cultural Anxiety and Narrative Form* (Durham, N.C.: Duke University Press, 1995); Jennifer Ashton, "Gertrude Stein for
Anyone," *ELH* 64:1 (1997): 289–331; and Lisi Schoenbach, *Pragmatic Modernism*
(New York: Oxford University Press, 2012), 49–67. Important for my concerns
here has also been the recent interest in pragmatism and radical empiricism's ties
to science, particularly the sciences of mind. Several recent critics have emphasized the influence of Stein's early work in genetics and neuropsychology on her

writing to argue that it is literally a scientific investigation into the way language functions physiologically and affectively. See, in particular, Meyer, *Irresistible Diction*, and Richardson, *A Natural History of Pragmatism*, 232–53.

8. On the relationship of Stein's celebrity status to her self-presentation as modernist "genius," see Kirk Curnutt, "Inside and Outside: Gertrude Stein on Identity, Celebrity, and Authenticity," *Journal of Modern Literature* 23:2 (Winter 1999–2000): 291–308; Timothy W. Galow, *Writing Celebrity: Stein, Fitzgerald, and the Modern(ist) Art of Self-Fashioning* (New York: Palgrave Macmillan, 2011); Jonathan Goldman, *Modernism Is the Literature of Celebrity* (Austin: University of Texas Press, 2011); and Deborah M. Mix, "Gertrude Stein's Currency," in *Modernist Star Maps*, ed. Jonathan Goldman and Aaron Jaffe (Burlington, Vt.: Ashgate, 2010). On Stein and new media in the 1930s, see Goble, *Beautiful Circuits*, and Sarah Wilson, "Gertrude Stein and the Radio," *Modernism/Modernity* 11:2 (April 2004). On Stein and progressive politics, see Michael Szalay, *New Deal Modernism: American Literature and the Invention of the Welfare State* (Durham, N.C.: Duke University Press, 2000), and Sean McCann, *A Pinnacle of Feeling: American Literature and Presidential Government* (Princeton, N.J.: Princeton University Press, 2008).

9. On Stein's turn to Weininger as a way to repudiate progressivism, see McCann, *A Pinnacle of Feeling*. On the similarities between Stein's and Rand's views of the New Deal, see Szalay, *New Deal Modernism*.

10. My account of the critical debates over Stein's work, and of the interpretations that have been proffered of her lectures, is by no means exhaustive. Stein's lectures were a less important source of insight into her work for the feminist critics in the 1980s who rediscovered her and who advocated for the academic and scholarly value of studying her experimental writing directly as a form of anti-patriarchal feminist practice. The same might be said of the many critics in the 1980s and 1990s who were concerned with Stein's exploration of semantic "indeterminacy" and the materiality of the linguistic medium, as well as with her ties to Cubism and the European avant-garde. For feminist recoveries of Stein's work, see, among others, Lisa Ruddick, *Reading Gertrude Stein: Body, Text, Gnosis* (Ithaca, N.Y.: Cornell University Press, 1990); Marianne DeKoven, *A Different Language: Gertrude Stein's Experimental Writing* (Madison: University of Wisconsin Press, 1983); and Harriet Scott Chessman, *The Public Is Invited to Dance: Representation, the Body, and Dialogue in Gertrude Stein* (Stanford, Calif.: Stanford University Press, 1989). On Stein's experiments with linguistic indeterminacy and materiality, see, among others, Marjorie Perloff, *The Poetics of Indeterminacy: Rimbaud to Cage* (Princeton, N.J.: Princeton University Press, 1981); Ellen E. Berry, *Curved Thought and Textual Wandering: Gertrude Stein's Postmodernism* (Ann Arbor: University of Michigan Press, 1992); and Peter Quartermain, *Disjunctive Poetics: From Gertrude Stein and Louis Zukofsky to Susan Howe* (New York: Cambridge University Press, 1992).

11. Adorno and Horkheimer's *Dialectic of Enlightenment: Philosophical Fragments*, trans. Edmund Jephcott (Stanford, Calif.: Stanford University Press, 2002), which coined the term "culture industry," emerged in 1944 as one of the most influential articulations of this fear.

12. As Karen Leick has shown, the interest aroused by the Armory Show artists also extended to their fellow traveler Stein, who was promoted in America by her friends Carl Van Vechten and Mabel Dodge and who published short works in *Vanity Fair* in 1917 and 1919. For a study of the criticism and reviews of Stein's work that she received in America throughout her career, and of the ways in which publishing strategies helped her success, see Leick, *Gertrude Stein and the Making of an American Celebrity* (New York: Routledge, 2009). On Stein's canny collaboration with Carl Van Vechten to publicize herself and her work, see Corinne E. Blackmer, "Selling Taboo Subjects: The Literary Commerce of Gertrude Stein and Carl Van Vechten," in Kevin J. H. Dettmer and Stephen Watt, eds., *Marketing Modernisms: Self-Promotion, Canonization, Rereading* (Ann Arbor: University of Michigan Press, 1996). On the surprisingly substantive attention Stein received within mass culture, see Alyson Tischler, "A Rose Is a Pose: Steinian Modernism and Mass Culture," *Journal of Modern Literature* 26:3/4 (Summer 2003): 12–27.

13. See Leick, Introduction to *Gertrude Stein*; Galow, *Writing Celebrity*; and Goldman *Modernism Is the Literature of Celebrity*.

14. Leick, *Gertrude Stein*, 2.

15. Jaffe argues that by making themselves recognizable in a broad array of cultural registers, these writers were able to effectively construct the distinctions among high, middlebrow, and low cultural tastes that endure today. See Aaron Jaffe, *Modernism and the Culture of Celebrity* (New York: Cambridge University Press, 2005).

16. See Goldman, *Modernism Is the Literature of Celebrity*, 2.

17. Important precursors to studies of modernism and celebrity in this respect include Dettmer and Watt, *Marketing Modernisms*; Rainey, *Institutions of Modernism*; Mark S. Morrisson, *The Public Face of Modernism: Little Magazines, Audiences, and Reception, 1905–1920* (Madison: University of Wisconsin Press, 2001); and Ardis, *Modernism and Cultural Conflict*.

18. See "Special Topic: Celebrity, Fame, Notoriety," *Publications of the Modern Language Association* 126:4 (October 2011).

19. Joseph A. Boone and Nancy J. Vickers, "Celebrity Rites," ibid.: 908.

20. On the limitations of Habermas's model for the American print public sphere, see Bonnie Carr O'Neill, "The Personal Public Sphere of Whitman's 1840s Journalism," ibid.: 983–98. Foundational feminist critiques of Habermas's separation of public reason from private emotion have been provided by Nancy Fraser, "Rethinking the Public Sphere: A Contribution to the Critique of Actually Existing Democracy," in *Habermas and the Public Sphere*, ed. Craig Calhoun

(Cambridge, Mass.: MIT Press, 1992), 109–42; and Rita Felski, *Beyond Feminist Aesthetics: Feminist Literature and Social Change* (Cambridge, Mass.: Harvard University Press, 1989), 164–75.

21. Theodore Hall, "No End of Books: Gertrude Stein, with Her Bell, Book, Candle and the Unsuspected Motley," *Washington Post*, May 7, 1935, 9.

22. "One Stein in Two Acts," *Golden Book* 21:51 (January 1935), 51.

23. See B. F. Skinner, "Has Gertrude Stein a Secret?" in Curnutt, ed., *The Critical Response to Gertrude Stein*, 207. As Tim Armstrong has noted, Skinner's condemnation of Stein seems to be motivated by something other than his own expertise: "What Skinner fears [in Stein] is something which his own work might seem to make an obvious subject: *writing as pure behaviour*, considered apart from a concept of mind." See Armstrong, *Modernism, Technology and the Body: A Cultural History* (New York: Cambridge University Press, 1998), 205.

24. See Curnutt, "Inside and Outside: Gertrude Stein on Identity, Celebrity, and Authenticity," *Journal of Modern Literature* 23:2 (Winter 1999/2000): 291–308. As Curnutt points out, moreover, much of Stein's own meditation on questions of audience and identity—some of which I discuss further in the next section—can be credited to her mastery of this aspect of celebrity discourse. Stein spilled much ink over the celebrity's dialectical relationship to her audience, describing in interviews and articles a writing block that resulted from her self-consciousness about her image—thus firing up still more interest in herself and her work—and investigating, in longer, more literary pieces, celebrity's strange dialectic of "identity" and "entity." On the celebrity identity crisis of the 1930s more broadly, see Leo Braudy, *The Frenzy of Renown: Fame and Its History* (New York: Oxford University Press, 1986).

25. "In Mayfair with Mme. Flutterbye," *New York Evening Journal*, November 17, 1934. Yale Collection of American Literature, Beinecke Rare Book and Manuscript Library, Yale University.

26. Karl Schriftgiesser, "Gibberish of Gertrude Stein Seen as Attempt to Freshen Language," *Washington Post*, December 23, 1934, B5.

27. On the ways in which radio personalized an increasingly impersonal and alienating mass public sphere in the 1930s, see Bruce Lenthall, *Radio's America: The Great Depression and the Rise of Modern Mass Culture* (Chicago: University of Chicago Press, 2007). Stein seemed to endorse this view of radio in her own account of broadcasting. See Stein, "I Came and Here I Am," *Hearst's International Combined with Cosmopolitan* (February 1935): 19+.

28. Joseph W. Alsop Jr., "Gertrude Stein Says Children Understand Her," *New York Herald Tribune*, November 3, 1934.

29. "Miss Stein Speaks to Bewildered 500," *New York Times*, November 2, 1934, 25.

30. See Floyd Simonton, "Gertrude Stein Arrives but 'Parks' Stutter: Interview

at Air Terminal Fails to Uncover Any Repetitive Words," *Hollywood Citizen-News,* March 30, 1935. Yale Collection of American Literature, Beinecke Rare Book and Manuscript Library, Yale University; and "Gertrude Stein Arrives and Baffles Reporters by Making Herself Clear," *New York Times,* October 25, 1934, 25.

31. "A mere prediction as yet, neutrino is not even singing behind the atomic scene. . . . Presently neutrino will step before the footlights and burst into a Gertrude Stein aria out of which the physicists will try to make sense." In "Introducing Neutrino," *New York Times,* March 11, 1934.

32. Ralph E. Renaud, "Matinee Idols Find Spotlight Is Boring," *Washington Post,* December 1, 1934.

33. Mark Goble's *Beautiful Circuits* also addresses the technological context of Stein's fame, crediting interest in Stein to the fact that "the life of fame she narrates, and which is pictured in the iconography that surrounds her, takes its particular shape within a world that depends on technologies of communication and representation whose influences are felt on a pervasive scale" (86).

34. See Kevin G. Barnhurst and John Nerone, *The Form of News: A History* (New York: Guilford, 2001).

35. See John Tagg, "Melancholy Realism: Walker Evans's Resistance to Meaning," *Narrative* 11:1 (2003): 13.

36. Prior to the development of post-synchronization and dubbing, directors had been forced to subordinate highly developed visual editing techniques to the dominance of the on-set microphone. This corporate, technical, and artistic struggle to synchronize during the transition to sound from 1927 to 1930 was undertaken in the shadow of audiences who were increasingly demanding, and willing to pay for, the new "talkies." On the coming of sound as a gradual process of experimentation, rather than a sudden break between old and new technologies, see Rick Altman, ed., *Sound Theory, Sound Practice* (New York: Routledge, 1992), and Donald Crafton, *The Talkies: American Cinema's Transition to Sound, 1926–1931* (New York: Scribner, 1997). On the attitudes of Stein's fellow writers toward the coming of sound, see Anne Friedberg, Laura Marcus, and James Donald, eds., *Close Up, 1927–33: Cinema and Modernism* (London: Continuum, 1998). See also David A. Cook, "The Theoretical Debate over Sound," in *A History of Narrative Film* (New York: Norton, 1981).

37. On media consolidation in the 1930s, see Michael Denning, *The Cultural Front: The Laboring of American Culture in the Twentieth Century* (New York: Verso, 1996) and Lenthall, *Radio's America.*

38. See Michael Schudson, *Discovering the News: A Social History of American Newspapers* (New York: Basic Books, 1978), 121–60.

39. Jennifer Wicke has argued that it is the face, more than the signature, that is the hallmark of celebrity. See Jennifer Wicke, "Epilogue: Celebrity's Face Book," *Publications of the Modern Language Association* 126:4 (2011): 1131–39.

40. "Exile's Return, and Other Celebrations," *Saturday Review of Literature,* November 3, 1934.

41. Stein made it clear that she disliked the "talkies" after witnessing herself in one. See "I Came and Here I Am." A subtle challenge to the talkies may also lie behind her many discussions of the complex relationship between sound and sight in her lectures and other writings in the 1930s. A good example can be found in her remarks on cinema and on theater "nervousness" in "Plays," *Gertrude Stein: Writings 1932–1946* (New York: Library of America, 1998), 250–51.

42. See John Durham Peters, *Speaking into the Air: A History of the Idea of Communication* (Chicago: University of Chicago Press, 1999).

43. Ibid., 12.

44. "Gertrude Stein Arrives and Baffles Reporters by Making Herself Clear," *New York Times,* October 25, 1934, 25.

45. Empirical communications research comprised social psychology, marketing research, and the analysis of public opinion and propaganda. See Daniel J. Czitrom, *Media and the American Mind: From Morse to McLuhan* (Chapel Hill: University of North Carolina Press, 1982), 122–47.

46. Peters ascribes mentalism primarily to the Ogden and Richards view of communication, but also notes that this view is related to the propaganda view "as cure is related to disease." See Peters, *Speaking into the Air,* 14, 12.

47. Ibid., 14.

48. Ibid., 18–19. On Dewey as a theorist of communication, see also Czitrom, *Media and the American Mind,* 102–13.

49. Ibid., 16–17.

50. John Dewey, *The Public and Its Problems* (New York: Henry Holt, 1927), 23. Hereafter cited parenthetically in the text.

51. Lippmann, who, like Dewey, had been profoundly influenced by William James, felt he had to explicitly break with James's radically empiricist account of perception to make this argument. The experience of the war and of war propaganda had challenged the political relevance Lippmann had once seen in the Jamesian notion of "virtual experience" (discussed in the Introduction). He writes, "For the most part we do not first see, and then define, we define first and then see. In the great blooming, buzzing confusion of the outer world we pick out what our culture has already defined for us, and we tend to perceive that which we have picked out in the form stereotyped for us by our culture. Of the great men who assembled at Paris to settle the affairs of mankind, how many were there who were able to see much of the Europe about them, rather than their commitments about Europe?" Despite his use of James's words for the infant's experience—a "great blooming, buzzing confusion"—Lippmann rejects the former's idea there is a virtual experience that precedes the differentiation into subject and object, along with the warrant James had thereby found to redefine philosophy on an

anti-foundational, nondualistic basis. "Stereotyping" was for James simply the way the mind worked, for better or for worse, because perception was a subtractive process leading to the formation of habits based on practical need. For Lippmann, by contrast, stereotyping and the formation of perceptual habits were aspects of human perception that were unequivocably harmful. Ordinary, non-expert human beings, he had come to conclude, are chained in the cave of their sensory worlds. See Lippmann, *Public Opinion* (New York: Free Press, 1922), 50.

52. It is important to note that Dewey contested Lippmann's definition of the public as either an ideal sphere of rational conversation and debate or a "mask for private desires for power and position." He refused to define the public, beyond the barest of functional terms. "The line between private and public is to be drawn on the basis of the extent and scope of the consequences of acts which are so important as to need control, whether by inhibition or by promotion," he notes (15). Ultimately, the formation of publics and of states must be "an experimental process," with their definitions changing with historical circumstances (33).

53. Throughout the 1930s, Dewey continued to explore the question of whether and how the reorganization of the press could produce recognition in its audience of consumers. See, for example, "Our Un-Free Press" (1935) and *Freedom and Culture* (1939) in Vols. 11 and 13 of J. A. Boydston and John Dewey, *John Dewey: The Later Works, 1925–1953* (Carbondale and London: Southern Illinois University Press, 1981).

54. On the Dewey–Lippmann debate and its implications for the Left, see Bruce Robbins, introduction to *The Phantom Public Sphere* (Minneapolis: University of Minnesota Press, 1993), vii–xxvi.

55. This debate was not always inchoate. In an interview with Stein conducted in Paris before her visit, a *Times* reporter, while painting an intimate picture of the private celebrity at home, asks Stein what her views are on "rule by intellectuals," Lippmann's solution to the decline of the public sphere. Stein replies that intellectuals are too "diverted . . . by their ideas and their theories, from responding to the instincts which ought to guide practical rule . . . in democracies this is more necessary than anywhere else." See Lansing Warren, "Gertrude Stein Views Life and Politics," *New York Times Magazine,* May 6, 1934.

56. Gertrude Stein, *Four in America* (New Haven, Conn.: Yale University Press, 1947)(written in 1932–33). Hereafter cited parenthetically in the text.

57. Gertrude Stein, *The Autobiography of Alice B. Toklas* (New York: Vintage, 1990), 78. (Originally published 1933)

58. See Sean McCann, *A Pinnacle of Feeling: American Literature and Presidential Government* (Princeton, N.J.: Princeton University Press, 2008), 33–66.

59. Ibid., 61.

60. Stein, *Everybody's Autobiography* (Cambridge, Mass.: Exact Change, 1993), 65.

61. McCann, *A Pinnacle of Feeling*, 49.

62. On radical empiricism, see the introduction to this volume and sources cited there. On Stein and radical empiricism, see sources cited in n. 7.

63. In making her portraits an extension, rather than a reflection, of the person, Stein is more specifically providing an acquaintance with both the sitter and with herself, since she adds her own organic rhythms in the act of writing. Stein's portrait of Picasso, discussed following, can better be understood as a portrait of "Stein-Picasso." Stein announced the project of her portraits in the title of a lecture, "An Acquaintance with Description," in *Gertrude Stein: Writings 1903–1932* (New York: Library of America, 1998), 530–65. On Stein's portrait phase and radical empiricism, see Meyer, *Irresistible Dictation*, 154–63 and 194–206.

64. Gertrude Stein, "If I Told Him: A Completed Portrait of Picasso," in *Gertrude Stein: Writings 1903–1932*, 506.

65. Gertrude Stein, *Writings: 1932–1946*, 276.

66. Ibid., 221.

67. In a late interview, Stein described the phase of her career in the early to mid-1930s as a time in which she solidified her interest in narrative, which she defines as the latter of the "two things" in which "all human beings are interested . . . the reality and . . . telling about it." Narrative, however, as Stein frames it, recalls the problem of mental transfer noted above, for the attempt to describe clearly to someone else "what happens," she points out, requires attention to "not what is in your mind but what is in somebody else's." Stein, "A Transatlantic Interview," *A Primer for the Gradual Understanding of Gertrude Stein*, ed. Robert Bartlett Haas (Los Angeles: Black Sparrow Press, 1971), 18.

68. Peters, *Speaking into the Air*, 5.

69. Stein's conception of habit recalls Dewey's definition of habits as flexible or plastic, and thus as standing in a dialectical rather than oppositional relationship to critical thought and awareness. On Dewey's definition of habit, the significance of habit in Stein, and the parallels between Stein and Dewey on this question, see Schoenbach, *Pragmatic Modernism*.

70. This suggests, in turn, why Stein also continually asks a curious question throughout *Four in America*: whether it is possible for a name to refer to a concept, rather than a particular person, place, or thing, such that, for example, all people named "Henry" might then have the same identity and do the same things. As Giorgio Agamben notes, names, insofar as they refer to specific people and arrive by means of descent, are signs whose "meaning must already have been explained for us to understand them." By contrast, "with propositions . . . we understand each other without any further explanations." See Agamben, *Potentialities*, 50. In emphasizing the *potential* generality—or truth value—of names, Stein thus launches a challenge to the duality at the heart of the idea of communication: an obsession with explanation and a fantasy of mental transfer. A similar challenge

can perhaps be seen in Stein's definition of poetry as "doing nothing but using losing refusing and pleasing and betraying and caressing nouns." See "Poetry and Grammar," *Gertrude Stein: Writings 1932–1946*, 327. For a discussion of the name's power to "stipulate" in Stein's work, with particular reference to *Four in America*, see Jennifer Ashton, "'Rose Is a Rose': Gertrude Stein and the Critique of Indeterminacy," *Modernism/Modernity* 9:4 (2002): 581–604.

71. As Sharon Marcus has noted in regard to celebrity in the nineteenth century, celebrity is also "theatrical in structure . . . organized around nonreciprocal exhibition and attention, around the asymmetrical interdependence that obtains between actors and audiences." See Marcus, "Salomé!! Sarah Bernhardt, Oscar Wilde, and the Drama of Celebrity," *Publications of the Modern Language Association* 126:4 (2011): 999–1021.

72. George Washington and Henry James's purely potential address to their audiences also makes them into saints. This is a hypothetical identity Stein explores only in relation to Ulysses S. Grant in *Four in America,* but it helps to explain how she imagined the "caress" of her writing might oppose presidential and corporate power. Jennifer Wicke has argued that the celebrity and saint have much in common, because the saint's appeal to worshippers historically exemplified Platonic *nous,* a knowledge "inspirited" by emotion, that "embraces, seduces, and impels, that relies on collectivity and on charismatic transmission" but that is understood to be "enfolding, not coercive," because it "intimates an epistemic union" with the divine. Stein invokes the figure of the saint frequently in her American lectures and articles, since her opera *Four Saints in Three Acts* had debuted to much success the previous year. See Jennifer Wicke, "Epilogue: Celebrity's Face Book," 1132.

73. Gertrude Stein, *How Writing Is Written: Volume II of the Previously Uncollected Writings of Gertrude Stein,* ed. Robert Bartlett Haas (Los Angeles: Black Sparrow Press, 1974), 93. Hereafter cited parenthetically in the text.

74. On the Bergsonian *durée,* see the introduction to this volume.

75. There is surely also a triple meaning here, as well, in the sense that *capital* can refer not only to government capitals and to capital letters, but also to wealth. Michael Szalay has pointed out the contemporaneous references to the WPA in this article, and has shown that Stein's opposition to Roosevelt—which she elaborated at length in a series she wrote for the *Saturday Evening Post* on money— had to do with fears about money losing its meaning. Stein might well also have feared that her writing was losing its capital—its potential to mean—in light of the new communicative transparency of the 1930s mass public sphere. See Szalay, *New Deal Modernism,* 88–91; 92–93.

76. Quoted in Richard Bridgman, *Gertrude Stein in Pieces* (New York: Oxford University Press, 1970), 306.

77. *Gertrude Stein: Writings: 1932–1946,* 620.

78. As Goble has suggested, in his account of the mediated nature of sexuality throughout Stein's writings in the 1930s, Ida's "dog Love" may well be a reference to Stein's and Toklas's sexuality. See Goble, *Beautiful Circuits,* 85–148.

79. See "The Geographical History of America or the Relation of Human Nature to the Human Mind," in *Gertrude Stein: Writings 1932–1946,* 401.

Index

Abbott, Lyman, 16

actual, 94; discontinuous and, 207n46; virtual and, 207n46

actualization, 66, 72, 91, 101

Adams, Henry, 7, 203n21

Adams, Rachel, 244n51

Adorno, Theodor, 41, 117

afterimage: metaphor of, 18

Agamben, Giorgio, 1, 209n67, 253n70

allegory, 51–53, 155–57

Alsop, Joseph, 179

"American Education and Colleges" (Stein), 195

"American Newspapers" (Stein), 192, 194

anti-imperialism, 43, 215n35, 217n58

Aristotle, 2, 3, 206n42

Armory Show, 176, 177, 248n12

Armstrong, Tim: on Barnes, 245n56

Arnold, Matthew, 100

Arsić, Branka, 211n80, 213n8, 255n59

"Art of Fiction, The" (James), 92, 94

"Art of the Novel, The" (James), 99

Autobiography of Alice B. Toklas, The (Stein), 177, 185, 186; popularity of, 173, 176

Autobiography of an Ex-Colored Man, The (Johnson), 31, 109, 111, 128–38, 233n52, 235n74, 236n81, 237n83; *Souls* and, 125, 234n65

autopoesis, 113, 122, 136

Baldwin, James Mark, 205n35

Bancroft, John Chandler, 106

Barnes, Djuna, 7, 17, 139–72, 238n2, 240n13, 245n57, 245n62; allegory and, 171; *The Antiphon,* 141, 238n4; Barney and, 238–39n4; baroque style and, 31, 141, 142, 153, 158, 163, 239n10; baroque theatricality and, 168, 244n50; boxing and, 162–64, 245n56; Chinatown and, 167, 168; criminals and, 149, 151, 156, 159, 243n44; Enright and, 149–51, 153, 157, 170; feminist readings of, 239n11; institutions/organizations and, 158; interviews by, 148; journalism of, 140–44, 158, 161, 164–65, 171; *The Ladies Almanack,* 141, 238n4; metaphors and, 142; mourning play and, 153–58; neobaroque style of, 141, 144, 162–63, 238n4; *Nightwood,* 139, 140, 141, 142, 143, 238n4, 239n5, 240n14, 245n62; reporting by, 243n38; *Ryder,* 141, 348n4; social problems and, 168; tropes of, 172; vertical cosmology of, 143; visual style of, 240n14; voluntarism and, 170

Barnes, Zadel, 238n2

Barney, Natalie, 238n2

baroque, 141, 147, 153–58, 163, 244n45

baroque style, 31, 142, 144

baroque theater, 153, 156, 158, 168, 244n50
Barthes, Roland, 231n34
Bataille, Georges, 203n20
Baudelaire, Charles, 17, 19, 153, 244n50
Beard, George M.: neurasthenia and, 116
"Beast in the Jungle, The" (James), 90, 93, 96
Beer, Thomas: Crane and, 213n16
Benfey, Christopher, 38, 213n18
Benjamin, Walter, 20, 168–69; afterimage and, 18; allegory and, 156; Barnes and, 243n38; baroque and, 144, 153–54, 156, 243n39, 243–44n44; on Baudelaire, 244n50; Bergson and, 17–19, 209n66; hidden index and, 19, 28; institutions/organizations and, 158; James and, 209n68; Kraus and, 143; modernity and, 21; mourning play (trauerspiel) and, 153–58, 161; The Origin of German Tragic Drama, 153, 157; Reformation and, 243n41
Bentley, Nancy, 5, 42, 60, 128n63
Bercovitch, Sacvan, 212n8, 213n8
Bergson, Henri, 2–3, 6–8, 10, 12–15, 17, 97, 201n7, 206n40, 208n57; Benjamin and, 17–19, 209n66; body/indetermination and, 13; choice/free will and, 25; conjunctive relations and, 12; Creative Evolution, 13, 16, 208n57, 260n42; Darwinism and, 13, 207n45; Deleuze and, 202n7; duration and, 13, 15, 19, 206n41; empiricism and, 206n36; experimental psychology and, 206n42; indirect value of, 18; James and, 7, 11–16, 21, 24, 205n35, 207n51, 208n61; Matter and Memory, 12,

13, 18; metaphysical language of, 207–8n51; mind and, 24; philosophy of, 16, 18; representation and, 12–13; Time and Free Will, 13; virtual experience and, 21; virtual mental image and, 206n43
Bergsonism, 208n57, 208n60
Bersani, Leo, 91, 93, 106; James and, 90, 225n62; on phenomenology of the look, 92
Bertillon, Alphonse, 242n34
Best, Stephen M., 230n14
black culture, 111, 113, 122, 126, 127, 128; popular/vernacular forms of, 235n72; state violence and, 230n14
blackness, 113, 127, 229n6, 230n12
black vernacular, 128, 236n77
Bly, Nellie, 140
Boone, Joseph, 177
Bosanquet, Theodora, 210n74
Boudreau, Kristin, 210n72
Bourke-White, Margaret, 180
Bourne, Randolph, 16, 122–24, 233n59; on American culture, 123; cultural criticism of, 233n55; radical democratic vision of, 209n62
boxing, women and, 162–64, 245n56
Brentano, Franz, 9, 204n26
Brooklyn Daily Eagle, 159, 167
Brown, Bill, 36, 62, 212n4, 237n83
Browne, Thomas, 239n10
Burrows, Stuart, 223n52, 227n78
Burton, Robert, 147, 239n10
Byrnes, Thomas, 148, 150

cakewalk, 130, 131, 231n18, 236n77
Calvinism, 145, 148, 149, 154
Cameron, Sharon, 68, 71, 89, 213n9, 228n88
Castronovo, Russ, 241n22
Cather, Willa, 7

Cavell, Stanley, 28, 37, 219n79, 246n7
celebrity, 177, 185–98, 203n13, 248n17
Chaplin, Charlie, 178
"Chinatown's Glories Crumbled to
    Dust" (Barnes), 167–68
Chisholm, Diane, 243n38
Chopin, Frédéric, 132, 135, 236n77
Chopin, Kate: *The Awakening*, 7
Citizen Kane (film), 41
clarity, 180, 181, 189, 197, 214n20
classical music, 115, 117, 128, 129;
    American, 119; ragging of, 132;
    spirituals and, 133
Coburn, Alvin Langdon, 228n92;
    James and, 94–95, 96, 108, 227n78;
    photography of, 94–95, 96, 107
color, 47, 52, 65–66, 67, 129; language
    and, 54; perception of, 65; poetics
    of, 35; textual investigation of, 51,
    56; virtual experience of, 53; virtual
    status of, 216n52
color *qualia*, 38, 51, 57, 65, 216n54
"Commissioner Enright and
    M. Voltaire" (Barnes), 148–50, 153,
    157, 158
communication, 176, 177, 178, 181–83,
    185, 190, 191–92, 197, 242n28; act of,
    191; debates about, 189; definitions
    of, 182–83; empirical, 183, 251n45;
    interwar notion of, 175; mentalism
    and, 183; public discourse about,
    180; representation and, 250n33;
    soundless/wordless, 209n70;
    theory of, 184, 191, 208n61, 242n27;
    wordless/ideal, 22
communicative labor: Stein and,
    176–85
Coney Island, 139, 140, 146, 161, 169
consciousness, 7, 9–10, 27, 134, 136,
    170, 232n48; class, 235n69; critical
    functions of, 71; experience and,

94; identity and, 91; impersonal, 99,
    225n57; loss of, 119; shared, 89, 182
coon songs, 116, 117, 129, 229n5, 229n6,
    231n30, 231n33
Cosmopolitan: Stein and, 173
"Coxon Fund, The" (James), 108
Crane, Jonathan Townley, 39
Crane, Stephen, 7, 17, 35–69, 213n12;
    Active Service, 54–60; allegory
    of, 53; aspirations/abilities of,
    36–37; Civil War and, 39, 216n45;
    color and, 47, 51–54, 56, 65–66,
    67, 216n52; experience and, 63,
    64; fact-fiction discourse and,
    219n74; Howells and, 37, 38, 39, 49,
    53; impersonal and, 68; indirect
    discourse and, 47–48; inspirations
    of, 49–50; Jamesian pragmatism
    and, 217n57; literary tradition and,
    33; *Maggie: A Girl of the Streets*,
    38, 213n12; mass culture/cultural
    elite and, 55; mass entertainment
    and, 51; realism and, 38; *The Red
    Badge of Courage*, 35, 36, 38, 39, 40,
    47–53, 216n44; social sympathy of,
    214n20; typological imagination of,
    213n18; as war reporter, 40, 61; war
    stories and, 56–57
Crary, Jonathan, 204n26, 204n29
criminals, 149, 150, 155–56, 168;
    potential, 153, 155, 156, 166
crowd mind, 147, 159, 164
culture industry, 1, 41, 248n11
Curnutt, Kirk, 178, 249n24
Czitrom, Daniel J., 241n27

dance, 117, 118
Dante, 151–52
Darwin, Charles, 13, 22
Darwinism, 8, 207n45
"Death and the Child" (Crane), 61, 62

"Death of the Lion" (James), 227n87
delay, 24, 26, 28, 211n76
Delbanco, Andrew: on Crane, 214n20
Deleuze, Gilles, 141, 206n36; Bergson
    and, 13, 202n7, 207n46; cinema and,
    201n7; philosophy of difference
    and, 201n7; virtual and, 3, 201n4
democracy, 98, 135, 191
Derrida, Jacques, 113, 131, 230n9
determinism, 13, 148, 216n54
Dewey, John, 8, 16, 122, 176,
    183–85, 225n57, 251n51, 252n53;
    communication and, 190–92,
    208n61; habits and, 253n69;
    instrumentalism/experimentation
    of, 208n61; Lippmann and, 185,
    252n52, 252n54; *The Public and
    Its Problems*, 183, 184; scientific
    techniques and, 184–85; Stein
    and, 183–85, 191, 195, 196; virtual
    experience and, 208n61
Dickens, Charles, 77
digital, 3, 33, 209n69; virtual and, 6
Dillinger, John, 194
Dilthey, Wilhelm, 8, 10
Dinerstein, Joel, 232n48
disciplinarity: emergence of, 6
Doane, Mary Ann, 232n48
Dodge, Mabel, 248n12
Dos Passos, John, 176
Douglass, Frederick, 235n70
Dracula (Stoker), 78, 232n38
Dreyfus Affair, 217n58
Du Bois, W. E. B., 5, 233n59, 234n66;
    American identity and, 124; black
    tradition and, 111; cultural pluralism
    and, 123; epigraphs of, 124–25; gift
    and, 234n62; idealism and, 123;
    Johnson and, 126; pragmatist/
    pluralist leanings of, 233n60; sonic
    mixing and, 234n63; sorrow songs

and, 125; *The Souls of Black Folk*, 123,
    124, 125, 234n63, 234n65; spirituals
    and, 234n64
du Maurier, George, 30, 135, 220n13,
    222n40, 228n92; captions by,
    92; death of, 99, 227n84; failing
    eyesight of, 72, 82, 88, 106;
    illustrations by, 81, 82–83, 84–85,
    88–89, 99, 102, 105, 106; James
    and, 71–108, 223n49; memoir of,
    78; obituary for, 99–100; *Partial
    Portraits*, 223n45; *Peter Ibbetson*,
    103, 104, 107; pictorialism and, 93;
    success for, 72, 108, 132; *Trilby*, 30,
    71–81, 99–108, 132, 220n12, 220n14,
    221n20, 221n27, 222n30, 228n91,
    236n81
"Du Maurier and London Society"
    (James), 81, 88, 91, 101
duration (*durée*), 12, 13, 15, 19, 206n37,
    209n66, 254n74
Dvořák, Antonín, 114, 115, 127

Edel, Leon, 71, 85, 223n42
Edison, Thomas Alva, 131, 236n80
"Editha" (Howells), 37, 44–45, 46, 47,
    48, 58, 65, 215n35
Edwards, Brent Hayes, 112, 230n12,
    235n72
Edwards, Jonathan, 29, 37, 213n9,
    241n22
Eliot, T. S., 143, 176, 233n52, 238n4
Ellington, Duke, 230n12
Emerson, Ralph Waldo, 4, 15, 29, 37,
    98, 174, 188, 225n59; on American
    scholar, 5; Bercovitch on, 213n8;
    Cavellian readings of, 211n80;
    influence of, 205n35; literary
    tradition of, 175; pragmatism and,
    89; revisionary reading of, 28; Stein
    and, 175; thinking and, 67

empiricism, 3, 8, 9, 10, 27, 198, 206n36, 210n72; idealism and, 21; narrow, 11, 23; radical, 11, 35, 37, 60, 174, 187, 204n32, 217n58, 246n7, 253n62, 253n63; superior, 206n36
Enlightenment, 141, 148
Enright, Richard E.: Barnes and, 148–53, 154, 155, 157, 170
entertainment, 4, 51, 181; mass, 62, 144, 150, 170, 171; reform and, 141, 147, 170; theatrical, 48
"Exile's Return, and Other Celebrations" (*Saturday Review of Literature*), 182
experience, 24, 42, 51, 64, 226n64; category of, 9; consciousness and, 94; expansion of, 27; holistic notion of, 18; inner/limit, 203n20; interactive, 145–46; media and, 29; philosophical implications of, 10–11; psychological, 10; pure, 2, 11–12, 25; quantification/materialization of, 27; shared, 184; thinking through, 29; virtual, 8–17, 40, 88, 146; visualization of, 7

Farwell, Arthur, 114
Fenner, Thomas P., 231n27
film, 42, 201n7, 214–15n26, 228n91; art and, 218n69; narrative, 158, 170, 171, 230n14; short, 170; spectatorship, 158; theater and, 215n26
Fisher, Philip, 55, 219n78
Fitzgerald, F. Scott, 176
Flower, Benjamin, 152
folk music, 115, 120, 136; black, 109, 118
form, crucible of, 122–28
Foucault, Michel, 141, 203n20, 211n82
Fouillée, Alfred, 8
Four in America (Stein), 175, 176, 185–88, 189–91, 198, 253n70, 254n70,

254n72; clarity and, 189; McCann on, 187
freedom, 17, 120, 121
free will, 25, 148, 149
Freud, Sigmund, 151, 152, 241n27
Fried, Michael, 36, 51, 52, 53
Friedberg, Anne, 201n4
Frost, Robert, 174
"Future of the Novel, The" (James), 92, 94

Galton, Francis, 228n89, 242n34
Garland, Hamlin, 43, 213n12
Gaskill, Nicholas, 51, 52
Goble, Mark, 91, 236n78, 250n33, 255n78
Godkin, E. L., 45
Golden Book: Stein and, 178
Goldman, Jonathan, 176–77
Goldsby, Jacqueline, 228n2, 230n14, 237n83
Goodrich, A. J., 117–18
"Gradual Making of the Making of Americans, The" (Stein), 173, 188
Graham, Wendy: on James/illustration, 226n72
grammar of latency, 31
grammatical tense: shifts in, 2, 12, 14
Grant, Ulysses S., 186, 254n72
graph: phone and, 112, 230n9
Great Depression, 174, 177, 186, 195, 196
Greco–Turkish War (1899), 36, 53–54
Green, Thomas Hill, 8
Grosz, Elizabeth, 206n41
Guattari, Félix, 201n7
Gunning, Tom, 215n26

Habermas, Jürgen, 5, 177, 203n14, 248n20
"Habits of Accuracy" (Reed), 119

handwriting: mind/word and, 217n56
Harlem Renaissance, 111, 126
Harper's, 99; *Trilby* in, 75, 77, 220n12
Hawthorne, Nathaniel, 188
Hayles, Katherine, 3, 209n69
Hearst, William Randolph, 40, 41, 54, 64
Hegel, G. W. F., 123, 234n66
Heidegger, Martin, 183, 204n31
Helmholtz, Hermann von, 115
"Hem of Manhattan, The" (Barnes), 165–67, 172
hidden index, 19, 28, 31, 32
"Himmel! The Roof of Your Mouth" (du Maurier), 103
Hitchcock, Ripley, 35, 37
Horkheimer, Max, 41
Howard, June, 241n22
"How It Feels to Be Forcibly Fed" (Barnes), 169
Howells, William Dean, 5, 63, 216n54; Crane and, 37, 38, 39, 49, 53; "Editha," 37, 44–45, 46, 47, 48, 58, 65, 215n35; James and, 84; mass culture and, 45; realist novel and, 35–36; *Red Badge* and, 38, 47; social realism and, 39; types and, 90
Huyssen, Andreas, 5

iconography, 241n21, 250n33
ideal, 60, 218n72; realizing, 77, 79
idealism, 3, 8, 9, 10, 14, 27, 111, 123, 136, 141, 210n72, 226n74; empiricism and, 21; religious, 145; secular, 145
identity, 25, 89, 249n24; American, 43, 124, 135; black, 129, 136, 237n86; consciousness and, 91; crisis, 249n24; cultural, 16, 122, 124; ethnic, 233n55; group, 159, 196, 218n71; immigrant, 123; individual, 159; national, 122; public, 218n71;

racial, 237n86; sexual, 31; social, 218n71
"If I Told Him" (Stein), 188, 197
illustrations, 86, 88, 95, 104; reproduction of, 145
images, 25, 50, 56, 105, 106, 171, 242n28; desire for, 172; false, 57; impressions of, 63; mental, 15–16, 26; values of, 85; virtual, 13, 15; voice and, 181
impressionism, 47, 218n69
inarticulacy, 113, 125, 138
individualism, 175, 187, 212n8
industrialism, 4, 16, 18
industrialization, 2, 97, 145
Inferno (Dante), 151–52
"In the Cage" (James), 1, 8, 19–28, 94, 96, 209n69
"Is There a Life after Death?" (James), 227–28n88

Jackson, Gregory, 145, 214n21, 241n22, 241n23
Jaffe, Aaron, 176, 248n15
James, Henry, 17, 174, 186, 190, 198, 204n26, 207n51, 223n44, 225n57, 226n66, 227–28n88; aesthetic judgment and, 210n71; aesthetic vocation and, 220n11; *The Ambassadors*, 89, 90; on American modernity, 97; *The American Scene*, 97, 105, 227n80; anti-mimetic theory and, 224n53; Benjamin and, 209n68; *The Bostonians*, 80; Coburn and, 94–97, 108, 227n78; du Maurier and, 71–108, 223n45; fictionalized treatment of, 71; *The Golden Bowl*, 89, 90, 95; grammar of latency and, 31, 104–5; *Guy Domville*, 80; illustrations and, 86, 226n72; images and, 26, 105, 106; late style of, 23–24, 30, 71, 73,

89–92, 225n61, 225n62; late works of, 91, 94, 99, 105; Leech and, 83, 84, 99; linguistic predication and, 106; literary publicity and, 227n87; mass culture and, 73; memory and, 105; metaphors of, 98; *Notes of a Son and Brother*, 105; photography and, 95, 227n78; pictorialism and, 30, 73, 81, 98–99, 102–3; *The Portrait of a Lady*, 84; pragmatism and, 89; *Roderick Hudson*, 89; shared consciousness and, 89–91; *A Small Boy and Others*, 72, 81, 91, 93, 226n65; Stein and, 187, 188, 189, 191; Stowe and, 93, 94; *The Tragic Muse*, 80; Trilby-mania and, 74, 81, 99–105; on *Uncle Tom's Cabin*, 93; utopian social imaginary and, 73; virtualizing syntax of, 101; *Washington Square*, 84, 90; *The Wings of the Dove*, 89

James, William, 2, 6, 8, 11–12, 13–16, 17, 25, 122, 174, 198, 202n7, 204n26, 205n35, 207n49, 211n77; anti-imperialism and, 217n58; Bergson and, 7, 11–16, 21, 24, 205n35, 207n51, 208n61; Crane and, 35, 59–61; experience and, 11–12, 14, 24, 26; Kallen and, 233n55; language/ literature and, 3, 14; metaphors and, 15; metaphysics and, 15; Peirce and, 15, 60, 205n35; philosophy of, 11–12, 13–16, 174, 207n51, 225n57; pluralism of, 60, 217n61; popular culture/yellow journalism and, 60; pragmatism and, 10; *The Principles of Psychology*, 9, 205n35, 207n49; psychology and, 216n58; public sphere and, 208n57, 220n11; pure experience and, 11–12, 203n20; as radical empiricist, 11, 206n37;

reason/pleasurable quickening and, 218n72; science/religion and, 8; sensory experience and, 63; Stein and, 175, 187; stereotyping and, 252n51; subjectivity and, 15; virtual and, 12, 13–16, 205n35

Jay, Martin, 6, 9, 202n8, 204n31

Jenkins, Emily, 222n30; *Trilby Triflet* and, 221–22n29

Johnson, James Weldon, 7, 17, 109–38, 228n2, 237n89, 326n81; aesthetics and, 230n8; African American culture and, 235n72; *The Autobiography of an Ex-Colored Man*, 31, 109, 111, 125, 128–38, 233n52, 234n65, 235n74, 236n81, 237n83; black alienation and, 109; black modernism and, 138; black music/ art and, 127, 128; *The Book of American Negro Poetry*, 109, 126; *The Book of American Negro Spirituals*, 126, 137; cultural preservation and, 128; Du Bois and, 126; Harlem Renaissance and, 129; popular culture and, 125; ragtime and, 110–11, 127; sonic materiality and, 128; spirituals and, 128; *Trilby* and, 132

Johnston, John, 322n35

Joplin, Scott, 229n5

Joseph W. Stern & Company, 233n52

journalism, 140, 142, 143, 161, 214n22; literature and, 64; music, 129; photo, 180; reform, 144, 165; sensational, 54; social problem, 140; stunt, 143; yellow, 55, 57, 60

Joyce, James, 176

Kallen, Horace, 122–23, 125, 126, 233n55, 233n59

Kaplan, Amy, 36

Kaup, Monika, 141, 238–39n4, 239n5, 243n38
Kittler, Friedrich, 10, 231n28, 232n35; classical music and, 115; criticism of, 211n81; on discourse network, 117; handwriting and, 217n56; influence of, 211n81; media/experience and, 29; synthesis by, 211–12n82
Kraus, Karl, 19, 139, 143, 169
Kristeva, Julia: semiotics and, 112–13
Kurnick, David: on James, 72, 91, 226n66

Lacan, Jacques: Kittler and, 211n82
Lacis, Asja: on Benjamin, 243n39
latency: grammar of, 96
Le Bon, Gustave, 147, 241n27, 242n28, 242n32
Lee, Gerald Stanley, 16
Leech, John, 81, 82, 83, 84, 99
Leick, Karen, 248n12
Lessing, Gotthold Ephraim, 221n25
Levin, Jonathan, 12
Lewis, Sinclair, 176
Life, 180, 197
Lindbergh, Charles, 194
Lippmann, Walter, 16, 147, 185, 190; communication and, 184; democratic politics and, 17; Dewey and, 185, 252n52, 252n54; informed public and, 17; media/wartime and, 242n30; Nietzsche and, 209n63; Stein and, 252n55; stereotyping and, 252n51
literacy, 112, 124
literary tradition, 33, 79; African American, 112; American, 28, 29; journalism and, 64; literature, 8, 28–32; mass culture and, 4, 73; media and, 29
Livingstone, James, 218n63

Locke, Alain, 233n59
Locke, John, 37, 213n9
Lodge, David, 71–72
Lott, Eric, 122
Luce, Henry Booth, 41
lynching, 114, 129, 135, 137

Mach, Ernst, 9, 204n26
Mackey, Nathaniel, 112, 113, 126
Maine: explosion on, 42, 55, 215n30, 215n36
Marcher, John, 90, 91, 93
Marcus, Sharon, 254n71
Marey, Etienne-Jules, 232n48
mass consumption, 185, 204n26
mass culture, 1, 17, 28, 37, 38–47, 51, 123, 144, 146, 175, 203n17, 240n20, 248n12; cultural elite and, 55; early, 4, 30–31; elite culture and, 5; literature and, 4, 73; mass witnessing and, 56; participation in, 7; rise of, 32; sensation-seeking, 5; spectacles of, 53; technology and, 32–33; visual, 224n53
mass public, 5, 28, 37, 55, 68, 73, 249n27, 254n75
Massumi, Brian, 201n4, 202n7
materiality, 4, 18, 166
Matthews, Brander, 76
Matthiessen, F. O., 85
McGann, Sean, 186, 187
McKinley, William, 40, 214n22
McLuhan, Marshall, 211n82
media, 2, 28–33, 47, 74, 91, 173, 176, 181, 241n27; arts and, 33; communications, 182; critical analysis of, 202n7; environment, 60; experience and, 29; expressive, 218n69; influence of, 214n22; language and, 4; mass, 4, 32, 41, 85, 185, 203n14, 245n57; materialities

of, 30; mechanical, 79; mind and,
59–60; objectivity, 180; pictorialist
transposition of, 94; variety of, 77;
war and, 44, 242n30
media forms, 28; relations between,
33, 95, 96
media studies, 4, 6, 8, 29, 33
media technology, 2, 17, 28, 29, 30, 33,
71–72, 91, 113, 181; arrival of, 73;
capabilities of, 4; rise of, 32
media theory, 4, 236n79, 242n27
Meisel, Martin, 76, 221n25
Melville, Herman, 29, 37
Memorial Hall, 13, 14, 15, 207n47
memory, 136, 231n28; Benjamin on,
18; intellect and, 12; literalizing/
visualizing, 135
Menand, Louis, 217n61
Mendelssohn, Felix, 130–31
Menke, Richard, 209n70
metaphors, 15, 18, 30, 98, 127, 142, 160,
163, 171; digressive, 166; media,
97; open-endedness of, 166;
proliferating, 141; writing, 58
metaphysics, 15, 154, 230n9
Miller, Bonnie, 41, 42
Miller, J. Hillis, 226n74, 228n92
Miller, Perry, 213n9, 214n24
mind, 24, 217n56; crowd, 147, 159, 164;
disordered, 49–50; embodied, 47,
60; homeless, 59; media and, 59–60
minstrelsy, 117, 230n12, 233n54, 236n76
modernism, 4, 31, 35, 36, 97, 177,
203n14, 248n17; black, 138;
critical stance toward, 17;
experience of, 21; literary, 7, 29;
postindustrial, 61; psychology
and, 205n34; spiritualizing, 2, 146;
technologized, 21, 30
"Monster, The" (Crane), 52
Montaigne, Michel de, 9

"Moral Equivalent of War, The"
(James), 60
Motherwell, Hiram K., 121, 122, 125,
130, 233n52
mourning play, 153–58
Muck, Karl, 130; musical development
and, 114–15; ragtime and, 116;
spirituals and, 133
muckraking, 144, 240n16, 244n46
Munsey's, 240n20
Museum of Modern Art: Stein and, 179
music, 234n63; African-American, 112,
114, 115, 124, 126, 127, 128; American,
122; classical, 115, 117, 119, 128, 129,
132, 133; development of, 114–15;
folk, 109, 115, 117, 118, 120, 136;
popular, 115, 117, 123, 127, 128; sacred,
128; vernacular, 127
Muybridge, Eadweard, 47, 232n48
"My Adventures Being Rescued"
(Barnes), 169
"My Sisters and I at a New York
Prizefight" (Barnes), 162–63

Nagel, James, 218n69
"Narration" (Stein), 174
narrative, 136, 230n14, 237n89
national expression, 116, 129
nationalism, 2, 40, 124
Negro vogue, 111, 132
neobaroque style, 141, 144, 162–63,
238n4
neurasthenia, 116, 120, 129, 231n32
neuropsychology, 246–47n7
New Deal, 174, 247n9
"New Negro" movement, 235n69
newsreels, 42, 173
New York Herald Tribune, 176, 179;
Stein in, 173, 192, 194, 195, 198
New York Times, 242n36; Stein and, 181,
246n2, 252n55

New York World, 40, 64, 140, 162, 165–66, 169

New York World Magazine, 169, 245n63

"Next Time, The" (James), 227n87

Nietzsche, Friedrich, 7, 8, 10, 16, 17, 206n36, 209n63

Nightwood (Barnes), 139, 140, 141, 142, 238n4, 240n14, 245n62; Kaup on, 239n5; modernist form of, 143

Norris, Frank, 159

Norton, Caroline, 67

Oehmler, Leo, 118, 119

Ogden, C. K., 182, 190, 251n46

O'Grady, Ellen, 150–51, 242n36; Barnes and, 151–53

Ohi, Kevin: on James, 92, 226n71

Ohmann, Richard, 203n17, 240n20

"On a Certain Blindness in Human Beings" (James), 60

"Open Boat, The" (Crane), 38, 39, 64, 66, 213n13; described, 65, 68

orality, 112, 124; aesthetics and, 230n8; black, 124

Pain, Henry J., 43

Pearson, Keith Ansell, 206n36

Peirce, C. S., 15, 35, 51, 59, 60, 66, 205n35

perception, 3, 11, 27, 65, 204n26

Peters, John Durham, 137, 182, 189; mentalism/communication and, 183, 251n46

Phaedrus, 226n74

phenomenology, 6, 86, 92, 224n56

Phillips, Adam, 221n20

philosophy, 6, 10, 12, 14, 18, 91, 182; pragmatist, 217n58; psychology and, 205n33

phone, 31; *graph* and, 112, 230n9

phonograph, 112, 115, 122, 128, 134, 137, 236n79

phonography, 117, 128–37, 237n83

Picasso, Pablo, 188, 253n63

Pickford, Mary, 178

pictorialism, 30, 73, 74, 77, 78, 79, 80, 102–3, 104, 222n33; lawless, 89–99; principles of, 81; superior, 88

"Pictures" (Stein), 173

"Plays" (Stein), 173, 188

pluralism, 60, 111, 123, 217n61

poetics, 119; modernist, 175; pragmatist, 175; virtual, 1–2, 6, 7, 17, 35, 175

"Poetry and Grammar" (Stein), 174

Poirier, Richard, 29

politics, 61, 177; critical analysis of, 202n7; cultural, 113; democratic, 17; progressive, 174

popular culture, 4, 5, 41, 91, 115, 123, 125, 132, 143, 145, 173; American, 118; intermedial citationality of, 92; literature/arts and, 73; yellow journalism and, 60

"Portraits and Repetition" (Stein), 174

Posnock, Ross, 227n80

potentiality, 1, 2, 17, 19, 83, 206n42, 206n43

Pound, Ezra, 176

pragmatism, 6, 10, 60, 89, 91, 174, 204n31, 217n57, 217n58, 224n56, 233n59, 246n7; Jamesian, 202n8; linear conception of, 98; philosophy of, 3; progress, 7, 8, 17; spirituality and, 16

Progressive Era, 31, 32, 97, 144, 145, 148, 197

progressive reform, 150, 154, 170

progressivism, 11, 141, 144, 149, 247n8, 247n9

propaganda, 41, 42, 147, 184, 242n28, 251n45

Protestantism, 37, 39, 146, 154, 213n18

Proust, Marcel, 19, 21, 201n7
psychoanalysis, 6, 90, 112, 151, 220n14
psychology, 10, 29, 31, 71, 90, 225n57;
    experimental, 3, 206n42;
    functionalism of, 11; modernism
    and, 205n34; philosophy and,
    205n33; scientific, 204n26
psychophysics, 118, 231n28
public: formation of, 252n52; as
    potentiality, 184; private and, 252n52
*Publications of the Modern Language
    Association*, 177 public discourse,
    177, 180, 184, 196
public sphere, 44, 45, 60, 63, 105, 163,
    185, 220n11; bourgeois, 42; decline
    of, 227n85; literary, 46, 53; mass,
    46, 55, 85; viability of, 7; virtual,
    185–98; visual/sonic, 74
Pulitzer, Joseph, 40, 41, 140
Punch, 105; du Maurier and, 82–83;
    James and, 84, 87; Leech and, 81
Puritanism, 37, 39, 51

queer politics, 98
queer theorists, 90, 91

race relations: nadir of, 31, 109
racial essentialism, 123, 126
racialization, 134, 135, 236n82
racism, 124, 128, 129, 130, 135
Radano, Ronald: on gift, 234n62
radical empiricism, 11–12, 35, 37, 60,
    174, 187, 204n32, 217n58, 246n7,
    253n62, 253n63
ragged time, 117, 120, 122, 137–38,
    238n90
ragtime, 114–22, 126, 128–31, 137, 229n5,
    229n6, 231n30, 231n34, 232n48,
    235n75, 236n76; classical music
    and, 129; controversy over, 112, 114;
    hidden index of, 31; legitimacy of,

110–11; peculiar charm of, 110–11;
    phonographic art of, 31, 111; playing,
    109–10, 125
"Ragtime: A Pernicious Evil and an
    Enemy of True Art" (Oehmler), 118
ragtime craze, 111, 114, 128
Rand, Ayn, 175, 247n9
real, 40; imitation and, 63; possible
    and, 207n46; representation and,
    46
realism, 2, 37, 38–47, 88, 137, 146,
    214n24, 228n2, 241n22; analytical,
    56; artificiality of, 224n52; literary,
    84; representation of, 161; secular,
    214n21; social, 39; visual, 2, 224n53
realist fiction, 39, 46, 99
realization, 48, 87, 95
"Real Thing, The" (James), 87, 88, 91,
    92; criticism of, 85; described, 84
reason: cultivation of, 74; pleasurable
    quickening and, 218n72; public
    exercise of, 203n14
Red Badge of Courage, The (Crane),
    35, 38, 39, 40, 47–53; body machine
    complex and, 216n44; corpse
    scene from, 50–51; Howells on,
    47; as photographic revelation,
    47; popular amusements in, 53;
    publication of, 36
Reed, Frank L., 119, 120
reform, 168; entertainment and, 141,
    147, 170; sanctimonious salvation
    of, 144; social, 157, 171
reformation, 148, 154, 157, 243n41
Reform Era, 142, 153, 162, 242n31
"Reluctant Voyagers, The" (Crane),
    213n13
representation, 89, 224n52, 232n38;
    communication and, 250n33;
    materiality of, 52; real and, 46, 161;
    virtual, 12–13; visual, 244n51

Richards, I. A., 182, 190, 251n46
Richardson, Joan, 213n9
Riis, Jacob, 145, 146, 152, 167
Robbins, Bruce, 203n14, 252n54
Robertson, Michael, 219n74
Rogin, Michael, 121
Rogues' Gallery, 144–53, 158, 242n34
Roosevelt, Franklin Delano, 186
Roosevelt, Theodore, 148, 198, 254n75
Rothenbuhler, Eric W., 137
Ryan, Judith, 10, 201n6, 205n34
Ryan, Marie-Laure, 2, 3

"Saltram's Seat" (Coburn), 107, 108
San Francisco Examiner: on Crane, 36
Santayana, George, 174, 225n57
Saturday Evening Post, 173, 254n75
Saturday Review of Literature, 181;
    clipping from, 182
Schopenhauer, Arthur, 7, 234n66
Sedgwick, Eve Kosofsky: James and,
    225n61
Sekula, Alan, 242n34
self: finding/founding, 219n79;
    subjectivity and, 28; virtual, 53
selfhood, 28, 30, 31, 53; experimental,
    198; moral contours of, 218n63;
    Puritan roots of, 212n8
self-making, 30, 121, 125
Seltzer, Mark, 218n71, 232n38
Shakespeare, William, 121, 233n52
Sidgwick, Henry, 8
Sidis, Boris, 241n27
signification, 61, 230n12, 232n34;
    potentiality of, 157
Singer, Alan, 142
Skinner, B. F., 178, 249n23
slavery, 110, 116, 131, 132, 134, 236n76,
    236n80, 242n36; dissonance of,
    123; legacies of, 31; music of, 115;
    violence of, 113

Smith, Victoria L., 142
social control, 10, 38
Social Darwinism, 13, 207n45
social evolution, 39, 145, 153
social forms, 84, 88, 91
Social Gospel, 145, 149, 214n21, 216n48,
    241n22, 243n37
social organization, 182, 190
social problems, 32, 40, 116, 145, 168,
    236n81, 241n22
social relations, 83, 225n64
social scene, 21, 86, 88, 105
social subjects: normative, 90
social types, portraying, 33
social world, 88–89, 213n15
sorrow songs, 125, 136
"Sorrow Songs, The" (Du Bois), 124
Souls of Black Folk, The (Du Bois), 123,
    124; *Autobiography* and, 234n65;
    epigrams to, 125; music in, 234n63
sounding telegraph, 20, 27, 33
Southern, Eileen, 229n5
Spanish–American War, 30, 33, 36,
    37, 40, 44, 45, 146, 214n22, 217n58;
    films about, 214–15n26; media
    coverage of, 42; racial/sexual
    iconography of, 215n34
spectacles, 10, 53; media, 37, 146, 147; of
    war, 38–47
Spillers, Hortense, 236n82
Spinoza, Baruch: empiricism and,
    206n36
spiritual experience, 8, 16, 37, 123, 146,
    152
spirituals, 124, 128, 137; classical music
    and, 129, 133; cultural gatekeepers
    and, 134; elusiveness of, 127
"Stanzas in Meditation" (Stein), 246n5
Stein, Gertrude, 7, 17, 173–98, 253n67,
    253n70, 255n78; aesthetics of, 174,
    175; American writing and, 198;

audience/identity and, 249n24; *The Autobiography of Alice B. Toklas*, 173, 176, 177, 185, 186; baroque style of, 31; celebrity of, 175–76, 181, 185, 191, 194, 197, 250n33; communication and, 178, 179, 180, 181–82, 189, 190, 191–92, 197; Dewey and, 183–84, 185, 191, 195, 196; education and, 195–96; experimental style of, 174; *Four in America*, 175, 176, 185–88, 189–91, 198, 253n70, 254n70, 254n72; *Four Saints in Three Acts*, 173, 254n72; genetics/neuropsychology and, 246–47n7; *The Geographical History of America*, 197, 246n5; habits and, 253n69; *Ida*, 196–97, 355n78; images of, 171; James and, 175, 187, 188, 189, 191; language and, 253–54n70; linguistic indeterminacy and, 247n10; Lippmann and, 252n55; *The Making of Americans*, 188; mass culture and, 248n12; New Deal and, 247n9; newspapers and, 194; Picasso and, 188, 253n63; pragmatism of, 246n7; progressivism and, 194, 195, 247n8, 247n9; publicity by, 173, 180, 246n3; public sphere and, 176, 177; radical empiricism and, 253n62, 253n63; Roosevelt and, 254n75; semantic indeterminacy and, 247n10; speaking and, 190; *Tender Buttons*, 177

Steiner, George, 243n38
"Stephen Crane's Own Story" (*New York Press*), 64, 65, 66
stereotypes, 117, 123, 132, 231n33, 252n51
Stowe, Harriet Beecher: *Uncle Tom's Cabin*, 77, 93, 94, 104, 222n31
style: virtuality of, 89–99
subjectivity, 4, 10, 11, 12, 26, 29, 207n49,

209n70; conception of, 9; fluidity of, 15; self and, 28
Sue, Eugene, 238n2
Sundquist, Eric, 234n63, 234n64, 238n90
symbolism, 46, 58–59, 148; portentous, 39–40
syncopation, 117, 118, 120, 122, 188
syncope, 118–19, 122, 135
Szalay, Michael, 254n75

tableaux vivants, 77, 78, 79, 85
Tagg, John, 180
technology, 45, 78, 112, 201n6; communication, 20, 92, 175; digital, 3; mass culture and, 32–33; old/new, 250n36; prosthetic effects of, 16; sound reproduction, 128. *See also* media technology
telegraph, 33, 71, 209n70
"That Shakespearian Rag," 233n52
theater, 91, 154; film and, 215n26; pictorialism in, 222n33
Theater Guild, 139, 244n50
thinking: as linguistic troping, 27n83; as sign-making, 59
Thoreau, Henry David, 29, 37
thought, 184; "language-form" of, 60; oppressive habits of, 196; virtual, 20
Thurschwell, Pamela, 210n74, 227n84
Tichi, Cecilia, 244n46
time: as duration/life force, 12
Time, 173, 176
Toklas, Alice B., 173, 179, 181, 197, 255n78
Top Hat (film): Stein reference in, 173, 179
tourism, 139, 166, 168, 172, 245n57
Trachtenberg, Alan, 241n22
Tree, Herbert Beerbohm, 78, 79
Trilby (du Maurier), 30, 99–108,

222n30, 228n91, 236n81; art of the situation and, 75–79; citable quality of, 72; critical readings of, 221n20; duality of, 101, 105; inspiration for, 80; James and, 81, 103; Johnson and, 132; origin of, 100, 101; parodies/burlesques of, 77; popularity of, 71, 72, 73, 74, 75, 77, 101, 102, 104, 132; publication of, 76, 220n12; reception for, 221n27; songs/illustrations from, 77; success of, 81, 101, 102, 107; suggestion and, 220n14; theatrical incarnations of, 71, 72; thematic resonance of, 77–78

Trilby-mania, 30, 73, 75, 77–81, 94, 100, 102, 104; beginning of, 99; citationality of, 105; impact of, 75

Trilby Triflet, A: productions of, 221–22n29

Trotter, Wilfred, 241n27

"Turn of the Screw, The" (James), 25, 89

"Twingeless Twitchell and His Tantalizing Tweezers" (Barnes), 159, 160–61, 172

Uncle Tom's Cabin (Stowe), 77, 104, 222n31; James on, 93; popularity of, 94

"Upturned Face, The" (Crane), 52

Vanity Fair, 139, 173, 248n12

Van Vechten, Carl, 248n12

Vickers, Nancy, 177

violence, 63, 113, 230n14

virtual, 2–4, 12, 13, 21, 103, 111, 161, 171, 205n35; actual and, 207n46; arts/technologies and, 201n4; continuous and, 207n46; digital and, 3, 6; evocation of, 112;

experience of, 20; importance of, 7; poetics of, 35

virtual-as-potential, 3, 206n43

virtual experience, 6, 8–20, 184, 203n21, 206n42, 208n61, 251n51; language and, 14; philosophers of, 8, 35

virtuality, 1, 2, 3, 17, 99

virtual knowers, 14, 24

virtual self, 19, 37, 45, 47, 53

virtual turn, 6, 7, 17, 32, 33, 204n32

vitalism, 1, 10, 11, 16, 17, 20, 27, 204n32, 208n57

voice: culture and, 228n2; image and, 181; narrative, 136, 137; virtual, 113, 138

Voltaire, 150

voluntarism, 143, 145, 149, 162, 167, 170, 216n48; rise of, 213n19

Wachtell, Cynthia, 45

Wagner, Bryan, 113, 114, 230n14

Wagner, Richard, 7, 234n66

war: media and, 44, 46; spectacle of, 38–47; technologies of, 45

Washington Post, 178, 179, 246n2

"Waste Land, The" (Eliot), 233n52

Weber, Samuel, 209n67, 232n36, 243n39, 243n43, 244n47, 244n48; on Benjamin, 155, 243n41; on mourning play, 244n45

"Wedding March" (Mendelssohn), 130–31, 235n75

"Wedding March Rag, The" (song), 131

Weheliye, Alexander G., 112

Weininger, Otto, 175

Weld, Arthur, 116, 117

Welles, Orson, 41

"What Is English Literature" (Stein), 173, 188

Whitman, Walt, 63, 66, 174, 218n72

Wicke, Jennifer, 75, 250n39, 254n72

Wilde, Oscar, 210n71
will, 17; motor activity and, 15
Wilson, Woodrow, 186, 189, 198
Winkiel, Laura: on Barnes, 146–47
Wolin, Richard: on allegories, 171
"Woman Police Deputy Is Writer of
    Poetry" (Barnes), 150–53
Works Progress Administration
    (WPA), 194, 254n75
"World of Pure Experience, A"
    (James), 208n56
Wright, Richard, 127

Wright, Wilbur, 185
writing, 185–98, 216n44, 232n38;
    afterlife of, 28–33; as dangerous
    supplement, 230n9; mass culture
    and, 38; materiality of, 61;
    metaphorics of, 30; realist, 30;
    superior medium of, 99

Young Americans, 209n62, 233n55
Young, Owen, 189, 191, 198

Ziff, Larzer: on Crane/events, 39

KATHERINE BIERS is assistant professor of English and comparative literature at Columbia University.